The French Terror Wave,
2015–2016

ALSO BY MARC E. VARGO
and from McFarland

*The Weaponizing of Biology: Bioterrorism,
Biocrime and Biohacking* (2017)

*The Mossad: Six Landmark Missions of the Israeli
Intelligence Agency, 1960–1990* (2015)

*Women of the Resistance:
Eight Who Defied the Third Reich* (2012)

The French Terror Wave, 2015–2016

Al-Qaeda and ISIS Attacks from Charlie Hebdo *to the Bataclan Theatre*

MARC E. VARGO

McFarland & Company, Inc., Publishers
Jefferson, North Carolina

ISBN (print) 978-1-4766-7918-1
ISBN (ebook) 978-1-4766-4131-7

Library of Congress and British Library
cataloguing data are available

Library of Congress Control Number 2020054556

© 2021 Marc E. Vargo. All rights reserved

No part of this book may be reproduced or transmitted in any form or by any means, electronic or mechanical, including photocopying or recording, or by any information storage and retrieval system, without permission in writing from the publisher.

Front cover image © 2021 Samot/Shutterstock

Printed in the United States of America

*McFarland & Company, Inc., Publishers
Box 611, Jefferson, North Carolina 28640
www.mcfarlandpub.com*

For Kay and Joe Allen

Table of Contents

Prologue: The Ascent of Radical Islamism in the French Republic 1

Part I. The Pen and the Sword: Freedom of the Press, Islamist Extremism, and the Massacre at *Charlie Hebdo* Magazine

1. *Charlie Hebdo* Magazine and the Grand Tradition of French Satire 8
2. Courting Conflict: The Muhammad Cartoon Controversies in Denmark and France 15
3. Stéphane Charbonnier: Satirist, Skeptic, Target 26
4. Al-Qaeda and the Radicalization of Saïd and Chérif Kouachi 35
5. Silencing Satire: The Assault on *Charlie Hebdo* 50

Part II. The Campaign to Demoralize: ISIS Attacks at the Bataclan Theatre, the Stade de France, and the Cafés of Paris

6. Belgium, Abdelhamid Abaaoud, and the Paris Terror Units 74
7. Carnival of Horror: The Bataclan Theatre, Stade de France, and the Café Attacks of Friday the Thirteenth 96
8. Responses to the Attacks: The Medical Community, the Military, and Law Enforcement Agencies 121

Part III. Radical Islamism and Single-Perpetrator Terrorist Offensives in France

9. Lone-Actor Terrorism, Encrypted Extremism, and Remote Control Attacks 136
10. Normandy: The Slaying of a Parish Priest 151

Table of Contents

11. Insanity by the Sea: The Bastille Day Ramming Attack   167
12. The Ramadan Murders: Ritualized Assault at an
    American-Owned Chemical Plant in France   184
13. Terror on the Tracks: Face-Off on a High-Speed Train to Paris   194

*Epilogue—France Today: Emotional Scars, Enhanced Security, and
    the Question of Future Attacks*   206
Chapter Notes   211
Bibliography   233
Index   251

Prologue

The Ascent of Radical Islamism in the French Republic

It was shortly before noon on Thursday, October 3, 2019, that computer scientist Mickaël Harpon left his office on a lunch break, walked to a nearby shop, and purchased an eight-inch ceramic kitchen knife. Forty-five minutes later, he returned to his job at the Paris Police Headquarters in the heart of the city, where he was assigned to the intelligence division. Holding a position of such trust presumably meant he was beyond reproach. Certainly as a computer scientist with a security clearance, he was privy to an assortment of highly sensitive information, not the least of which were the classified files of numerous terrorism suspects. And like his co-workers, Harpon also enjoyed extensive access to the fortified, Neo-Florentine building itself.

By this point in 2019, the Paris police had amassed an impressive amount of material about scores of potential terrorists, but it had slipped up when it came to one of its own staff members. What the authorities did not know about Mickaël Harpon is that, following the al-Qaeda-supported attack on the satirical magazine *Charlie Hebdo* in 2015, he told his colleagues that he was sympathetic to the terrorists' cause. Troubled by the startling disclosure, his coworkers filed a report about the incident, but their higher-ups in the police prefecture do not appear to have pursued the matter. Then, in the ensuing years, Harpon, a passionate Muslim, ramped up his attendance at a mosque headed by a radical imam; a divisive, militant figure whom officials considered expelling from France. As well, he stopped having certain types of customary contact with women, even as he set about posting on Facebook an array of radical Islamist videos. In one, a beheading was simulated, while another implied the slashing of throats. "Everyone knew that he was troubled," said Linda Kebbab, an official of the city's police union.[1]

So it was that the computer scientist, on this autumn day, returned to police headquarters armed with the ceramic knife, which, owing to its composition, was not sensed by the facility's metal detectors. Once inside the massive building, he walked into an office and slashed the throat of a 50-year-old man, a police major. Seconds later, he stabbed a 38-year-old police officer in the stomach. These two killings were followed by that of a 37-year-old administrator, after which Harpon murdered a 38-year-old policewoman before leaving the building and walking into the expansive courtyard. Here he seized another man, but then a young police officer suddenly materialized. Releasing the victim, the assailant, knife raised, lunged at the policeman, who shot him dead. It may never be known if Harpon, during the years he worked in the intelligence division, shared sensitive, terrorism-related information.

For the city of Paris, the incident, which was clearly an act of terrorism, stunned a population that had been shocked numerous times in the past four years. "The attack immediately raised fears of a return to the waves of terrorism that hit Paris in 2015 and 2016," reported the *New York Times*.[2] This two-year surge of terrorist assaults is the subject of this book, and the memory of the attacks is still very much alive in France today. It is an open wound as demonstrated by the city's reaction to the brutal assault at police headquarters. "(T)he attack has contributed to a latent sense of unease here, a reminder, after years of relative calm, that the terrorist threat is still high; that the country is a semi-dormant volcano, one that could erupt at any time; that the state itself—embodied by the police department, on the Île de la Cité, just steps from Notre-Dame, the very center of Paris— is vulnerable to infiltration by rogue elements," wrote Rachel Donadio, a Paris-based journalist.[3]

The fact is, France, of all of the Western European nations, holds the unenviable distinction of being the number-one target of Islamist terrorist organizations, namely al-Qaeda and the Islamic State (ISIS). Not only that, the operatives who have carried out these attacks have been, in numerous cases, citizens of France. Their purported aim: to punish *La République* for a host of supposed misdeeds. These offenses have ranged from its participation in U.S.-led military actions in the Middle East to the contention that the French people, as a whole, are infidels; that French society, due to its liberal values and customs, is an affront to Allah and the prophet Mohammad. Of course, other European nations also contribute troops to U.S. military operations in the Middle East and are culturally liberal as well, yet these countries are not attacked nearly as often or as ruthlessly by Islamist extremists. So the question arises: *Why is it that France faces the greatest threat from radical Islamists, particularly from home-grown terrorists?*

The answer may stem, in part, from the long-term experience of

France's Muslim population; the fact that the nation, while once having encouraged the adherents of Islam to relocate to it, has been indifferent in more recent decades in ensuring that Muslims are recognized, valued, and offered the same opportunities to involve themselves in French life as non-Muslim citizens. At least this is the charge that has been leveled repeatedly against France since the early years of the twenty-first century, a charge suggesting that the nation may not be furnishing its Muslim citizenry, especially the younger generation, with sufficient opportunities to participate and advance in society. If this is true, it was not always the case.

A look back at the country's history reveals that the followers of the Islamic faith have lived in France for hundreds of years, originally as episodic conquerors in southern France and thereafter as residents who enriched French culture in numerous ways. Their number was small, however; it was during the twentieth century that the steady movement of immigrants to France caused the Muslim presence to become truly substantial. According to the Pew Research Center, France currently boasts the largest Muslim population in Western Europe: nearly six million people or roughly nine percent of the country's total population.[4]

The most recent migration, a century-long process, commenced in the early decades of the 1900s, when a small share of Muslims arrived from the Middle East, the sub–Saharan regions of Africa, and western Asia (Turkey). A larger portion hailed from the North African nations of Morocco and Tunisia, both of which were once French colonies with Muslim majorities. It was after World War II, however, that the lion's share of Muslims immigrated to France, most of whom came from Algeria. Because Algeria was a French colony until the Algerian Revolution led to its autonomy in 1962, France could, and did, draft Algeria's men—they were predominantly Islamic—to fight on its side in World War II.[5] The upshot: a considerable number of these veterans and their families resettled in France in the postwar era. Subsequent to this, French businesses in the 1960s and 1970s capitalized on Algeria's ample pool of inexpensive labor, prompting thousands of Algerian-Muslim families to relocate to France on the prospect of better lives. Among their number were also those who were fleeing the political turmoil that continued to afflict the newly liberated Algeria. And the result was a sizable and robust Islamic presence in France. Generally speaking, it was also an orderly, constructive presence between the 1940s and the 1990s, one in which a healthy share of the country's Muslims established themselves in the middle class and integrated into mainstream society.

A poll conducted in 1995 found that 71 percent of all Muslims living in France, immigrants and native-born citizens alike, reported feeling welcomed by the non–Muslim population.[6] And yet, while this figure is heartening, it implies that up to 29 percent may not have felt fully accepted, which perhaps reflects the political disputes that erupted occasionally between Muslims and non–Muslims. Clashes broke out, for instance, over the French government's support of the Algerian military during the Algerian Civil War (1991–2002). A "dirty war," 200,000 Algerians, mostly Muslims, perished in the course of it.[7] As well, many Franco-Muslims became alienated by the animosity toward Muslims voiced by political firebrands on France's far right, men and women who advocated nativism and extreme nationalism. Yet it was not until the current century that a significant segment of France's Muslim population, primarily a younger component, became deeply disconnected from mainstream society.

It came after al-Qaeda's cinematic attacks on the World Trade Center and the Pentagon on September 11, 2001; unprecedented acts of political violence that shook the world. In response, the White House, under the direction of George W. Bush and Dick Cheney, made the decision in 2003 to invade Iraq. Of course, doing so constituted an act of war against a sovereign Middle Eastern nation, a violation of international norms triggered by the erroneous White House claim that Iraq possessed weapons of mass destruction. And one consequence, a rather predictable one, was that many Franco-Muslims, sympathetic to their beleaguered Iraqi brethren, developed an anti–American mindset. Moreover, as other nations joined the misguided U.S. campaign, this frame of mind mushroomed into a broader anti–Western outlook, and even took on a measure of animosity toward France itself. This is notwithstanding the fact that the French government opposed the American invasion of Iraq, both before and during its occurrence.

Compounding the wrath over the preemptive assault and ensuing occupation of Iraq, many French Muslims became further outraged upon learning about the war crimes that were purportedly being committed in Iraq, Afghanistan, Guantanamo Bay (Cuba), and other spots. First and foremost was the U.S. Army's abuse of male and female detainees at Abu Ghraib prison twenty miles west of Baghdad, where, according to investigative journalist Seymour Hersch, "more than sixty per cent of the civilian inmates … were deemed not to be a threat to society, which should have enabled them to be released."[8] At this facility, the unlawful treatment of captives included isolation and sensory deprivation, canine attacks, and rapes of both male and female captives. They were atrocities that convinced scores of Franco-Muslims of the need to take action against the Western coalition forces in the Middle East and more broadly against Western interests in Europe and beyond. As could be predicted, subsequent American and French military actions in the region, most notably the 2014–2019 campaign in Syria to eliminate the Islamic State's self-proclaimed caliphate, further inflamed young French Muslims. And these were not the only reasons for their discontentment.

During this same period, a sizable sector of the Franco-Muslim community found itself struggling with an escalating xenophobia on the part of the general population, yet another toxic consequence of the September 11 attacks in the United States and ensuing terrorist strikes in Western Europe. It was an aversion to foreigners, immigrants, and their offspring that a segment of the public was expressing through intensified discrimination against, and occasionally overt hostility toward, those who abided by the teachings of the Koran. Case in point: the mounting anti–Muslim rhetoric of the Front National (FN), France's far-right political party. No friend of the Muslim community, the FN was founded in 1972 by Jean-Marie Le Pen, a Holocaust revisionist and former French intelligence agent who had operated in Algeria in the 1950s and whom the French media later nicknamed "the devil of the [French] Republic."[9] In the twenty-first century, the Front National, renamed the Rassemblement National in 2018, escalated its opposition to Muslim immigration while propagating a pervasive anti–Islamic message.

Unfortunately, as these adverse political and social developments were weighing on France's Muslims, a significant number found themselves living in discouraging circumstances. Whereas numerous Muslims across France, especially those of previous generations, were enjoying successful careers and healthy earnings, a growing number of Muslims, younger ones in particular, were enduring life among the country's economic underclass. All too often, they and their loved ones resided in sequestered communities in metropolitan areas in which violence was rife. For them, the future looked bleak.

For such reasons, the first two decades of the twenty-first century became fertile ground for the recruitment and radicalization of young, disenfranchised French Muslims, such as those subsisting in the public housing districts of Paris and other cities. Aching to vent their rage at what they viewed as Western military conceit coupled with their own domestic constraints, some of these disillusioned individuals were willing to consider the extreme messaging of persuasive, if toxic, figures among the growing ranks of France's radical Islamists.

All too often, a pattern was discernible: Young French Muslims from disadvantaged backgrounds, nearly always men, would fall into petty crime and end up in prison. Once they were behind bars, militant Islamists would befriend them, then proceed to recruit them. Alternatively, the new inmates, intimidated by their circumstances, would seek out "the protection of a powerful group in prison, which can be the jihadi," says Belgian terrorism expert Thomas Renard.[10] In still other instances, first-time inmates, feeling alone and depressed inside the walls of the penitentiary, would seek comfort, meaning, and redemption through the religion of their childhoods. "Islam has become very popular, very successful within French prisons as a rebirth for these people," says Paris-based research scholar Myriam Benraad.[11] Unfortunately, Islamist recruiters would often detect and exploit these vulnerable individuals. Regardless of the particular scenario, such inmates, upon their release from prison, would be partially or fully radicalized or they would at least have acquired a penchant for militant Islamism together with personal ties to violent extremists.

Unfortunately, the number of inmates who could potentially be indoctrinated in French prisons continues to be considerable. Whereas Muslims in France, as previously noted, account for approximately 9 percent of the general population, they constitute 40 to 50 percent of the country's prison population, a grossly disproportionate share.[12] Given that France's prisons are estimated to contain a total of 70,000 inmates, this suggests that up to 35,000 are adherents of the Islamic faith, a segment of whom may be susceptible to the recruitment efforts of Islamist extremists.

In this book, seven terrorist attacks that were committed on French soil are examined, together with the historical and social contexts in which they transpired. All took place during the years 2015 and 2016 in what were the aforementioned "waves" of militant Islamist attacks in the European nation. As to their origins, they were conceived and executed by male terrorists acting, formally or informally, on behalf of al-Qaeda or ISIS; that is to say, some were organizational operations and thus officially sanctioned, while others were the work of individual actors aided by a small number of abettors. And lastly, of the 20 terrorists who committed the acts of violence against France and the French people to be examined in this book, 14 of them, or 70 percent of the assailants, were citizens of France.

The text begins by revisiting the attack on the staff of *Charlie Hebdo* magazine in Paris, an assault that was backed by al-Qaeda. Commensurate with the above-mentioned characteristics, the assault was carried out by two French brothers, both of them Muslims, whose parents immigrated to France from Algeria. The assailants' childhoods in Paris were disadvantaged and their family, impoverished. In due course, the two were arrested for petty crimes and sent to prison, where they were introduced to radical Islamism.

PART I

The Pen and the Sword
Freedom of the Press, Islamist Extremism, and the Massacre at Charlie Hebdo Magazine

1

Charlie Hebdo Magazine and the Grand Tradition of French Satire

The terrorist attack on the satirical magazine *Charlie Hebdo*, a grisly paroxysm of rage and indignation, was a calculated assault designed to silence a cadre of artists and writers who sought to express, in print and with wit, their thoughts on controversial issues of the day. The assailants: a pair of French brothers, radical Islamists, who had been programmed for violence. Their grievance: the weekly magazine's send-ups of their prophet Muhammad. The *Charlie Hebdo* bloodbath, then, was an attack not only on the freedom of expression but also on a specific literary form, satire, which holds a special place in an open society as well as in the history of French literature.

By its nature, satire tends to be perceptive, risky, and spirited. When weighed against other forms of expression, it is also among the most resistant to political, social, and financial forces that so often attempt to shape or even suppress the journalistic effort. And it is precisely because this distinctive literary form refuses to be muzzled or otherwise reined in by the powers-that-be that it plays such a valuable role in a free society, an insightful and informative one.

"Satire without mercy remains fundamental to democracy, in that it goes where mainstream journalism often does not," writes journalist Emma Hurt.[1] As to the way in which this bold approach relates to *Charlie Hebdo*, the impertinent French weekly has, for nearly forty years, tackled those subjects that the mainstream press has approached in an overly-cautious manner or, in countless cases, dodged entirely. It has done so, moreover, by deliberately overstepping the bounds of good taste and genteel critical analysis to drive home its point. Of course, some readers claim to be startled or offended by *Charlie Hebdo*'s uncompromising content, especially those who live beyond France's borders and are unfamiliar with that nation's upfront approach to satire. What such critics may not realize is that the cartoons and commentaries that grace the publication's pages, while provocative and often crude, are in keeping with the nation's extensive history of spiky social humor. "[*Hebdo*'s] trademark features—scatology, vivid sexual humor, and the breaking of taboos, above [all] with respect to, but showing no respect for, religious beliefs—are nothing new," writes Laurence Grove in the *Jewish Quarterly*.[2]

Although *Charlie Hebdo* is a recent manifestation of a nearly six-hundred-year French satirical tradition, the literary form itself can be traced back to ancient Rome, where Horace (first century BCE) and later Juvenal (late first–second centuries CE) introduced mockery into verse and promoted its use. From this pair of poets, satire evolved into an art form seeking to expose and critique the shortcomings and vices of the existing social, religious, or political orders through the use of ridicule, sarcasm, parody, irony, and hyperbole.

As to the emergence of satire in French publishing, it was in the mid-fifteenth century that a collection of illustrated stories was printed under the title, *Les Cent Nouvelles Nouvelles*, and later the English title, "One Hundred Merrie and Delightsome Stories."[3] Parodying society's eccentricities, the text and corresponding drawings reserved their sharpest barbs for the quirks and pretenses of nuns and priests, who were portrayed as oversexed and self-deluded. A shot across the literary bow, this cheeky offering marked the dawn of French satire.

While the sixteenth and seventeenth centuries showed an appreciable rise in the literary form, it was during the eighteenth century that sardonic visual and written humor truly came into its own. A sterling era of French satire and one that shaped its modern-day incarnation, this revitalization of the art form was a gift of The Enlightenment, the philosophical and intellectual movement that emerged in western Europe and gave rise to advances in scientific thought, philosophy, and politics. It also gave birth to some of France's paramount humorists. Yet on the heels of this resurgence of satirical writings and illustrations came a backlash in the form of a suppression campaign directed at its creators. By punching upward at those in power, a preferred stance of satire across the ages, writers and artists placed themselves in a vulnerable position vis-à-vis their targets, who possessed both the authority and the will to stifle them.

The French royal family, for one, was often the butt of scathing humor, with the clergy receiving its fair share as well. Regarding those satirists who were admonished for their controversial productions, Voltaire (1694–1778) was perhaps the most celebrated. Poet, essayist, and champion of unimpeded political and religious thought, Voltaire found himself rebuked because his satirical works crossed the line of acceptability—acceptable, that is, to its ecclesiastical and royal targets. This meant exile to England, and, on another occasion, imprisonment in the Bastille for penning poetry that was deemed defamatory. But while the decision to punish Voltaire and his fellow satirists was high-handed at best, those who held the reins of power surely had reason to worry about the political influence that such productions, both textual and pictorial, were exerting on the masses. Caricatures of the queen, for instance, are thought to have punctured her aura of superiority and untouchable grandeur at a moment when populist sentiment was already running high. "Historians have argued that cartoonists' undignified depictions of French royals in the eighteenth century lessened the prestige of the monarchy, helping pave the way for revolution," writes Alice Robb.[4] It is also worth noting that parallels have been drawn in recent times between these literary and visual challenges to the kingdom's religious and political elite and the cartoons of *Charlie Hebdo* magazine. "*Charlie Hebdo* is part of a venerable tradition in French journalism going back to the scandal sheets that denounced Marie-Antoinette in the run-up to the French Revolution," writes the *BBC*'s Hugh Schofield.[5]

In the years following this period of political unrest and social upheaval, the production of satirical works not only continued but proliferated, particularly in the case of illustrations. This was due mainly to the advent of lithography in 1796, a process in which a drawing or a piece of writing is transferred from an external surface—originally, a stone surface—onto paper. Together with the mechanical printing press, lithography led to the mass production of pictorial material. The upshot: cartoons and picture books flourished and, in the case of satirical works, became even more influential since they could now reach a more socially and economically diverse audience.

Among the nineteenth-century French artists and illustrators who created such widely distributed drawings was Honoré Daumier (1808–1879), the caricaturist, printmaker, and sculptor, who turned out thousands of lithographs lampooning French political and social life. A staff member of the humor magazines *La Caricature* and later the progressive *Le Charivari* (Pandemonium), Daumier's illustrations poked fun at the avaricious middle class as well as the legal profession and France's political leadership. But whereas the public took great delight in his plucky drawings, his targets did not, and Daumier, like Voltaire before him, paid a steep price for his irreverent wit. In an 1831 caricature skewering King Louis-Philippe I— the artist was careful not to name the monarch in the drawing—Daumier drew a portly giant ensconced in an oversized chair with a chute leading up to its mouth. Townsfolk loaded food onto the chute, which resembled a modern-day conveyor belt and ascended to the goliath's mouth. No food remained for the people.

1. Charlie Hebdo *Magazine and the Tradition of French Satire* 11

"There's something truly vile about his tiny dead eyes and gross paunch—he's a brainless, heartless eating machine," writes art critic Jonathan Jones.[6] As could be predicted, the king was not amused by the personification of gluttony and greed. And worsening matters for the monarch, Daumier's self-centered monstrosity inspired spinoffs. Because the behemoth's head was pear-shaped, the public had no difficulty recognizing the figure as Louis-Philippe, so the caricaturist and his colleagues thereafter portrayed the king simply as a giant pear. Regrettably for Daumier, his lithograph, dubbed *Gargantua*, landed him behind bars for six months.

Four years later, more bad news was visited upon French cartoonists when the authorities banned political caricatures entirely. "(T)here is nothing more dangerous, Gentlemen, than these infamous caricatures, these seditious designs," railed Marie-Charles Duchatel, the Minister of Commerce, before the French legislature. "(T)here is no more direct provocation to crimes which we all deplore."[7] Seconding his overwrought argument was Eugene Janvier, a legislative deputy, who joined him in berating political caricaturists. "(T)hey address themselves only to the low chord of the heart, play with crime, and frolic with assassination!" he declared.[8]

Fortunately, the law outlawing the publication of political caricatures was lifted in 1881; this, despite an increase in satirical productions, including caricatures. Indeed, the vibrant era known as La Belle Époque (1871–1914) unleashed a torrent of social and political satire, such as that on parade in the cabarets of the Montmartre district of Paris, a bohemian playground at the time. As historian Michael L.J. Wilson explains, it was during this glorious age of French theater, literature, music, and the visual arts that a style of satire emerged known as *le fumisme*, which Wilson translates informally as "blowing smoke" and compares to "the joking hyperbole and buffoonery of the artist's studio."[9] Spearing the usual suspects—politicians, priests, and the social elite—fumisme also mocked middle class materialists. "Practiced by performers in the cafés of then-exotic Montmartre, fumisme was part disdain, part mockery and zesty provocation, shuffled and dealt with cutting accuracy," writes Robert Zaretsky.[10]

Among the more prominent and prosperous Montmartre cabarets was Le Chat Noire, which not only staged floorshows but published three satirical newspapers as well. Mixing feisty text with mischievous illustrations, the periodicals sent up newsworthy figures and topics of the day, taking particular aim at political and clerical scandals. A synergistic alliance of essayists and illustrators, it was an approach *Charlie Hebdo* would adopt nearly ninety years later. "The intimate collaboration between writers and artists … stands as a testament to the possibilities created through cooperation," writes art historian Janet Whitmore. "Together, they created work that made a point while raising a smile."[11]

As the success of the Chat Noir newspapers suggests, their readership devoured the wry observations and satirical cartoons even if others found the barbed humor not to their taste. "The Chat Noir publications, like the cabaret, were an acquired habit that appealed to audiences with an absurdist sense of humor and a willingness to accept, if not endorse, socially outrageous behavior," writes Whitmore.[12] Regardless of whether their work was loved or loathed, however, the satirists were performing a vital function in scrutinizing and appraising society at large. "Central to these publications is the role of the creative artist as the social conscience of a world run amok."[13]

As the outbreak of the First World War in 1914 revealed, the world would continue running amok into the twentieth century, and exposing and evaluating the goings-on would be satirical newspapers. Predictably, satirical images would climb sharply in number during the 1930s and 1940s, paralleling Hitler's rise to power and ruinous reign. And more often than not, the artists who created these illustrations were ahead of the curve. "You can see during the build-up to the war that cartoonists were warning of the grim nature of events to come, the stupidity of failing to learn from history and the shock felt in the aftermath," writes American cartoonist Tony Husband.[14]

Collectively, France's cartoonists were an adored lot during the war—the public hailed their inspired creations—yet their illustrations occasionally annoyed the country's political leadership and enraged the Nazis themselves owing to the commanding influence of the images. Not surprisingly, some French cartoonists found their names on *der Führer*'s hit list. "(T)he cartoon was what people would remember," writes Husband, "not the headline, not the thousands of printed words, but the image."[15]

This disparity between the impact of visual imagery compared to that of the written word is an intriguing subject and one that Victor S. Navasky, publisher emeritus of *The Nation*, tackled in his fascinating book, *The Art of Controversy: Political Cartoons and Their Enduring Power*.[16] At this juncture, it will be worthwhile to briefly examine Navasky's insights into the "inescapable immediacy" of illustrations, as he so aptly phrased it.[17]

"Cartoons and caricatures have historically had and continue to have a unique emotional power and capacity to enrage, upset, and discombobulate otherwise rational people and groups," writes Navasky, adding that illustrations can drive their audiences to "disproportionate-to-the-occasion, sometimes violent, emotionally charged behavior."[18] This was, of course, the case for the assailants in the *Charlie Hebdo* massacre. And while it remains unclear why cartoons and caricatures have such an instant and intense effect, Navasky explored various possibilities, one of which entails the manner in which the brain processes various types of input. A cognitive explanation, this notion holds that the interpretation of the written word requires an intermediate or transitional stage of mental processing that a visual image does not. By circumventing the reading and interpreting of printed language, comprehension is accelerated and the resultant emotional reaction, pure and raw. "(L)ike the sharpest knife," says Navasky, "the condensed exaggeration of caricature carves its way into your brain and yields a conceptual blend that, unlike text, which must be studied, arrives with the speed of light."[19] The effect is visceral and immediate; it hits the gut and cannot be unseen. "Cartoons may ... be easy to describe in words, but that is not the same as experiencing them."[20]

Such arresting images were especially ferocious in France and other western nations during the politically and socially chaotic 1960s. Among the satirical magazines that began publication during this period was *Hara-Kiri*, whose chosen marks were the French leadership, political parties, and the Church. Boasting an impressive list of contributors, its stable of artists included cartoonist Georges Wolinski and caricaturist Jean Maurice Jules Cabu, best known by his penname, "Cabu." Although the authorities twice shut down the cheeky *Hara-Kiri*, the closures were temporary and the publication thrived. Not only that, it expanded its operations at the end of the decade to include a weekly version of itself called *Hara-Kiri Hebdo*.

It was the following year, 1970, that president Charles de Gaulle died at his home in northeastern France, and *Hara-Kiri Hebdo*, being a satirical vehicle, led with a provocative headline about the cause of his death. To the chagrin of the weekly's editor-in-chief, however, the joke was condemned for besmirching the dignity of the office of the president, and on this pretext the government took legal action against the publication, isolating and thereby suffocating it. The editors, writers, and cartoonists remained unfazed, though, and the weekly soon sprang to life again, retaining its staff and adopting the name *Charlie Hebdo*. While "hebdo" translates into English as "weekly," the "Charlie" in the title was an inside joke about Charles de Gaulle as well as a tribute to the American cartoon-strip character Charlie Brown, which was still enjoying worldwide popularity even after a quarter of a century. To make it official, a Peanuts comic strip featuring the put-upon, everyman protagonist was reprinted in the inaugural version of *Charlie Hebdo* magazine.

Beyond merely reflecting the rebelliousness of its sixties predecessor, however, *Charlie Hebdo*, from the get-go, strove to push the literary envelope to its limits. With guns blazing, it set out to exemplify France's centuries-old history of satire and in a most belligerent form. Thus, the upstart magazine was not a one-off, a sophomoric whim, or an artistic quirk meant to titillate or aggravate the public, but rather the latest manifestation of a truly grand tradition, a satirical publication created by a top-tier collection of France's artists and geared toward a public accustomed and amenable to satire. It is also is important to note, especially in light of the terrorist attack that was to come, that the French public, by and large, understood that it is the satirist's job is to scrutinize the political, religious, and social issues of the day, along with those figures who play critical roles in these matters.

In its early stages in the 1970s, *Charlie Hebdo* confidently took on numerous influential entities, with a propensity to confront prominent ecclesiastical figures. "I've seen defecating popes, nuns in sex orgies; nuns in sex orgies defecating on popes," writes Hugh Schofield.[21] But while the content was audacious and, in the view of its critics, insulting, the magazine swiftly earned a small but loyal following and became a feature of the nation's literary life. In a sense, *Charlie Hebdo* was like a naughty but affectionate uncle, scandalous yet benign, its impudent and often tawdry illustrations splashed unapologetically across its front page and engaging passersby from train station kiosks and street-side newsstands. And so it remained until 1981, when, due to declining revenue, the weekly had little choice but to shutter its operations. But this was not the end of the story.

In 1992, the publication re-emerged under the editorship of writer, musician, and comedian Phillipe Val. Resurrecting the defiant *Charlie Hebdo* wit, the operation took pride in its distinguished cadre of cartoonists, caricaturists, and writers, among them such *Hara-Kiri* alumni as Georges Wolinski and Cabu. And joining them would be an extraordinary caricaturist by the name of Stéphane Charbonnier, who would work full-time at the magazine and, in 2009, take the reins as editor-in-chief during a highly-combustible period for satirical cartoonists in Europe. Commencing with an explosive 2005 controversy involving the provocative publication of "blasphemous" cartoons in a Danish newspaper, this fight would be extended into 2006 and years thereafter by Stéphane Charbonnier and his staff of French cartoonists and writers.

In the ensuing chapter, we revisit the artistic, social, and political clashes in Denmark and later France that occurred between segments of the Muslim population and political caricaturists, clashes in which Stéphane Charbonnier became a central figure. Ultimately, these ideological disputes climaxed in the diabolic massacre that transpired in 2015 in the Paris offices of *Charlie Hebdo* magazine.

2

Courting Conflict
The Muhammad Cartoon Controversies in Denmark and France

In September 2005, the people of Denmark were witness to a passionate and protracted controversy known as the "Muhammad Cartoon Conflict," a media-generated event that brought to the surface a marked disparity in values between the nation's Muslim and non–Muslim citizens.[1] It was also a clash that resulted in two hundred deaths in the Middle East, as well as a conflict that served as a prelude to the Islamist attack on *Charlie Hebdo* in Paris five years later. And although there were certain differences between the Danish and French cartoon controversies, the social and political conditions that laid the foundations for both of them had been in the making for years.

In the case of Denmark, the toxic atmosphere had its origins in the mid–1990s, when a segment of the non–Muslim citizenry began taking a stand, nastily at times, against Muslims seeking to resettle in Denmark. More than merely an impulse to be found in conservative sectors of the general population, it was shared by the government's immigration office, which set about reducing the number of Muslim applicants it would permit to emigrate to Denmark. And the ensuing reduction was drastic. The *Washington Post* reports that Muslim refugee families seeking asylum in Denmark in the 1990s were "eight times less likely to be successful than families that adhered to another religion."[2] In that the Scandinavian nation had historically taken pride in its open-mindedness, social tolerance, and compassion, its growing opposition to the admission of Muslims, including those from war-torn regions who were seeking sanctuary, was a unique development. At issue: the concern, especially by those on the extreme right, that Denmark was in danger of becoming too heavily populated by the followers of Muhammad; a demographic trend, they argued, that threatened to dilute, if not destroy, the country's distinctive culture.

As was its function, the Danish press covered the burgeoning anti-immigrant sentiment, a matter with both immediate and far-reaching implications, with admirable diligence. But while it was important for the public to have access to news reports describing and dissecting the mounting discord, the reportage itself was not without bias. *Jyllands-Posten* (*JP*), for instance, one of Denmark's oldest and largest news dailies, increasingly sided with the country's nationalist elements in their belief that Muslim newcomers constituted a threat to Danish society; this, despite the fact that the newspaper professed to be impartial on such matters.

Into the twenty-first century, *Jyllands-Posten* continued publishing material, mostly editorials, disparaging those Muslims who were aspiring to migrate to Denmark, with its anti-immigrant posture gradually expanding to include jingoistic slams against the nation's existent Muslim community. Portraying the latter as insular and disconnected from Danish society, the newspaper painted individual Muslim citizens as backward, coarse, and loath to adapt to the country's comparatively liberal norms. More harmful still, *JP*'s news reports and editorials, particularly in the wake of the horrific events of September 11, increasingly equated the Islamic faith with terrorism. Yet even before the al-Qaeda attacks in the United States, the Danish press, including *Jyllands-Posten*, had not been averse to advancing the pernicious notion of an intrinsic association between terrorism and Islam. And among those creating such associations, in this case through the graphic arts, was the distinguished cartoonist Kurt Westergaard.

Hired by *Jyllands-Posten* in the early eighties, Westergaard began crafting unflattering images of Muslims in the mid-nineties. It was an aspect of his job as an illustrator for the newspaper's items, including those pieces casting aspersions on the followers of Muhammad. It could be posited, of course, that Westergaard's images not only reflected the intensifying hostility with which the nation's Muslim minority was being met, but may actually have fanned the flames to some degree. Regarding the cartoonist himself, Westergaard has asserted over the years that he is not adverse to Muslims or immigrants as such. Instead, he explains that his concerns center on what he perceives to be a risk to the long-established personality of his homeland, and especially to its fundamental liberties, that is posed by unchecked immigration and immigration without assimilation.[3] "We [give] them everything," Westergaard said in an interview with the *National Post*; "money, apartments, their own schools, free university, health care."[4] In return, the cartoonist argued, the newcomers owe it to their adopted home to respect and abide by its democratic precepts, first and foremost the freedom of speech.[5]

2. Courting Conflict

The *Jyllands-Posten* Cartoon Controversy

In 2005, Westergaard would play a conspicuous role in Denmark's escalating conflict over Islam and immigration when he would be among a dozen cartoonists whom *Jyllands-Posten* would invite to submit drawings of the prophet Muhammad. Because the newspaper explicitly encouraged visual satire in its project, observers suspected it was stage-managing the exercise to lampoon the founder of Islam, a messenger of God in the eyes of nearly two billion people worldwide.[6]

The project itself grew out of a claim by Kåre Bluitgen, a Danish author and atheist known for his harsh views on Islam and other world religions. In a publication a couple of years earlier, Bluitgen drew a distinction between what he characterized as "Muslims-by-culture" and "Muslims-by-practice," praising the former while sounding the alarm about the latter. According to researchers Mona Konwal Sheikh and Manni Crone at the Danish Institute of International Studies, Bluitgen believed that "Muslims-by-culture (*kulturmuslimerne*) who are not practicing Muslims, should be regarded as an enrichment to society while the practicing Muslims constitute a problem, because ... they regard democracy and human rights as contrasting values to Islam."[7] That same year, Bluitgen would recommend that non–Muslim Danes confront what he deemed the nation's "political correctness" on the matter by orchestrating a protest in the streets of Copenhagen dressed in burkas and pushing baby strollers. "Then they should throw everything in the trash and splash the Qu'ran with menstrual blood," he said.[8]

As the story goes, Bluitgen subsequently had difficulty securing a narrative illustrator to create drawings for a children's book he was writing on the subject of Islam. Perhaps this should not have come as a surprise. As to those who turned down his offer, Bluitgen claims that, for three of them, it was a case of self-censorship; that they were afraid of violent reprisals by the Muslim community, since the assignment would require that they illustrate the prophet Muhammad.

Here it should be noted that a substantial share of the Muslim population considers it irreverent to create images of Muhammad. Although the Koran (Qu'ran), the sacred text of Islam, does not explicitly forbid pictorial representations of the religion's founder, ancient Hebrew writings do discourage it as part of their proscriptions against idol worship, and Muslims borrowed this rationale. Muhammad had reservations about the practice as well. "The prophet himself was aware that if people saw his face portrayed by people, they would soon start worshiping him," says Islamic scholar and author Akbar Ahmed of the American University.[9] Viewing himself as a person like any other, Muhammad did not wish to be perceived as distinct from ordinary mortals nor exalted by them. It was the creator, Allah, who was to be worshipped. Accordingly, Muhammad's likeness has seldom been rendered over the centuries, and on those occasions when it has been pictured, it has usually been as a veiled figure or in shadow.

So it was that *Jyllands-Posten*, animated by Bluitgen's claim about self-censorship among Danish illustrators, set out to explore the issue by inviting the members of a Danish society of cartoonists to draw the prophet Muhammad's face for publication in the newspaper. It was, in effect, a test to determine if the organization's twenty-five active members would turn down such a request due to a fear of retaliation. Imposing a very short deadline, the editors of *JP* evaluated the results of their experiment a few days later.

To their surprise, the editors discovered that Denmark's cartoonists would not self-censor, thereby disproving the experiment's hypothesis. "According to Flemming Rose, *Jyllands-Posten*'s cultural editor, only one person ... declined to draw [citing a] fear of violent reactions from Muslims," writes Danish anthropologist, researcher, and writer Peter Hervik.[10] Twelve invitees nixed the offer for other reasons, such as contractual affiliations with competing publications or previously-scheduled commitments. Most of these artists, however, also expressed their opposition to the nature of the project itself.[11] In terms of the remaining twelve, Kurt Westergaard among them, they agreed to the offer.

Curiously, *Jyllands-Posten* did not terminate the project once it had been determined that most Danish illustrators would not, in fact, silence themselves. Instead, the newspaper steamed ahead. As mentioned earlier, it also appears that the editorial staff may have elicited the types of images that a judicious observer would expect to rattle the followers of Muhammad. Writes Hervik: "Instead of repeating Bluitgen's call for illustrators, *Jyllands-Posten* asked satirical cartoonists to draw caricatures of the prophet Muhammad 'as they saw him.'" He adds, "(s)atirical cartoonists are by definition more provocative than illustrators."[12] This raises the question of why the newspaper concocted the project knowing it could ignite a firestorm in the Muslim community.

On this question, three possible answers have been offered. One is that *Jyllands-Posten* was trying to spark a debate, a national conversation on the issue of freedom of the press. In this scenario, one the newspaper itself promulgated, *JP* was performing a service to society by putting to the test a fundamental aspect of democracy. "This is the sort of debate that Jyllands-Posten had hoped to generate when it chose to test the limits of self-censorship by calling on cartoonists to challenge a Muslim taboo," writes Flemming Rose in a *Washington Post* editorial.[13]

Another view is that *Jyllands-Posten* was merely continuing its pattern of publishing news articles and editorials critical of Muslim immigrants and the Islamic faith. "Jyllands-Posten's cartoons did not emerge in a vacuum as a test of freedom of speech," writes Hervik, "but as part of an ongoing set of anti–Islamic discourses."[14] More than anything else, the "Draw Muhammad" endeavor, as it became known, may simply have been business-as-usual for the right-wing newspaper, except that it was now using Bluitgen's debunked claim of Danish self-censorship as a pretext for amping up its vitriol toward the adherents of Islam.

On top of that, there was speculation that *JP* may have been trying to engineer a public confrontation with Denmark's imams and mullahs, who were sure to rise up in defense of their beloved prophet. Lending support to this premise, *Jyllands-Posten*, on its front page, printed an explanation of the Draw Muhammad project on the day the satirical images appeared, one stating that citizens living in a secular democracy with a free press must accept being "scorned, mocked and ridiculed."[15] Tellingly, *Jyllands-Posten* abandoned plans to publish an unrelated set of cartoons that poked fun at the resurrection of Jesus Christ. As stated on the CBS news program *60 Minutes*, the newspaper did not wish to offend Christian readers by printing the images.[16]

Finally, there are those who suggest that the decision to publish the Muhammad images was based, at least in part, on a desire for publicity and revenue; that *Jyllands-Posten* purposely set up the conditions for a clash between Muslims and non–Muslims in order to bring attention to itself and increase its sales. It is a point of view Michael Coren touches upon in his article, "The 'Draw Mohammad' Contest Was Not an Attempt to Start a Conversation but a Single Act of Bravado."[17] In the piece, Coren underscores the visibility that *Jyllands-Posten* sought from its disruptive undertaking, while also calling attention to the pointlessness—and the destructiveness—of the project. "Empty, self-promoting gestures with fatal consequences advance no meaningful cause at all," he writes.[18] Peter Hervik adds that *JP*'s decision to publish the images "must be seen in the growing competition in the domestic news market."[19]

The Draw Muhammad Project

Regarding the cartoons themselves, *Jyllands-Posten* published the collection of twelve images on September 30, 2005, under the headline, "The Face of Muhammad."[20] For the most part, the drawings were benign, notwithstanding the fact that their mere existence riled many Muslims. It further appears that most of participating cartoonists were skeptical of Kåre Bluitgen and *Jyllands-Posten*, the upshot being that over half of the drawings satirized Bluitgen or the newspaper in relation to the Muhammad project itself. Some of the cartoons, for instance, pointedly implied that the

Draw Muhammad venture was a publicity stunt designed to promote Bluitgen's forthcoming children's book or *Jyllands-Posten* newspaper. Other images, however, were more disparaging of Muhammad and Islam. "The cartoons included one of the prophet as a crazed, knife-wielding Bedouin and another of him at the gates of heaven telling suicide bombers: 'Stop. Stop. We have run out of virgins!'—a reference to the belief of some Muslim extremists that male suicide bombers are rewarded in heaven with 72 virgins," reports the *Washington Post*.[21]

In terms of the four cartoons that focused exclusively on Muhammad and were widely regarded as the most belligerent, they were submitted by cartoonists employed by, or otherwise affiliated with, *Jyllands-Posten* itself. Of these drawings, the most inflammatory was that which flowed from the pencil of Kurt Westergaard. The face of a bushy-browed Muhammad with a penetrating gaze, the prophet is wearing a turban adorned by the Shahada, or Islamic creed, in Arabic ("There is no god but Allah, and Muhammad is his messenger").[22] And then comes the kicker: swathed in the prophet's turban is a bomb, its fuse lit. A visual punch to the gut, the image was widely interpreted as accusing Muhammad himself of being the wellspring of Islamist terrorism.

Predictably, reaction to the cartoons was swift, with Westergaard's contribution triggering the most intense response. The nation's Muslims, most notably its imams and Islamic organizations, cried foul, insisting the images were demeaning to Muhammad and those who observe his teachings. Accordingly, they demanded that *Jyllands-Posten* make amends by issuing an apology to the country's Muslims. It was a demand that would fall on deaf ears. A defiant Carsten Juste, *JP*'s editor-in-chief, scoffed at the idea of expressing regret, adamant that he "wouldn't dream of" apologizing to the Muslim community.[23] And it was now that the conflict careened onto the global stage.

In mid–October, the fifty-seven-nation Organization of the Islamic Conference released a statement denouncing the *Jyllands-Posten* cartoons, while, in a separate action, eleven ambassadors, led by Egyptian ambassador Mona Omar Attia, dispatched a letter of concern to the Prime Minister of Denmark, Anders Fogh Rasmussen. Troubled by the cartoons and related matters, the diplomats asked to meet with him.

Several days later, Prime Minister Rasmussen responded to the emissaries' request by rejecting it, his explanation being that it was not his role to police the nation's media. In actuality, the ambassadors were not asking that he censor the press; their aim was to review a spate of anti–Islamic incidents in Denmark, the *Jyllands-Posten* controversy being the most recent. Although Rasmussen did not meet with the diplomats of the predominantly Islamic countries, however, he did agree to an interview with

Jyllands-Posten newspaper, a disparity that did not go unnoticed in the Muslim world.

In the weeks that followed, several nations recalled their ambassadors from Denmark either in protest or to debrief them on the situation in the Scandinavian nation. At the same time, polls showed that a majority of the Danish citizenry supported the actions of *Jyllands-Posten*, accepting as fact the newspaper's claim that it was standing up for the freedom of the press.[24] News outlets in other countries expressed solidarity with *JP* as well, some of them going so far as to take comparable risks. "Newspapers all around the world began to republish the cartoons, saying they supported a fight against self-censorship," writes journalist Adam Taylor.[25] Among such publications was *Magazinet*, an evangelical Christian newspaper in Norway whose actions further aggravated the situation. In a departure from this practice, newspapers in the United States were reluctant to reprint the offending images. Their explanation: they did not wish to offend Muslim readers, and, moreover, considered a written description of the images to be sufficient for informational purposes.

By the start of 2006, matters had grown even more volatile. There was now profound blowback against both Denmark and *Jyllands-Posten*, repercussions that included boycotts of Danish goods, flag burnings, and a lawsuit against the newspaper. (A court would dismiss the latter defamation allegation.) Violence was also erupting, aggression that reached such a pitch that Denmark's Foreign Ministry warned Danish travelers to be on their guard when visiting nearly a dozen countries and territories having large Muslim populations. Certainly the advice was reasonable, since demonstrators had recently been killed in Libya and Afghanistan. Elsewhere, European embassies were targeted. Protestors set fire to the Danish embassies in Lebanon and Iran, while in Syria both the Norwegian and Danish embassies were torched. In all, an estimated two hundred people died protesting *JP*'s Muhammad cartoons.

It was during this same period that Osama bin Laden, from his mountain sanctuary in Pakistan, demanded that Danish authorities hand over the cartoonists who, in his view, had blasphemed the prophet. To the surprise of no one, the authorities refused, not least because the cartoonists had committed no crimes under Danish law and were not bound by religious laws.

Finally, in late January 2006, *Jyllands-Posten* apologized to the Muslim community, claiming that it had never intended to insult Muslims or the Islamic faith. Carsten Juste said he was sorry if Muslims had been offended, then reminded readers that the newspaper's actions were within Danish law.[26] Similarly, Prime Minister Rasmussen made a public statement, albeit without mentioning *Jyllands-Posten* or the Draw Muhammad project, in which he denounced efforts to "demonise groups of people on the basis of their religion or ethnic background."[27] For many Muslims in Europe and the Middle East, such generic expressions of contrition were a case of too little, too late. It would prove to be an injury that would not heal.

For Kurt Westergaard, it became a hell of its own, one marked by a lifetime of twenty-four-hour security. In 2008, Danish police arrested three North African men who were plotting to kill the cartoonist, the result being that seven newspapers in Denmark reprinted the original Muhammad cartoons as a way of thumbing their nose at the would-be assassins. In response, Osama bin Laden released an audiotape blasting those who republished the images, concluding with an ominous statement. "I tell you: if there is no check on the freedom of your words, then let your hearts be open to the freedom of our actions," he said.[28]

Unfortunately, the attempts on the Westergaard's life did not cease. Two years later, Muhudiin Mohamed Geele, a twenty-eight-year-old Somali man with ties to al-Qaeda and the militant organization al-Shabaab, crashed through a window in the cartoonist's home in Århus on New Year's Day while Westergaard and his five-year-old granddaughter were watching *The Wizard of Oz*. Wielding an axe and a knife, the assailant sprang at his target. "We will get our revenge!," he shouted.[29] With foresight, authorities had equipped the cartoonist's home with a panic button and a safe room— an armored bathroom—and it was here that the artist took cover until the police arrived.

Charlie Hebdo and the Danish Cartoon Controversy

In terms of *Charlie Hebdo*'s role in the *Jyllands-Posten* affair, four months after the Muhammad images appeared in Danish newspaper, the French cartoonists weighed the pros and cons of entering the ongoing debate. Their aim was two-fold. First, they wished to show public support for their beleaguered colleague Jacques Lefranc, the editorial director of the newspaper *France Soir*, who had been fired a few days earlier by the French-Egyptian magnate who owned the newspaper. Lefranc was sacked for republishing the collection of twelve Danish cartoons. And second, *Charlie Hebdo*, as a publishing entity, wished to take a public stand against the suppression of free expression, and to do so by exercising its rights as preserved in the French Constitution. To its editors and artists, this meant republishing a small sample of Muhammad images—two cartoons—from the *Jyllands-Posten* collection. Based on the timing coupled with Hebdo's relatively constrained approach to the topic—and unlike the questionable motives of the *Jyllands-Posten* team—it does not appear that the French magazine was seeking to stir up hostility toward the Muslim population or pursuing quick profits.

The *Charlie Hebdo* team arrived at the decision to join the fray in the course of an editorial meeting, a weekly get-together during which the staff generated ideas for the magazine's next edition. Also present at the gathering were two filmmakers, Jérôme Lambert and Philippe Picard, who were making a documentary about a brilliant *Hebdo* cartoonist in attendance, Jean Cabut, or "Cabu." The filmmakers would later say that they had been impressed by the artists and their dynamic process of brainstorming, as well as by the cartoon of the prophet that Cabu subsequently produced for the Muhammad edition. "We were just amazed by the collaborative, creative, joyful process that led to the cover and caption," Lambert and Picard recalled.[30]

On February 8, 2006, *Charlie Hebdo* republished a pair of *Jyllands-Posten* cartoons that had received considerable attention across the globe during the previous four months: the Westergaard caricature of the bomb-wielding Muhammad, and the one in which the prophet complains that paradise is running out of virgins owing to the number of terrorists arriving in the afterlife. On its front cover, the edition also featured Cabu's new caricature of Muhammad so as to affix *Hebdo*'s ironic stamp to the controversy. A tragicomic image, it revealed a weeping prophet, his face buried in his hands (and therefore not visible), with a caption reading, "Muhammad overwhelmed by fundamentalists" ("Mahomet débordé par les intégristes").[31] A subcaption adds, "It's hard to be loved by imbeciles" ("C'est dur d'être aimé par des cons").[32] It was an allusion, of course, to the explosive reactions that were on display by scores of Muslims in Europe and the Middle East. Notably, Cabu's portrayal of the prophet was careful to respect the widespread Muslim belief that it is sacrilegious to depict his face. It also presented Muhammad as blameless in the international uproar and even seemed to offer him a measure of sympathy.

Despite the fact that the caricature's focus was less on Muhammad than on his followers—the violent ones—it was still not well-received by France's Muslim community, which by now had become sensitized to the raging cartoon controversies in Denmark. Even so, violence did not break out as it had in other parts of the world; rather, legal action ensued.

On February 7, 2007, the Grand Mosque of Paris and the Union of Islamic Organizations of France filed a lawsuit against *Charlie Hebdo*, editor-in-chief Philippe Val, and publisher Les Editions Rotative. The accusation: the magazine, by publishing the three cartoons, was "publicly abusing a group of people because of their religion."[33] It was an allegation the plaintiffs framed as racism, even though Islam, like other world religions, welcomes adherents of all skin colors. As to the judicial relevance of the charge, it is a crime under French law to incite racial hatred, an offense carrying the possibility of a six-month jail sentence and a five-figure fine.

When the case came to trial six weeks later, the *Charlie Hebdo* defendants insisted that their decision to print the images was in no way calculated to inflame racial tensions, but instead to comment on a specific category of people—combative adherents of Islam, terrorists in particular—who adopt the mantle of piety. "One should not confuse criticism of an ideology with racism," said Val.[34] The plaintiffs, however, remained unshakeable in their assertion that *Charlie Hebdo* was purposely insulting Muslims in order to generate racial animus, rejecting outright the magazine's argument that it was simply expressing an opinion. "Racism is not an opinion," said Francis Szpiner, an attorney for the Grand Mosque.[35]

In the end, the *Hebdo* team presented the more compelling argument, one that was in harmony with France's stalwart commitment to secularism and freedom of expression. Buttressing the defense was the testimony of such authoritative figures as François Hollande and Nicolas Sarkozy, the latter declaring that he much preferred "an excess of caricatures to an absence of caricatures."[36] So it was that the court, after two days of proceedings, ruled unanimously in favor of the defense, stating that two of the cartoons, Cabu's weeping prophet and the jest about the shortage of virgins, were targeting extremists, not ordinary Muslims. The third image, Westergaard's caricature of the prophet Muhammad with an incendiary device in his turban, was addressed as well. "(T)he court said that while the cartoon picturing the bomb in the Prophet's turban could offend Muslims if seen on its own, the picture had to be judged in the context of the magazine issue, which had treated religious fundamentalism," writes Thierry Leveque.[37] "(C)artoons step beyond the bounds of good taste in order to parody," the court explained; "the literary nature of caricature, while deliberately provocative, in this instance falls under freedom of expression and a vehicle for thoughts and opinions."[38] A ruling of considerable magnitude, it was one that the French media celebrated and free-speech advocates heralded as a triumph for freedom of the press. "It is," Val said, "good news for all of us, those who defend the principle to the right to publish satire."[39] He further stated that the followers of Islam, particularly secular Muslims who support France's democratic principles, should likewise be in favor of the ruling.

In the intervening years, *Charlie Hebdo* persisted in publishing cartoons and caricatures spoofing Judaism, Christianity, and Islam, just as it had done since the 1970s. Its humor also retained the magazine's trademark coarseness, while the publication itself continued to enjoy success in both print and digital formats.

In 2009, an adjustment to the magazine's organizational structure

2. Courting Conflict

occurred when editor-in-chief Phillipe Val was appointed director of *France Inter*, the national public radio station and a component of *Radio France*. Replacing him at the helm: Stephane Charbonnier ("Charb"), who, by all accounts, had earned the promotion during his seventeen years at the publication. In terms of his stance on Muslim sensitivity to religious satire, Charb, like Val before him, argued that cartoonists must not be intimidated into putting down their pencils. In his view, humor, by offering a unique perspective on reality, is essential when dealing with what he regarded as religious and political extremism.

In the next chapter, we explore the life of Charb, from his birth in a picturesque French town to his death at the hands of extremists in the capital city. Along the way, we examine his growth into a unique voice in contemporary French satire, and explore the events that led to the forty-seven-year-old caricaturist being selected as the primary target of the terrorist attack on *Charlie Hebdo*.

3

Stéphane Charbonnier
Satirist, Skeptic, Target

It would be a bloodstained collision between radicalized religion and the free press, one that would take place on an overcast winter day in the city of Paris. And although over a dozen people would perish in the course of the horrific affair, the principal target would be Stéphane Charbonnier, the mild-mannered editor-in-chief of *Charlie Hebdo*. Known throughout France by his nom de plume, Charb, he was a cartoonist whom al-Qaeda had branded an enemy of Islam and whose assassination it had solicited years earlier.

Born near Paris on August 21, 1967, Charb spent his childhood and adolescence in Pontoise. A picturesque town situated fifteen miles northwest of the capital city, it was here that he enjoyed an auspicious upbringing, one that fostered independent thinking and creativity and instilled in him an appreciation of the arts. Given the town's heritage, perhaps the latter was inevitable.

Once a Roman settlement and later renowned for its medieval architecture, Pontoise has long been associated with intellectual and artistic brilliance. Among the town's illustrious progeny are its twentieth-century hometown son, the astronomer-author Jacques Vallée, and the nineteenth-century Impressionist painter Camille Pissarro, who lived and worked in Pontoise for nearly twenty years. Paul Cézanne, Vincent van Gogh, and Paul Gauguin also found inspiration in the quaint town with its bygone structures and verdant landscape, their distinctive portrayals establishing it forever as a corner of earthly beauty. As for Charb, he would join the ranks of such inventive minds when he discovered, very early on, the joy of drawing.

It was during his childhood that he set about sketching, with his initial fans being his parents, Michel and Denise Charbonnier, both of whom were freethinking communists. Bolstered by their support, the budding artist published a handful of drawings in *Echo des collégiens*, a newspaper operated by the first school he attended, the Collège des Louvrais. He was fourteen years old at the time. During his ensuing years at the Lycée Camille Pissarro, a secondary school, Charb's fascination with the form intensified and expanded to include satirical caricatures, this being a natural and perhaps foreseeable development.

Sylvie Premisler, one of his teachers, recalls that the nascent cartoonist had an expansive, generous personality that was reflected in his work, with his drawings covering a spectrum of subjects marked by boldness and infused with humanity and fair-mindedness.[1] Charb's illustrations also bristled with what was becoming his signature sense of humor, and they invariably delighted his classmates. "He had a lot of humor and bite, a critical mind, and was already very responsive to the news" ("Il avait beaucoup d'humour et de mordant, un esprit critique et il était déjà très réactif à l'actualité"), says Frédéric Legendre, a fellow student who befriended the seventeen-year-old Charb in 1984 at the Lycée Camille Pissarro.[2] As could be expected, Charb's artwork, with its sharp wit and individualized style of presentation, would soon attract notice beyond the walls of academia.

In the late 1980s, for instance, his drawings were featured in a parochial newspaper, *les Nouvelles du Val-d'Oise* (The Val-d'Oise News), and from here they came to the attention of executives at Utopia, a company that operates a network of cinemas in France. Impressed with his talent, the latter hired him to provide illustrations for the company's monthly publication, *Gazette d'Utopia*, this being the first time the company had employed a person in such a capacity. Charb's responsibilities included creating cartoons and providing other drawings to accompany film reviews, announcements of cinematic events, and commentaries on germane topics of the day. As had been the case at Lycée Camille Pissarro and *les Nouvelles du Val-d'Oise*, the up-and-coming artist quickly earned praise for his social and political astuteness, keen eye for detail, and remarkable energy and productivity.[3]

In the years that followed, Charb's cartoons were further exhibited in a pair of acclaimed publications, the top-rated Franco-Belgian comics magazines *L'Echo des savanes* and *Fluide Glacial*, each boasting its own international roster of cartoonists. Among his fellow contributors were the American artists Robert Crumb and Art Spiegelman, along with Chilean-French filmmaker, composer, and cartoonist Alejandro Jodorowsky. Charb additionally provided artwork for the large-circulation *Télérama*, a Paris-based weekly magazine focusing on television and cultural issues, and *L'Humanité*, a daily newspaper espousing collectivist values and a former publication of the French Communist Party.[4] It would be in 1992, however, that the rising star of satirical caricature would secure a permanent, full-time position at *Charlie Hebdo* in Paris, and, in 1998, create at this publication two one of his most entertaining characters in a long-running comic strip known as *Maurice et Patapon*.

In the series of three-frame *Maurice et Patapon* escapades, Maurice was an orange dog, a wild-eyed anarchist who was narrow-minded and intolerant. He was also pansexual and partial to sodomy. His accomplice, Patapon, was an uptight, sexually disinterested, condescending cat who leaned toward fascism. While the anti-capitalist pair, whose offbeat humor impaled everyone from chain-smokers to politicians, might have been regarded as insufferable in other milieus, in the context of humor—more precisely, in Charb's capable hands—the duo radiated a childlike irreverence together with an exuberant free-spiritedness and affability. In this respect, they resembled their creator himself.

"In private, he was one of the gentlest and sweetest men," says Lionel Hoëbeke, Charb's publisher and longtime friend.[5] In an interview with *Le Figaro*, Hoëbeke portrayed Charb as a benign soul, a man whose personal qualities permeated the playful characters he brought to the page.[6] Accordingly, it was rather paradoxical when Charb, a pacifist cherished by his family, friends, colleagues, and readers, became a central target in the wave of Islamist terrorism that traumatized the Western world beginning on September 11, 2001.

Stéphane Charbonnier (right), editor-in-chief of *Charlie Hebdo* and the principal target of the al-Qaeda-inspired attack on the satirical weekly. Pictured with Voice of America interviewer Arzu Çakır, 2012 (Arzu Çakır/Voice of America [VOA]).

Osama Bin Laden Meets *Charlie Hebdo*

As is well known, it was on this fateful day that nearly three thousand men, women, and children, everyday people from all walks of life, met their deaths in the attacks on the World Trade Center and the Pentagon. The terrorist unit delivering the horror was composed of fifteen Saudi nationals and four others from Lebanon, Egypt, and the United Arab Emirates, all of them radical Islamists and members of al-Qaeda. Presumably, their actions were guided by the Saudi militant and founder of the al-Qaeda network, Osama bin Laden, who conceived of, and orchestrated, the attacks in conjunction with his uppermost associates.

As the United States reeled, countries around the globe expressed their sympathy and support, with France being among the most demonstrative. From candlelight vigils on the streets of Paris to the hundreds of French citizens who gathered at Notre Dame Cathedral to sing "The Star-Spangled Banner," *la République* grieved for its longtime friend and ally. Emblematic of this solidary was an editorial in *Le Monde*, a heartfelt piece leading with the headline, "We Are All Americans" ("Nous sommes tous Américains").[7]

In the days following the attacks, the crew at *Charlie Hebdo* got to work. Even though irony was the magazine's lifeblood and its staff members were experts in incisive political art and commentary, the periodical nevertheless faced a challenge in illustrating the diabolical occurrence on the other side of the Atlantic. It was a dicey situation by any measure. It terms of the single most precarious task, that of producing the cartoon for the weekly's front cover, the assignment was handed to Charb, his task being to address the cataclysmic attack in such a way as to neither minimize it nor disrespect the victims, but rather, in a clever fashion, offer political insight into the momentous occurrence.

On September 19, 2001, his political art hit the newsstands. Heralded by a top-of-the-page banner proclaiming, "Special: the shit hits the fan!" ("Spécial ça va chier!"), it depicted a panoramic view from a large window of a Manhattan skyscraper.[8] An airline piloted by a frenzied, keffiyeh-wearing Arab is barreling toward this room in which sit several stock-traders, nearly all of them busily conducting business on their computers. One trader has spotted the plane heading toward them, though, and is shouting to his colleagues to sell their stocks.[9] A jab at Islamist fanaticism, Charb's cartoon was also a swipe at the purported American fixation on money and the accumulation of wealth.

Inevitably, criticism of the magazine ensued, namely accusations that Charb and his colleagues had been offensive in the face of America's calamity. The *Hebdo* staff took the grumbling in stride, however, aware that political cartooning is not meant to be a feel-good enterprise nor is it expected to avoid wrestling with controversial events and developments. But aside from the predictable smattering of criticism over the magazine's approach to the attacks, the September 19 issue of *Charlie Hebdo* was noteworthy in that it represented the opening salvo in what was to become its years-long satirical assault on radical Islamism, with extremists' destructive and self-destructive exploits furnishing the magazine's writers and illustrators with abundant fodder. And Stéphane Charbonnier, pencil in hand, would be ready to perform his alchemy of transforming their ghastly goings-on into smart visual humor.

A non-religious man, Charb considered himself to be clear-headed when assessing religious beliefs and practices. He had no inclination toward any faith, but rather viewed the three leading Western religions—Christianism, Judaism, and Islam—as mythologies that could be, and in fact had been, detrimental to humanity in several respects. And he voiced this opinion often. Consistent with his position, he refused to accede to any religion and dismissed categorically their dictates, a situation that sometimes led to his being accused of blasphemy. It was an allegation he rejected as illogical.

"A nonbeliever," Charb said, "*cannot* blaspheme." In his book, published posthumously under the title, *Open Letter: On Blasphemy, Islamophobia, and the True Enemies of Free Expression*, the caricaturist explains that "God is sacred only to those who believe in him."[10] Charb's argument was that an individual cannot insult a deity that, in the person's opinion, does not exist, and that other people, even pious believers, should grasp this fact. Addressing complaints from the Islamic community, Charb continued to express this line of reasoning, namely, that because he was not a Muslim, he was under no obligation to adhere to Islamic standards of behavior. And to Charb, this included the act of sketching the image of Mohammad in his cartoons and caricatures, which some, but not all, Muslims contend is blasphemous. Instead, he insisted that he was free to discuss, criticize, illustrate, and poke fun at the religion, and, moreover, that the French legal system protected his right to do so. It was a matter of freedom of expression.

As it turned out, editor-in-chief Charb's commitment to press freedom would land *Charlie Hebdo* in hot water once again in November 2011, when he decided that the magazine would celebrate—tongue-in-cheek, of course—the electoral victory of Ennahda, the Islamist party in Tunisia. To this end, the forthcoming edition of the magazine was to be rechristened "Charia Hebdo," a play on the term "Sharia law," and Muhammad was to serve as guest editor. To be showcased on the cover, moreover, was a caricature created by staff cartoonist Rénald

Luzier ("Luz"), an amusing image of a comical Muslim man warning, "100 lashes if you don't die laughing!" ("100 coups de fouet, si vous n'êtes pas morts de rire!").[11] Explains Charb, "It was a joke where the topic was to imagine a world where Sharia would be applied."[12] Although it was designed to be a light-hearted spoof, it would be met with a heavy-handed response.

At one o'clock in the morning on the day the "Charia" edition was scheduled for release, Molotov cocktails smashed through the windows of the *Charlie Hebdo* offices. The publishing operation was wrecked in an instant. "The stocks are burned, smoke is everywhere, the paste-up board is unusable, everything is melted, there's no more electricity," Charb reported to the media.[13] Presumed to be the work of radical Islamists, the perpetrators were never apprehended. As for the 75,000 print-run of the special edition, it had been stored at a separate facility and thus made it to the newsstands later that day. Meanwhile, a sympathetic newspaper in Paris, *Libération*, promptly provided *Charlie Hebdo*'s twenty-five staff members with workspace until the magazine could secure new accommodations.

An inquiry into the firebombing revealed that the magazine had received menacing letters and emails before the incident. And shortly after the attack, the periodical's website was hacked and visitors redirected to a site brandishing the Islamic creed and photographs of mosques. Naturally, condemnation of these intrusions was swift.

"Freedom of expression is an inalienable right in our democracy," railed French prime minister François Fillon, "and all attacks on the freedom of the press must be condemned with the greatest firmness."[14] France's interior minister Claude Guéant also issued a forthright response. "If some think they can impose their way of thinking on the Republic," he said, "they are mistaken, they will be fought."[15] And Charb weighed in, predicting that Islamist extremists, if left to their own devices, would ensure that Islam would be the only topic in France that would be untouchable by the press. "If we can poke fun at everything in France," Charb said, "if we can talk about anything in France apart from Islam or the consequences of Islamism, that is annoying."[16] It was an aggravation with which he would continue to struggle.

Years later, Philippe Val would recount how his resilient colleagues at the periodical, as they were resurrecting the satirical magazine in another district of Paris, laughed at the attack that had demolished their home.[17] And in a retort to the firebombing, the irrepressible Luz would publish a cartoon depicting two men, a French cartoonist and a Muslim, locked in a deep, sloppy kiss, with a caption reading, "Love is greater than hate" ("L'amour puis fort que la haine").[18]

The Innocence of Muslims

Hate would reign supreme once again the following year when an anti–Islamic video was uploaded to YouTube. Created by Nakoula Basseley Nakoula (AKA Sam Basile), a convicted felon and self-described "Israeli Jew" living in California, the short film was called *The Innocence of Muslims* and it depicted Muhammad as a lout, sadist, and pedophile.[19] Although the video was cheaply made, poorly presented, and thoroughly preposterous, its affront to the prophet nevertheless set off riots in the Middle East. In the course of the unrest, fifty people died and hundreds more suffered injuries. And it was in the midst of this maelstrom that *Charlie Hebdo*, as a publication that comments on important political and social topics of the day, decided to address the heated reaction to the video's public scorning of the prophet.

For the September 19 issue, Charb decided the magazine would again feature caricatures of Muhammad. As always, a portion of the images were risqué and offensive to some viewers, with one in particular rankling a disproportionate share of them. "The most objectionable," according to Jon Wiener at *The Nation*, "is labeled 'Mohammed,' and shows the Prophet naked on his hands and knees with his ass in the air, inviting anal sex; the cartoonist has drawn a star over his anus, and the caption says 'a star is born.'"[20] The cartoon was an allusion to the prophet's starring role in *The Innocence of Muslims*.

The same edition contained a spirited editorial as well, one titled, "Laugh, for God's Sake."[21] Likening Islamist extremists to fascists, it argued that compromise was not the solution to the incompatibility between cast-iron religious edicts and the freedom and flexibility of the press.

In terms of the cartoons themselves, leading the pack was an image created by Charb, that of a Muslim in a wheelchair being pushed by an Orthodox Jew. "The wheelchair-bound figure on the front page said 'You mustn't mock' under the headline 'Intouchables 2,' a reference to a popular French movie … about a paralyzed rich white man and his black assistant," reports *Der Spiegel*.[22] The cartoon expressed, yet again, Charb's complaint that Islamist extremists all too often demand that their religion be immune to criticism in the press, including satirical humor. It further suggested that these same individuals, as represented by the infirm Muslim in a wheelchair, treat Islam as if it were a delicate, vulnerable religion that lacks resilience. Charb, in fact, had long contended that extremists had no reason to appoint themselves the sentries of the Islamic faith, that the religion has survived and flourished since its inception in the seventh century and is more than capable of bearing the occasional affront in the media.

The French government, for its part, had its own set of concerns at this juncture, first and foremost the safety of its citizens and the security of the nation's interests. In light of the riots in the Middle East brought about by *The Innocence of Muslims* video together with the firebombing of the *Charlie Hebdo* offices eleven months earlier, officials feared that the publication of the latest *Hebdo* cartoons would provoke a grave response. Besides presenting a danger to French citizens at home, officials worried that Muslims in the Middle East might retaliate against French operations in that region. Accordingly, the government took the unusual step of temporarily shuttering France's embassies and schools in twenty nations having large Muslim populations, while also deploying riot police to protect the *Charlie Hebdo* offices in Paris. French officials also made no secret of the fact that they were perturbed by the magazine's decision to proceed with publishing the challenging material.

As it turned out, significant violence did not break out in protest of the *Charlie Hebdo* cartoons, although the episode proved to be an expensive and disruptive one for the French government. It also gave a boost to a mounting counterargument, shifting attention from the magazine's Constitutional right to publish provocative material to its wisdom in doing so. "Is it really sensible or intelligent to pour fuel on the fire?," asked French foreign minister Laurent Fabius in a public rebuke of Charb's publishing decision.[23] It was a question that was echoed on the other side of the Atlantic as well. "We don't question the right of something like this to be published," said Jay Carney, speaking on behalf of the Obama White House, "we just question the judgment behind the decision to publish it."[24] The emergent position, then, was that merely because one had the right to perform an action, in this case the publishing of controversial cartoons, does not mean that one should necessarily exercise that right; that there are other factors besides Constitutional protections to be weighed when contemplating the release of potentially inflammatory material.

Such opinions notwithstanding, Charb remained resolute in his conviction that the press must not allow extremists to coerce it into silence. It was not, in his view, a case of pouring fuel on a fire but rather that of a satirical weekly simply doing the job it had done for decades, that of providing levity and insight into important social and political events. In the present case, it was doing so in the face of hypersensitive, intolerant, and aggressive adversaries.[25] In effect, Charb was taking the same stand as those risk-taking figures discussed in Chapter 1, such as Voltaire when faced with exile for his tongue-in-cheek verse about the French regent's family or Daumier when gambling with the prospect of imprisonment for his lithograph portraying the rapacious king as a giant pear. And like Voltaire and Daumier, whose actions did indeed lead to their exile and incarceration,

Charb and his colleagues would face harsh consequences. In the case of the *Charlie Hebdo* team, however, the consequences would not be delivered by legal authorities—the magazine had committed no crimes—but by Saïd and Chérif Kouachi, two French brothers and staunch Islamists determined to silence the satirical magazine and its editor-in-chief.

4

Al-Qaeda and the Radicalization of Saïd and Chérif Kouachi

Unlike *Charlie Hebdo*'s editor-in-chief, Stéphane Charbonnier, who was raised by doting parents in a small, pristine town in the French countryside, his eventual killers, the Kouachi brothers, were dealt a hand that was anything but promising. Born in Paris to parents who hailed from Constantine, Algeria, the boys were two years apart in age, with Saïd coming into the world on September 7, 1980, and Chérif on November 29, 1982. Besides their mother and father, Freiha and Mokhtar Kouachi, they lived with their sisters, Aïcha and Salima, and a younger brother, Chabanne, in government-subsidized housing in Paris' tenth and nineteenth arrondissements, or districts.

The brothers' early years were austere, their father struggling to support the family and the children having little in the way of material comforts. To lend a hand, a charitable organization invited Saïd and Chérif to take part in the social and recreational activities it offered to the neighborhood's impoverished youth, and the boys seized the opportunity. Shortly thereafter, their contrasting personalities became evident to others in the group.

Evelyne, the woman who supervised it, remembered Saïd as an introverted child who wept often and tended to follow the younger Chérif's lead.[1] She portrayed Chérif, on the other hand, as extroverted and gregarious as well as mischievous and rambunctious. Even so, she did not consider him unpleasant or a "problem child." More the opposite. "You only had to sweet-talk him and take him in your arms and he would calm down," she says, adding that she was quite fond of Chérif in those days.[2]

As if the Kouachi brothers' underprivileged childhoods weren't tough enough, their lives would be ruptured in 1991 when their father succumbed to cancer. Because of his absence, the family's financial situation spiraled downward, a situation worsened by the fact that Freiha was unemployed, ill, and, according to her neighbors, intoxicated much of the time.[3] For such reasons, a social welfare agency removed Saïd and Chérif from the home and dispatched them to a center for orphaned and troubled youth in October 1994. A therapeutic "country home," it was called La Fonda and was operated by the Claude Pompidou Foundation.

The region in which the facility was situated is known as Corrèze, in southwestern France, and is distinguished by gently sloping hills, old-world villages, and stately châteaux. The town itself was the small municipality of Treignac, which rests on the banks of the Vézère River and is renowned for its historic architecture and air of tranquility. But whereas the local adults appreciated Treignac's medieval vestiges together with its serenity, younger residents complained that the town of 1,700 was mind-numbingly dull. And this included the Kouachi brothers, whose number-one aim, according to a fellow classmate, was to leave it behind and return to Paris.[4]

As things stood, the two youths did travel to the capital city three times a year to visit their mother, sisters, and brother, but these trips came to halt in January 1995, when there occurred another fracture in the family. It seems that young Aïcha came home from school one day to find their mother Freiha dead, an empty pill bottle resting near her body. Although officials classified the death as illness-related, the presence of the empty container coupled with the fact that the widowed mother of five had recently become pregnant caused her neighbors to suspect that she had taken her own life.[5] Whatever the cause of death, Saïd, in particular, never completely recovered from the loss but rather remained heartbroken by it, with his bitterest, most blistering episode at La Fonda stemming from his classmates' sneers about his deceased mother.[6]

Since both of their parents had now passed away, Saïd and Chérif would not be returning to Paris anytime soon; henceforth their lives would be centered at La Fonda. But this was not necessarily an adverse development in that both youths appear to have profited from their ensuing five years in the French countryside. "They laughed and played like normal teenagers," says Alain Lascaux, who supervised an athletic club in Treignac.[7] It was an observation that was voiced often, the siblings' stability in the face of family heartbreak and displacement being praised by many who knew them, according to journalist Marion Von Renterghem in his account of the Kouachis in *Le Monde*.[8]

Through La Fonda, Saïd and Chérif enjoyed excursions to the Alps and the Pyrénées, played music and sports, and took part in an array of courses and workshops. In many respects, their new lifestyle was far superior to the one they had left behind in Paris, with the youths flourishing both at the residential center and their schools, which included middle school at the Collège Lakanal in Treignac and high school near Limoges.

Older brother Saïd, for his part, acquired self-confidence and became more outspoken, his leadership skills prompting his classmates to elect him as their representative to the student government. He also continued being the more serious, conscientious, and pious brother, steering clear of tobacco and alcohol, praying in his room each night, and devoting himself to a romantic relationship with another student by the name of Stephanie.

Chérif remained the opposite. A bit of a scoundrel as well as the class clown, he dated several girls but did not commit to any of them. Demonstrating no interest in Islam even when harangued by his older brother, Chérif eschewed prayer and other Muslim practices, smoked and drank, and formed a rap band. Above all, he played soccer, a sport at which he excelled, with there being talk that he might make a career of it.

So intense was Chérif's love of soccer that he enrolled in a regional sports-studies program to earn an instructor's certificate, while Saïd signed up for a hotel culinary program with the aim of becoming a chef. The two were full of hope, their prospects bright. But then came a change as the pair began morphing into largely unrecognizable youths. Toward the end of the 1990s, Saïd became socially aloof and more dogmatic about his Islamic practices, while Chérif became unaccountably hostile and detached. He also dropped out of the sports-studies program and lost interest in his other studies. And while the reasons behind the abrupt shifts in the brothers' attitudes and actions are not known for certain, what is known is that they were now spending a considerable amount of their time at the apartment of an uncle in Paris. Mohamed was his name, and the La Fonda staff suspected him of exerting a harmful influence over the pair, especially when it was discovered that they had lied about their whereabouts on numerous occasions to spend more time at his city apartment.

In short order, representatives from Child Welfare convened a family meeting during which they conferred with Mohamed and the four Kouachi children, including young Aïcha whom the uncle had purportedly expressed an interest in marrying. Contending that Mohamed's effect on the children had been corrosive, the authorities denied him further contact with them.[9] But prohibiting future visits was an unpopular decision with the Kouachi brothers and ultimately did not stand. Distraught by the injunction, Saïd left La Fonda a year later, in 2000, and moved into Mohamed's flat in Paris' nineteenth arrondissement, with Chérif joining them shortly thereafter.

In the French capital, the brothers continued drifting away from mainstream French life, spending an increasing amount of time in the company of those whose backgrounds and circumstances were more akin to their own. These were, for the most part, the sons and daughters of Algerian immigrants whose standards of living were far from sufficient. As well, the Kouachis were evincing a mounting rebelliousness, one that would intensify in the coming years and culminate in a dramatic turn to militant Islamism.

Radicalization

Based on Chérif's accounts when interrogated by the authorities, he and his brother were drawn into the orbit of radical Islam in two distinct stages, with Chérif, rather than the older Saïd, taking the lead at both points. It is not clear to what extent Mohamad, their Parisian uncle, fostered their pivot toward religious and political extremism; Chérif, under police interrogation, claimed his uncle did not play a significant role. Whatever the truth of the matter, we do know that Mohamad kicked Chérif out of the apartment after a few months. We also know that the Kouachi brothers proceeded to form close relationships with two figures outside of their family, two militant Muslims, who appear to have been instrumental in facilitating the Kouachis' conversion from aimless, adrift young men to fixated jihadists.

It was in the early 2000s and conditions were harsh in the district in which Saïd and Chérif were living, one described in an *NBC News* report as a "multi-national neighborhood where families with roots in one-time

Saïd Kouachi (left) and Chérif Kouachi (Photo Booth [public domain]).

French colonies in North Africa crowd into housing projects that rise above street markets offering Moroccan melons and pungent French cheese."[10] While savory food may have been plentiful, rewarding jobs for young Muslims were not, the norm being low-paying positions that offered no real prospects for advancement. And this was the case for Saïd and Chérif, the latter being employed as a pizza deliveryman even as he committed robberies and peddled hashish for extra cash.[11]

During this same period, Chérif dated women but remained uncommitted to them, which may have been due partly to his nomadic existence. Because his uncle that had thrown him out of the apartment, Chérif was more or less rootless. "He was living almost like a homeless person," says journalist Angelique Chrisafis, "staying with someone but it was more of a mattress on the floor than a real home."[12] That said, the younger Kouachi's days were not without sunshine. He played soccer and video games in his spare time, as well as club-hopping, smoking hashish, making rap music, and appearing in an amateur rap video. It was when he met up with a former classmate from Treignac, however, a man whose mother offered Chérif lodging, that he set about reexamining his priorities. The upshot: he began attending, with Saïd by his side, the Pré-Saint-Gervais Mosque, and his participation seemingly had a palliative effect on him. "It helped me calm down," Chérif later said, "which is why I started going frequently."[13]

Chérif also spent much of his time at the nearby Buttes-Chaumont Park, a rambling, hilly green space replete with meadows, ponds, and even an ersatz Roman temple. In this park, he mixed with other young men like himself: Muslims, at least nominally, in their late teens and early twenties, many of whom were the sons or grandsons of Algerian immigrants. More often than not, their homes were chaotic and their families impoverished, conditions that prompted some of the group's members to resort to petty crime.

In 2003, the authorities began to detect a change in this ragtag band of comrades as its participants coalesced into what the police began calling the "Buttes-Chaumont Gang." Among other developments, its members now championed fundamentalist Islam. Entailing a narrow, isolated, and concrete interpretation of religious writings, fundamentalism involves, in the words of British scholar and imam Usama Hasan, "the reading of scripture out of context with no reference to history or a holistic view of the world."[14] They also began espousing a set of positions in line with Islamism, or politically-directed Islam. This movement toward militant Islamism suggested to the authorities that the boisterous group was heading into stormy seas, which indeed would prove to be the case. Regarding Chérif, who had remained rather guileless in spite of his sporadic forays into minor crime, his Buttes-Chaumont mates educated him in the ways of their world and swayed him with their opinions and beliefs—religious, political, or otherwise. "They ran rings around him because he was relatively fragile and allowed himself to be led by the nose," says educator Francoise Ronfet.[15]

Farid Benyettou

Fast becoming a persuasive figure to those in the Buttes-Chaumont group—and a person who seems to have led Chérif Kouachi by the nose—was a self-styled imam by the name of Farid Benyettou. A twenty-two-year-old janitor, Benyettou was the Paris-born son of Algerian immigrants and the brother-in-law of terrorist Youssef Zemmouri, who plotted in 1998 to unleash horror at the World Cup soccer tournament in France. As an adolescent, Benyettou lived with Zemmouri before the latter was convicted and deported, and through this relative became acquainted with jihadist ideas. Benyettou was specifically drawn to Salafism, an ultraconservative, reformist application of Islam, and to Salafi jihadism, a militant, transnational ideology that was gaining devotees in France during this period. The Islamic State (ISIS) and al-Qaeda are considered examples of Salafi-jihadist organizations.

Into his early twenties, Benyettou remained a staunch Salafist, unlike the preponderance of Moslems in his Paris neighborhood who neither shared his approach to Islam nor countenanced his overdramatic means of expressing it. In fact, a local religious facility, the Adda'wa Mosque, ejected him because he not only failed to show respect for its imams but went so far as to accost them in public.[16] After being expelled, the young zealot, who dressed in white robes and swathed his head in a traditional keffiyeh, joined another mosque in the nineteenth arrondissement. Even more consequential, he began handpicking a small group of lost souls from Buttes-Chaumont Park and assembling them in his flat ostensibly for religious lessons. Chérif was among the attendees.

Without delay, Benyettou embarked on a scheme to indoctrinate the younger Kouachi brother and his comrades into the Salafist, or "early Muslim," approach to the Islamic faith, which emphasizes devotion to the teachings of Allah and the necessity of proper conduct as outlined in the Koran. It was a message that resonated with Chérif, as did the mentor-pupil relationship itself, the teacher and his teachings providing him with a much-needed sense of belonging and direction. "I think in Mr. Benyettou he found someone who could tell him what to do, like an older brother," Vincent Ollivier, Chérif's attorney, told reporters.[17] And Chérif's behavior did in fact become more constructive, at least for a while, as he himself

4. Al-Qaeda and the Radicalization of Saïd and Chérif Kouachi 41

attested. "Going to see Farid helps me behave better," he told gendarmes.[18] Quickly becoming an enthusiastic devotee of Benyettou, Chérif ensured that his brother Saïd became a follower as well.

After the lay imam had secured the confidence of his band of acolytes, he altered his message. Within a few months, he was stressing the value of jihad, a holy war or crusade, against those he considered infidels and adversaries of Islam. His uppermost targets: the United States because of its unprovoked attack on Iraq and the French government for having banned female Muslims from donning the traditional veil in public schools. Benyettou argued that a struggle was the agency by which faithful Muslims should respond to acts of this nature. All the same, he was careful not to advocate violence in these discourses, teaching instead that nonviolent means could be effective. "We have to fight in France, but we should not fight with weapons nor throw bombs," he told his adherents.[19]

For Chérif, who had placed his trust in Benyettou, it was only a matter of time before he embraced wholesale the lay imam's proposition that jihad was essential, although it is unclear if Chérif fully grasped what he was advocating. When the police interrogated him after one of his arrests, they discovered that the younger Kouachi brother knew surprisingly little about Islam in general or Salafism, al-Qaeda, or the Middle Eastern political situation in particular despite having spent months under Benyettou's tutelage.[20] Symbiotically attached to the lay imam, Chérif may simply have been parroting Benyettou's words and mirroring his militancy, identifying with him while striving for acceptance and continued guidance. Unfortunately, Benyettou's directives would soon descend into more sinister territory.

A year later, in 2004, the passionate Salafist supplanted his pacifistic teachings with the suggestion that the Buttes-Chaumont Gang consider taking up arms against the infidels. His method of persuasion was roundabout and largely risk-free, however, in that he did not order them to engage in physical aggression but rather taught that doing so for the cause of jihad was a noble choice for a pious Muslim. As to why he did not command his followers to become violent, it may have been that he assumed a hands-off position that would afford him a degree of deniability in the event that one or more of them were to be arrested for a threat or act of violence. In such a circumstance, Benyettou could claim that he did not explicitly call for the crime to be committed and perhaps avoid legal repercussions. Alternatively, he may have respected the free will of his acolytes and truly believed the decision to pursue jihad should come from them, not from him; that it should arise from their own convictions instead of being a knee-jerk response to an authority figure's directive. Whatever the case, Benyettou, while refraining from demanding that his followers become bloodthirsty jihadists, did steer them into a position to do so, making it known that he would place his full support behind those who resolved to take part in a holy war and were prepared to accept martyrdom. Sacrificing oneself for the sake of Allah, he taught, was an honorable death; a death endorsed by holy Muslim texts and rewarded with paradise in the afterlife.

In the present life, meanwhile, Benyettou set about helping those who wished to pursue jihad by arranging for them to travel to the Middle East to undergo arms training. Afterward, they could either remain in the Middle East and carry out strikes against the Western coalition forces or return to France and take action at home. By and large, his followers, who he had successfully primed by this point, were eager to comply.

The first to go was Boubaker al-Hakim, a brawny combatant who had already spent time in Iraq as a human shield before being arrested in Syria and deported to France. After a stretch in Paris with his longtime friend Benyettou and Benyettou's acolytes, al-Hakim decided to return to Iraq, reconnect with the anti-coalition forces, and help coordinate the training of other members of the Buttes-Chaumont Park Gang upon their arrival. "Benyettou recruited Boubaker because he [Benyettou] was a softy preaching in Paris and Boubaker was the muscle," explains Jean-Pierre Filiu, an academic specializing in French-Islamist terrorism.[21] Their strategy would not be up to standard, however, as demonstrated by the fate of the first set of gang members to alight in the Middle East.

This initial group consisted for four men and included, among others, al-Hakim's nineteen-year-old brother Redouane. Before long, Redouane was killed during an American bombing raid, another two died as well, and the sole survivor lost his limb and his sight. Clearly, the Buttes-Chaumont Gang's track record in the Middle Eastern cauldron was proving to be abysmal.

Regarding Chérif, he and a few other aspiring jihadists in the gang, which officials would soon rename the "Buttes-Chaumont Jihadist Network," began preparing on their own turf. In the Paris park, they exercised, competed in soccer, and ran laps each day to increase their endurance. On top of this, they studied weaponry and tactics. To familiarize themselves with AK-47s, for instance, they spent time in the city's internet cafés, sketching diagrams of the weapon retrieved from online sources and speculating about how to operate it. For Chérif, the objective was to enhance his physical and mental readiness until he could slip into the Middle East for arms training.

It would be in late 2004 that such an undertaking would be set into motion when arrangements were finalized for him to fly to Syria. From there, Chérif, who had taken to calling himself Abu Issen when in the company of those in the Buttes-Chaumont network, would travel to Iraq where, upon completing his training, he would oppose through guerrilla warfare

4. Al-Qaeda and the Radicalization of Saïd and Chérif Kouachi   43

the American forces stationed in that country. Yet despite the feasibility of the plan, events took an unexpected turn when the time arrived to initiate it. It seems that French authorities had wiretapped the Buttes-Chaumont network, a practice that led to the arrest of Chérif Kouachi and Thameur Bouchnak, a fellow jihadist-in-the-making, on January 24, 2005, shortly before they were to fly to Damascus. Officials promptly subjected the pair to serial interrogations.

During three such sessions, Chérif lied about his motives, insisting his purpose in traveling to the Syrian capital had been to purchase goods he could resell in France for a profit. Only in the fourth grilling did he concede that his intention had been to engage in a holy war in Iraq, a course of action he claimed to have chosen upon learning about the rogue band of American soldiers who had tortured and murdered Muslim detainees at Abu Ghraib prison. But while he disclosed that he had been willing to forfeit his own life in the Middle East—Chérif explained that Benyettou had enlightened him about the magnificent mansion and scores of virgins who awaited the martyr in paradise—Chérif claimed that he had recently developed a case of cold feet and was relieved the authorities had prevented him from proceeding. He added that he had come to realize that the devil had led him down the reckless path from which the police had rescued him.[22]

Altogether, the authorities detained five people in addition to Chérif in the course of this operation aimed at thwarting travel to the Middle East for illicit purposes. Among them was Saïd Kouachi, whom the authorities released a short time later, and Farid Benyettou, whom they did not. Instead, they incarcerated the lay imam just as they did Chérif, who spent nearly twenty months behind bars in Fleury-Mérogis Prison in anticipation of his trial. Subsequent to this, the younger Kouachi brother spent several more months at home until, at last, the proceedings were held.

By all accounts, it was a very different Chérif who came before the judge in 2008. A more serious and sullen one had replaced the wayward yet ingenuous youth, a stark change in demeanor that reflected the degree to which he had been influenced by his stint in Fleury-Mérogis Prison. Among other affronts, this more belligerent Chérif snubbed the court when he appeared before it, refusing to stand in the courtroom because the judge was a woman and because she represented the French judicial system. Nevertheless, the judge let slide Chérif's display of disrespect and sentenced him only to the amount of time he had already served while awaiting trial, meaning he was back on the street within hours.

It has since become known that it was while Chérif was being held in prison that the second, more intensive stage of his radicalization transpired, and it commenced when he found himself face to face with fellow inmate Djamel Beghal. An al-Qaeda recruiter, this forty-year-old prisoner appears to have singlehandedly recalibrated the trajectory of Chérif's life. In terms of the arc of Beghal's own life, his personal journey illustrates the way in which an otherwise unexceptional individual may, under a particular set of circumstances, develop into a formidable personality who wields tremendous influence over others and uses it masterfully to inflict harm on his fellow beings.

Djamel Beghal

Like Chérif and Saïd's parents who immigrated to France from Algeria, Djamel Beghal came from an Algerian town, Bordj Bou Arréridj, a hundred miles to the west of the city of Constantine. Beghal's mother had been a nurse known for her iron will—her nickname was "the panther"—while his father had fought against the French in the War of Independence.[23] Beghal also had an uncle to whom he was close, but their relationship was cut short. Owing to the "long-term effects of the torture the uncle had endured at the hands of French forces during the same war, he succumbed at the age of forty."[24]

Arriving in Paris in 1986, the twenty-one-year-old Beghal held a few conventional jobs and, four years later, married a French citizen: a Breton named Sylvie Gueguen. He met her while he was employed as a youth worker in the town of Corbeil-Essonnes. In addition to forging a life with Sylvie and carrying out his job responsibilities in this southern suburb of the capital city, the devout Muslim found time to recruit local residents into the Islamic faith.[25] Beghal's interests, it should be noted, were not only in Islam, but in Islamic fundamentalism in particular and soon thereafter, militant Islamism.

In terms of his clashes with the French legal system, Beghal first landed on officials' radar twelve years later when investigators unearthed in his belongings the telephone number of a suspected terrorist. Although they interrogated Beghal, who by now held citizenship in both France and Algeria, they did not charge him, since, strictly speaking, he had not committed a crime. All the same, officials kept him under a watchful eye, and it may have been partly for this reason that he relocated to England a few months later.

Residing with his wife and four children in the East Midlands city of Leicester from 1997 to 1999, Beghal worked for a charitable organization that provided services to the homeless. He also studied computer science and, for extra income, made sandwiches. More tellingly, he made the hundred-mile trip to London frequently, where he attended services at the Finsbury Park Mosque. Suffice it to say, it should have been a red flag given

4. Al-Qaeda and the Radicalization of Saïd and Chérif Kouachi 45

Beghal's recent past in France, one capturing the attention of British terrorism experts in that the London mosque was known to be home to a pair of radical figures. Their names were Abu Hamza, an imam from Egypt, and Abu Qatada, a Salafi cleric from Jordan, and it was through these men that Beghal proceeded to become fully radicalized. It was Qatada, moreover, who thereafter directed him to travel to the Middle East to prepare for jihad.

"As he moved more deeply into radical circles, Beghal spent the year 2000 at a training camp in Afghanistan," write Alexandria Sage and Chine Labbé.[26] His efforts quickly paid dividends. Within months, he earned the confidence of the al-Qaeda leadership, most importantly Osama bin Laden himself, who summoned Beghal to his mountain hideout for a personal appraisal. Concluding that the thirty-five-year-old extremist would make a suitable operative, bin Laden handed him over to Abu Zubeida, a senior deputy who offered Beghal the lead role in a prospective attack on a pair of U.S. concerns in Paris.[27] It was to be a precarious mission, yet Beghal seized the opportunity to orchestrate it.

A two-pronged strike, a nine-person cell was to carry out the attack. In the first phase, Nizar Trabelsi, a former pro-soccer player from Tunisia, would stroll into the American embassy in Paris wearing a bomb belt concealed under his business suit. Comprised of acetone and sulfate, the incendiary device, when activated, would obliterate the building along with Trabelsi himself. In the second phase, which was to occur moments later, another cell member would drive a van loaded with explosives into the American cultural center at the Place de la Madeleine and detonate them. While the double-suicide plan was feasible, however, it would not see the light of day, instead being disrupted well in advance of its scheduled target date.

In July 2001, six weeks before the al-Qaeda attacks on the World Trade Center and the Pentagon, Beghal departed Afghanistan for France to oversee the bombings in the capital. Unbeknownst to him, his journey was about to be cut short. Only a few hours into his trip, authorities arrested the would-be terrorist during a layover at the Dubai International Airport and wasted no time subjecting him to intensive interrogations. In the course of the grillings, which ground on for two months, Beghal let loose with a torrent of information, most crucially the al-Qaeda plot against American interests in Paris. Naturally, officials leapt into action.

"Beghal's confessions in Dubai, reportedly made after religious authorities there convinced him that terrorism was contrary to Islam, led immediately to more than a dozen arrests in France, Holland and Belgium in the wake of the September 11 attacks," journalist Jon Henley wrote at the time.[28] Certainly it is true that Beghal's revelations marked the end for one of Europe's widespread terrorism networks, an operation that spanned several countries and included cells in the aspiring terrorist's former haunts of Corbeil-Essonnes, France, and Leicester, England.

In the weeks that followed, authorities made arrests in four additional countries, even as their original source sought to reverse his guilty plea. "Beghal said the confession was extracted through torture that he claimed included inserting instruments such as knitting needles into his genitals," reads a *New York Times* account.[29] Widely assumed to be true were the other tortures he described, not least because his body bore the evidence. "(H)is toenails were pulled out, his fingers were bent backward 'with a sort of bottle opener' ... a wisdom tooth was drilled without the use of anesthetic, and he was injected with 'products producing much pain, vomiting,'" according to a separate report.[30] Beghal's assertions of abuse notwithstanding, a French court, when his case came to trial in March 2005, convicted him of organizing a conspiracy to commit terrorist acts and sentenced him to ten years in prison, the maximum penalty. Numerous co-conspirators were likewise convicted but were handed shorter sentences.

It was during this same year, 2005, that the forty-year-old Beghal was joined in Fleury-Mérogis Prison by twenty-three-year-old Chérif Kouachi, who, as we noted earlier, was confined in the facility while awaiting trial for attempting to travel to the Middle East for arms training. Chérif, in turn, befriended Amedy Coulibaly, another twenty-three-year-old inmate. French by birth and Malian by ancestry, Coulibaly, also a militant Islamist, was serving time for armed robbery, and, together with Chérif, would eventually play a role in the diabolical plot of which the *Charlie Hebdo* assassinations were the chief component. It would be Djamel Beghal, moreover, who would ultimately set the pair on the path to such unfathomable violence, and it would begin here at the Fleury-Mérogis penitentiary.

Situated in a southern suburb of Paris and housing nearly four thousand inmates, this notorious correctional facility was a hub of Islamist radicalization when the two younger men arrived. According to Coulibaly, the prisoners, although restricted to their cells for twenty-two hours each day, communicated with one another through notes passed from cell to cell, lowered from windows using bed sheets, and verbally through windows and other openings.[31] Among the messages passed in this labyrinthine practice were those traveling to and from Djamel Beghal, who was supposedly being held in isolation. Further contributing to Beghal's ability to communicate within the walls of the institution was one of the prison's directors, who permitted him to conduct religious services for Muslim prisoners and preside over their weddings.[32] Intimidated by Beghal's power over the other inmates, the director was seeking to keep matters under control by allowing Beghal to connect with them periodically. Through such means, the manipulative inmate was able to spend his years at Fleury-Mérogis molding rudderless, pliable men into hard-bitten jihadists. "(A) sorcerer, [a] seducer," is how the former deputy chief of France's domestic counter-terrorism unit, Louis Caprioli, described the al-Qaeda recruiter. "(A)nyone who came in contact with him could not have helped but become more radicalised."[33]

Certainly there existed a sizable pool from which Beghal could select prospective jihadists. Forty to fifty percent of inmate population in French prisons was Muslim, a sizable share of which was easy prey for Islamists seeking new blood. Furthermore, conditions in facilities like Fleury-Mérogis were, and continue to be, highly conducive to such exploitation. "Prisons are ripe for radicalization because you have people in a confined space who have nothing else to do than talk to one another," says political scientist Francesco Ragazzi.[34] Worsening matters, guards were swamped by the sheer number of inmates, a single correctional officer often being responsible for up to a hundred prisoners. "If we have such a hard time regulating something as simple as cigarettes," says David Dulondel, a representative of a prison-guard union, "how do you expect us to regulate something as abstract as ideas, as religion?"[35]

So it was that Beghal, in this institution in which inmates taped posters of Osama bin Laden to their cell walls, schooled Chérif Kouachi and Amedy Coulibaly in jihadist ideology and methods of visiting terror upon nonbelievers. This programming in religious fanaticism and the use of violence for political ends took place over the course of a seven-month period, one that straddled 2005 and 2006.[36] And it took hold. As the recruiter had intended, the two young men, by the time of their releases, had become well-acquainted with terrorist tactics, were wholly under Beghal's spell, and were keen to do his bidding.

The latter would come about in 2009 when the pair is believed to have conspired with him in another crime. At this point, Chérif was residing with his wife Izzana, whom he had married the previous year, and working in the seafood section of a grocery store. In terms of their living arrangements, the couple rented an apartment in Gennevilliers, a pallid, proletarian suburb of Paris, where Chérif outwardly appeared to have found a sense of belonging. Rather than presenting himself as an alienated recluse or religious extremist, Chérif came across as a composed, socially-integrated husband and neighbor. "(W)ell-behaved, friendly, polite, clean-looking and above all, which is very important, he was willing to help old and disabled people," is how Eric Bade, who also lived in Gennevilliers, described him.[37] It is not known if Chérif's revamped demeanor reflected a genuine enhancement in his empathy, sociability, and self-control or if it was merely a façade he had perfected in prison, a means of averting any suspicions his new neighbors might otherwise harbor. What is known is that he attended a nearby mosque with his brother Saïd on a regular basis, as well as preserving his friendship with Amedy Coulibaly, whom the Buttes-Chaumont network now welcomed into the fold. Even more consequential, Chérif and his comrade Coulibaly began visiting Djamel Beghal after the latter's release from prison in May of that year.

Due to a legal hitch, the French government was unable to deport Beghal to Algeria and so, determined to keep a tight rein on him, formulated an arrangement whereby he essentially would remain under house arrest in the village of Murat. Located four hours south of Paris in the mountainous Auvergne-Rhône-Alpes region, it was an excursion Chérif and Coulibaly made regularly to meet with him. During such visits, the trio hiked and chatted, with the two Parisians supplying their mentor with food from the city. But this is not all they did. The two acolytes and their al-Qaeda recruiter also appear to have set aside the pleasures of the Auvergne to focus on organizing a convicted killer's escape from a penitentiary.

"The prison break plot was known as the BELKACEM Project," reports CNN, citing an undisclosed source.[38] The aim was to liberate Algerian terrorist Smaïn Aït Ali Belkacem, a member of a lethal Algerian organization, the Islamic Armed Group (GIA), and a key figure in the 1995 bombings of Parisian railway stations. Scores of civilians were injured or killed in this series of attacks for which Belkacem was sentenced to life in prison, the crimes being a reaction to France's support for the Algerian government in the Algerian Civil War (1991–2002). In terms of the plot to spring him from prison, it was thwarted by a string of sunrise raids in May 2010, that led to the arrests of Beghal, Saïd and Chérif Kouachi, Amedy Coulibaly, and a handful of suspected co-conspirators. But while Beghal was given another ten-year sentence for consorting with terrorists and Coulibaly was handed five more years behind bars, neither of the Kouachi brothers was convicted due to a lack of evidence.

Commencing at this juncture and continuing into the spring of 2014, French law enforcement and intelligence services intermittently monitored the siblings' whereabouts and activities. In so doing, the authorities discovered, after the fact, that Saïd had traveled to Syria in 2009 on a student visa ostensibly to study at the San'a Institute for the Arabic Language. While in residence, he befriended a fellow student who lived across the hall, the would-be "underwear bomber" Umar Farouk Abdulmutallab. A few months later, on Christmas Day, Abdulmutallab would attempt, but fail, to blow up a Northwest Airlines plane over the city of Detroit, a holiday suicide bombing that was the brainchild of Anwar al-Awlaki.[39] An American-Yemeni imam, al-Awlaki, with whom Abdulmutallab had been in close contact, was a senior recruiter for al-Qaeda in the Arabian Peninsula, or AQAP.

4. Al-Qaeda and the Radicalization of Saïd and Chérif Kouachi   49

Two years later, Saïd Kouachi returned to Yemen, where he too established contact with Anwar al-Awlaki and underwent arms training with the AQAP. In this, he was joined by Chérif, who confirmed four years later that he had received such instruction. "I went there, and it was Sheikh Anwar al-Awlaki who financed me," he told police, adding that he had willingly become an instrument of AQAP, long considered to be the deadliest of the al-Qaeda affiliates.[40]

After wrapping up his indoctrination and training in the Middle East, Saïd returned to France and settled in the city of Reims, northeast of Paris, and in 2012 married a woman by the name of Soumya. The couple had two children. Chérif, meanwhile, remained in the French capital with his wife Izzana, and, like Saïd, bided his time. "(B)oth brothers appeared to have refrained from any activities that might have drawn the attention of French law enforcement or spy agencies," writes Mark Hosenball.[41] Evidently, their low-profile veneers paid off, since law enforcement and intelligence agencies stopped monitoring them in 2014. Officials no longer believed the pair posed a risk to the public. Of course, they were very much mistaken.

By this point—it was only eight weeks before the *Charlie Hebdo* attack—Chérif and Izzana had dropped any pretense of being model residents of Gennevilliers. During the couple's six years in the Paris suburb, the composition of their household had also undergone a change, along with the appearances, attitudes, and lifestyles of those within it. "Neighbours say Saïd and 32-year-old Chérif shared their apartment with a third man … who was believed to be their brother-in-law, as well as a woman who always wore a head-to-toe jilbab, a tightly wrapped headscarf whenever she went outdoors," writes Mark MacKinnon.[42] The neighbors were alarmed because, among other developments, they had begun hearing the Koran being chanted through the walls of the family's apartment and worried that the Kouachis might be moving toward religious or political fanaticism. Accordingly, two of these neighbors slipped into the flat while Chérif and Saïd were away on an errand, and inside they came upon a cache of weapons. Despite the gravity of their discovery, however, the pair did not alert the police, because Chérif and Saïd returned home unexpectedly, manhandled them, and threatened to retaliate if they did so.

It was during this same period that Chérif Kouachi paid a visit to his old friend and former mentor Farid Benyettou. In this, their final tête-à-tête, Chérif set about touting the virtues of executing infidels in the name of Islam. "With him," said Benyettou, "it always came back to the same conversation, everything revolved around combat."[43] Two months later, Chérif and his brother would unleash their rage.

5

Silencing Satire
The Assault on Charlie Hebdo

The feral savagery unleashed upon the artists, writers, and editors of *Charlie Hebdo* shocked Parisians and led to the implementation of heightened security measures across the French republic. Predictably, these measures were the most vigorous and most visible in the capital city itself, not only because it was the site of the al-Qaeda–inspired bloodbath but also because it was home to the largest Muslim community in the European Union. And in the same way that the terrorist attacks at the World Trade Centers forever changed Manhattan's security landscape, so too would the *Charlie Hebdo* massacre alter that of the city of Paris. It was a fateful chain of events that began, innocently enough, on a weekday shortly after the New Year's celebrations as shoppers were enjoying the after–Christmas sales.

Day One

More precisely, it started on Wednesday, January 7, 2015, a cold, misty morning in the City of Light. Corinne Rey, a thirty-two-year-old cartoonist at *Charlie Hebdo*, had just dropped off her daughter at a nursery and was hurrying to her office at the publication's nondescript headquarters at 10 rue Nicolas-Appert. The artist, known to readers by the pen name "Coco," was planning to attend the weekly editorial meeting at 10:00 that morning.

The Kouachi brothers, Saïd and Chérif, were also in Paris on this day, but unlike Coco they were not on their way to work. They were mobilizing for a massacre that some counterterrorism experts speculate may have been cooked up by smarter, more experienced operatives within the al-Qaeda terrorist network. Certainly it was not unusual for higher-ranking members to recruit and steer would-be terrorists like Saïd and Chérif, suggestible and submissive Muslims, into committing monstrous strikes on

5. Silencing Satire   51

unwary targets. To what extent the Kouachi brothers were being deployed by al-Qaeda handlers on this day and thus were serving as such expendable pawns may never be known with certainty.

We do know that the cartoonists at *Charlie Hebdo*, in contrast to the Kouachis, were anything but suggestible or submissive. They also were nonviolent. Independent and inventive men and women, their pencils were their weapons and they wielded them like samurai. The issue of the magazine that would be hitting the newsstands on this particular day, for instance, was taking aim at those Islamist militants the artists regarded as indoctrinated and dangerous. In the lead cartoon by editor-in-chief Stéphane Charbonnier, a New Year's message boasts that France had not seen an episode of terrorist violence thus far in 2015. "Still no attacks in France" ("Toujours pas d'attentas en France"), it read.[1] Yet below this optimistic pronouncement stands a wall-eyed, bearded jihadist with an AK-47 slung over his shoulder, a comical figure who informs readers that militants still have until the end of January to let loose their New Year's "wishes" ("voeux") upon the French populace.[2] The cartoon, of course, was precisely the type known to annoy Islamists—fundamentalist hardliners, many of whom advocate militancy.

In terms of the Kouachis' familiarity with *Charlie Hebdo*, al-Qaeda publicly branded the publication an enemy of Islam while the two brothers were in the Middle East between 2009 and 2012. Intermittently during this period, Saïd and Chérif undertook arms training through the terrorist network. Then, in 2013, al-Qaeda published a hit list in *Inspire*, its online propaganda magazine, which included Stéphane Charbonnier's name and *Charlie Hebdo* affiliation. Ten targets in other nations made the list as well, among them the Indian-born British writer Salman Rushdie and Danish cartoonist Kurt Westergaard. The headline: "Wanted, dead or alive for crimes against Islam."[3] In all likelihood, Saïd and Chérif were well aware of al-Qaeda's fatwā against Stéphane Charbonnier and were more than willing to carry it out.

So it was that Coco, as planned, attended the editorial meeting on this gray January morning, a gathering during which the staff selected a cartoon for the cover of the upcoming issue and also enjoyed a spirited debate about the motives of young Muslims who wage jihad.[4] Present at the meeting as well were Stéphane Charbonnier ("Charb"), his police-bodyguard Franck Brinsolaro, staff members Mustapha Ourra, Sigolène Vinson, and Laurent Léger, and most of the *Hebdo* team of renowned cartoonists. The latter included Jean Cabut ("Cabu"), Bernard Verlhac ("Tignous"), Philippe Honoré ("Honoré"), Laurent Sourisseau ("Riss"), and Georges Wolinski. A handful of guests also attended the meeting, among them the economist Bernard Maris, psychoanalyst Elsa Cayat, book designer Gérard Gaillard,

Headquarters of *Charlie Hebdo* magazine, 10 rue Nicolas-Appert, Paris. Site of the al-Qaeda–inspired attack on January 7, 2015. Twelve were killed and several more injured in the terrorist operation.

travel writer Michel Renaud, and journalists Fabrice Nicolino and Philippe Lançon.

The Charlie Hebdo *Massacre*

At 11:30 a.m., as the meeting was winding down, a black Citroën sedan drew to a halt in front of 10 rue Nicolas-Appert and the Kouachi brothers bounded out of it. Clad in black, they wore combat boots, ammunition vests, and, to conceal their identities, balaclavas that covered their heads and faces. Only their eyes were visible. Their cache of weapons included Russian semi-automatic pistols, submachine guns, AK-47 assault rifles, a pump-action shotgun, Molotov cocktails, and a rocket-propelled grenade launcher. Some of these weapons they carried with them, while others they left behind in the Citroën. Their prey, by comparison, would be an unarmed, unsuspecting clutch of men and women.

Storming into the lobby of the four-story building, the Kouachis sprayed a volley of gunfire so earsplitting that one onlooker likened it to the clatter of a scaffold collapsing.[5] Another bystander, Jeremy Ganz, recounted the gut-wrenching spectacle of his workmate being gunned down. "I saw a door opening, a guy was shouting, 'Charlie!' and he fired," said Ganz.[6] The casualty, seated at the reception desk, was Frederic Boisseau, the forty-two-year-old father of two adolescents.

Darting up a staircase to the top floor, Chérif and Saïd stopped when they spotted a female postal worker delivering mail to a commercial firm. As she opened the door to the agency, one of the gunmen fired a warning shot and shouted, "Is this *Charlie Hebdo*?"[7] The brothers' preparations, it seems, had been shoddy. Although the two had nailed down the day and time of the magazine's weekly editorial meeting, they had failed to obtain the precise location of its suite of offices. They had only secured the street address, perhaps on the assumption that the magazine's name would be listed on the directory in the building's lobby. In reality, the satirical publication, having been the target of a firebombing in 2011, made sure its name was no longer displayed on public directories or even at the entrance to its headquarters.

As Chérif and Saïd proceeded to scour the halls for the magazine's quarters, tenants throughout the building alerted one another, as well as the police, to the incursion. No one contacted the *Charlie Hebdo* offices, however, most conspicuously Premières Lignes Télévision, the firm situated directly across the hall from them. A news and documentary production agency, the Premières Lignes staff did not have the magazine's telephone number at hand and deemed it too risky to venture across the corridor to warn their endangered neighbor. An employee did phone the police, however, then barricaded the door and watched through a peephole. Several others took cover beneath their desks, while a handful, worried that bullets might come through the walls, scurried up a private internal staircase to the roof.

It was at this juncture that Coco, still in the *Hebdo* conference room and unaware that anything was amiss, decided to take a break. Her plan was to buy a baguette, pick up her daughter, and enjoy lunch. First, though, she decided to smoke a cigarette with Angélique, the subscriptions manager, and it was as the two women were walking downstairs that it happened. The Kouachi brothers materialized in the stairwell, shouted at Coco, and rushed toward her. Startled by their abrupt appearance and puzzled that they knew her name, she became even more flustered when the men began shoving her and demanding that she take them to the *Charlie Hebdo* offices. The cartoonist, holding her hands behind her head, attempted to comply, but in her bewilderment she walked the gunmen to the wrong floor. Livid at being thrown off course and believing she had done it on purpose, the Kouachis now threatened Coco and delivered an unnerving declaration: they represented al-Qaeda in Yemen. As they no doubt intended, their claim of allegiance to the terrorist organization compounded the cartoonist's fears, although she did manage to compose herself sufficiently to lead them to the magazine's center of operations on the third floor.

Jabbing an AK-47 into her back, one of the brothers ordered the panic-stricken cartoonist to enter the door code. "We want Charb!" he barked.[8] Coco would later recall how conflicted she felt, not wishing to place her colleagues in mortal danger but, at the same time, thinking about her little girl.[9] She punched in the code.

Charging inside, the lead gunman headed for the first staff member he saw. It was Simon Fieschi, the magazine's webmaster. At nearly point-blank range, the assailant shot Fieschi, the bullets striking the thirty-year-old's spine and lancing his lung, with the blast itself thrusting him out of his chair. Although he survived, the staffer would suffer a buildup of spinal fluid that would produce extensive nerve damage and cause his doctors to fear that he might spend the rest of his life in a state of partial paralysis. Then too, Fieschi's recovery would be grueling and protracted. Following a month-long coma and a lengthy hospitalization in an intensive care unit, the webmaster, unable to walk, would spend the next several months in a full-time rehabilitation program. "I was shaking all over," said Maisie Dubosarsky, Fieschi's fiancée, upon learning that Islamist militants had attacked her prospective husband's workplace.[10]

As the Kouachi brothers strode toward the conference room to continue their homicidal mission, Coco scrambled under a desk. She would be among the few to make it through the massacre alive. Not so lucky would be the lion's share of *Charlie Hebdo* staffers.

One employee who attended the editorial meeting, the cartoonist Laurent Sourisseau, recalled that he and his colleagues heard gunfire outside the conference room as they were preparing to leave.[11] Although one person thought firecrackers might be the cause, Charb's bodyguard recognized the sound at once, jumping to his feet and pulling his gun. But it was too late. The assailants, their faces still concealed, kicked open the door to the conference room and shouted, "Allah is the greatest!" in Arabic.[12] "I thought, 'Shit, this is it,'" said Eric Portheault, the co-owner and financial manager of *Charlie Hebdo*, who overheard the frenzy from an adjacent office.[13] "Where is Charb?" the terrorists bellowed.[14]

Unlike some of the others in the room who were frozen in place, Sourisseau dropped to the floor as the shooting resumed. A canny response, it may have saved his life. In a matter of seconds, the Kouachi brothers, recognizing Charb, opened fire on him, then strode from person to person discharging a burst of gunfire into each victim. The cartoonists, writers, editors, and visitors were hemmed in; there was no escape route. Minutes later, believing they had executed everyone in the room, one of the assassins returned to Charb who was lying face down on the floor and pulled the trigger one last time. In all, the gunmen fired thirty-six shots during their rampage. Sourisseau, for his part, lay injured and pretending to be dead.

While lives were being extinguished in the conference room, the Première Lignes employees who had fled to the roof could hear the evenly-spaced bursts of gunfire below them, with one witness recounting the heartbreak of knowing the magazine's workers were being executed one by one. "You know each bullet is for someone and that's hard," said Martin Boudot, a television producer.[15]

Unscathed in the maelstrom was Eric Portheault's dog, Lila, a friend and mascot of the *Charlie Hebdo* staff. Merely an hour earlier, the cartoonist Jean Cabut had been feeding treats to Lila in the conference room while the editorial meeting was in progress. Now the dog padded to Portheault's side in the office where he was hiding behind his desk, lying on the floor. In what may have been a life-saving act, she curled up on his face, obscuring it from the terrorists as they passed by and evidently causing them to assume he was dead. Portheault, as a result, remained untouched. Also spared from injury were Gérard Gaillard, Laurent Léger, and Sigolène Vinson. Three others were hurt, however: Philippe Lançon (shot in the face), Fabrice Nicolino (shot in the leg), and, as noted earlier, Laurent Sourisseau, who sustained a bullet wound to the shoulder. Eleven others lay dead or dying, among them Frédéric Boisseau, Franck Brinsolaro, Jean Cabut, Elsa Cayat, Stéphane Charbonnier, Philippe Honoré, Bernard Maris, Mustapha Ourrad, Michel Renaud, Bernard Verlhac, and Georges Wolinski. Three of those murdered were in their sixties, two were in their seventies, and one was eighty years old.

By all accounts, the scene in the conference room was stomach-churning. "All the bodies were on the ground, there was gore on the tables, windows had been shot out and there was glass everywhere," said Julien Beaupé, a post-production director at Premières Lignes, who arrived shortly after the slaughter.[16] Another witness described the scene as "a total shock, an apocalyptic vision."[17] And a particularly poignant account was offered by Patrick Pelloux, an emergency room physician and the medical columnist for *Charlie Hebdo*, who arrived at 10 rue Nicolas-Appert a few minutes after the massacre. Fortunately for the doctor, he had missed the editorial meeting due to an earlier obligation. Entering the bullet-riddled quarters, Pelloux knew at once the sight would be a grisly one. "It smelled of death," he said.[18] Recounting the moans of the dying in the small conference room, the physician was devastated that the lives of his friends and colleagues had ended in such a harrowing, diabolic manner, at the hands of faceless figures wielding weapons of war.

After their vicious assault on the *Charlie Hebdo* staff, Saïd and Chérif returned to their Citroën as several Première Lignes employees watched from the roof. The brothers did not rush, nor did they act as if they felt vulnerable. In fact, they appeared to feel supremely confident, a video of the incident suggests.[19] And it was precisely at this moment that three police officers on bicycles appeared a few yards away, just around the corner from the assailants, and were moving toward the crime scene in a way that suggested they were unaware that a terrorist attack had taken place. To alert them, a Première Lignes employee who was in a position to observe the movements of both the gunmen and the police yelled down to officers. Seconds later, the crack of gunfire echoed through the streets and the police scattered.

"We have avenged the Prophet Muhammad!" shouted one of the brothers, adding once again that they represented al-Qaeda in Yemen.[20] Climbing into their car, the Kouachis traveled down Allée Vert, a narrow lane situated alongside the building that houses the *Charlie Hebdo* offices, where they encountered a police cruiser coming toward them head-on, its light-bar flashing. Without hesitation, Saïd and Chérif leapt out and peppered the police car with gunfire, leaving seventeen bullet holes in its windshield and causing the officers to throw the cruiser into reverse.[21] The gunmen then drove forward a few more yards to Boulevard Richard-Lenoir, a broad, tree-lined thoroughfare, where another opportunity for bloodshed would present itself.

As the two traveled along the boulevard—they were still only six hundred feet from *Charlie Hebdo* headquarters—Ahmed Merabet, a forty-two-year-old police officer patrolling the area, confronted them on foot. Facing the oncoming Citroën, he took a shot at it, prompting Saïd and Chérif to stop and return fire, their bullets striking him in the leg and causing Merabet to collapse onto the sidewalk. As he rolled from side to side howling in pain, the terrorists ran toward him, with one of them asking the fallen officer, sarcastically, if he wanted to kill them. "No, it's okay boss," Merabet uttered, lifting his hands in capitulation.[22] But his surrender was ignored. Training his AK-47 downward at Merabet's head, the masked gunman squeezed the trigger. It was a cold-blooded execution caught on video by a witness in a building overlooking the boulevard. "Come to the car," the assassin called out to his brother, "it's done."[23]

Like the Kouachi brothers, Ahmed Merabet, the murdered policeman, was a Muslim and the son of Algerian immigrants. Popular with his fellow officers, he lived in a predominantly Muslim suburb, one that was rife with immigrants. Merabet was also engaged to be married in the spring. "He was a nice person, very likable, always with a smile and very professional," said Rocco Contento, a trustee of the police officers' union.[24] In the aftermath of the killing, Merabet's brother, Malek, would denounce Saïd and Chérif Kouachi and reject outright their claims of piety. "My brother was Muslim," Malek would say, "and he was killed by people who pretend to be Muslims."[25] Echoing this sentiment would be French President François Hollande. "Ahmed Merabet knew better than anyone that radical Islam has nothing to do with Islam and that fanaticism kills Muslims."[26] By the end of the day, the media would report that Merabet was not the only adherent of Islam whose blood was spilled by the Kouachi brothers. Mustapha Ourrad, the Algeria-born copy editor whom the two jihadists executed in the *Charlie Hebdo* conference room, was Muslim as well.

Loping back to their getaway car after killing Officer Merabet, the assailants began driving toward the northeast of the city. Quite possibly, they were en route to Reims, ninety miles away, where Saïd and his wife lived in a rental unit in the Croix-Rouge district. Since they had been masked during the shootings and supposedly were unidentifiable, Saïd and Chérif may have assumed they could return to Saïd's apartment and proceed with their lives. Alternatively, they may have banked on receiving sanctuary in the Croix-Rouge community or perhaps had already arranged to do so. Certainly there were denizens of the district who could be expected to support the brothers' militancy, the locality containing high-rise complexes known to house a sizable number of discontented young Muslims. Whatever the Kouachis' strategy of escape, however, it was not to be.

The problems started when the fugitives crashed their Citroën into another car. It was in the nineteenth arrondissement, a couple of miles north of the *Hebdo* offices near the park where the two brothers had originally become involved in the notorious Buttes-Chaumont Jihadist Network. Undaunted by the wreck, Saïd and Chérif commandeered a gray Renault Clio and ejected its owner. "If the media ask you anything," one of them told the man, "tell them it's al-Qaida [sic] in Yemen."[27] With this, the killers were on the run again, but in their haste they left behind incriminating materials in the Citroën, evidence that included not only their fingerprints but also Molotov cocktails, two jihadist flags, and Saïd Kouachi's identification card. The latter would spur the pair's defenders in the radical Islamist community to insist that Saïd and Chérif were innocent, that they had been framed. "(A) red herring, planted deliberately," one avid supporter asserted about Saïd's identification card.[28] Such conspiratorial thinking would soon prove to be unfounded, however, and by the Kouachi brothers themselves, who wanted it known that they had committed the murders and, equally important, that they were associated with al-Qaeda.

As Saïd and Chérif resumed their flight out of the city, the French government jumped into action. Prime Minister Manuel Valls activated the nation's anti-terrorism alert system within an hour of the *Charlie Hebdo* attack, setting the severity rating at four—scarlet. It was the highest level of threat. As a component of this pre-programmed response, an additional three thousand law enforcement officers throughout the nation took to the streets, including five hundred in Paris alone, with concentrations at media outlets, synagogues, and other centers of worship. Supplementary defense measures were put into motion as well, some of which were disruptive to public life but deemed necessary under the circumstances.

Within ninety minutes of the horrific massacre, President Hollande visited the site of the killings. Afterward, he held an emergency meeting with cabinet members and officials at Élysée Palace, and subsequently made a televised statement about the atrocity. "Today, France was attacked at its very heart in Paris, at the offices of a newspaper," said Hollande.

> This extremely violent shooting killed 12 people and injured several others; highly talented cartoonists [and] courageous columnists were killed. Their impertinence and independence influenced generations and generations of French people. I want to tell them that we will continue to defend this message, this message of freedom, in their name.[29]

Lauding the *Charlie Hebdo* victims as "our heroes," the French leader concluded his statement by calling for a day of national mourning.[30]

Across the Atlantic, President Barack Obama released a statement as well, one of American solidarity with the people of France. And weighing in too was Vice President Joe Biden. "What the ... terrorists don't understand, will never understand, is that bravery and decency will never bow down to intimidation and terror," said Biden.[31]

On the evening of the attack, and acting on the lead offered by Saïd's abandoned identification card, law enforcement officials identified three suspects: the two Kouachi brothers and Mourad Hamyd. The latter was Chérif's eighteen-year-old brother-in-law and was believed to have been the driver of the getaway car. Because the authorities were still analyzing closed-circuit footage of the assault, they were not yet ready to conclude that there had been only two terrorists. So it was that Hamyd, who discovered through social media that he was a suspect, presented himself to the police in the small town of Charleville-Mézières, where he lived near the French-Belgian border. Interrogated at length, counterterrorism agents released him after his friends confirmed his alibi, namely, that he had been attending class when the Paris attacks occurred. Officials nevertheless placed Hamyd's name on France's terrorist watchlist.

Rattled by his brief stint as a suspect, the college freshman opened up to reporters. "I'm in shock, people said horrible and false things about me on social media even though I am a normal student who lives quietly with his parents."[32] Hamyd also said he was worried about the adverse publicity he had received, fearing it might damage his reputation and hurt his prospects. "I only hope this won't taint my future," he said.[33] As it happened, Turkish forces would intercept Hamyd eighteen months later as he was trekking to Syria to join ISIS. Deported to France, he would be charged with associating with terrorists.[34]

Shortly after the *Charlie Hebdo* bloodbath, the police subjected Izzana Hamyd to serial interrogations as well, she being Mourad's sister and Chérif Kouachi's wife. Seventy-two hours later, convinced that her husband had kept her in the dark about his lethal plans, officials released her.

While the authorities were questioning the Hamyds on the evening of the attack, tens of thousands of Parisians poured into the streets to share their grief, candles in hand. "Je Suis Charlie" became their rallying cry—"I Am Charlie"—a phrase that appeared on a sea of improvised signs at the Place de la République and a message of unity that the American embassy in Paris featured prominently on its Twitter page. One participant in the vigil, a young man named Adrian, held a sign aloft that read, "Charb mort libre" ("Charb died free").[35] It was a salute to the courage and convictions of Stéphane Charbonnier, the cartoonist and editor-in-chief of *Charlie Hebdo*, who refused to be cowed by threats and previous acts of violence against the satirical publication.

As the night wore on, counterterrorism experts employed video technology to track the Kouachi brothers' movements, with footage from closed-circuit cameras positioned throughout the city allowing them to piece together a visual record of the gunmen's getaway. But there was a hitch: the imagery was incomplete, most notably after Saïd and Chérif left the metropolitan area, the upshot being that their whereabouts were unknown.

Day Two

As if Parisians were not already on edge, the next morning would bring another jarring development. At the outset of the workday—it was shortly after 8:00 a.m. on Thursday, January 8, 2015—a police spokesperson announced that an unknown assailant had shot a black female police officer in Montrouge, a suburb four miles south of Paris. A twenty-seven-year-old native of the Caribbean island of Martinique, the unarmed policewoman's name was Clarissa Jean-Philippe and she had only been on the job for a fortnight. "Her colleagues called her the 'little brother' of the police station," said David Merseray of the municipal police union.[36] By all accounts, Jean-Philippe had been excited to embark on her new career.

As for the attack, a heavily-armed man wearing a bulletproof vest and a balaclava approached a municipal worker, a middle-aged man named Laurent, and aimed an AK-47 at him. Instinctively, Laurent fought him off, in the process yanking the balaclava off the assailant's head to reveal a thirty-three-year-old black man. Undaunted, the latter pulled the trigger, but it was not Laurent who was struck by the bullet but rather Jean-Philippe, the policewoman. She had been responding to a traffic mishap when the violence erupted and she died three hours later. Determined to complete his attack, the assailant next struck Laurent in the head with a pistol and once again took aim at him, but the gun jammed. Stymied, the aggressor fled on foot, leaving behind his balaclava in the confusion of the moment.

At first, the authorities did not connect the Montrouge killing to the *Charlie Hebdo* massacre of the previous day, partly because of the race of the assailant and deceased police officer. But an ensuing review of the city's overnight crime log suggested that the inexplicable act of violence may in fact have constituted another terrorist incident. For one thing, the municipal worker and the policewoman had been standing near a synagogue and a Jewish school when they were attacked, meaning that these institutions may have been the original targets and that the gunman, for whatever reason, could not complete his initial plan. For another, an attempt had been made on the life of a thirty-two-year-old man a few hours earlier, a jogger in the suburb of Fontenay-aux-Roses. Shot five times by a man wielding a Russian Tokarev pistol, the same type of pistol favored by Islamist extremists, the Kouachi brothers among them, it was a vicious deed having no apparent motive other than striking fear in the citizenry. In this respect, it was akin to the Jean-Phillipe homicide. The police therefore braced for more shootings, the assumption being that they were dealing with a copycat killer, an Islamist sympathizer, or an accomplice of the Kouachi brothers.

And there was more to come on this tense Thursday, with officials providing an update on the manhunt for the Kouachis. Among other developments in the case, the police revealed that residents had caught a glimpse of Saïd and Chérif in the northeastern municipality of Villers-Cotterêts.

Situated in the Aines region, a wine-growing expanse known for its Champagne, Villers-Cotterêts is midway between Paris and Reims.

A police spokesperson reported that the two gunmen had robbed a service station of food and gasoline near Villers-Cotterêts, a conclusion backed up by surveillance footage. During the holdup, which occurred at 9:30 a.m., a bystander spotted assault rifles and a rocket launcher in the back of the pair's car, while another recounted that the terrorists had subsequently driven in the direction of a neighboring forest. Accordingly, counterterrorism forces set about combing the woodlands, forces that included an elite tactical corps from the GIGN, or National Gendarmerie Intervention Group (Groupe d'intervention de la Gendarmerie nationale), and a special-operations unit from the National Police Intervention Force. Military transport helicopters carrying rapid-response teams were deployed as well. Within a few hours, nearly ninety thousand police and anti-terrorism officers joined in the search, making it the largest manhunt in the history of France.

Not surprisingly given the gravity of the situation, eyewitness reports poured in throughout the day, unconfirmed observations that often turned out to be inaccurate. That said, the police did converge on Crépy-en-Valois after receiving credible descriptions of the fugitives, the town being situated slightly south of Villers-Cotterêts where the Kouachi brothers had last been observed. Here, the authorities trained their sights on shops, restaurants, and service stations. "French police seem to be aiming to capture the suspects if and when they surface to get resources, such as food and petrol," explained *Al Jazeera* correspondent Barnaby Phillips.[37]

Ensuing accounts had the two terrorists heading back toward Paris, prompting officials to beef up police presence on all major roadways leading into the capital. "The atmosphere around the edge of the city, where police were awaiting the potential arrival of the two suspects, was described as one of 'extreme anticipation' bordering on fear," *The Guardian* reported.[38]

Owing to the possibility that the Kouachi brothers might nevertheless manage to slip into Paris, officials set about securing additional sites. Focusing on those that were either symbolic or "sensitive," they blocked streets near the Arc de Triomphe and the Champs-Elysées, the presidential palace, and the headquarters of the French Intelligence Services. Other prospective targets were likewise sealed off, the upshot being more disruption for those living and working in the city.

Finally, as Thursday drew to a close, thousands of Parisians returned to the Place de la République to express their grief and now their rising anger. Certainly they were not alone in their fury: outrage about the heinous attacks on artists and writers was mounting around the world.

Into the night, police tactical units continued their pursuit of Saïd and Chérif Kouachi, paying particular attention to vacant houses and cabins, abandoned properties, and the remote side roads north of Paris. In the capital city, meanwhile, police were on the hunt for Amedy Coulibaly, the Mali-born friend of the Kouachi brothers who had murdered the policewoman in Montrouge. By this point, the authorities had determined that he was her killer, a forensic team having identified him through a DNA analysis performed on fibers from the balaclava he had dropped at the crime scene.

In the end, one thing seemed assured: the terrorists' parade of violence had not yet run its course. It would persist into a third day in a final drama that would commence at sunrise.

Day Three

After passing the night in a forest near Crépy-en-Valois, Saïd and Chérif discovered at dawn that their stolen Renault had become mired in the mud. Trudging back to the highway, they commandeered the first vehicle that came into view, a Peugeot, and ejected its driver unharmed. The pair did not succeed in concealing the hijacking, however. A woman who was traveling along the same roadway, an attentive schoolteacher, spotted the fugitives as they were seizing the Peugeot and, suspecting them of being the Kouachi brothers, notified the police. The time was 8:32 a.m.[39]

As a result of the teacher's tip, the elite police tactical unit, the GIGN, determined that the gunmen were most likely returning southward toward Paris. Accordingly, the unit dispatched additional aerial crews to surveil the roads north of the capital and closed those highways leading into the city itself. By design, the GIGN was shoe-horning the Kouachi brothers onto the N2 roadway with an eye toward isolating and containing them. It was, as it turned out, an effective strategy. The gendarmerie funneled the terrorists into the town of Dammartin-en-Goële, where, shortly after a shoot-out between the Kouachis and police that left no one injured, Saïd and Chérif found themselves in the parking lot of Création Tendance Découverte, a printing plant that had not yet opened for the day. With AK-47s draped over their shoulders and with one of the brothers packing the rocket launcher, they approached the entrance.

In a second floor office overlooking the grounds, the owner of the facility, Michel Catalano, was drinking coffee with a young male employee, Lilian. They were awaiting a delivery before the start of the work day. When the doorbell rang, Catalano assumed it was the expected shipment, but instead he glimpsed through the window the two heavily armed men. "I told Lilian to hide and turn his mobile off," said Catalano.[40] Racing into the adjoining room, the worker managed to fold his body into a cabinet beneath a wash basin as the Kouachis stormed into the printing plant and confronted Catalano.

The jihadists began by proclaiming that they were planning to die as martyrs. As they continued holding forth, a GIGN officer staked out a spot near the building's side door in the event that the pair tried to exit. And indeed, Saïd, apparently sensing the officer's presence, burst outside a few moments later, shouting "Allahu akbar" and taking aim at him.[41] But the officer shot him in the throat, the blood gushing from Saïd's neck as the jihadist stumbled back inside the facility.

Worried about his own survival, Michel Catalano tried to calm the terrorists by explaining that he was trained in emergency medical care, and he set to work applying a tourniquet to Saïd's neck. During the next two hours, Catalano would apply two more tourniquets to the hemorrhaging man in a humanitarian act for which Chérif would eventually allow Catalano to go free. Lilian, on the other hand, would remain hidden beneath the wash basin, his presence still unknown to the fugitives.

While isolated inside the printing plant with his wounded brother, Chérif spoke by phone to the media, a terse exchange during which the Islamist claimed yet again that he and Saïd represented al-Qaeda in Yemen. He stated further that the late Anwar al-Awlaki had bankrolled their activities, and in the same breath insisted that neither he nor Saïd had behaved horrifically in their blood-drenched attack on the *Charlie Hebdo* staff.[42] "You are the ones killing women and children in Syria, Iraq and Afghanistan," Chérif told the interviewer, pointing out that Islam has a code of honor.[43]

While the younger Kouachi was struggling to portray himself and his brother as the principled defenders of the prophet Muhammad, the GIGN was stealthily surrounding the printing plant, having dropped a considerable number of gendarmes onto the building by helicopter and trucked in additional forces. Snipers, meanwhile, positioned themselves on neighboring buildings, with one marksman in particular securing an unimpeded view into the facility's second-floor bay window. From this vantage point, he could observe simultaneously Michel Catalano and both of the Kouachi brothers. And there were further preparations and precautions as well. At Charles de Gaulle Airport, for instance, two runways were shut down as a safety measure, the airport being only six miles from the printing plant. And then came a pause, a pause that would last several hours as the GIGN sought to out-wait the terrorists in the hope that, unlikely though it might be, the Kouachis would tire out and surrender. Since the two could no doubt deliver valuable information under interrogation, the objective was to arrest them, although the GIGN had already decided to use lethal force if necessary to prevent them from leaving the scene. And it was during this taut stretch that an unforeseen development unfolded, complicating matters further.

The Hyper Cacher Market Siege

Four hours after the Kouachi brothers took refuge in the printing plant, Amedy Coulibaly resurfaced in eastern Paris, the jihadist having passed the night in a safe house to elude capture. In a predominantly Jewish neighborhood in Port de Vincennes, he now materialized with the aim of continuing the orgy of violence that he and the Kouachi brothers had embarked upon during the previous days. Wearing a bulletproof jacket, a camouflage vest, a backpack, and combat boots, Coulibaly stormed into a kosher market at 1:00 in the afternoon armed with a submachine gun, two AK-47s, and a set of Tokarev pistols. As if this were not enough, he was also toting a duffel bag stuffed with twenty sticks of dynamite, a quantity sufficient to obliterate everything within a forty-five-yard radius. And he had a GoPro video camera strapped to his chest so he could upload his acts of carnage onto the internet.

Regarding the retailer, it was a small grocery store, one in a chain of Hyper Cacher markets, and it was about to close for Shabbat, the Jewish Sabbath. As was typically the case on a Friday afternoon, the store was brimming with last-minute shoppers preparing for the religious observance. Unfortunately, on this day the hapless customers would find themselves face to face with an attention-seeking Islamist, one bent on traumatizing them in an episode that would end with the slaughter of innocents.

Striding into the kosher market, Coulibaly spotted a twenty-year-old employee who was arranging shopping carts. The young man's name was Yohan Cohen, and the gunman, without warning, shot him in the face. Shrieking in agony, Cohen crumpled to the floor and died minutes later.[44] The arbitrary murder was a message, a demonstration of the terrorist's willingness to kill and be killed without a moment's hesitation.

"I was heading for the check-out with ... goods in my hand when I heard a bang—very loud," said Michael B, a customer.[45] Clutching his three-year-old son, Michael rushed to the rear of the store, where the pair found themselves in the company of fifteen other panicked customers. Thirteen were adults, two were children.

Detecting the group's presence, the gunman hurried to the back of the market, where he came upon François-Michel Saada, one of these unlucky shoppers. Saada was a sixty-four-year-old retiree, a resident of Paris, and the father of two adult children who were living in Israel. Grasping him, Coulibaly asked about Saada's origins and the latter replied that he was

Jewish. "So you know why I am here then," the terrorist said, and fired into him."[46]

Shortly after this second murder, Philippe Braham entered the store. Forty-five years old, Braham was employed at an information-technology firm and his children attended a Jewish school in Montrouge near the spot where Coulibaly had murdered the policewoman a day earlier. Braham had come to the store to buy bread and was unaware that anything was awry. In an attempt to protect him, the cashier, a young woman, rushed over to him, claimed the store was closed, and tried to usher him out the door. But the devout Jew persisted, explaining that he needed the bread for Shabbat. And it was at this moment that Coulibaly shot him. After convulsing for several seconds, Braham died.[47]

The terrorist now began firing in all directions, seemingly at random. In the hope of preventing further injuries, the cashier offered him all of the money in the cash register, but he scoffed at the suggestion. Identifying himself as an ISIS-connected jihadist, Coulibaly explained that he had not come to rob the store; he was there to die as a martyr. He stated further that his targets were Jews and that he was coordinating his actions with Saïd and Chérif Kouachi, who were holed up in a printing plant in Dammartin-en-Goëlle. Counterterrorism experts would later confirm that Saïd and Chérif Kouachi had indeed texted Coulibaly less than an hour before he launched the Hyper Cacher attack.[48] The three were also in contact during the grocery store siege itself.[49]

In terms of this lethal alliance between the Kouachi brothers and Amedy Coulibaly, the former claimed to represent al-Qaeda in Yemen while the latter insisted that he represented ISIS. But this is problematic. According to counterterrorism specialists, al-Qaeda and ISIS were fierce rivals at the time and were locked in a struggle for power in the jihadist movement.[50] Then too, the groups were at variance in key respects. "The two organizations differ fundamentally on whom they see as their main enemy, which strategies and tactics to use in attacking that enemy, and which social issues and other concerns to emphasize," write Daniel Byman and Jennifer R. Williams of the Brookings Institution.[51] Accordingly, the two competing organizations would not have joined forces in the Paris killing spree, nor would they have been willing to share the credit for this or any other operation.

The more plausible scenario is that Saïd and Chérif Kouachi were conducting a terrorist mission that was sanctioned, perhaps even abetted or overseen, by al-Qaeda, whereas Coulibaly was carrying out a separate ISIS operation, or at least one that he claimed was ISIS-related. In this setup, the three terrorists would have chosen to schedule their respective missions in close proximity so as to increase the attacks' collective shock value, yet they would have done so in the absence of a formal, organizational partnership between al-Qaeda and ISIS. Supporting this notion is an assertion Coulibaly made in a video released posthumously on the internet, one describing the way in which he and the Kouachi brothers choreographed their killings. "We did some things together, some things separate," the Islamist said, "that way we would have more of an impact."[52] Further bolstering the idea that the assaults were purposely bunched in time, yet ideologically distinct, is the fact that their motives and targets were different. Saïd and Chérif Kouachi sought to make an example of those French cartoonists and writers whom they felt had disparaged the prophet Muhammad, whereas Coulibaly was on an anti–Semitic killing binge. "He targeted Jews specifically with his choice of the Kosher [market], claiming to defend 'oppressed Muslims' in Palestine," writes Lizzie Dearden in *The Independent*.[53] Dearden derived her information from a telephone interview that Coulibaly gave to a local television station while he was carrying out the assault.

Fortunately for those shoppers—they had since become hostages—who were huddled in the rear of the grocery store, they would not be without help for long. An employee by the name of Lassana Bathily promptly appeared and hurried them down a spiral staircase to the basement, his intention being to hide them from view. A twenty-four-year-old stock clerk, Bathily, like Coulibaly, was a Muslim who hailed from Mali. So it was that the worker, upon herding the flustered group downstairs, guided them into the store's two cold-storage rooms and instructed them to remain silent. Moments later, he climbed into a freight elevator and escaped from the store through a ground-level exit. In the hours ahead, Bathily would furnish the police with a detailed layout of the facility and other vital material. To reward the Muslim immigrant for his life-saving deeds, the president of France would grant him full citizenship eleven days later.

By this point in the Hyper Cacher massacre, the Research and Intervention Brigade (Brigade de Recherche et d'Intervention), or BRI, had gathered outside the store. A component of the French National Police, the BRI specializes in crimes such as kidnappings, robberies, and other gang-related offenses. "As many as 20 officers crammed into [a] cafe and others crouched behind cars in the street," reported the *Sydney Morning Herald*.[54] Authorities also shut down schools and businesses in the vicinity so as to shield the public from harm, even as more BRI officers poured onto on the scene and tacticians created a command center by positioning armored police vans in a circle at the site.

Inside the market, meanwhile, Coulibaly demanded that the cashier retrieve the hostages who were hiding downstairs. Although only a few of them agreed to accompany the clerk upstairs, among those who did was a twenty-one-year-old university student. Yoav Hattab was his name, and he had come to Paris to earn a degree in international business studies. A citizen of Tunisia, he was the son of Binyamin Hattab, the chief rabbi of the capital city of Tunis.

Upon returning to the main floor, Hattab saw before him the terrorist's three causalities as well as the two assault rifles, one of which was leaned against a wall. Snatching the AK-47, the student took aim, but evidently did not know how to operate the weapon. Straightway, Coulibaly fired two bullets into him, then led the cashier to Hattab's mangled corpse and forced her to view it. It was a warning to her.

As the news broke about the young man's attempt, against all odds, to save himself and his fellow captives, those who knew him well were not surprised by his valor. "I was sure he would fight, would do anything he could, even risk his life, to try and stop the savage murderer," said his heartbroken father.[55] Fittingly, Yoav Hattab would receive a hero's burial at Har HaMenuchot, a cemetery near parliament in Jerusalem. The other three victims would be laid to rest at Har HaMenuchot as well.

Having recorded the murders of Cohen, Braham, and Saada, Coulibaly next turned the GoPro camera on himself in order to speak directly to the viewer. It was, in effect, a martyrdom video, one in which he voiced yet again his uncompromising political views. As he was doing so, the beleaguered hostages who were still hiding in the cold-storage rooms were likewise trying to make contact with the outside world. "We're very afraid, and we're very cold," one captive, Noemi, texted to a friend.[56]

After Coulibaly recorded his self-statement, he attempted to upload the two videos he had made in the kosher market using a laptop computer he had brought along in his backpack for this purpose. However, he was unable to secure an internet connection on his device, so he forced a hostage to help him operate the store's computer. It was what came next, though, that proved to be the game-changer.

In a telephone exchange with a police negotiator, Coulibaly said he had killed four hostages and threatened to execute the remaining captives if the authorities attacked Saïd or Chérif Kouachi. The Kouachi brothers, of course, were still inside the printing plant in Dammartin-en-Goële at this time, surrounded by scores of gendarmes, while Amedy Coulibaly, whether or not he was aware of it, was likewise cornered inside the Hyper Cacher market. Police had formed a cordon around the building, and three BRI tactical teams were in position and awaiting authorization to act.

Sorties and Solidarity

When the end came for Saïd Kouachi, Chérif Kouachi, and Amedy Coulibaly, it was as cold and brutal as the terrorists themselves. Late afternoon was approaching when a police negotiator at the printing plant phoned Saïd and Chérif Kouachi inside the facility. The intention was to establish a truce, one whereby students at a nearby school could be evacuated safely. But in what would prove to be their final opportunity to communicate with the outside world—a lifeline—the Kouachi brothers refused to speak to the negotiator.

Then, shortly before 5:00 p.m., Saïd and Chérif bolted from the building and exchanged gunfire with the gendarmes. Within ninety seconds, the two brothers lay dead. After liquidating them, the GIGN blew out the building's main window and liberated Lilian, who had been in hiding for eight hours. Uninjured, he and Michel Catalano embraced and wept. Unavoidably, the printing plant suffered such extensive damage from the blast as to require ten months of reconstruction work.

Because Amedy Coulibaly had threatened to kill the Hyper Cacher hostages if the gendarmes attacked Saïd and Chérif, law enforcement officials decided it was time to eliminate the heavily-armed jihadist. To this end, a brace of police units prepared to raid the Hyper Cacher market. The strategy was to simultaneously breach two discrete entrances to the store: the large rolling-steel shutter at the front of the market, the key to which the stock clerk, Lassana Bathily, had given to the BRI, and a service entrance on the side of the building. Knowing that Coulibaly could not respond to both incursions at once, it would be the entrance he forfeited through which the police would enter and attempt to save the hostages. And indeed, this is precisely what transpired.

The first team of BRI officers blew off the door to the service entrance, then hurried inside and set about liberating the hostages. A testament to the BRI's proficiency, the officers freed all of captives, who were unharmed. As this was happening, the second team unlocked the rolling-steel shutter at the front of the store and the lead officer rushed inside. Twelve seconds later, he deployed a flash grenade, with the ear-splitting boom and dazzling light stunning and disorienting Coulibaly. In a frenzied effort to flee, the terrorist dashed toward the front entrance, but the police were awaiting him on the sidewalk and sprayed him with forty bullets. He died at their feet within moments. One of the officers subsequently disclosed that the BRI had felt no sympathy for the jihadist or, for that matter, for the Kouachi brothers; that the police were ready, even eager, when the time came to confront him. "Sincerely, one of the things that most motivated us was that video of the odious assassination of our colleague Ahmed Merabet outside Charlie," said the officer.[57]

After the three terrorists' deaths, the French government ordered Saïd Kouachi's body to be buried without public notice in an unmarked grave in a Muslim cemetery in Reims. Chérif's remains were to be interred in the Paris suburb of Gennevilliers under identical conditions, while those of Amedy Coulibaly were to be laid to rest, anonymously, in the suburb of Thiais. The reason for the secrecy was to prevent the burial sites from inviting violence, incurring damage, or being converted into shrines by Islamist sympathizers.

In terms of the sites of the gruesome attacks, both the Hyper Cacher market and the printing company, Création Tendance Découverte, reopened in their original locations after repairs were completed, while *Charlie Hebdo* secured a new center of operations elsewhere in the capital. It was here that Coco and other surviving artists and writers carried on skewering a range of social and political targets, the magazine now being under the editorship of Lawrence Sourisseau. As noted earlier, cartoonist Sourisseau was one of the victims of the attack, having been shot in the shoulder.

As to the terrorists' claims that they were acting on behalf of al-Qaeda and ISIS, al-Qaeda in the Arabian Peninsula (AQAP) released a video asserting that the Kouachi brothers had indeed been fulfilling its global jihad in their assault on *Charlie Hebdo*. "When the heroes were assigned, they accepted," said Nasr Ibn Ali al-Ansi, a commander in the Yemen-based organization.[58] In the video, al-Ansi featured photos of himself with the Kouachis and claimed that the late Anwar al-Awlaki, killed in a drone strike in 2011, had masterminded the 2015 *Charlie Hebdo* massacre in retaliation for the magazine's comical depictions of the prophet Muhammad.[59] In reality, it has never been proven that al-Awlaki or AQAP engineered the Paris operation. It is known, however, that AQAP did give Chérif Kouachi $20,000 while he was training in Yemen, money that French intelligence experts believe was almost certainly earmarked for such a mission.[60] Related to this, Amedy Coulibaly, in his own video, also claimed to have given the Kouachis money for supplies, saying the brothers needed it to finalize their preparations for the attack.

Certainly Coulibaly had access to such cash, having secured a bank loan of 25,000 euros shortly before he murdered the policewoman in Montrouge and killed the four Jewish men at the kosher market. Investigators concluded that he had used the loan to purchase weapons and combat gear for his suicidal mission. And it is partly because the jihadist financed his own attack that there remains a question as to whether he truly represented ISIS. Had the terrorist organization authorized the assault, it likely would have covered the expenses. Then too, another video that Coulibaly uploaded to the internet, purportedly an ISIS production made shortly before the Hyper Cacher attack, was amateurishly constructed and inconsistent with the style of the organization's verified videos. "It shows Coulibaly had no direct connection to the organisation's main

70 Part I—The Pen and the Sword

propaganda unit, and he is unlikely to have had a direct line to the leadership either," says Charlie Winter, a researcher at The Quilliam Foundation, the London-based think tank.[61] All the same, ISIS was quick to accept responsibility for the Hyper Cacher massacre, since such barbarity, regardless of its origins, bolstered the image of the organization as bloodthirsty and ruthless. Regarding al-Qaeda's reaction to the massacre at the kosher market, it praised Coulibaly's rampage, calling it a blessing, but claimed no part in its planning or execution.

Postscript

Two days after the police killed the trio of terrorists—the date was Sunday, January 11, 2015—Parisians gathered yet again at the Place de la République. From the early morning onward, their number swelled until 3:00 in the afternoon, at which time the crowd of one million people set off on a peaceful march to the Place de la Nation, two and a half miles away. "This is the first [terrorist] attack I can really remember, and it has really affected me," said one demonstrator, an eighteen-year-old woman. "The idea that people can come into central Paris with Kalashnikovs and kill people, it's something I could never have imagined."[62]

The purpose of the march, one in which participants clutched pencils and pens and waved French flags, was to honor the eleven artists and

Wall mural near *Charlie Hebdo* headquarters following the al-Qaeda-inspired massacre. The painting pays tribute to the magazine's editorial and artistic staff.

journalists, four hostages, and two police officers murdered by Saïd and Chérif Kouachi and Amedy Coulibaly. But it was also a display of defiance, a sweeping public declaration by Parisians of their support for the nation's free press and their unified opposition to those forces that would suppress it. The largest demonstration of its kind in the history of the French republic, participants included not only the upper echelon of the French government, but also an array of political figures from Europe, the Middle East, and North Africa. Among the dignitaries: Angela Merkel (Germany), David Cameron (Great Britain), Benjamin Netanyahu (Israel), Mahmoud Abbas (Occupied Territories), King Abdullah II (Jordan), and Sergei Lavrov (Russia).

As one might expect, France's artists, writers, editors, and publishers reacted to the *Charlie Hebdo* massacre like that of the public at large: with utter outrage. Viewing it as a devastating assault on the freedom of expression, specifically in its satirical form, associations of writers and artists were forthright in their support for the magazine and their castigation of the mindset behind the diabolical effort to destroy it. Among such advocates was the novelist Salman Rushdie, who released a statement through PEN, the international writers' association, in which he addressed the mounting political pressure on journalists and artists to respect religion. In the current milieu, he explained, the term "respect religion" was actually a code of sorts, one meaning that writers and artists should not to criticize or lampoon religion. The unspoken reason: a fear of its zealots. Championing the opposite approach, Rushdie argued that religious ideas, like all substantive concepts that directly affect vast swaths of the population, deserve our scrutiny, our humor, and even our disrespect at times. Such is the functioning of an active, unrestricted mind and a healthy society.

"(R)eligious totalitarianism has caused a deadly mutation in the heart of Islam and we see the tragic consequences in Paris today," Rushdie wrote. "I stand with *Charlie Hebdo*, as we all must, to defend the art of satire, which has always been a force for liberty and against tyranny, dishonesty and stupidity."[63]

Voltaire would have agreed. In an assertion that is as true today as it was in the eighteenth century, the brilliant French philosopher, social critic, and author declared, "To hold a pen is to be at war."[64]

PART II

The Campaign to Demoralize

ISIS Attacks at the Bataclan Theatre, the Stade de France, and the Cafés of Paris

6

Belgium, Abdelhamid Abaaoud, and the Paris Terror Units

"He's exactly the kind of person you would expect to plan something like this," says Charlie Winter, Associate Fellow at the International Centre for Counter-Terrorism in The Hague.[1] The "kind of person" to whom Winter was referring was Abdelhamid Abaaoud, a twenty-eight-year-old jihadist and the on-the-ground organizer of the most lethal string of terrorist attacks in France since World War II. To support the assertion that Abaaoud fit the profile of a seasoned terrorist, Winter pointed to the intricate mass murder that the jihadist and his operatives visited upon the people of Paris on the night of November 13, 2015. A complex undertaking distinguished by numerous targets and multiple hit squads, it was obvious that Abaaoud was no rookie; a neophyte could not have overseen such a sophisticated mission. And indeed, it came to light that Abaaoud, a Belgian by birth, had trained with ISIS in Syria, been featured in its online propaganda magazine, and directed terrorist strikes at other sites before helping devise this grand mission to be perpetrated in the City of Light. In terms of his conversion to militant Islamism three years earlier, it came as a shock to those who had known him when he was a boy, a fairly regular occurrence in such cases.

Born into a family that was both financially secure and socially engaged in the community, Abdelhamid Abaaoud's upbringing was sunnier than many of those who become jihadists. His Morocco-born father and mother, Omar and Badi, had resettled in Belgium, where they launched a clothing store in the Brussels municipality of Molenbeek. Here, they were considered an upright Muslim couple who chose to assimilate, as well as conscientious parents who raised their seven children to respect society and the law. Omar and Badi's objective was to ensure that their sons and daughters would lead respectable, productive lives. Yet this aim, while commendable, was not without its challenges, most notably in the case of young Abdelhamid. In large measure, this is because of the neighborhood, Molenbeek, in which the Abaaoud family lived.

Molenbeek

A heavily Muslim municipality situated adjacent to central Brussels, Molenbeek is a stone's throw from the headquarters of the European Commission and the Palais de Bruxelles. In contrast to the latter neighborhood, however, with its Art Nouveau architecture and numerous national and EU executive offices, much of Molenbeek is marred by overcrowding, financial hardship, social marginalization, and the scent of desperation. It is also saddled with an off-putting reputation, that of a high-crime area which serves as a magnet for both potential and active terrorists. But this wasn't always the case.

An agricultural village in the ninth century, Molenbeek became a prosperous manufacturing center in the nineteenth century as the Industrial Revolution took root in the West. And although the first half of the twentieth century was a discouraging period of de-industrialization due to the two world wars and the Great Depression, the municipality nevertheless continued to attract those in need of work. During the 1960s and 1970s, in particular, Molenbeek witnessed an unprecedented influx of Moroccan Muslims looking for employment, with a smaller number of Muslim newcomers immigrating from Turkey, Libya, and Egypt. It would be in 1975 that Omar and Badi Abaaoud joined their ranks.

During the decades that followed, this wave of immigrants unwittingly contributed to a detrimental change in the Molenbeek way of life, one marked by an overabundance of new arrivals, a further loss of manufacturing jobs, and a consequent financial strain. And there was another important development as well, one arising on foreign soil. The Persian Gulf states, most notably Saudi Arabia, began funding mosques in Molenbeek in which they placed Saudi-trained, ultra-conservative Sunni imams. Disciples of Wahhabism, a form of Salafism, these imams rejected the contemporary interpretation of the Koran and other sacred Islamic texts that were the norm in Molenbeek's Islamic community, and insisted instead on a rigid, concrete, and puritanical reading of the ancient works. In short order, the chasm between the fundamentalists' beliefs and those of the community's more established imams led to antagonism. Even more far-reaching, the fundamentalists' mounting influence in Molenbeek's mosques and religious schools helped create the conditions for the eventual radicalization of young Belgian Muslims who felt disenfranchised and frustrated and yearned for a sense of purpose.

Terrorism experts point to the 1990s as the period during which such political radicalization in Belgium took hold, a time when jihadist cells began setting up shop in the Brussels area. For the most part, they converged on Molenbeek with its 40 percent Muslim population, their plan being to use the municipality as a hub from which to recruit prospective assailants and organize terrorist missions to be executed in Western European nations. It was, unfortunately, a strategy that proved to be remarkably effective. "Almost every time there is a terrorist attack, there is a link with Molenbeek," says Charles Michel, the prime minister of Belgium.[2]

The Islamists' strategy picked up steam in the early years of the twenty-first century, a rejuvenation that came on the heels of al-Qaeda's attack on the Twin Towers in Manhattan and the resultant Western military intervention in Iraq and Afghanistan. In 2003, recruiters added the U.S.-led intervention in the Syrian Civil War to their list of reasons that Muslims should pursue the path of militant Islamism. A one-dimensional message aimed at demoralized Muslim youth, such simplistic yet compelling propaganda by ISIS, in particular, appears to have captivated Abdelhamid Abaaoud in 2013; this, despite the fact that he was not devoted to Islam and enjoyed far greater privilege than other young Muslims in his neighborhood. "We had a nice life," said his father, "even a fantastic life."[3]

The Conversion of Abdelhamid Abaaoud

By all accounts, Omar and Badi had high hopes for their son, Abdelhamid, who was born on April 8, 1987, in Anderlecht, a municipality in the Brussels region. Showering him with affection, the pair sought to instill in him the same sense of ambition that Omar possessed. To bolster young Abaaoud's chances of forging a successful life for himself, for instance, Omar and Badi enrolled him in Collège Saint-Pierre, an exclusive school in Brussels, when he was twelve years old. And it was here, at a Catholic school favored by prominent families, that Abaaoud came to be known as a friendly, flirtatious, and feisty boy, one whom the Christian staff and students treated respectfully and who blended well with the other pupils. "He was one of us, he was never sidelined, never a dispute or a hint of racism" ("Il était l'un des nôtres, il n'a jamais été mis à l'écart, jamais de dispute ou d'allusion un peu raciste"), recalls one of his classmates.[4] Such praise notwithstanding, it has also been said that young Abaaoud developed a fondness for marijuana while at Collège Saint-Pierre and performed inadequately in his studies.[5] And another person who attended classes with him claimed that Abaaoud pinched wallets while at the school.[6] Whatever the case, Abaaoud did not return to Collège Saint-Pierre after the first year, but instead spent his days getting into mischief with a new group of friends. "Like a significant number of youngsters living in 'inner-city' areas like Molenbeek," writes Belgian journalist Guy van Vlierden, "Abaaoud fell in with a loosely organized gang of local youths, whose members included several future co-conspirators in the Paris attack."[7] Before long, Abaaoud and his friends were committing criminal acts, often to obtain money for drugs. Even more concerning was the pattern of Abaaoud's offenses, his infractions becoming increasingly serious and culminating in a troubling rap sheet.

Whereas Abaaoud's initial run-in with the police occurred in 2002 when he was fifteen years old, his first encounter with the Belgian courts took place in 2006 after he was discovered with stolen property. Nineteen years old, he was ordered to perform community service. Three years later, in 2009, he was again found guilty, this time of crimes centering on violent behavior and resisting arrest. Then, in 2010, police spotted Abaaoud trying to break into a parking garage, a predicament from which he tried frantically to escape. "Fleeing from the police," writes van Vlierden, "Abaaoud jumped in a river, where he was found suffering from hypothermia."[8]

Unchastened, Abaaoud was arrested on two more occasions the following year, with these latest crimes, theft and assault, resulting in an eighteen-month prison sentence. Even so, he was not deterred. Shortly after his release from prison, Abaaoud was convicted of assault. Twenty three years old, he was returned to lockup, and it was in the course of this final incarceration that an ISIS recruiter hooked him.

ISIS Behind Bars

Extremist organizations across the globe have long sought new members among prison populations, but ISIS's exploitation of this source took the practice to a whole new level. "ISIS is perhaps the first jihadist group that has explicitly targeted this demographic, and they've done it very consciously and especially in Europe," says Peter Neumann, director of London's International Centre for the Study of Radicalisation and Political Violence.[9] The reason is simple: inmates often possess skills that ISIS can use; skills such as stealing, forging documents, attaining arms on the black market, and much more.[10] The organization is not all that choosy if the potential recruit possesses something of value. "ISIS attracts and accepts devout Muslims," says Bruce Hoffman, "but it also actively recruits recent converts, opportunists, profiteers, sadists and thrill-seekers—essentially anyone who can contribute to the cause."[11] Supporting this contention, while Belgians who become ISIS members are usually Muslim, a sizable percentage come from Christian backgrounds or are non-religious. Of course, when potential terrorists are sought after by recruiters, they may have no idea that it is due partly to their hands-on value to the Islamist organization.

It is also worth noting that prospective Muslim extremists in prison, especially those in European penitentiaries who come from marginalizing circumstances, often have pre-existing antisocial attitudes. Moreover, they frequently evince a strong disdain for key aspects of Western society. Thus, they may already be primed for political manipulation as well as receptive to the religious sheen that will be added to the mix in the course of their programming.

Alain Grignard, a counterterrorism expert with the Brussels Federal Police, elaborates on this subject. "We're increasingly dealing with what are best described as 'Islamized radicals,'" he says. "The young Muslims from 'inner-city' areas of Belgium, France, and other European countries joining up with the Islamic States were radical before they were religious."[12] Grignard continues:

> Their revolt from society manifested itself through petty crime and delinquency. Many are essentially part of street gangs. What the Islamic State brought in its wake was a new strain of Islam which legitimized their radical approach. These youngsters are getting quickly and completely sucked in.... The Islamic State has legitimized their violent street credo.[13]

While conversion to jihadism during confinement is one of the most common means by which youthful male offenders in Europe are drawn into Islamic extremism, it is not merely because they spend months or years in close quarters with other prisoners and are therefore literally a captive audience for ISIS recruiters who are likewise incarcerated. It is also because the recruiters' message is highly effective in penetrating the souls of such adrift, down-on-their-luck inmates. Whereas a youthful Muslim may enter prison viewing himself as a failure in society, those who seek to influence him will offer him justifications for his criminal behavior coupled with an unorthodox route to spiritual deliverance. The Islamists' message, Grignard writes, proceeds along these lines:

> You had no choice but to carry out criminal actions because you were part of a discriminated against community. You were only defending yourself. And if you now put yourself in service of the [Islamist] cause ... not only are these actions legitimate but they will win you redemption and reward in paradise.[14]

From miscreant to martyr, from hooligan to hero, the ideas espoused by recruiters can be very seductive to a directionless prisoner, a young person with a criminal record whose future seems bleak. And if the recruiters' messaging takes hold, the inmate may become convinced that he now has a path to transforming his seemingly irrelevant existence into a purposeful, if violent, life within a close-knit, accommodating brotherhood. This appears to have been the case for Abdelhamid Abaaoud.

Abaaoud in Syria

"After his release from Forest prison on September 29, 2012, Abaaoud grew his beard and cut off some of his friendship ties," writes van Vlierden.[15] Single and living alone in Molenbeek, Abaaoud turned down an offer from his father to become a merchant. Although Omar had long thought his son might be adept in the retail field and had even opened a shop for him to manage, Abaaoud turned his attention to a militant outfit in Molenbeek led by Khalid Zerkani, a middle-aged Moroccan immigrant. The group was seeking to persuade young Muslims to fight in Syria, would-be converts like Abaaoud who were already experienced criminals. Abaaoud, moreover, promptly acceded to Zerkani's request that he travel to Syria and participate in jihad, the cost of the trip being covered by money obtained from robberies in Molenbeek. And so, in February of 2013, Abaaoud and six fellow recruits made their way to the Middle Eastern nation. The twenty-five-year-old Belgian had no way of knowing that the State Security Services—Belgian Intelligence—would be making a concerted effort to monitor his movements and communications.

To this end, intelligence agents listened in on a call Abaaoud made using a Turkish man's cellphone the following month. GPS coordinates placed Abaaoud at the Syrian-Turkish border, where he was plotting with this Turkish accomplice to send funds to Yassine, one of Abaaoud's younger brothers back in Belgium. It was part of an effort to create a monetary channel through which money could be funneled from Syria to an ISIS cell in Molenbeek. Unfortunately for Belgian Intelligence, the surveillance team lost its target shortly thereafter when Abaaoud vanished into the Syrian underground; that is, until autumn, when he resurfaced in Belgium.

"From a police source," reads a statement in a declassified intelligence report, "[Abaaoud] has been seen at the end of September walking around Molenbeek-Saint-Jean" ("De source policière, il a été aperçu à la fin du mois de septembre en train de se promener dans Molenbeek-Saint-Jean").[16] To the frustration of Belgian Intelligence, however, the jihadist, who had long been adroit at shaking off his pursuers, quickly disappeared yet again, this time until January 2014, when he showed up at an airport in Cologne, Germany. It was at this juncture that intelligence officials concluded that Abaaoud was working exclusively with ISIS, that he was not involved more broadly in the jihadist movement. Accompanying him on the trip was another of his brothers, thirteen-year-old Younes, along with a Molenbeek-based jihadist of Moroccan descent and a superior of Abaaoud in ISIS, Dniel Mahi. The latter was also known as "Padre." As to their destination, the trio was traveling to Syria, Abaaoud having taken his younger brother out of school for the journey without their parents' knowledge. Of course, Omar's reaction was foreseeable. Angry and distraught, the father tracked down Abdelhamid by phone in the Middle East a few months later and insisted on speaking to Younes, but Abdelhamid refused Omar's request. Abdelhamid further made it clear that he planned for Younes to receive a Muslim education, not a European one, and that the youth would not be returning to Belgium anytime soon. The upshot: a permanent rupture in the family. "I will never forgive Abdelhamid" ("Je ne le pardonnerai jamais à Abdelhamid"), Omar told an interviewer.[17]

As it turned out, Younes, who would become the youngest known member of ISIS, to say nothing of a recurring headache for Belgian Intelligence, would not survive his stint with the Islamist organization. In January 2018, a French official announced that Younes had been killed. And while this same official, Isabelle Prevost-Desprez, noted that he had perished in Iraq or Syria, she did not specify when he had died, although Younes could not have been more than seventeen years old. (With regard to Abdelhamid Abaaoud's other brother, Yassine, the one who had been asked to collaborate with ISIS in setting up a monetary channel between Syria and Belgium, he would eventually be arrested in Morocco and sentenced to two years in prison for being an "apologist for terrorism."[18])

So it was that Abaaoud returned to Syria in 2014, where he became increasingly combative and brutal. It was a development the public would witness through a handful of videos released online at the time. In the most infamous one, recorded on the front lines in Syria, he is shown driving a pickup truck that is dragging several mangled corpses. "It's not fun seeing blood spilled," Abaaoud comments to the camera, grinning, "but it gives me pleasure from time to time to see [the] blood of the disbelievers run because we grew up watching the blood of Muslims being spilled in the whole world on TV."[19]

It was also during 2014 that Abaaoud began his rapid ascent within the ISIS hierarchy. To understand his rise, his responsibilities, and ultimately his role in the horrendous attacks in Paris the following year, it will serve us well to examine briefly the ISIS special division, Emni, in which he became such an important player.

"Lord of the Shadows" and the Creation of Emni

When Abaaoud joined ISIS in 2013, he initially served in a standard capacity alongside other rank-and-file members.[20] And like these fellow recruits, he was observed and assessed by higher-ups in the organization,

6. Belgium, Abdelhamid Abaaoud, and the Paris Terror Units 81

a standard practice aimed at identifying nascent jihadists who possess special qualities or advantageous circumstances. Typically, ISIS superiors pluck these exceptional individuals from the ranks and move them into more sensitive and vital roles in the organization. In the case of Abaaoud, he was promoted rather quickly to the ISIS security apparatus known as the "Amniyat," most likely because he was a Belgian national with criminal experience and connections in Molenbeek, was fluent in both French and Arabic, and was inordinately ruthless.

Regarding the configuration of the Amniyat, it was designed to be a comprehensive entity that contained four divisions, three of which were committed to military intelligence (Amn al-Askari), internal security (Amn al-Dawla), and the protection of ISIS territories (Amn Dakhili).[21] But it was the fourth division—Amn al-Kharji, commonly referred to as the Emni—for which Abaaoud was chosen.

The word "Emni" is the English-language transliteration of the Arabic word "Amn," which is itself a shortened version of the term "Amniyat," meaning "trust" or "safety" in Arabic. The Emni, specifically the Amn al-Kharji, is the division responsible for terrorist operations outside of Syria and Iraq. After hand-picking its members, it trains them in special techniques and dispatches them to carry out sabotage or armed attacks thousands of miles away.

The Emni was the brainchild of Samir Abd Muhammad al-Khlifawi, better known by his *nom de guerre*, Haji Bakr. Before the U.S. invasion of Iraq in 2003, Bakr, who was also known by the theatrical nickname, "Lord of the Shadows," had been a colonel in Saddam Hussein's intelligence service. Following the collapse of Iraq's dictatorial regime, however, he became a principal figure in the construction of ISIS.[22] While a senior leader in the organization's formative years, Bakr contributed significantly to strategizing its takeovers in Iraq and Syria, an endeavor informed by his days in the autocratic Hussein regime.

From the start, Bakr's concept of ISIS had less to do with religion and more to do with power and control, based on his detailed blueprint for the organization that was unearthed after his death in 2014.[23] In his scheme, the Islamic faith was to be used as a mechanism for attracting recruits, a marketing strategy of sorts. It was an approach that was evident in his written master plan for the organization. "It was not a manifesto of faith, but a technically precise plan for an 'Islamic Intelligence State,'" writes *Der Spiegel* reporter Christophe Reuter, "a caliphate run by an organization that resembled East Germany's notorious Stasi domestic intelligence agency."[24] Tellingly, two searches of Bakr's home yielded his edifying ISIS master plan, passports, computers, and a surfeit of relevant papers, but failed to produce a single copy of the Koran.

Characteristics of the Emni

As Bakr had intended, the Emni was tightly regimented and highly controlling of its members. In fact, it routinely spied on them. But it was most fascistic when bringing to heel those outside of ISIS it regarded as enemies or potential enemies of the envisioned caliphate. "The ISIS Emni, following the plans of Haji Bakr, relied on surveillance, espionage, murder, and kidnapping to pave the way for the creation of the powerful totalitarian state structure of the 'Islamic State,'" write Anne Speckhard and Ahmet Yayla. "At the same time, [the Emni] also sought to disguise their subversion under the religious cover of Islam, thereby exploiting the religious faith of others to gain ultimate power."[25] The external operations division, then, reflected the devious and dictatorial nature of ISIS itself as Bakr and his collaborators had conceived of it.

Concerning the chain of command, Abu Mohammed al-Adnani was in charge of it throughout most of Abdelhamid Abaaoud's stretch with the Emni. When Adnani was killed in a drone strike in August 2016, Oussama Atar, whose *nom de guerre* was Abu Ahmad, assumed his functions. And Atar, it turned out, would play a cardinal role in the Paris 2015 attacks.

Oussama Atar

A Belgian-Moroccan citizen, Atar was born on May 4, 1984, in Laeken, Belgium, and began traveling to Syria when he was eighteen years old. It wasn't until five years later, however, that western intelligence agencies became interested in him. At this time, he was arrested Ramadi, Iraq, for entering the country illegally and was suspected of weapons smuggling as well. Sentenced to ten years in prison, he proceeded to serve his sentence in a string of facilities, among them the infamous Abu Ghraib Prison, al-Rusafa Prison, and Camp Bucca. And it was in the latter that he met and bonded with Abu Bakr al-Baghdadi, the future leader of ISIS.

Abu Bakr al-Baghdadi, while he was detained by U.S. armed forces at Camp Bucca in Iraq, 2004 (U.S. Army).

While Atar was an inmate in al-Rusafa Prison, his family spearheaded a public campaign on his behalf, one demanding that he receive immediate medical attention for a life-threatening condition. According to Atar's mother, a Belgian official had contacted her with alarming news. "She said that the Belgian Foreign Ministry told her that [Atar] was about to die of kidney cancer if he didn't get surgery," said Belgian attorney Vincent Lurquin.[26] Adding its august voice to the family's campaign, Amnesty International, the human rights organization, issued a call to action. "Amnesty International believes the denial of medical care to Oussama Atar may amount to cruel, inhuman or degrading treatment," read its September 9, 2010, statement.[27]

As it happened, Atar did not, in fact, have a life-threatening medical condition, only an infection, but he did exploit the misdiagnosis to escape captivity. After being transferred to Belgium to receive the medical treatment that proved unnecessary, he vanished, eventually resurfacing in the Middle East. In the ensuing years, Atar was responsible for several ISIS terror attacks, ultimately earning the notorious distinction of being the top Islamic State figure to be directly associated with the November 2015 attacks in Paris. And while he was regarded as their mastermind, it was Atar's protégé, Abdelhamid Abaaoud, who would be responsible for organizing and directing the specific assaults in Paris. (In 2018, Atar would be killed in an airstrike in Syria, one conducted by the international anti–ISIS coalition.)

Returning to our discussion of the structure of Emni, beneath Abu Mohammed al-Adnani, and subsequently Oussama Atar, in the organizational chart were three emirs, each of whom was in charge of a region of terrorist activity—Europe, Asia, or the Middle East. Beneath each of these emirs, moreover, was an unknown number of theater commanders and local commanders; unknown, that is, to Western intelligence. One theater commander in Europe was Salim Banghalem, who emerged from the same Buttes-Chaumont Network in Paris as the Kouachi brothers, Saïd and Chérif, perpetrators of the *Charlie Hebdo* massacre. It is also known that Abdelhamid Abaaoud became a commander in 2014 during his rise in ISIS, and that a year later he was considered one of the most formidable in the European arena. Indeed, it was during this year, 2015, that European intelligence agencies placed his name at the top of their most-wanted lists.

The Roles of Abdelhamid Abaaoud

Known for his determination, proficiency, and callousness as a commander, Abaaoud was effective at attracting young European Muslims to Islamism and thereafter manipulating them. As for Abaaoud's modus operandi, the former French Prime Minister, Bernard Cazeneuve, described it as such: the Belgian jihadist would conceive, often from his post in Syria, a terrorist attack to be carried out on the European continent. After formulating it, he would choose one or more European jihadists to execute it, typically individuals who had traveled clandestinely to the Middle East to receive arms training through ISIS.[28] The targeted countries most often consisted of France, Spain, and Germany. In a 2015 interview with CNN, Cazeneuve said Abaaoud is believed to have been involved in four of six attempted terrorist attacks in France alone.[29] Given Abaaoud's influence, reach, and the fact that ISIS was increasingly focusing its attacks on European sites because Western forces were systematically destroying its stronghold in the Middle East, the consensus of European counter-intelligence agencies in 2015 was that Abaaoud, as an Emni commander whose territory was Europe, must be stopped.

By this point, Abaaoud is believed to have gained considerable autonomy in choosing targets and conceiving the overall design of attacks. That said, he did offer substantial leeway to his operatives once they were on the ground, making sure they understood that they had the freedom to modify the proposed missions depending on the circumstances that confronted them when it came time to act. As it happened, such independence sometimes resulted in failed missions, especially if the operatives were substandard.

In one such episode, Abaaoud, from his post in Syria, is believed to have assigned a jihadist to perpetrate a lethal plot against a church in the town of Villejuif, four miles south of Paris. Abaaoud did not select a particular church, however; he left that decision up to the man carrying out the mission. In this case, that man was Sid Ahmed Ghlam, an Algerian citizen who was ostensibly in France to study computer science at the Sorbonne. One thing was certain, though: he was not the best person for the job. Before Ghlam could carry out the mass murder, the would-be terrorist inexplicably murdered an innocent woman, a dancer, then accidently shot himself. When law officers searched his home, they recovered a Kalashnikov, a computer, and a cell phone, with the two electronic devices yielding evidence that he had undertaken arms training with ISIS in Syria. The devices further revealed that an unidentified figure had instructed him to target a Villeneuf church of his choice. The latter person, counter-terrorism experts concluded, was Abaaoud acting in his capacity as a commander of European operations.

Other missions that Abaaoud conceived were more successful. In one operation in 2014, Belgian Intelligence detected a cellphone connection between Abaaoud, speaking from a Turkish number, and Mehdi Nemmouch, a French citizen and fellow jihadist who first traveled to Syria in 2012 after his release from prison. Nemmouch had a lengthy criminal record and, as so often happens, had become radicalized while locked up. What Belgian Intelligence found curious is that a few weeks after Abaaoud's phone call to Nemmouch in Europe, the latter stormed into the Jewish Museum in Brussels, a video camera strapped to his chest, and gunned down four people. Two of them were Israelis. The question, then, is to what extent Abaaoud may have been behind the anti–Semitic assault, he and Nemmouch having been members of the same unit in Syria. Of course, this question may never be answered with confidence, although we do know that Abaaoud was by now working hand-in-hand not only with his immediate Emni superior, Adnani, but also with ISIS leader Abu Bakr al-Baghdadi. (The latter would be killed in Delta Force operation on October 26, 2019.)

Abaaoud would continue performing his high-level role in ISIS well into 2015, the final and most fateful year of his life and one that was supposed to commence with a string of out-of-the-blue assaults on police officers in various parts of Belgium. Fortunately, counter-intelligence experts uncovered the plot shortly before the killing spree was slated to occur. Further, they knew Abaaoud was in charge of it and pinpointed the whereabouts of the principal group of would-be perpetrators. Accordingly, the authorities formulated a plan of action that would both prevent the multiple assaults and lead to the capture of Abaaoud.

With this in mind, security forces leapt into action on January 15, 2015, in what was a unique Belgian-Greek counter-terrorism operation. In the Belgian component of it, officers staged early evening raids in nearly a dozen locales. The most significant was in Verviers, a city in the eastern part of the country, where a handful of senior ISIS members were known to be readying for the next day's mission. And while the Verviers raid proved to be a success, it was nevertheless a dicey undertaking, security forces being met with a barrage of gunfire as they approached the entrance to the terrorist-occupied apartment. Amplifying the risk, the flat was situated above a bakery in a densely populated district. To fend off the officers, ISIS members used both handguns and military-grade weapons.

"I heard the sound of grenades, bursts of gunfire," said onlooker Emrick Bertholet, "I'm a bit shocked, a bit afraid, surprised it could happen here."[30] Two terrorists, both of whom held high-level positions in the cell, were killed in the raid, while a third was severely wounded.

In the ensuing months, sixteen members of the ISIS cell were indicted, nine of whom the authorities could not locate. In terms of the leader, Abdelhamid Abaaoud, he avoided capture. The jihadist had been directing the terrorist cell by phone from Athens, where the Belgian-Greek special-ops strategy called for Greek counter-intelligence agents to seize him immediately before the raids in Belgium. For reasons unknown, though, this did not happen. Instead, Greek security forces launched their raids two days after those in Belgium, the upshot being that Abaaoud had already fled. True to form, his elusiveness became a point of pride. "My name and picture were all over the news yet I was able to stay in their homeland, plan operations against them, and leave safely when doing so became necessary," he bragged to *Dabiq*, the online magazine of ISIS.[31]

In much the same way that Abaaoud slipped out of Greece in January, a few months later he again traveled undetected from Syria to Belgium to set up a safe house from which to organize future attacks. While in Belgium, Abaaoud, using a false passport, managed to board a ferry and cross the English Channel to Dover, ferry ports being less secure than airports. Using an alias, he is believed to have met with a handful of Moroccans who were holed up in London and in the Bordesley Green and Alum Rock suburbs of Birmingham. It was information obtained a year later and based on contact numbers found in Abaaoud's cellphone.

Also contained in the phone were photos he had taken of some of London's most celebrated landmarks, although his reason for doing so is a mystery. While he may have been trying to pass himself off as a tourist, it is also plausible that he and his accomplices were envisioning attacks on British soil. Whatever the case, Abaaoud's mere presence in England was unsettling. "An international terrorist who is on watch lists and is subject to an international arrest warrant doesn't take the risk of moving about unless he's doing something operational," says Marc Trevidic, a former anti-terror judge in France who oversaw cases involving violent extremism in Pakistan, Afghanistan, and, of course, France.[32] Thanks to the police raid in Paris that would soon liquidate Abaaoud, England may have dodged the proverbial bullet.

In August 2015, shortly after Abaaoud's surreptitious visit to England, French intelligence experts found themselves deluged with incoming reports pointing to an impending terrorist attack, a major one, to be executed somewhere in Europe. Consistent with these reports was a disconcerting rise in cyber chatter. Then there was the jihadist, a man who had just returned from Syria, who uttered a chilling warning to officials that corroborated their intelligence reports. His named was Reda Hame, he was Parisian, and the police took him into custody on August 11, 2015, as he reentered France. Under interrogation, the twenty-nine-year-old computer technician admitted that he had recently undergone an abbreviated one-week training course in the city of Raqqa, where his sponsor, Abdelhamid Abaaoud, had given him $2,300 and advised him to pass through Prague on the way back to France. It was a route that benign backpackers often use and was therefore unlikely to draw the notice of intelligence agencies. Hame added that Abaaoud instructed him to carry out an attack on an easy target in France, and that he specifically suggested a setting guaranteed to produce a large number of casualties.[33] "Imagine a rock concert," Abaaoud told Hame.[34] Most alarming, Hame disclosed that a large-scale attack in Europe was also in the works, the preparations for which were nearly complete. "All I can tell you is that it will happen very soon" ("Tout ce que je peux vous dire, c'est que cela va arriver très bientôt"), he said.[35] The aspiring terrorist divulged this time-sensitive information to French intelligence officials just twelve weeks before Abaaoud stage-managed ISIS's string of lethal attacks at a rock concert, a national sporting event, and at five bustling cafés in Paris.

Assembling the Assassination Squads

In organizing this multi-faceted terrorist mission, Abaaoud was fastidious in choosing assailants for the job, with his method of selection reflecting the approach ISIS had previously found effective in attracting prospective terrorists in the Molenbeek district. It centered on relationships. Whereas recruiters in other locales employed an array of strategies to draw in prospective fighters, social media being among the more successful tools, word of mouth worked best in the close-knit Moroccan community of Molenbeek. And more often than not, this meant private communications between close friends or family members; people who could be trusted not to inform on one another.

In assembling his team to carry out the Paris attacks of November 13, 2015, Abaaoud selected several individuals, ten of whom are described below and who were directly involved in perpetrating the assaults. Two of them were brothers, Salah and Brahim Abdeslam. Salah was also a close friend of Abaaoud, their connection dating back to their childhood years together in Molenbeek.

Salah Abdeslam

Despite being born and reared in Belgium, Salah Abdeslam was a French citizen. His parents were Moroccan immigrants who had once lived in what was, at the time, French Algeria before resettling in Belgium in 1960. Accordingly, the family was legally French.

Growing up in Molenbeek, Salah Abdeslam was similar to other boys. Like many others this age, he acquired a keenness for motorbikes and soccer when he reached his teen years. But also like some of his friends, most notably Abdelhamid Abaaoud, Salah began having run-ins with law enforcement at an early age, with multiple arrests for petty and no-so-petty crimes. Among the latter: armed robbery. It is Salah who was Abaaoud's accomplice when the pair tried to break into a parking garage and were arrested. There is also the possibility that Salah earned money through same-sex prostitution, although this is not certain.

For many months and continuing up to the time he took part in the Paris terrorist attacks, Salah patronized gay bars on a regular basis in Brussels' "gay village." Certainly, his face was well-known to the bartenders. And while it has been speculated that he may have been gay, or that he may have been attempting to steal patrons' identification papers, or even that he was perhaps casing the establishments for a future terrorist attack, the theory of sex work became the dominant one, most of all among those who worked in the district. "We had him down as a rent boy, he was always hanging out with that kind of crowd," said one bartender, Julien, in an interview with *The Sunday Times* of London.[36] Whatever Salah's reason for being in gay clubs, he was well-known for socializing with the other men and smoking marijuana while there.[37]

The speculation about sex work aside, Salah did have regular jobs much of the time. For instance, he was employed as a technician with Brussels' tram system for several months, although he was eventually terminated. The reason for his firing is unclear, with rumors ranging from workplace theft to recurrent absences.

Subsequent to his stint as a technician, Salah and his brother Brahim managed a small grocery store and, beginning in August of 2015, operated their own bar called *Les Béguines* in Molenbeek. Because the latter was known for catering to marijuana smokers along with users of more substantial substances, police raided the establishment in August 2015. In the course of it, they recovered hallucinogens.[38] "The bar appears to be a point where you can buy and consume drugs, causing problems for the neighbourhood and public order in general," stated the official police report.[39] The bar's closure was immediate and five patrons were booked for possession of illegal substances. The following month, just a few weeks before the scheduled Paris attacks, the Abdeslam brothers unloaded the defunct enterprise and purportedly turned a tidy profit in the process. It was later discovered that Salah had swindled the Belgian government out of $20,000 in unemployment compensation while he was running the grocery store and bar, since he had been gainfully employed during the period he was receiving the funds.

In the forthcoming Paris attacks, Abaaoud would select Salah to be in charge of logistics. Among his duties, Salah would rent cars and lodgings for the terrorists, as well as drive a getaway car following the attacks. Abdelhamid Abaaoud would be among the passengers.

Brahim Abdeslam

Like Salah, his brother Brahim Abdeslam was born in Belgium and grew up in the Molenbeek district, yet was technically a French national. A thirty-one-year-old electrician, Brahim had a police record, with his criminal acts dating back to at least 2005. Most were thefts and scams, one of which included Abaaoud as an accomplice. Despite the elder Abdeslam's intermittent scrapes with the law, however, he also performed good deeds from time to time, most notably in the autumn of 2014.

At that time, he was praised for saving the lives of five children who were trapped inside a burning building in Molenbeek. A dangerous, unselfish feat, it was the polar opposite of his actions a year later in the course of the Paris attacks. "I'm grateful to Brahim for saving my children, but I can't understand what he did in Paris," the children's father would say.[40] It was an observation shared by countless other denizens of the district.

Brahim was also the affable, sociable sort who enjoyed drinking with comrades at the *Les Beguines*. And he had other past-times as well. "His favourite activities were smoking weed and sleeping," said his estranged wife.[41] She added that Brahim smoked three or four joints a day, was nearly always mellow and easy-going, and did not behave violently toward her or other people.[42]

Regarding Brahim's political views, friends and neighbors denied that he was radical in any sense of the word, with one acquaintance pointing out that he spent his Fridays not at the local mosque, like observant Muslims, but chilling with customers at his bar. That said, Brahim did try to sneak into Syria by way of Turkey in 2014, but he was caught and sent back to Belgium. This suggests that Brahim, like other would-be terrorists, was scrupulously keeping his extremist tendencies under wraps in Molenbeek. Indeed, an interrogation conducted after he returned to Belgian prompted officials to classify him as "radicalized." It was later discovered that, in 2015, Brahim Abdeslam would succeed in entering Syria and training or fighting with ISIS.

Foued Mohamed-Aggad

A French citizen brought up in the Alsace region of northeastern France, Mohamed-Aggad was the son of Algerian and Moroccan immigrants. When his mother divorced, she took responsibility for rearing him and his siblings.

While there is little information publicly available that describes Mohamed-Aggad's childhood years, those who knew him describe the future jihadist as well-behaved, if a bit bashful. "(A) nice boy who did not wave" ("Un gentil garçon qui ne faisait pas de vague"), is how the president of his high school soccer club depicted him.⁴³ Unlike others who become ISIS terrorists, Mohamed-Aggad did not have a history of petty crime. For that matter, some have said he had no meaningful history at all.⁴⁴

After graduating from a technical high school, Mohamed-Aggad applied to a police academy but failed the entrance exam. He was likewise unsuccessful in enlisting in the army. Instead, he held intermittent employment in restoration work and locksmithing.

The turning point came in 2012, when the twenty-year-old began attending a local mosque. Soon, he allowed his beard to grow, and his family and friends noticed a marked change in his demeanor. Then, the following year—it was December 2013—Mohamed-Aggad and his older brother traveled to Syria to fight with ISIS, this being another instance of family members being brought together into the Islamist organization. While there, Mohamed-Aggad fought in Aleppo and appeared in an internet video, a grisly cavalcade of beheadings and shootings in which he was shown slaying a defenseless man. Subsequent to this, his superiors selected him to lead a battalion of 300 combatants.

Although Mohamed-Aggad was expected to return to France in 2014, he chose to stay in Syria. "If I go back to France, it is not to go to prison, it is to explode everything" ("Si je rentre en France, c'est pas pour aller en prison, c'est pour tout exploser"), he said in an intercepted message.⁴⁵

The following spring, the fervent Islamist, who was still in contact with his mother in France, told her that he hoped to die a martyr. From his communiqués, it is evident that he planned to do so in France, the land of his birth. And sure enough, Mohamed-Aggad was back in France a few months later, preparing to bring about his self-styled martyrdom in the Paris attacks.

Chakib Akrouh

Born in Brussels and raised in the Molenbeek district, Akrouh held Belgian-Moroccan citizenship. It is believed that he knew Abaaoud from their years in Molenbeek prior to their radicalization.

In 2013, Akrouh traveled to Syria to take part in the Syrian Civil War, and while there he became an ISIS sympathizer. Eventually devoting himself totally to the Islamist organization, he would make an appearance in an ISIS video warning the nation of France about the likely repercussions of its military presence in Syria.

In a 2015 proceeding, a court found Chakib Akrouh guilty of helping send jihadists to Syria. Although he was sentenced to five years in prison, he would not serve any time, his whereabouts being unknown.

"Ahmad al-Mohammad"

Although Ahmad al-Mohammad was not his real name—it was the name on the forged passport found near his remains after the Paris attacks—officials would nevertheless identify him as such in the wake of the terrorist assaults. Months later, ISIS would publicly identify the jihadist by his *nom de guerre*, Ukasah al-Iraqi, which suggests he was a citizen of Iraq.

While virtually nothing is known about him, a trace of the fake passport reveals that the terrorist traveled by boat with nearly 200 Syrian refugees from Turkey to the Greek island of Leros, arriving on October 3, 2015. Next, he made his way to Athens, then followed the route taken by hundreds of thousands of desperate refugees, passing through Macedonia and Serbia and eventually reaching Western Europe. Beyond these bare bones, "al-Mohammad" is still a mystery.

"M. al-Mahmod"

Accompanying al-Mohammad to the isle of Leros, Greece, and likewise using false papers, was a man by the false name of "M. al-Mahmod." After the Paris attacks, ISIS publicly identified him by the *nom de guerre* Ali al-Iraqi, which indicates that he too was most likely an Iraqi national. As with al-Mohammad, "M. al-Mahmod" continues to be a question mark.

Samy Amimour

A French citizen and the son of Algerian immigrants, Samy Amimour grew up in Drancy, a northeastern suburb of Paris. Although Muslim, the Amimour family was both westernized and progressive, Amimour's mother being a feminist and his father, who left the family when Amimour was a boy, a clothing salesman and an aficionado of French literature.

Those who knew him as a youth describe Amimour as bright, shy, and inward. "Not mean at all" ("Pas méchant du tout)," is how one acquaintance depicted him.[46] After graduating from high school, Amimour studied pre-law at the University of Paris in Villetaneuse, but he encountered academic difficulties and switched to an industrial logistics program at a technical college. In 2012, he left academia altogether and secured a job as a bus driver for the RATP, a public transportation operation based in Paris. While in this position, Amimour paid a visit to a local mosque and soon began a striking transformation, one that entailed shaving his head and adopting traditional Salafist Muslim attire. He also stopped kissing women and children, and started taking firearms lessons from a law enforcement organization. Finally, Amimour walked away from his position as a driver and withdrew from his family and friends. "He got radicalised, he quit his job, he closed up, cut himself off from his parents," says Jean-Christophe Lagarde, the mayor of Drancy.[47] Lagarde theorizes that Amimour's shyness, his apparent insecurity, made him a target for recruiters at the mosque he attended.[48]

It the autumn of 2012, counter-terrorism agents learned that Amimour was preparing to travel to Yemen with two other men to take part in jihad. Pulling him in for questioning, French authorities released him afterward—he had not yet committed a crime—but they did affix his name to the nation's terrorist watchlist.

In September of the following year, the budding Islamist told his father that he, Samy Amimour, was heading to the South of France. In reality, he was heading to Syria to join up with ISIS. And sure enough, he made his way through Turkey to Syria, where he enlisted in the Islamic State. In short order, Amimour married and settled in Raqqa, which was about to become an ISIS-controlled metropolis. As to his role in the organization, he was a combatant until early in 2014, when he was wounded near the war-torn city of Aleppo. A leg injury, it brought to an end his days as a fighter.

Throughout this period, Mohamed Amimour was worried about his son, who he now knew was waging war in Syria. For this reason, the sixty-seven-year-old man decided to make a secret, circuitous, three-week trek from Paris to ISIS territory in Syria to persuade the twenty-seven-year-old to come home. Although returning to France would mean Samy would be taken into custody—an international arrest warrant had been issued in 2013 in response to an indictment for criminal conspiracy associated with a terrorist entity—staying in Syria would be even more perilous in that he could face death at the hands of enemy troops. Mohamed hoped he could help his son recognize the error of remaining on the frontline in the Middle Eastern country.

Arriving at the border of Turkey and Syria in the summer of 2014, Mohamed, who had not told Samy he was coming to visit, was taken aback by his son's iciness when contacted by phone from the border. And although Samy did meet his father at the border and accompany him into ISIS territory, their visit was anything but affectionate. "He did not take me to his house, did not tell me how he was hurt, or whether he was fighting" ("Il ne m'a pas emmené chez lui, ne m'a pas dit comment il s'était blessé, ni s'il combattait"), says Mohamed.[49] Not surprisingly given the sea change in his son, Mohamed would soon be returning to France without him. As for Samy, he and his wife would resettle temporarily in Mosul, Iraq. It is not know when or how he returned to Paris to play his part in the killings.

Bilal Hadfi

A twenty-year-old French national whose childhood and adolescence were spent in Belgium, Hadfi's life was unremarkable until he reached his teens. At that time, his circumstances changed owing to the death of his father, a tragedy that scarred young Hadfi and produced a struggle with grief would last for the rest of his short life. Aside from this emotional rupture and its effects, he was otherwise an ordinary youth, according to his family, friends, and teachers; a boy drawn to soccer and girls but not to religion or politics.

As a high school student in Brussels in 2013, Hadfi studied information technology, but he told his instructors that he was more interested in becoming a truck driver than a computer technician. In fact, he would become neither, since he failed his year-end exams. What he did instead was to transfer to another school, while remaining the same person he had always been. "But a year later everything changed," says Brigitte Colliege, one of his teachers.[50]

It was in 2014 that Hadfi was faced with difficulties at home, where he lived with his mother and two brothers. While the nature of the family's problems is hazy, records reveal that his mother was hospitalized during this period. As for Hadfi, he started skipping school, turning away from his friends, and smoking marijuana.

By the following January, he had changed profoundly and in a worrisome direction. At his new school, he made it a point to declare his opposition to its stance on the importance of social and religious tolerance. He also made homophobic slurs, praised Boko Haram for its blood-drenched territorial victories, and stopped listening to music because Islamic law forbade it, historically. Most upsetting to his teachers and classmates, he praised Saïd and Chérif Kouachi's slaughter at *Charlie Hebdo* in Paris when it happened. "Hadfi said the *Charlie Hebdo* employees who were killed deserved it because they had repeatedly been warned for insulting Islam," recalls Kasmi M'Hamed, another of Hadfi's teachers.[51] In the wake of the *Charlie Hebdo* massacre, which seemed to galvanize Hadfi, he told his classmates he would soon be going to Syria, and subsequently featured on his Facebook page his newly-adopted *nom de guerre* together with a photo of himself with a jihadist flag.

The following month, when he didn't return to school, his teachers paid a visit to his mother. Although she claimed that her son had moved to Morocco to live with relatives, his classmates insisted that he had gone to fight with ISIS in the Syrian Civil War. Alarmed, his instructors reported their concerns about his radicalization to school administrators, but their warnings were not forwarded to law enforcement or to Belgian counter-intelligence officials.

Meanwhile, in Syria, Hadfi maintained a presence on social media. Among other cyber-activities, he communicated with members of a Libyan spinoff of ISIS, uploaded photos of his weapons arsenal, and posted an image of Islamists vandalizing a police car. In addition, he shared a photo of himself aiming an AK-47 at a resort hotel. Finally, a post that Hadfi presumably had written appeared on his Facebook page, an unnerving statement likening Westerners to dogs and calling for acts of violence. "Strike them in their community of pigs so they can't feel safe again in their own dreams," read the statement.[52] It was posted on June 2015, five months before the Paris attacks. In the end, French and Belgian officials never determined when or how Bilal Hadfi returned to Europe to take part in the Paris atrocities.

Ismaël Omar Mostefaï

Born and brought up in the Paris suburb of Courcouronnes, Ismaël Omar Mostefaï and his family moved to Chartres while he was in his teens. His mother had immigrated from Portugal and his Algeria-born father had fought in the Algerian War. Upon moving to France, the elder Mostefaï is further believed to have become involved with a military group that was active in Pakistan and Afghanistan.

By all accounts, Mostefaï's childhood was emotionally sound, his parents being attentive to him and his four siblings. Regarding the family itself, the Mostefaïs were well-liked and respected in their working-class community.

As a youth, Mostefaï was described as being a bit timid at times, but otherwise was amiable and athletic. He was especially proficient in the sport he loved the most, soccer, which he played with a group of neighborhood friends. They were a rambunctious blend of black, white, and Arabic youths. "Omar, as we called him, was a normal guy in sneakers and baggy pants," says a neighbor.[53]

In his twenties, Mostefaï landed a job as a baker's apprentice, a position in which he appears to have performed up to expectations. Yet side by side with this socially responsible conduct were repeated incidents of defiance. The fact is, he was arrested eight times between 2004 and 2010, albeit for comparatively minor infractions such as driving a car without carrying a license. Even though he was never sent to jail, however, his actions nevertheless revealed a propensity toward rebelliousness.

A practicing Muslim, Mostefaï had a spiritual side too, one that was fostered by his father with whom he attended a mosque in Chartres. Counter-terrorism experts now suspect it was while Mostefaï was attending this house of worship in 2009 that he fell under the spell of a

Moroccan-born, Belgian imam, a radical one, and began his slide into extremism. Soon, Mostefaï would metamorphose into a militant Islamist.

A year later, he married, and he and his wife had a child. Also in 2010, French intelligence experts identified Mostefaï as a person who was at a high risk of becoming radicalized. It was a prediction that proved to be spot-on. Counter-intelligence experts determined three years later that Mostefaï was in Syria fighting against Assad's forces in the Syrian Civil War, and they had reason to believe that he was becoming further radicalized while in the war-torn country. Presumably, he left Syria in the late spring of 2014, although it is possible, even probable, that he returned to the Middle East on other occasions, since by this point he had become an ardent jihadist.

In an exasperating twist that came about in October 2014, Turkish officials concluded that Mostefaï, a French national, was indeed a terror suspect and they notified French authorities two months later. Among other insights, Turkish intelligence experts were now in the position to confirm that he had trained with ISIS. When no response was forthcoming from their French counterparts, Turkish officials again warned them that Mostefaï was likely a terrorist. Yet as before, French intelligence officials did not act on this crucial tip. Instead, they relayed back to their Turkish colleagues that they were powerless to intervene, that their hands were tied. It was in June 2015, that French officials received this second warning, just three months prior to the attacks in French capital, where the twenty-nine-year-old father, husband, and jihadist would carry out his horrific assignment.

So it was that Abdelhamid Abaaoud, the on-the-ground orchestrator of the forthcoming assaults in Paris, was ready. It was now early November 2015. He had hand-picked the members of the three hit teams that would carry out the killings, and Oussama Atar, his superior who was currently helming the Emni, had green-lit the operation. On board, too, was a prominent ISIS commander, Abu Suleyman al-Firansi, who monitored the organization's European attacks from Syria and who possessed detailed knowledge of the forthcoming terror mission in France's capital city. It was now just a matter of time.

7

Carnival of Horror

*The Bataclan Theatre,
Stade de France, and the Café
Attacks of Friday the Thirteenth*

The air was brisk and the skies over Paris were clear on the evening of November 13, 2015. On the tree-lined Boulevard Voltaire, traffic was dense, the thoroughfare teeming with Parisians relishing the arrival of the weekend. Some were on their way to nightclubs, bars, and *café terraces*—sidewalk cafés—while others were en route to the Bataclan Theatre, where they planned to unfetter themselves at a high-voltage concert by an American rock band. Still others amassed at the Stade de France, the national rugby and soccer stadium, situated north of Paris in the crime-ridden municipality of Saint-Denis. An exhibition match was set to take place between the national soccer teams of France and Germany, and President François Hollande and other dignitaries were slated to be in attendance. To be sure, it promised to be an exhilarating night in the City of Light. And no doubt it would have been if Abdelhamid Abaaoud and his ten operatives had not made other, darker plans.

While Paris bustled, the militant Islamists were elsewhere in and around the city priming for their massacres. Salah Abdeslam, the operative responsible for logistics, had entered France several weeks earlier after passing through Austria and Germany, and had managed to secure lodgings and transportation for the mission. Among other preparations, he had rented a black Volkswagen Polo and two hotel rooms in the town of Alfortville, just south of Paris, while his brother Brahim had leased a house northeast of the capital city in Bobigny. The former locations were to serve as drop-off points on the night of the attacks, while the latter, in Bobigny, was to be the spot at which members and supplies were coordinated. Investigators would later determine that two additional cars were rented for the operation, a black Seat Leon and a Volkswagen Golf, with the transactions having been conducted in Belgium.

7. Carnival of Horror

Regarding weapons, they included AK-47s and Serbian-designed Zastava M70 assault rifles, along with explosive vests to be worn by seven of the operatives who were designated suicide bombers. All of the explosive outfits were identical in design. Unfortunately, investigators were unable to determine who constructed the vests, which had the appearance of a pair of suspenders with explosives affixed to the bottom, at waist level. What we do know is that they were similar to those used in terrorist missions conducted in North African and Middle Eastern nations. In European attacks, radical Islamists ordinarily use backpacks to hold their incendiary devices. Moreover, due to the volatility of the chemicals involved, it is believed that the vests were assembled in Europe, probably in France, and that their maker was not among the attackers. The reason: bomb-making skills are at once specialized and scarce and thus highly valued by terrorist organizations. The bomb-maker would have been kept at a distance from the attack sites so as to be shielded from harm or discovery.

In terms of the devices themselves, each bomb contained a battery, detonator, screws and bolts, and a homemade compound, TATP. Similar to TNT in its power and nicknamed the "Mother of Satan" by terrorist organizations owing to its destructive effects, TATP, or triacetone triperoxide, is easily formulated. "Anyone who could follow a recipe to make a pumpkin pie could follow the recipe to make TATP," says Kenneth Suslick, a research professor at the University of Illinois.[1] Certainly the components are easy to purchase. "Common household ingredients—paint thinners (acetone), bleach or antiseptic (hydrogen peroxide), and a powerful drain unblocker (>85 per cent sulphuric acid)—can be obtained from hardware stores and pharmacies," write Bea Perks and Lionel Milgrom.[2] When blended in the proper proportions, the chemical reaction can be devastating. Then too, TATP is easy to detonate. Merely touching the compound can ignite it, which is why bomb-makers who work with it are notable for their missing fingers. As an explosive to be deployed in the Paris terrorist attacks, TATP could be expected to produce mass casualties.

In keeping with Abaaoud's scheme, three teams were to target six discrete sites, all of which were sure to be packed with unsuspecting women, men, and children enjoying leisure activities. Addressing the choice of Paris as the target, an official statement from ISIS subsequently explained that the assaults were a reply to France's military actions in the Middle East, and that the city was in the crosshairs because it was "the capital of prostitution and obscenity, the carrier of the banner of the Cross in Europe."[3]

The sites themselves were to be composed of the national sports stadium, a cluster of cafés and bars, and a concert hall. Presumably, Abaaoud kept each of his three teams in the dark regarding the details of the other teams' assignments, a familiar practice in ISIS operations. Structurally, it is known as a "bamboo" configuration. "(M)ost militant groups have cells intended to operate separately and in parallel to ensure that if one member is killed or a plot is aborted, the demise would not affect other plots," writes Eric Schmitt in the *New York Times*.[4]

By early evening, Abaaoud's three teams would have been awaiting the go-ahead. By comparison, the city of Paris was unprepared for the violence that was about to be visited upon it, a state of vulnerability that has since become the subject of controversy and criticism. Only ten days earlier, a classified report was circulated warning that six ISIS terrorists had managed to enter France, but inexplicably this critical information was not forwarded to the General Directorate for Internal Security (DGSI), the French intelligence agency charged with counter-espionage and counterterrorism. Furthermore, French intelligence was operating on the assumption that ISIS was plotting a campaign in Paris on or around November 30, when the UN Climate Change Conference was scheduled to convene in capital city. For such reasons, a string of terrorist strikes was not expected to rock Paris on this Friday evening in the midpoint of the month.

While the city as a whole may have been unwary, however, the target that was intended to be "ground zero" of the ISIS operation was well-prepared. The site: the national stadium, an arena with a seating capacity of 80,000 and one that had already distinguished itself with its exceptional perimeter security. It is common knowledge that providing protection, thoroughly and visibly, at the boundary of a stadium is essential if potential intruders are to be dissuaded, or directly blocked, from entering it. "It is the point at which security teams have the greatest ability to ensure the safety and security of everyone in attendance," says Miranda Tomic of MSA Security.[5] On this front, the Stade de France would exceed expectations.

Stade de France

The soccer match set to take place between the German and French teams was projected to draw an immense audience, with millions watching on television and 78,000 spectators in the venue itself. Besides the French president and numerous cabinet ministers, a delegation of prominent German officials would also be in attendance, with the event set to commence at 9:00 p.m.

As the match kicked off, Salah Abdeslam drove up to the Stade de France in a Renault Clio and dropped off three suicide bombers: twenty-year-old Bilal Hadfi and two operatives using false names, Ahmad al-Mohammed and M. al-Mahmod. The strategy was for al-Mohammed to enter the stadium at the start of the match, while Hadfi and al-Mahmod remained outside. Authorities believe this to be the case because al-Mohammed was the only one of the trio to possess a ticket to the event. Once inside, he was to detonate his explosive device amongst the spectators, which would not only guarantee a sizable number of deaths and injuries but also trigger a disastrous stampede out of the stadium. Then, as the crush of spectators ran outside, Hadfi and al-Mahmod would be waiting at separate exits, detonating their bombs and killing even more people. It was a diabolical plan, but fortunately for the tens of thousands of attendees it would not unfold as envisioned.

"A security guard," reports CNN, "told French police that starting at 9:05 p.m., he blocked a man resembling one of the Iraqi stadium attackers four times from trying to trick his way in."[6] Because the would-be gatecrasher, presumably al-Mohammed, was unsuccessful in slipping past the guard, the terrorist decided at 9:20 p.m. to take his chances with his ticket. Striding up to Gate D near Avenue Jules Rimet, he presented it to the attendant, and at once a security guard began searching him for weapons. When the guard, a man by the name of Zouheir, detected the suicide vest beneath al-Mohammed's jacket, the terrorist backed away and seconds later set off his explosive device, killing himself and a bystander.[7] In effect, Zouheir's vigilance at the facility's perimeter foiled the foundational act of the Stade de France scheme, the upshot being that Hadfi and al-Mohmad would now have to improvise.

Inside the sports facility, meanwhile, the audience remained calm. "(W)e are used to hearing fireworks or loud noises in stadiums," says spectator Franck Benarroch, "so we just assumed it was that."[8] No one, it seems, perceived the sound to be that of a bomb blast, not even those who had served in war zones, perhaps because the arena's reinforced walls had muffled or otherwise distorted the sound. Of course, those in the vicinity of the explosion knew exactly what had happened and, seconds later, officers jumped into action.

Surveillance data reveal that Bilal Hadfi, at this same moment, was on his cellphone speaking to organizer Abdelhamid Abaaoud. The latter was en route to one of Paris's café districts to carry out his own succession of attacks.

While the coaches for the German and French teams, the players, and the audience were not told that anything was amiss, an emergency meeting was set up in the security station on the top floor of the stadium. President Hollande would preside over it. Present, too, would be the head of the French Football Federation, Noël Le Graët, who was also at the venue watching the match. "Don't move, no need to show panic," he recalls being told, "but you're going to meet the president in two minutes, but very calmly, leave with your hands in your pockets so you don't show any sign of panic."[9]

At the emergency gathering, President Hollande explained that the Interior Ministry was ensuring that all of the arena's entrances and exits were secured and that the match would continue as if nothing had happened. Le Graët was specifically told not to alert anyone to the situation, and to make certain that all televisions in the facility were turned off, including those in the locker rooms. Le Graët would later contend that these decisions by the French president helped prevent a mass slaughter, since scores of spectators were not evacuated into the streets where Hadfi and al-Mahmod, the remaining suicide bombers, were lying in wait.[10] Shortly after the meeting, Hollande was escorted out of the building, a sight that unsettled some of the spectators. Underlining his belief that his stadium decision was sound, the French leader advised his adult son, who was also present in the arena on this night, to remain seated, stating that it was safer for him to be inside than outside.[11]

At 9:30 p.m., the second suicide bomber, M. al-Mahmod, decided to set off his explosive device even though the hoped-for pandemonium had not broken out in the wake of the first bombing. Dressed in a jogging suit emblazoned with the logo of the Bayern Munich soccer team, al-Mahmod detonated his device at Gate H, situated on Avenue Jules Rimet. For whatever reason, it proved to be a more powerful blast than the initial explosion. "I felt like I was in a video game," said one onlooker.[12] People in the surrounding area suffered injuries, while the bomber, of course, died instantly.

As before, spectators in the Stade de France were told nothing. That said, concern was mounting, particularly as audience members began receiving texts from family and friends alarmed about the situation at the facility. One spectator who did not remain oblivious to the facts was General Philippe Boutinaud, commander of the Paris Fire Brigade and a former member of NATO's Military Committee. Whereas Boutinaud, like most everyone else, mistook the first explosion for fireworks, he was less certain about the second one. Even so, he did not suspect a bombing, although he would soon learn the truth.

Five minutes after the second detonation, Jean-Pierre Tourtier, the Paris Fire Brigade's chief physician, phoned Boutinaud and explained that shootings were now taking place in the city and, as Boutinaud already knew, that two explosions had occurred at the Stade de France. Leaving the arena at once, Boutinaud found himself on Avenue Jules Rimet minutes later, where he tripped over a leg. It was the severed limb of a bomber. Across the street, Boutinaud spotted the other leg together with remains of the terrorist's mutilated body, as well as what appeared to be puffs of cotton strewn across the area. Recognizing the latter to be the stuffing from a jacket, the seasoned military veteran now grasped that the explosions had been the work of suicide bombers.[13]

At 9:53 p.m., coinciding with half time, Bilal Hadfi detonated his device, making him the third and final Islamist to kill himself at the Stade de France. Unlike his two accomplices, the twenty-year-old triggered his bomb near a McDonald's restaurant at the intersection of rue des Trémés and rue de la Cokerie, a tenth of a mile from the sports venue. It has been speculated that he had been waiting for the half-time crowd to gather outside the stadium, but since the exits had been closed temporarily, he shifted his attack site to the McDonald's restaurant. Hadfi's reasoning may have been that McDonald's would likely be brimming with customers, and, moreover, that the fast-food chain is associated with the United States. This would make the bombing a secondary strike against America.[14] Sadly, over fifty people were wounded in this third blast.[15]

It was also at half time that Didier Deschamps, coach of the French team, and Joachim Löw, that of the German team, were notified of the bombings. Although Deschamps initially considered sharing this information with the French players, he ultimately kept it to himself, as did Löw. As a result, players on the two teams dismissed the explosions as hoaxes, and the match carried on into the second half. "The coaches' decisions, along with typically spotty cellphone reception during major events at the cavernous Stade de France just north of Paris, made for a surreal atmosphere: The players played and most of the fans cheered as usual, unaware of what was going on around them, while a smattering of coaches, officials and journalists (all of whom had access to the Internet) grimly followed the escalating carnage of the coordinated terrorist attacks," writes Sam Borden.[16] As previously noted, the decision to withhold from the audience the source of the explosions was meant to avert a mass panic and thus further injuries and deaths. Moreover, it achieved its aim, although the strategy would attract its share of critics in the aftermath of the Paris massacres.

When the match wrapped up at 10:50 p.m., Franck Bargine, the sports announcer, informed the audience that acts of violence had transpired outside the facility and that a few parking lots and exits were closed as a result.[17] As could be expected, the spectators, at least those who were still unaware of the terrorist campaign underway in Paris, became unsettled. Had they checked the internet at this juncture, they would have become even more upset by the wild rumors circulating online, among them false reports about terrorist squads attacking the Louvre, Les Halles, and the Pompidou Center. Not surprisingly, when firecrackers were set off outside the stadium shortly after Bargine's announcement, scores of exiting spectators rushed back inside and onto the playing field fearing that the noise was gunfire. Meanwhile, helicopters hovered above the stadium as police ushered throngs of flustered soccer fans away from the arena.

Slate journalist Robin Panfili, who found himself hurrying toward a nearby metro station, described his encounter with a hundred or so people fleeing toward him. "The crush of the crowd carries people," he writes "some of them are pushing without knowing where to go, others fall and grab onto the ankles of those who manage to weave through."[18] Such accounts reveal the chaos and confusion of the scene.

At this point, the French and German soccer teams began to learn about the bombings, with some of the players finding out as they walked through the passageways leading to their dressing rooms. In these covered walkways, the televisions that were suspended from the ceilings had been turned on again and numerous players stood stock-still in front of them, glued to the images of the violence in the city.

Two players on the French team were especially alarmed. Antoine Griezmann, a forward, knew that his sister Maud was attending a rock concert at the Bataclan Theatre, and he did not know if she was safe. "May God take care of my sister and the rest of France," he wrote on Twitter.[19] Also distraught was midfielder Lassana Diarra, a Muslim, who was worried about his cousin, Asta Diakite. Asta was likewise a Muslim, and she was at a café in a targeted area of Paris. As it turned out, Maud Griezmann would survive, but Asta Diakite would perish.

Owing to the immediate danger of traveling on an unsecured team bus—and to the fact that there had been a bomb scare at the German team's hotel earlier in the day—it was decided that the German players would stay at the Stade de France overnight and catch an early morning flight back to Frankfurt. To this end, mattresses were hauled out and the Germans, who admitted to being shaken by the ongoing assaults, prepared to sleep in the arena. Then something unexpected occurred, says Reinhard Rauball, acting president of the German Football Association. "The French said that they were staying as long as Germany had to stay."[20] So it was that the French players also took to the stadium's mattresses in a stirring show of solidarity, camaraderie, and sportsmanship.

In all, three terrorists and one bystander died in the Stade de France bombings. Another 54 people were injured, some critically.[21]

The Café District

Within minutes of the terrorists launching their assault at the Stade de France, the second team initiated its attacks on a handful of establishments five miles south of the stadium in the 10th and 11th arrondissements. They focused on the Canal-Saint-Martin area of Paris, an area favored by local denizens because of its easygoing bars and *café terraces*, and sweetened by its reasonable prices.

Le Carillon and Le Petite Cambodge

One such bar is Le Carillon, situated on rue Alibert. "For many locals," writes Kevin Ponniah of the BBC, "it's unpretentious and inviting, with old sofas and low lighting—a place to meet friends in the evening or stop by for coffee during the day."[22] Proximate to Le Carillon on the same street is Le Petit Cambodge, a restaurant specializing in Asian cuisine and another popular haunt in the neighborhood. On this evening, both would become the targets of ISIS extremists bent on mass destruction.

The killing spree erupted only minutes after the first suicide bombing at the Stade de France, the plan apparently being for the assaults at the stadium and the café district to transpire nearly simultaneously. Here in the restaurant and bar zone, the bloodshed commenced at 9:25 p.m., when five shots were fired from a black Seat Leon with Belgian license plates. The target was the man driving the car in front of it, which was holding up traffic. After killing him, Abdelhamid Abaaoud, ringleader of the entire Paris operation and the driver of the Seat, activated its hazard lights, following which he, Brahim Abdeslam, and Chakib Akrouh sprinted a few yards to Le Carillon and Le Petit Cambodge. Clad in black, the three were described by witnesses as young-looking, physically fit, and professional-acting, as well as being likened to combat soldiers because of their discipline and determination.[23]

"Allahu Ahkbar," one of terrorists shouted as they set about killing

Le Carillon, 18 rue Alibert, Paris. One of six café-bars targeted during the Islamic State-sponsored attacks on November 13, 2015.

customers, with the gunfire stunning patrons and knocking them out of their chairs on the front terrace of Le Carillon.[24] Over fifty customers were at Le Carillon—the bar was packed, this being soccer night in Paris—and it was in the establishment's interior that the assailants continued their violence after executing those on the terrace. The volley of gunfire was so substantial that it caused a smoke cloud to drift across the room.

At the neighboring Asian restaurant, there were an estimated forty diners and staff who were similarly dumbfounded. "All of a sudden we heard huge gunshots and glass coming through the windows," recalls Charlotte Brehaut.[25] Customers and workers dropped to the floor. As to those who lived near the restaurant, they too heard the commotion and were perplexed by it. Resident Pierre Montfort, for instance, thought the metallic, staccato clack of AK-47s was that of fireworks, and he noted that it seemed never to end.[26]

At the entrance to Le Petit Cambodge, one of the terrorists repeatedly pivoted left and right, firing three to four precision shots in each direction.[27] As he did so, some of the wounded, as well as those who were still unharmed, crawled across the floor and took cover underneath tables, while shards of glass rained down on them.[28] Another gunman targeted people running through the streets in search of refuge. Within minutes, there was a cluster of bodies in the restaurant's main dining room, along with victims lying incapacitated or lifeless on the pavement.

Back at the neighboring bar, Le Carillon, multiple casualties were suffered as well, with a handful of corpses on the terrace. But among the bar's patrons on this night had been medical personnel. "Doctors and nurses from the nearby Hôpital Saint-Louis were in Le Carillon when the attacks happened, and [they] supplied emergency assistance to the wounded," writes Robert Burke, a hazardous materials expert at the University of Maryland.[29] One such Samaritan was dermatologist Barouyr Baroudjian, who had brought with him to the bar a handful of interns. Even though Baroudjian and his fellow doctors were dazed by the paroxysm of savagery and found their own emotions blunted, they nevertheless tried, if somewhat mechanically, to provide the victims with emergency medical care.[30] Baroudjian later recounted his feelings of futility in the face of the profound carnage, noting the obstacles that he and his fellow caregivers confronted. "I'm not sure we had any use because we had nothing, nothing but our hands," he said.[31]

Other helpers included a city medic who arrived within minutes. He and his two coworkers were in the immediate area attending to an unrelated crisis when the shootings erupted. The medic provided oxygen, applied tourniquets, and performed other life-saving measures while waiting for backup.

Also vital were those Parisians who lived in the surrounding apartments. In one case, a young girl opened her family's doors to over a dozen patrons of Le Carillon who were fleeing the gunmen.

In this initial strike in the café district by the second team of terrorists, over a hundred shell casings were recovered. As to the death toll, fifteen people were killed and ten more were critically injured. Among the murdered were identical twins Charlotte and Emilie Meaud, twenty-nine-years-old, who perished side by side. One of the sisters was an architect, and the other had earned a degree in economics and worked at a firm that assists start-ups. "Absolutely shattered," is how one of their former teachers described his reaction to the Meauds' deaths.[32]

Another fatality was Mohamed Amine Ibnolmobarak, who was twenty-nine years old. A Morocco-born architect, his thesis had centered on his pilgrimage to Mecca. Amine's wife, who was with him at Le Carillon, was shot three times, but survived.

À la Bonne Bière and La Casa Nostra

After carrying out their strikes on Le Petit Cambodge and Le Carillon, Abaaoud drove his two accomplices 750 yards to the south and to a fashionable district known as Folie-Mélancourt. At 9:32 p.m., one of the jihadists climbed out of the car at 32 rue du Faubourg du Temple, shouted the Takbīr ("Allahu akbar"), and opened fire on patrons at À la Bonne Bière. A bustling bistro, five people were killed and eight others were severely wounded. As in the earlier shootings, police recovered an estimated one hundred shell casings.

Four minutes later, Abaaoud and his accomplices arrived at another soft target, La Casa Nostra, an Italian eatery situated only 130 feet away. Like the other restaurants the assailants targeted on this mild autumn evening, it was packed with customers both indoors and outdoors. Unlike the others, though, it would suffer no fatalities. This is partly because the shooter's gun jammed as he was about to execute diners on the front terrace, a malfunction investigators later observed on closed-circuit video from the restaurant.

La Belle Équipe

Racing to 92 rue de Charonne, Abaaoud and his accomplices next came to a halt at 9:36 p.m. at La Belle Équipe ("The Great Team"). A trendy neighborhood bistro adored by locals and visitors alike, it was operating at full capacity on this Friday evening, meaning its sidewalk terrace was replete with patrons. And it was here, in the exposed dining area, that the gunmen first opened fire. Overpowering the al fresco diners, a slaughter ensued, with the shooting lasting three minutes and resulting in the second deadliest attack of the evening, according to the BBC.[33] While one assailant mowed down those on the terrace and inside the café—as at Le Petit Cambodge, the shooter swiveled left and right while delivering a torrent of gunfire—another gunman targeted cars passing by the establishment. To complete the job, the shooter pointed his weapon downward and picked off, one by one, those who lay suffering on the ground. For the third time, police would recover approximately a hundred shell casing at La Belle Équipe, suggesting that the serial restaurant attacks had been conducted in a prearranged, uniform fashion, even to the point of the number of clips used.

Predictably, the scene was ghastly. One witness, a man who arrived moments after the onslaught, found himself in a nightmarish landscape. "I see a guy crying because his wife was dead, then we go on and we realize we are in the middle of a pond of blood."[34] The witness added that the dead and dying were sprawled on the ground and slumped across tables. So copious was the blood that it was spilling into the gutter.[35]

Another witness, one who arrived at the restaurant just as the assault commenced, described being momentarily confounded by one of the victims, a woman. She appeared to be asleep on a table, yet she was holding a drink. "Then I saw a hole in her face, and I realised she had been shot," the witness said.[36]

In all, nineteen diners were killed at La Belle Équipe and nine others were critically wounded.[37] Among the murdered were a young Romanian couple, Ciprian Calciu and Lacramioara Pop, the parents of an eighteen-month-old son; Barcelona-born Victor Munoz, an online marketing specialist; and Guillaume Le Dramp, a waiter whose dream was to become an elementary school teacher. "Charming, warm, truly kind with a wicked sense of humour," is how one of Le Dramp's loved ones described him.[38]

Other victims were directly associated with La Belle Équipe itself. Gregory Reibenberg, the Jewish owner of the bistro, held the hand of his wife, Djamila Houd, as she passed away. "She asked me to take care of our daughter, and I promised I would," he said.[39] Also killed were Hodda and Halima Saadi, ages thirty five and thirty seven years old. Hodda was the manager of La Belle Équipe, and she was a Muslim. "(A) free-spirited and determined woman with a wide smile and a passion for yoga and vintage clothing," read the *New York Times*' depiction of her.[40] On this night, Hodda was celebrating her birthday with her sister Halima and nine friends, this being one of two commemorations at the establishment.

Hodda and Halima's brother, Khaled, was a server at the restaurant and he was waiting tables when the shootings started. Dropping to the floor, he managed to escape serious injury, but moments later he came upon the lifeless body of Hodda, who had been shot twice in the back. Distraught, he carried her to another café with the help of a friend. As for Halima, the mother of two, she succumbed to her injuries shortly thereafter at a Paris hospital. It was one more instance of the militant Islamists killing ordinary Muslims who were going about their business, a violation of Islam that was not lost on France's Muslim community. "There were black people, Arab people, Jewish people, all of us were hit," said Abdallah Saadi, another member of the Saadi family.[41] "These people are fascists," interjected a gentleman of Tunisian descent who worked near La Belle Équipe. "(I)t's got nothing to do with Islam."[42]

Le Comptoir Voltaire

Abdelhamid Abaaoud, Chakib Akrouh, and Brahim Abdelslam finalized their portion of the Paris mission when the three arrived at the Place de la Nation. At this busy historic circle, Abaaoud dropped off Abdelslam and sped away. Abdelslam then walked the 300 yards to Le Comptoir Voltaire, a restaurant and bar located at 253 Boulevard Voltaire. Starting with Le Carillon, all of the café, bar, bistro, and restaurant attacks had been committed in a progressively southward direction.

At Le Comptoir Voltaire, Abdelslam strode across the front terrace a few feet and into the center of the interior dining room. Although he was described as neat and trim in appearance, his demeanor was another matter. "I gradually see his face and his gaze, which is both determined and full of hatred," says Vincent, a customer.[43] When a waitress approached Abdelslam, he bowed his head and placed his left hand to his face. An instant later he detonated his incendiary device. A blinding blast of white light, it temporarily deafened the diners and staff, as well as seriously harming one person and wounding fourteen others.[44]

Among those present was a nurse, David, who set about helping the victims after what he thought was a gas explosion. One of those who he attempted to save was a man with a gaping hole in his side, his body entangled in tables and chairs. Freeing him and placing him on the ground, David began performing cardiac massage, pausing momentarily to remove the man's shirt for better contact. Then came the shocker. "When you lift a t-shirt and you see wires, you know that's not normal," says David.[45] The nurse also noticed numerous nuts and bolts, shiny and new, strewn around the mangled man, who was in fact dead. And it was at this moment that David realized the "victim" was a terrorist—and still wired. Moments later, a fireman arrived and told David the bomb had not fully detonated. "Everyone get out of the way, we evacuate everyone!" shouted the fireman.[46]

By this time, Abdelhamid Abaaoud and Chakib Akrouh were headed three miles east to Montreuil, a Paris suburb. It would be two days later that a Belgian resident of Montreuil noticed a black Seat Leon with Belgian plates parked on rue Edouard Vaillant, a side street. Finding this odd, she peered through the car windows and spied three AK-47s and several sixteen-bullet magazines. Law enforcement promptly sealed off the street, then secured, examined, impounded the car.

A congested neighborhood with reserved parking, one resident asserted that a vacant space would not have been available on a Friday night. "(T)hey must have arranged to park at this spot after the attack and swap vehicles before escaping."[47] If correct, this attests to the thoroughness of Abaaoud's plan for the Paris operation, as well as pointing to the participation of others who were not directly involved in the shootings and bombings; in this case, a car exchange maneuver.

In all, this second group of operatives—the café team—murdered thirty-eight people in their offensive. Investigators would subsequently determine that Abdelhamid Abaaoud, after leaving the Seat Leon in Montreuil, traveled to the Bataclan neighborhood by Métro, presumably to watch from a distance as the third and final attack transpired. It is not known if he made direct contact with the three men who comprised this last team—Samy Amimour, Ismaël Omar Mostefaï, and Foued Mohamed-Aggad—but he most likely had the opportunity, since the trio had been parked near the concert hall since 7:30 p.m. So suspicious was the team's appearance and demeanor that a passerby tried numerous times to notify law enforcement officials, but the authorities did not accept or return the man's phone calls about the strangers in the black Volkswagen Polo stationed at the renowned venue.[48] The city's police force was already up to its neck in other crises on this November night.

The Bataclan Theatre

A fanciful, multicolored building constructed in 1865 in an East Asia-inspired style and topped with a pagoda roof, the Bataclan theatre was named after the Asia-influenced operetta by Jacques Offenbach, "Ba-ta-clan." Registered as a national historical landmark in 1991, the building is located at 50 Boulevard Voltaire in a vibrant neighborhood within walking distance of the six cafés targeted by the terrorists. In its 150-plus years, the venue has hosted such varied acts as Buffalo Bill Cody, Edith Piaf, Maurice Chevalier, Kraftwerk, and Prince.

In keeping with its tradition of diversity, the theater on this night was hosting an American band from Palm Desert, California—the Eagles

7. Belgium, Abdelhamid Abaaoud, and the Paris Terror Units 109

The Bataclan Theatre, 50 Boulevard Voltaire, Paris. One of the sites of the Islamic State-sponsored attack on November 13, 2015. Ninety were killed and over 200 injured.

of Death Metal—which, despite its name, is not a death-metal outfit. "Eagles of Death Metal," explains the Genius Media Group, "is a fun, tongue-in-cheek, rock and roll band."[49] Not surprisingly given its thousands of devoted fans in France, tickets to its 9:00 p.m. performance had sold out. The warm-up act, an Austrian duo called White Miles, had already wrapped up its show and left the building, and the Eagles of Death Metal was now forty-five minutes into its performance. It was as the band was finishing the song, "Kiss the Devil," that it began.

"We left, we're starting" ("On est parti, on commence").[50] So read the text message that one of the terrorists sitting in the black Volkswagen sent to a Belgian phone number. A bystander noticed the phone's screen illuminating the face of the man texting on it, and investigators would later discover that the device, which the man would toss into a garbage can, contained a floor plan of the concert hall.

At 9:49 p.m., Amimour, Mostefaï, and twenty-three-year-old Mohamed-Aggad walked to the front of the distinctive red and yellow Bataclan building. Next to the theater's entrance sits the Bataclan Café, and it was here, on its sidewalk terrace, that the gunmen began firing on customers. The three shooters were unmasked, and were deliberate and measured in their actions.

One minute later, the terrorists entered the theater and stationed themselves near the back wall of its central, two-story ballroom. The band was performing on the stage in the front, and between the stage and the assailants was the "pit," where 1,200 concertgoers were packed shoulder-to-shoulder in the darkness, dancing. Above the pit was a wrap-around, horseshoe-shaped balcony from which another 300 to 350 spectators were enjoying the show.

Shouting "Allahu akbar" and railing against France's military actions in Syria and Iraq, the gunmen fired their AK-47s into the crowd.[51] "At the moment I thought it was part of the show," said Fahmi B., a twenty-three-year-old Turkish woman, "then.... I saw a person who had just caught a bullet in the eye" ("Sur le moment j'ai pensé que ça faisait parti du show, puis ... j'ai vu une personne qui venait de prendre une balle dans l'œil").[52] Many of those on the balcony likewise assumed that the mechanical clatter was pyrotechnics and a feature of the concert. The Eagles of Death Metal, however, knew exactly what was happening, since the band was facing the assailants from across the ballroom and could see the flames surging from their Kalashnikovs. "I saw two guys out front and that just might be the most awful thing ever," said drummer Julian Dorio, "them just relentlessly shooting into the audience."[53] Dorio dove behind his drum set as the other four band members darted off the stage. Fortunately, all of the musicians managed to escape, although the group's merchandising manager, Nick Alexander, would not be so lucky. The twenty-six-year-old Alexander and a companion, Helen Wilson, were standing near the terrorists when the shooting began, and Alexander was among those who were hit. "I tried to keep him talking and then I tried to give him mouth-to-mouth resuscitation and [the gunmen] were just sort of in the shadows and they would shoot if anyone said anything," said Wilson.[54] Alexander expired a short time later.

Minutes after the ambush started, a staff member switched on the house lights in spite of the fact that a gunman was aiming his AK-47 at her.

7. Belgium, Abdelhamid Abaaoud, and the Paris Terror Units 111

He did, in fact, proceed to kill her. As the staffer had evidently hoped, the sudden illumination allowed some of the audience members to better find their way to exits or to hiding places within the theater, although it also made it easier for the shooters to detect and execute their targets.

As Amimour, Mostefaï, and Mohamed-Aggad continued shelling the audience, rows of victims tumbled like dominoes. "(T)he shots kept going and going and going, and people started screaming and ducking, hiding behind the chairs," said spectator Jenny Watson.[55] Some attempted to flee by rushing instinctively in the opposite direction of the terrorists, meaning that the front of the concert hall became a magnet for those desperate to escape. "Everybody ran to the stage, there were scenes of stampeding," said another audience member.[56] Michael O'Connor, who was visiting from England, found himself situated near the stage as a mass of individuals bolted forward. "(P)eople falling all over the place, people screaming and just clawing and running and pushing to get away," said O'Connor.[57] Most spectators dropped to the floor. Some of them were dead, others were wounded or dying, and still others were feigning death by lying motionless.

As the terrorists mowed down the crowd—witnesses likened the image to that of a wheat field bowing in the wind—the Paris Fire Brigade dispatched a unit to the Bataclan. It left the station at 9:55 p.m. Around the same time, the Bataclan's chief of security wrestled his way through the crowd in order to unlock an emergency exit. A Frenchman of Algerian descent who prefers to be known publicly as "Didi," the security chief opened the fire exit located on the back left side of the ballroom, outside of which was Passage Saint-Pierre-Amelot, a side street. At once, throngs of people burst through the door and onto this street, although the exit's narrowness quickly produced a bottleneck, making escape more difficult.

Cristian Movilă, a Romanian photographer who was in Paris for a photography festival, happened to be on Passage Saint-Pierre-Amelot and used his cellphone to photograph the throng of humanity spilling out of the concert hall. "I saw terrified people running for their lives," said Movilă, "their screams intermittently drowned out by the sound of gunfire."[58] Most of these people would survive, thanks in no small measure to Didi's smart, bold actions. The thirty-five-year-old Muslim had saved numerous lives, even as he risked his own by returning to his post in the theater to help more of those penned within it. "He's a guy who, when he managed to get out, be in the street—and we all dreamed of that street," said survivor and fellow Muslim, Ismaël El Iraki, "he went back in."[59]

Didi next gathered his security staff and tried frantically to make his way to the front of the theater, his aim being to open another emergency exit onto Passage Saint-Pierre-Amelot. As he was doing so, the three assailants fanned out across the audience and continued firing, occasionally tossing grenades into the pit well. "(T)hey were shouting at people to lie down and stay down, they shot anyone who tried to run, then also shot at people on the ground, it was carnage," recalled a survivor.[60] "(I)t lasted for ten minutes, ten minutes, ten horrific minutes," a witness told CNN's Wolf Blitzer. "(W)e heard so many gunshots."[61]

In the course of the onslaught, the gunmen changed their strategy. Rather than the three men firing simultaneously into the room, two of them began working in tandem. This was because some of the audience members were now trying to incapacitate them. "One [terrorist] shot into the front of the venue while another covered the shooter to make sure nobody was able to approach," said John Leader, an Australian visitor who had taken his preteen son to the concert.[62] The assailants also hunted for members of the Eagles of Death Metal band, asking spectators in flawless French about the musicians' whereabouts and alluding to French and American military campaigns in the Middle East. "It's an American group, you're bombing us with the Americans, so we're going to hit the Americans and you," shouted one of the gunmen, according to police reports.[63] Authorities would later determine that the terrorists had conducted an online search of the Eagles of Death Metal prior to the attack.

During this phase of the Bataclan assault, Amimour, Mostefaï, and Mohamed-Aggad paused three or four times to reload their AK-47s, and it was during these brief intervals that concertgoers tried to escape. Sixty of them scrambled through a door that led to the theater's rooftop, and from here climbed through a window into an adjoining apartment. "We could hear explosions, gunshots, screams but we didn't know what was going on really," said one of those hiding in the flat.[64] Others made it to the ground-floor exits, while a group of nearly two dozen spectators on the balcony climbed above a false ceiling. Then there were those who dashed for cover inside the venue's dressing rooms, offices, bathrooms, and electrical closets—not that these places were necessarily safe. In one case, several spectators decided to huddle inside the band's dressing room only to be murdered. Yet in another case, a clutch of thirty people took cover in a small room, barricaded the door, and remained silent. When one of the terrorists tried but failed to kick down the door, he resorted to trickery. "Open the door, it's the police, we're here to rescue you," he said, according to survivor Kelly Le Guen.[65] Those in the room, still silent, took a vote by hand and decided not to open the door, unsure if the man was a police officer or an assailant. Ceding, he left and went elsewhere in pursuit of targets.

Two of the shooters, Mostefaï and Mohamed-Aggad, prowled the theater and checked its rooms for prey, with one of assailants snatching a concertgoer's cellphone and sending a text from it. Evidently, there was no reply. "One of the gunmen turned to a second and said in fluent French,

7. Belgium, Abdelhamid Abaaoud, and the Paris Terror Units 113

'I haven't gotten any news yet,' suggesting they were waiting for an update from an accomplice," reported the *New York Times*.[66]

Samy Amimour, for his part, stood on the stage and eyed the vast carpet of bodies that lay before him in the pit. Knowing that many of those lying on the floor or on top of one another were pretending to be dead, he shot arbitrarily into the mass hoping to maim or murder them.

It was a few minutes into the massacre when first responders began arriving outside the theater, in particular the brigade of firefighters mentioned earlier and an elite team of eight heavily-armed soldiers. The latter were members of Operation Sentinelle and by chance were on patrol in the area. A major counterterrorism operation entailing 10,000 troops, Sentinelle was created in the wake of the *Charlie Hebdo* assault earlier in the year and was designed to protect "sensitive areas" of France from extremist threats.

Although the sound of gunfire was coming from within the theater, the firefighters at the venue could not go inside because the police had not yet arrived. As for the eight counterterrorism soldiers, their superiors ordered them to stand down. "They were forbidden from launching a physical intervention—in other words from entering [the Bataclan]—but also from giving any medical equipment to police officers carrying out first aid," said attorney Samia Maktouf.[67] The counterterrorism soldiers were further barred from loaning their military weapons to the police officers who would soon be on the scene to respond to the massacre.[68] Instead, the police would have to rely on their side arms when confronting the terrorists and their AK-47s, grenades, and suicide bombs.

Predictably, this decision by Sentinelle commanders would be widely regarded as a grave mistake. It may also be assumed that the stand-down order frustrated the Sentinelle forces who were at the Bataclan and heard the bloodbath as it was happening. It should be noted, however, that these soldiers were not idle: they did help protect people who managed to escape from the theater, and they furnished secondary support to those forces that would, in fact, take action inside the venue to stop the carnage.

In 2016, the French parliament would conduct an inquiry into the police and military response to the ISIS attack at the Bataclan, and it would include a review of the Sentinelle's inaction. The probe would be spearheaded by former magistrate Georges Fenech, who, upon its completion, would discuss the Sentinelle controversy and the commanders' reasons for not deploying their soldiers. In terms of the explanations, they would range from differing interpretations of the rules of engagement to organizational and jurisdictional confusion. Then there was the viewpoint expressed by Bruno Le Ray, the military governor of Paris; a stance that centered on preserving the Sentinelle's highly-trained, elite troops when confronted with an ambiguous situation. "It is unthinkable to put soldiers at risk in the hypothetical hope of saving others" ("Il est impensable de mettre des soldats en danger dans l'espoir hypothétique de sauver d'autres personnes"), said Le Ray.[69] "They are not meant to throw themselves into the mouth of the wolf" ("Ils n'ont pas vocation à se jeter dans la gueule du loup").[70] Ultimately, the intervention issue would be resolved, and Sentinelle's counterterrorism forces would thereafter respond promptly and decisively to terrorist strikes in Paris and beyond.

As it turned out, there were, in fact, people who would willingly throw themselves into "the mouth of the wolf," starting with two Paris police officers who arrived at the venue at 10:02 p.m. It was twelve minutes into the assault. "We decided," said one of the policeman, "that we couldn't leave these people without us."[71] Accordingly, the officers entered the concert hall and positioned themselves at the back of the ballroom. They were approximately eighty feet from the stage on which Samy Amimour was preparing to execute a spectator, and they fired six shots at him. Wounded, Amimour toppled forward, causing his suicide belt to activate and blowing him up. The deafening blast shook the building, with witnesses comparing the horrific spectacle to a burst of confetti.[72] In all likelihood, those who were near the Amimour were likewise killed or seriously wounded judging from the types of trauma observed on the casualties.

With Amimour having been removed from the equation, Mostefaï and Mohamed-Aggad's strategy began to shift from offensive to defensive, but not before they opened fire on the pair of intrepid police officers who had eliminated their accomplice. The two officers, convinced they were about to be killed, crouched behind a pillar and phoned their loved ones to say goodbye.[73] Moments later, their commander ordered them to halt their intervention, explaining that the operation was to be taken over by the BRI (Brigades de Recherche et d'Intervention), which was en route to the Bataclan. Regarding the Paris police, its officers would remain at the site but would serve in a support capacity. Mostefaï and Mohamed-Aggad, meanwhile, would continue murdering concertgoers until the BRI arrived.

Unfortunately, at this moment when time was of the essence, the BRI was sent to the wrong address. It was dispatched to La Belle Équipe bistro, where the shootings had already ended and the gunmen had left the scene. Such miscommunications reveal the effectiveness of the ISIS operation, one that targeted multiple, diverse locations in rapid succession and thus overwhelmed and confused those whose job it was counter it.

Within minutes of Samy Amimour's death, Mostefaï and Mohamed-Aggad, realizing they were no longer the predators but about to become the prey, set about collecting hostages, twenty of them. Subsequent to this, they led their captives, who were to be used as human shields or pawns in negotiations, upstairs to the balcony on the left side of the ballroom. From here, Mostefaï and Mohamed-Aggad would occasionally fire down into the pit, picking off those who still showed signs of life. When the gunmen saw people twisting in pain and pleading for help, their reaction was telling. "That more or less made them laugh," said a witness.[74] One of the terrorists also grinned when, though a balcony window, he shot a man across the street who was watching television in an apartment.[75]

In terms of those individuals who were lying in the pit, whether wounded or feigning death, they were in torment. "I saw my final hour unfurl before me," said Marc Coupris, a fifty-seven-year-old Frenchman. "I thought this was the end."[76] Another spectator, Audrey, found herself on the floor with her back exposed to the gunmen and was sure she was about to be executed. And her experience was transcendent. Reconciling herself to her impending death, a sense of grace embraced her and a deep inner peace swept over her. "It's such a personal and intimate feeling, I want to keep this to myself what goes on in that moment," she said.[77]

The experiences of other concertgoers were not as sublime. Some people were enraged, and they railed at the assailants. "You cocksuckers!" yelled one man, who was executed on the spot.[78] Other people went blank, unable to think at all, or they focused on their loved ones whom they would be leaving behind. Many found themselves concentrating exclusively on survival, calculating distances and escape routes. And then there were the ones who entered into a state of denial, convinced, against all odds, that they would emerge unscathed from the slaughter. Because they were unable to grasp the reality of their circumstances, these people remained relatively composed. And while a number of witnesses described, often with a touch of shame, a temporary loss of empathy that caused them to ignore those around them who were calling out for help, others spoke of the humanity that manifested during the ordeal. "There was a brave French man who was in the exact danger as me, who managed to assure me—a complete stranger—in English that everything was going to be O.K. whilst he was risking his life to save mine," said Isobel Bowdery, a twenty-two-year-old Sorbonne student from South Africa.[79] In another case, a twenty-four-year-old man, Gauthier, was wedged in a pile of bodies when he noticed another man, a stranger in a red shirt, coming toward him. "He grabbed me by my arms, yanked me with all his force, and he pulled me out," said Gauthier.[80] Such accounts reveal the resilience, benevolence, and selflessness that can surface unexpectedly in harrowing situations, even when such altruism may come at a steep price. "A great reason why so many were killed is because so many people wouldn't leave their friends," said Jesse Hughes of the Eagles of Death Metal. "So many people put themselves in front of [other] people," he said, referring to the way in which friends, lovers, and family members used their own bodies to shield one another from harm.[81]

Forty minutes into the massacre, the air in the theater reeked of gunpowder and blood, and the spectators were still in shock. They would speak of feeling disoriented, of sensing that they were outside of their bodies, and of being suspended in space and time. Unbeknownst to them, a large number of police officers and firefighters had now gathered outside the building, and the BRI, which had arrived at 10:17 p.m., had completed its assessment of the situation and was ready to penetrate the theater.

At 10:30 p.m., a team of BRI commandos, fifteen of them, rushed into the Bataclan. Dressed in black and heavily armed, they wore bulletproof vests and, underneath their helmets, balaclavas. Entering the ballroom, they were met with silence, one punctuated only by the ringing of cellphones. The victims would soon start shouting for help, however, as they came to realize that the BRI was there to rescue them. The commandos were also saturated in a dazzling white light from the venue's intense, industrial lamps. And before them in this light lay a mound of bodies. "It is Dante's inferno" ("C'est l'enfer de Dante"), is how one commando described the tableau.[82] An estimated 700 to 800 people were sprawled in the pit, in what the team's commander called, "hell on earth."[83] Unbeknownst to the BRI, many were pretending to be dead.

Although the BRI's primary objective was to locate and liquidate the terrorists, a certain amount of time would be required to carry out this operation since the two assailants were nowhere to be seen. For that matter, the BRI had no way of knowing if Mostefaï and Mohamed-Aggad had secreted themselves inside the concert hall or absconded altogether. The victims who lay wounded in the pit or in the Bataclan's offices and dressing rooms, however, could not wait. They needed medical treatment. The BRI therefore set about securing the ground floor so these victims could be transferred to hospitals.

To this end, commandos began by speaking to the crowd, instructing those who were unharmed to stand up and place their hands on their heads. These people were then escorted out of the building. Yet not everyone complied with the commandos' instructions, with some people being reluctant to trust the masked figures who were dressed in black and clutching automatic weapons.

After the BRI had secured the pit and evacuated those who were uninjured, the brigade's doctor, Denis Safran, and the chief physician from RAID, Matthieu Langlois, entered the venue.[84] RAID, an acronym for Recherche, Assistance, Intervention, Dissuasion (Research, Assistance, Intervention, Dissuasion), is another tactical team specializing in domestic counterterrorism. Safran and Langlois would oversee the evacuation of the wounded.

7. Belgium, Abdelhamid Abaaoud, and the Paris Terror Units   117

As to the severity of the injuries, a considerable portion were catastrophic. "The majority were gunshot wounds inflicted with weapons of war, of high caliber," said Philippe Juvin, an emergency room physician.[85] But unlike a combat situation in which soldiers may be protected by body armor, the women, men, and children at the Bataclan were dressed only in street clothes. And it wasn't just the caliber of the weapons that was significant; the points of impact were also key. "Most [shots] were aimed to kill, at the head, thorax, abdomen," said emergency medicine specialist Patrick Pelloux, the upshot being that there was little that caregivers could do to ensure survival.[86]

Beyond the walls of the Bataclan Theatre, in the meantime, the city of Paris was reeling, the airwaves inundated with dramatic accounts of the bombings at the Stade de France and the killings at the six cafés. All the while, family members and friends, beside themselves with worry, phoned their loved ones inside the concert hall. All too often, their calls went unanswered.

By 11:00 p.m., thirty minutes after the arrival of Denis Safran and Matthieu Langlois, the injured spectators had been removed from the theater; only the deceased remained. Backed by RAID officers, two columns of BRI commandos now set about combing the building for any survivors who might still be hiding, and it turns out there were quite a few of them. Feeling more assured at this juncture, traumatized spectators began revealing themselves and leaving the venue.

The BRI and RAID units also searched for Mostefaï and Mohamed-Aggad during this phase of the operation, even though the authorities were beginning to believe that the terrorists had probably escaped. The reason was because the commandos had not seen any sign of them in the course of the evacuation operation on the ground floor. Of course, the BRI had no way of knowing that the assailants were hiding on the balcony and holding at gunpoint a score of hostages. At 11:15 p.m., however, the commandos would find out.

As matters stood, the BRI and RAID teams had opened all of the doors in the theater except for one: a wooden door situated on the left side of the balcony. Behind it was a narrow hallway ten yards long, and crammed into it were Mostefaï, Mohamed-Aggad, and their hostages. The terrorists were forcing some of the captives to block the door with their bodies, while compelling others to serve as lookouts at the windows.

"When police tried to open the door," writes journalist Lucie Aubourg, "one of the hostages—a messenger designated by the terrorists—yelled at the police not to enter, saying the attackers would begin killing hostages."[87] The captive, a young man, also shouted a telephone number to the BRI, one they could use to speak with the terrorists.

Minutes later, a negotiator did in fact initiate a dialogue with the gunmen, but it proved to be less than encouraging. All the same, the talks would continue over the next forty-five minutes.

Unknown to the terrorists and their hostages, they were not alone in the immediate area. When the two assailants checked a door in the hallway, they discovered that it opened into a dressing room with a small bathroom. Inside were panicked concertgoers, among them a tearful young woman and a man by the name of Pierre Janaszak, a radio-show host. Janaszak later recalled how the terrorists explained to this knot of frightened spectators that the ISIS assault was in response to France purportedly murdering innocent people in Syria; that it was meant to show the French people how it felt to be targeted. Concerning the tearful woman, one of the gunmen asked her why she was crying, and she said it was because she was afraid. Janaszak, who overheard this exchange, quoted the gunman's reply. "You don't have to be scared, you will be dead in a few minutes, so don't worry."[88]

The telephone negotiations continued for nearly an hour, but to no avail. Unlike typical hostage negotiations in which abductors demand cash, transportation, or protection, Mostefaï and Mohamed-Aggad made unrealistic political demands involving military actions in Syria as well as insisting that the team of commandos leave the Bataclan. Naturally, both sets of demands were nonstarters; France would not agree to change its foreign policy to comply with a terrorist threat, and the BRI had no intention of abandoning the hostages. When this was pointed out to the terrorists—self-described soldiers of the caliphate—they became flustered. "They threatened to decapitate a hostage and throw the corpse out the window," writes Robert Burke.[89]

So it was that four more phone conversations took place between the assailants and the negotiator, fraught discussions during which Mostefaï and Mohamed-Aggad threatened to blow themselves up. In due course, the authorities concluded that the assailants were not negotiating in good faith, that they were now merely stalling for time. "They [wanted] just to prepare themselves for the final assault," said the captain of the commando unit.[90] As could be expected, the BRI was preparing itself as well; for instance, by sending more commandos into the building. As to the final assault, it would come at 12:20 a.m., when a higher command would give the go-ahead for the BRI to breach the wooden door.[91]

By all accounts, the raid was a stunner. Armed with Glocks and H&K G36 assault rifles, the BRI beat down the door. Configured with two commandos at the head of the column, the team stormed into the hallway, while taking shelter behind a Ramses-style ballistic shield. Four-feet tall with a bullet-proof window at the top, the 175-pound shield was capable of weathering both AK-47 rounds and grenade fragments.

7. Belgium, Abdelhamid Abaaoud, and the Paris Terror Units 119

At once, a terrorist unleashed a volley of gunfire, up to 35 rounds from his assault rifle, causing a commando to be struck in the hand by a ricochet. The wounded man collapsed, but because the team had agree beforehand not to pause to help their own, they pushed on without him. Moments later, a heavy-set commando who was bearing the shield stumbled over an obstacle and lost his grip on the device, causing it to fall onto a female hostage's hip. Fortunately, she was not seriously harmed, not even by the other hostages whom the commandos now grabbed and shoved behind the shield. "I [was] trampled," said the woman, "but it was the happiest pain of my life and I was protected."[92] Although the shield was momentarily out of commission, the two officers at the head of the column nevertheless continued rushing forward into the corridor.

The brigade next set about deploying stun grenades, six of them, to temporarily blind, deafen, and disorient Mostefaï and Mohamed-Aggad. Although the "flashbang" grenades had the same effect on the hostages, these men and women, determined to survive, charged behind the shield and out of the hallway to safety.

As the BRI shunted hostages out of harm's way, a commando opened a side door in the corridor and discovered a little boy, a woman, and five men inside a dressing room and its bathroom. This was the group that was mentioned earlier, the one that included the tearful woman and the radio-show host. The commandos evacuated these people as well.

Finally, the commandos were alone with Mostefaï and Mohamed-Aggad and were ready to liquidate them. No doubt realizing the end had arrived, Mostefaï set off his explosive device, killing himself and injuring Mohamed-Aggad who was standing nearby. Falling to the floor, Mohamed-Aggad patted himself hectically, searching for his detonator with the intention of blowing himself up as well, but a commando spotted the danger and killed him with two shots. In the coming days, Mohamed-Aggad's father would learn about his estranged son's actions at the Bataclan Theatre and would be repulsed. "If I had known he would have done something like that, I would have killed him beforehand," he told a reporter.[93]

The BRI had carried out its spectacular raid in three minutes. In this audacious operation, no hostages were killed and the injured commando recovered. Tellingly, the ballistic shield had over two dozen AK-47 bullet-holes in it.

For the next hour, police officers would scour the Bataclan searching for more survivors in hiding. It would take another ten hours to remove the deceased and identify them, a task that would prove difficult since several of them had left their identification papers in the cloak room.

In all, ninety people died in the Bataclan massacre, and more than 200 others were wounded. As in the other attacks in Paris, victims included the followers of Islam, such as Salah Emad el-Gebaly, a devout young Muslim from Cairo. El-Gebaly was one in an array of humanity whose lives ended at the venerated theater. Others victims of the assault included a clinical psychologist, a carpenter, a florist, a television editor, a BMX aficionado, a guitar maker, and a makeup artist for fashion shoots. One fatality, Jean-Jacques Amiot, who was nearly seventy years old, was a silkscreen printer and peace lover, while two others, a young couple named Anne and Pierre-Yves Guyomard, were looking forward to starting a family in the near future.[94]

In the end, a total of 130 people died in the string of ISIS terrorist attacks on this night, nearly 500 more were injured, and 302 of these people required hospitalization. Forty-one of the latter were wounded so severely as to require treatment in intensive care units.[95]

On Saturday 14, 2015, the Islamic State released a statement in French, Arabic, and English on a messaging platform deemed authentic by counter-intelligence experts. "Eight brothers, wrapped in explosive belts and armed with machine rifles, targeted sites that were accurately chosen in the heart of the capital of France," read the statement, "including the Stade de France during the match between the Crusader German and French teams, where the fool of France, François Hollande, was present."[96] The statement proceeded to declare that the November attacks were merely the beginning, and that ISIS would inflict further catastrophic strikes on France in the future.

8

Responses to the Attacks
The Medical Community, the Military, and Law Enforcement Agencies

The Paris attacks blasted into all levels of French society, horrifying the public and immobilizing the capital city. It was, moreover, a shock and anguish that was experienced far beyond France. In the days after the atrocities, public displays of mourning coupled with tributes to the victims were held around the world, from Australia and South Korea to Russia and India, with several impromptu memorials taking place across the United States as well. In Paris itself, one night after the attacks, heartbroken citizens ignored the advice of police and gathered at the Place de la République to share their grief. Still others in the capital city came together to convey their rage at the terrorists who slaughtered their compatriots. And then there were those who defiantly refused to give ISIS the pleasure of seeing them suffer at all. Among the latter: an American attorney whose job took him to France. "I went to a party in the 10th [arrondissement] and danced," he said, "because fuck those guys."[1]

In this chapter, we examine the responses of three specialized communities to the horrendous string of attacks. The first consists of the French government, and its measures within France to contain the terrorist threat, along with its ensuing military counter-attack in Syria. The second consists of the law enforcement community, and its scores of domestic raids in the weeks following the ISIS affront. Included in the account is its manhunt for, and elimination of, the surviving terrorists of the Paris attacks. And the third consists of Paris's medical community, with an exploration of the short-and long-term reactions of those professionals and para-professionals who were on duty the night of the shootings and bombings. It is with the latter individuals, many of whom were first responders at the scenes of the crimes, that we begin our discussion.

Response by the Medical Community

The medical response to the terrorist strikes was exemplary. Most of the 302 people who were hospitalized after the attacks were the victims of high-energy ballistic trauma, with their injuries consisting not only of entry wounds from bullets but also bone fractures and nerve damage. Predictably, the severity of their injuries was often extreme and in many cases atypical, making treatment challenging. One of the physicians caring for the victims, Youri Yordanov of Hôpital Saint-Antoine, described the case of a woman who was brought in with a bullet wedged between her skin and her skull. "The fact she was there," said Yordanov, "was a miracle."[2] Still, despite the complex nature of the damage and the immense number of victims, the quality of care was so outstanding that the mortality rate for the hospitalized patients was only one percent, or four people.

While there are likely numerous reasons for this remarkably low figure, three factors stand out. First, the medical professionals, firefighters, and police officers were well-prepared, their knowledge of disaster procedures having just been refreshed. More precisely, on the morning of the attacks, a number of these responders participated in a simulated terrorist attack, one that entailed multiple shootings, which no doubt helped ready them for the real-life attacks that would transpire a few hours later. That said, a minor downside to the serendipitous simulation was observed, according to an article in the medical journal, *The Lancet*. "In the evening, when the same doctors were confronted with this situation in reality, some of them believed it was another simulation exercise."[3]

A second factor involves the timing of the terrorist strikes. They happened at night, when hospitals tend to be relatively calm, and at the onset of the weekend. "Some of the aspects might have been more difficult if [the attacks] had happened during a working day when the sterile stock is partly unavailable and when doctors and staff are already busy," write physician Martin Hirsch and his colleagues.[4]

Third, and most important, the Director General of the APHP (Assistance Publique-Hôpitaux de Paris), activated the "White Plan."[5] Created twenty years ago but not implemented until the November 2015 assaults, the White Plan was developed for a major crisis like the multi-site ISIS attacks. As for the strategy's features, it brings together forty hospitals in the city of Paris and its environs and coordinates them so that they function as a single entity. As a part of this integrated force, the White Plan requires off-duty medical professionals to return to work, which, in the November 2015 attacks, resulted in a potential corps of 100,000 caregivers. It also makes available 200 surgical suites and 22,000 hospital beds. As a result, Paris did not suffer from a shortage of medical personnel or facilities when responding to the terrorist strikes, nor were any surgical procedures significantly delayed.[6]

Besides ensuring hospital and staff availability, the White Plan further called for forty-five medical teams to be dispatched to the seven attack sites, with each of these mobile units consisting of a doctor, a nurse, and a driver. (An additional fifteen teams were kept on standby.) Their purpose was to assess victims at the scene and transfer them to medical facilities that could meet their particular needs. Upon arrival at the receiving hospitals, these same patients were met by triage teams that classified their conditions as either relative or absolute emergencies and admitted them for treatment. Incoming victims of penetrating traumas were, of course, fast-tracked. An impressive, well-designed system, the White Plan made certain that victims at the locations of the attacks could be managed swiftly and suitably. Moreover, by dispersing patients to numerous facilities, it ensured that none of the city's hospitals became overburdened.

On the interpersonal side, a review of the medical community's response revealed that the professionals and para-professionals who provided care during the disaster, including operating room staffs, were exceptionally cooperative. "Trust and communication between the different specialties and jobs were apparent," stated the report. "The common goal was so clear that no [one] tried to impose an individual view."[7]

The excellence of the medical care notwithstanding, many of the wounds inflicted by the terrorists' weapons of war were so devastating as to produce lasting damage, physically and emotionally. Illustrating this fact, one year after the attacks, twenty victims were still hospitalized for injury-related conditions.[8] Another 2,000 were receiving outpatient treatment for emotional trauma, a number that included not only those who directly experienced the assaults but also their loved ones who were not at the scene. Certainly there was reason for such distress: 1,000 people had lost a relative in the terrorist strikes, among this number being fifty children who lost one or both parents. Then there was the disheartening case of a thirty-one-year-old survivor, still distraught two years later, who killed himself shortly after a 2017 memorial service. He had been receiving treatment from a psychiatrist and a psychologist. "The psychological trauma suffered on the occasion of these attacks is profound, it is long-lasting, it must be considered and treated," reads a statement from *13Onze15 Fraternité-Vérité*, a support organization that serves survivors of the Paris assaults.[9]

Regarding the emotional status of those healthcare professionals and para-professionals who participated in the rescue and inpatient treatment of the victims, a study conducted four weeks after the attacks found that these individuals reported "a significantly higher psychological impact, defined by PTSD [post-traumatic stress disorder] symptoms, than those not directly involved."[10] Although another study conducted many month later, one that examined a somewhat different pool of responders, found a lower incidence of PTSD symptoms, it nevertheless appears that the terrorist attacks did take a human toll on many of those who provided help in the midst of the disaster, with their symptoms being the most intense during the weeks immediately following the assaults.[11]

Response by the Government and Military

On the night of Friday the 13th, 2015, while the Bataclan massacre was underway, French President François Hollande met with Prime Minister Manuel Valls and Interior Minister Bernard Cazeneuve at the Interior Ministry. Two on-the-spot results: the city's anti-terrorism prosecutor was placed in charge of investigating the attacks even as they were still occurring, and the French president set about instituting special measures to protect the capital city and the country.

At one minute past midnight, Hollande, in a televised address, declared a state of emergency and announced he was closing France's borders. "We must ensure that no one enters to commit any crimes and that those who have committed the crimes that we have unfortunately seen can also be arrested if they should leave the territory," he said.[12] As a part of the declaration, a citywide curfew was implemented, the first since World War II, and it produced an unsettling atmosphere. One resident likened the empty streets, the closed businesses, and the blaring sirens to a civil war.[13] Beyond the formal curfew, officials asked Parisians to remain indoors regardless of the time of day until it could be confirmed that the terrorist threat had ended. In these early hours, it was not known if ISIS was planning further acts of violence. And indeed, investigators later surmised that another strike had been intended, but for reasons unknown it did not happen.

At 2:25 a.m., the government released a summary of an ad hoc cabinet meeting, one that listed the elements of Hollande's emergency declaration. The synopsis stated that an additional 15,000 troops were being deployed to Paris. It also explained that local prefects anywhere in France could now establish "protection security zones" in areas they deemed warranted. "(L)aw enforcement officers could check people's identification papers and search their bags and vehicles without cause" in these sectors, reads a legal précis from the U.S. Library of Congress.[14] Also across France, border controls, including the mobilization of Customs, were implemented.

As to those procedures that applied exclusively to the city of Paris, the cabinet summary asserted that local authorities could restrict the movements of individuals if the latter were judged to be a potential threat. For instance, anyone suspected of being engaged in a dangerous activity could be confined to his or her home.

Other measures allowed for officials to shut down theaters, meeting halls, sports arenas, and other entertainment venues without prior notice. As well, authorities would henceforth exercise greater latitude in searching people, even those who were not in protection security zones, and police could confiscate citizens' weapons. The rationale behind these procedures was that the measures allowed local authorities to act quickly and autonomously to avert a potential terrorist strike, even if the intrusive police action infringed on the public's freedom of movement and other civil rights. In light of the circumstances—anticipated ISIS attacks—the government deemed the provisional compromises to be acceptable.

Lastly, schools and school trips were to be cancelled the following day, Saturday 14, 2015. Tourist sites, including the Eiffel Tower, were to be closed as well, along with markets, shops, cinemas, libraries, museums, and even swimming pools, while sporting matches were to be postponed. In addition, a handful of companies, such as American Airlines and Uber, opted to suspend their services to, and within, the French capital in the wake of the attacks, while Disneyland Paris (Euro Disney) closed as a sign of respect for the victims. Since the emergency declaration also called for certain types of public gatherings to be deferred, a

Police on patrol at a memorial site near the Bataclan Theatre on November 14, 2015, one day after the ISIS-inspired assault at the concert hall (Voice of America [VOA]).

handful of preciously-scheduled environmental protests were called off. Large and possibly unruly gatherings of this type could invite another terrorist attack, as well as burdening those law enforcement resources that were needed during the national emergency.

Two days after the Paris attacks, the Senate, at Hollande's request, extended the emergency declaration for three months. Subsequent to this, it was reinstated again, causing it to be in effect for the ensuing two years. While certain components of it eventually became controversial, one feature was so contentious as to be challenged in France's constitutional court. It centered on local prefects' freedom to establish protection security zones at their own discretion and the infringement of civil rights such zones tolerated. During the first year of France's emergency declaration, the security-zone component was utilized over 5,000 times, and it continued being employed frequently into the second year; that is, until November 1, 2017, when the entire emergency declaration itself expired.[15] One month later, on December 1, 2017, a French court ruled the security-zone measure, which technically was no longer in effect, to be unconstitutional. Except that it *was* still in effect, but in another incarnation. On the day the emergency declaration expired, the French government replaced it with new anti-terrorism legislation that included many of the same controversial elements that the declaration had contained. These components, with slight adjustments, had simply been made into law. As could be expected, opponents of this legislation, like the critics of the emergency declaration before it, argued that the new anti-terrorism law was susceptible to abuse, most notably against racial and religious minorities, and that it sacrificed the protection of individual liberties for national security.

Public warning on the front door of the Bataclan Theatre, 2018. Translation: *Reinforced (Heightened) Security, Risk of Attack.*"

International Condemnation

On Saturday, November 14, 2015, President Hollande addressed the public a second time, confirming ISIS's claim that it was behind the attacks. Describing the terrorist assaults as an act of war, he proclaimed three days of national mourning.

On this day too, political and religious leaders around the globe denounced the terrorist attacks, among them the presidents and other representatives of nations having large Muslim populations. These figures included Iranian president Hassan Rouhani, Indonesian president Joko Widodo, Qatari foreign minister Khaled al-Attiyah, and Kuwaiti Emir Sheikh Sabah al-Sabah, who stated that the Paris attacks were "counter to all teachings of holy faith and humanitarian values."[16] Even Syrian president Bashar al-Assad slammed the assaults, despite ISIS's assertion that its gruesome violence was an act of retaliation for French military involvement in Syria. And prominent Islamic organizations expressed dismay, among them the Union of Islamic Organizations of France, an umbrella organization that today is called "French Muslims."

U.S. President Barack Obama (right), French President François Hollande (center), and Paris Mayor Anne Hidalgo (left) visit the Bataclan Theatre memorial display shortly after midnight in Paris, November 29, 2015 (official White House photo by Pete Souza, Washington, D.C.).

Military Intervention in Syria

Sunday, November 15, 2015, would bring a dramatic development in France's reaction to the Paris attacks. At 7:50 p.m., in the ISIS stronghold of Raqqa, Syria, the French Air Force launched air strikes. Departing from Jordan and the United Arab Emirates, air crews bombed Raqqa intermittently over a four-hour period, in the process destroying numerous ISIS-related targets in what was the largest such raid by the French military since it began operations in the Middle Eastern country in September 2014. Among other hits, the city's stadium was demolished, the sports arena having been commandeered by the Islamic State and used as its headquarters.

The next day, the French Air Force conducted more sorties, with confirmed strikes on a terrorist training camp, an ISIS command post, a recruitment center, and an arms depot. A museum was targeted as well, one that ISIS had been using as a makeshift jail. In terms of unconfirmed accounts of damage and fatalities, they were inconsistent. While anti–ISIS activists in Raqqa reported that no civilian casualties had been incurred, they also stated that clinics had been hit.[17] Yet one thing was certain: the military intervention immobilized the ISIS stronghold, at least for the time being. "It was a heavier barrage than had typically hit the city and its environs," the *New York Times* reported, "and it knocked out electricity and water service, spreading more fear than usual among civilians."[18]

In France, meanwhile, the raid in Raqqa was welcomed, which no doubt was part of the French government's plan. For the moment, the airstrikes helped furnish the people of France with a sense of justice and resolution, while simultaneously serving as a warning to militant jihadists inside of France. Major General James Marks, formerly of the U.S. Army Intelligence Center, addressed this function in a CNN interview. "Clearly, it's a military activity, but it really sends a very strong political message, and it's all for internal consumption within France," he said.[19]

The notion that France was endangered and would aggressively protect itself was one that resonated with the public, judging from the number of men and women who sought to enlist in the French Army following the nightmare in Paris. Ordinarily, one hundred to 150 potential applicants contact the army each day, but this figure soared to 1,500 contacts per day, a ten-fold increase, during the week after the terrorist attacks.[20] The applicants' motives, moreover, did not appear unusually pugnacious. "They are not [seeking] vengeance, they want to help" ("Ils ne sont pas dans la vengeance, ils veulent aider"), said Colonel de Lapresle, chief of recruiting for the French army.[21] Defending the republic was the dominant intention.

Response by Law Enforcement

In France during the weekend that its military was conducting sorties in Syria, law enforcement officers were carrying out a sweeping operation on the home front. It involved seizing those who may have been involved in the terrorist attacks in the capital city.

During the bombings at the Stade de France, Salah Abdelslam, the driver of the black Renault Clio that carried three suicide bombers to the arena, failed to detonate his own suicide vest in the operation. Instead, he, along with two people not directly involved in the attacks, drove to Belgium a few hours later. Arriving at the border in the early morning hours of Saturday, November 14, 2015, the three presented their identification papers, and, because Abdelslam had not yet been named as a suspect, were allowed to continue on their journey.

The next day, investigators determined that Abdelslam had rented, in Belgium, the black Volkswagen Polo that was parked at the Bataclan Theatre, the one in which the concert-hall killers had arrived. Police had seized the discarded vehicle after the Bataclan massacre. Abdelslam's name also appeared on rental agreements for others cars and apartments associated with the Paris attacks. Accordingly, manhunts were launched in both Belgium and France for Abdelslam as well as other possible participants in the assaults. While most of the actual assailants had been killed in the attacks, Abdelhamid Abaaoud and Chakib Akrouh, like Abdelslam, were still on the lam, hiding out in a Saint-Denis neighborhood of Paris. Counter-intelligence officials surmised that Abaaoud, as a key organizer of the attacks, was probably in Syria by now, unaware that he was right under their nose. Soon, though, they would pinpoint his whereabouts.

Uncertain of the number of terrorists who had helped plan, execute, or furnish post-attack support in the Paris shootings and bombings, police teams from RAID and GIPN (Groupes d'Intervention de la Police Nationale) carried out a series of raids Sunday night and early Monday morning, November 15–16, 2015. A total of 168 were conducted in northern and southern France, with targeted neighborhoods including those in Bobigny, Grenoble, Lyon, and Toulouse. The emergency declaration gave the authorities the power to arrest or detain Islamist militants and others suspecting of having played a role in the Paris operation or potentially possessing information that could help the authorities identify and capture the perpetrators. In all, twenty-three people were arrested in these raids and another 104 were detained, with confiscated items consisting of bulletproof vests, guns, and rocket launchers. Raids were likewise carried out in Germany, Serbia, and Spain. And in Belgium, as one would expect, several were conducted, most notably in Molenbeek, where it was surmised that Salah Abdelslam may have taken refuge. During one such search, Mohamed Abdeslam, brother of Salah and the recently-deceased Brahim, was detained but released twenty-four hours later. As it turned out, Salah Abdelslam was able to evade the police, at least for now, although the end was near for Abdelhamid Abaaoud and Chakib Akrouh.

Raid in Saint-Denis

It was in the northeastern outskirts of Paris, one mile from the Stade de France, that Abaaoud and Akrouh arranged for shelter in the frenzied days after the Paris attacks. The location was Saint-Denis, an arrondissement in which nearly twenty percent of the residents are Maghrebian immigrants (i.e., Moroccan, Algerian, Tunisian, Libyan, and Mauritanian), many of them *sans documentation*. It is also an area in which the crime rate is steep, with offenses ranging from robbery to murder. Then too, the district, as one might expect, is marked by a decidedly pro–Arab attitude. When a reporter asked a resident of Saint-Denis about the ISIS assaults in Paris that had transpired a few days earlier, the man's response was revealing. "The Paris attacks lasted three hours," he said, "but this happens everyday in Syria."[22]

It was here, in Saint-Denis, that a thirty-one-year-old man, Jawad Bendaoud, sub-let his apartment to a twenty-six-year-old woman by the name of Hasna Aït Boulahcen shortly after the ISIS assaults, she being the cousin of Abdelhamid Abaaoud. The woman told Bendaoud that the apartment would be used to lodge two men. When he was later questioned by the police, Bendaoud insisted that he was unaware of the men's backgrounds and deeds, and thus the extraordinary risk he would be taking by sub-letting to them. "I swear on the head of my son that I didn't know they were terrorists," he said tearfully.[23] Although a French court would eventually find the Bendaoud not guilty, prosecutors would appeal the decision such that, in the end, he would be sentenced to four years in prison for harboring terrorists.

A few days after the attacks, French intelligence officials received a tip-off from their Moroccan counterparts indicating that Abaaoud was still in France, not Syria. Because of this information, the authorities believed he would attempt to make contact with others in the city. Among the possibilities: Hasna Aït Boulahcen, who lived in Saint-Denis and who was already under surveillance for her involvement in the drug trade. Officials had tapped her phone and were monitoring the movement of funds through her bank account. So it was that intelligence officers now listened in on her phone calls, in the course of which they heard as she rented a flat at 8 rue du Corbillon in Saint-Denis. It had only been four days since the Paris attacks. Placing the apartment under observation, officers next watched as she and Abaaoud entered it a day later. Counter-intelligence experts speculated that it was supposed to become home to a new ISIS cell, one headed by Abaaoud, from which further terrorist strikes in the capital city could be carried out.

At 4:20 a.m., on the morning of November 18, 2015, police, including RAID teams, arrived on rue du Corbillon. Owing to the early hour and the fact that the emergency curfew was still in effect, the street was empty. Moving stealthily and sealing off the block, commandos entered the apartment building and instructed the tenants to turn off their lights, stay inside, and lie on the floor. To ensure that the tenants did not stray outside of their flats, the officers also blocked the doors.

Having established that Abaaoud was in the second-story flat and that Chakib Akrouh was probably there as well, the police knew the pair would be heavily armed. And indeed, when commandos set off an explosive device meant to blow off the apartment's front door, they discovered that the door had been barricaded to give the terrorists and their accomplices time prepare for such an incursion.

The commandos persisted until they succeeded in breaching the entrance, then used stun grenades to disorient the extremists. To determine if the rooms might now be safe to enter, the officers sent in a police dog, a Belgian shepherd named Diesel who was due to retire soon. Sadly, the militants shot her to death. Diesel's life had been sacrificed for the lives of the police, and tributes to her would pour in from around the world.

At approximately 6:00 a.m., more ambulances arrived at the scene, along with police helicopters and truckloads of soldiers, while grenade blasts and the sounds of a firefight echoed through the streets. "(H)elp me, help me, help me!" shouted a woman believed to have been Boulachcen, according to a neighbor.[24] In the midst of the maelstrom, a terrorist tried to lure commandos into a proximity that would endanger them, after which the man, Chakib Akrouh, detonated his suicide vest. As it turned out, however, no officers were killed in the explosion, although both Akrouh and Hasna Aït Boulahcen were blown up.

It would be five hours later that the siege would finally come to an end. Damage to the building was extensive, an entire floor having collapsed during the battle. In all, three people were dead, including Abdelhamid Abaaoud, although the police were not yet able to confirm it due to the condition of the corpse. Seven others were arrested. In the high-risk operation, police had fired over 5,000 shots and five officers had been mildly injured.

During the next twenty-four hours, a body believed to be that of Abaaoud was examined. Mutilated, it had been lacerated by shrapnel from grenades and was riddled with bullets. When a forensics team lifted fingerprints from it, they were found to match those Abaaoud, as were the prints on an AK-47 discovered in an abandoned vehicle. Chakib Akrouh's identity was also confirmed, in his case through DNA analysis of recovered body tissue.

All of the ISIS attackers who had taken part in the Paris attacks had now been eliminated with the exception of Salah Abdelslam, who would survive in hiding for another four months. It would be on March 15, 2016, that a police operation in Forest, Belgium, would expose him, who by this point had become the most-wanted man in Europe. In the ensuing clash, Abdelslam and two accomplices opened fire on law enforcement officers and managed to escape to Molenbeek, but Belgian authorities tracked down the terrorist and took him into custody. In 2018, a Belgian court handed him a twenty-year prison sentence for his violent actions against the police. Still in prison, Abdelslam has steadfastly refused to cooperate with French and Belgian authorities.

Paris After the Attacks

Life in the capital city would gradually return to normal, but it would never be quite the same. Moreover, the ferocity of the attacks themselves would be forever imbedded in Paris' psyche, a viciousness illustrated by the amount of work that was required to restore, for instance, the Bataclan Theatre. Removing the bloodstains from the concert hall took three full days, and it required a year to return the venue to its previous condition. On November 12, 2016, the theater would finally return to life with a concert by Sting.

Regarding the bistros, bars, and restaurants, they too required considerable work, although they were able to reopen sooner than the concert hall. Café Bonne Bière returned to business after three weeks, while Le Carillon was ready to receive customers two months after the attacks. La Belle Equipe, the most extensively damaged, was out of commission for the lengthiest period. "Nothing is reparable," the popular bistro posted on its Facebook page shortly after the attacks, "so we're going to have to start from scratch."[25] La Belle Equipe would reopen four months after the ISIS assaults.

Although the targeted businesses were finally up and running again, ISIS's savagery would not be forgotten nor would the public's empathy for the victims wane. In a case of the latter, a painting appeared on the exit door of the Bataclan Theatre in June of 2018, the door through which throngs of traumatized concert-goers had escaped or tried to escape. It was a mural created by Banksy, the anonymous British street artist whose work often addresses consequential social and political issues, and it was a tribute to

8. Belgium, Abdelhamid Abaaoud, and the Paris Terror Units 133

Painting of a grieving figure on an emergency exit door at the Bataclan Theatre through which survivors escaped during the ISIS-sponsored attack. The painting, believed to be the work of the anonymous British street artist Banksy, was stolen in 2019.

those who were murdered in the massacre. Stenciled in a ghostlike white, the image was that of a veiled girl in mourning, her head bowed. Unfortunately, the painting, which touched the hearts of those who came to the Bataclan to view it, was stolen five months later. In the dark of night, a van of thieves removed the theater's door and made off with the artwork in what was yet another blow to the people who had lost loved ones in the shootings and bombings. "The work of Banksy, a symbol of remembrance belonging to all: locals, Parisians, citizens of the world, has been taken from us," declared a statement released by the concert hall.[26] In much the same way, Paris' innocence had been taken from it by the comparatively small band of militant Islamists headed by Abdelhamid Abaaoud. And such grisly assaults, such acts of unspeakable malice committed on dubious political and religious grounds, would continue being perpetrated in the years to come, although they would not always be the work of terrorist networks or organizations. In some cases, they would be carried out by individuals who were unaffiliated with any formal terrorist structures but who nevertheless chose to act in the name of them. In Part III, we revisit four operations conducted by so-called "lone actors" in France, all of whom claimed to be acting in support of the Islamic State.

Part III
Radical Islamism and Single-Perpetrator Terrorist Offensives in France

9

Lone-Actor Terrorism, Encrypted Extremism, and Remote Control Attacks

The phenomenon of the man or woman who plans and executes a terrorist strike without the involvement of others, most notably without being trained, managed, or otherwise abetted by an established terrorist organization, has received considerable notice in recent years. It is a concern that stems from the unique nature and lethality of single-perpetrator attacks, as well as from a disturbing upsurge in their occurrence. The latter increase is the work of ISIS, and it can be traced back to 2014, when the organization began losing territory in Syria and Iraq owing to a sustained military operation led by the Syrian Democratic Front (SDF). It was territory that ISIS had seized and claimed as its caliphate, an unforgiving Islamic jurisdiction the size of Great Britain in which the self-proclaimed theocratic "state" controlled the lives of twelve million people. But while the liberation of its stolen land may have been demoralizing to the ISIS leadership and rank-and-file membership, it did not mark the end of the Islamist organization itself. ISIS stills exists. "It may be weaker in the immediate term, but there is not a chance in hell that it has been defeated," said Charlie Winter of the International Center for the Study of Radicalization in 2019.[1]

Supporting Winter's argument, the militant organization, to ensure its survival, set about revising its strategy in the face of the SDF's victories. Recognizing that a large, permanent base of operations was no match for the SDF—or, for that matter, for other nations' military machines—ISIS began decentralizing. Among other acts, it galvanized its spinoffs in Africa and Asia, as well as calling on individuals who were sympathetic to the Islamic State to commit acts of violence on their own, in their own lands. By spreading the threat of bloodshed far beyond its declared caliphate, a threat to be carried out by those who had not set foot in ISIS's training camps in Syria or Iraq, the organization sought to make it more difficult for counter-intelligence agencies to detect the assailants and prevent their attacks.

Decentralization of this sort had occurred previously in another terrorist outfit, al-Qaeda. As the U.S-led coalition increasingly liquidated the network's leaders in Afghanistan and Pakistan, it began splintering. The result: a rise in new branches of al-Qaeda in Somalia, Syria, Yemen, and Iraq. In addition, the network boosted its calls for individuals who were unaffiliated with it to inflict damage on Western targets.

In the case of ISIS, to date its most blatant push for this strain of single-perpetrator aggression came when in 2015 a spokesman, Abu Muhammad al-Adnani, urged non-members to carry out attacks worldwide during the Muslim holy month of Ramadan. "The smallest action you do in their heartland is better and more enduring to us than what you would if you were with us," al-Adnani proclaimed.[2] And his entreaty was granted. During Ramadan, terrorist attacks were committed in Orlando, Florida, along with France, Jordan, Yemen, Lebanon, Iraq, Bangladesh, and Turkey, most of which were confirmed to have been in response to his call. The killings, moreover, returned the world's attention to the waning Islamic State, as the organization had no doubt hoped. "The recent spate of attacks could be less about Ramadan than about the Islamic State's desire to project strength as it loses territory," writes journalist Ben Hubbard.[3]

Today, organizations such as ISIS and al-Qaeda continue pressing for individuals who are not closely tied to their group or network to conduct brutal deeds, and both entities are quick to take credit for those assaults that turn out to be successful. It is important to keep in mind, however, that there are also those lone actors who have no contact with any terrorist organization, but who decide wholly on their own to stage an attack. Former math professor Ted Kaczynski, the American domestic terrorist who was nicknamed the "Unabomber," comes to mind. To be sure, there is substantial diversity in both the personality features and the strategies for violence among lone-actor terrorists, as will become evident in the following sections.

Research Findings on the Lone-Actor Terrort

There is reason to be troubled by the presence of potential lone-actor terrorists in our society, and to learn as much as possible about them so as to prevent their attacks. Unfortunately, a share of the existent body of research that focuses on these outwardly solitary figures suffers from various shortcomings, starting with issues related to the choice of terms and definitions.

Concerning the first of these, individuals who plot and carry out acts of violence ostensibly for religious or political reasons, and who do so on their own, have long been referred to as "lone wolf" terrorists. It is a label that many in the social sciences persist in using, as do those in the media. Yet critics of this moniker point out that the lone-wolf designation may inadvertently glorify the extremist in that it could be taken to suggest a gutsy, if misguided, maverick. Accordingly, the term "lone-actor" terrorist is gaining currency in many quarters, a label that is more descriptive, less sensational, and thus unlikely to romanticize the attacker. It is also the term used in this book.

As to the second issue, a handful of definitions of the lone-actor terrorist have been provided in recent years, with the result being a muddling of the topic. Perhaps the most stringent definition is the one used by the Danish Security and Intelligence Service, which identifies the lone-actor terrorist as a person who has no connection whatsoever to any other extremist or to an extremist organization, and who independently plans and executes an attack. Other definitions are broader, however, and include the individual who belongs to, and perhaps was trained by, an established terrorist organization, but who decides to carry out an assault autonomously. In other words, the strike transpires without the organization's knowledge or consent, outside of its command and control structure. And there is a third definition that is even more inclusive, one that encompasses two people ("isolated dyad") or a small, sovereign group of people ("wolf pack") who share a radical ideology and commit a terrorist attack. (Here it is important to distinguish between the lone actor, regardless of the particular definition, and the "solo terrorist," the latter being a man or woman who is an active member of a terrorist organization and who is selected, assigned, and dispatched to perform a specific, violent mission.)

As to the characteristics of the lone actor as reported by a share of researchers and the media, they appear to be imprecise in numerous respects. Until now, the prevailing image of the lone-actor terrorist has been that of a person who is socially inept and, being uncomfortable around people, has few relationships with others, even with like-minded extremists. Because his or her social uneasiness extends to groups, the person also has no connections to radical political movements or terrorist organizations. The modern mythos of the lone actor further suggests that the individual is poorly integrated, excitable, and impulsive, such that the decision to carry out an assault occurs precipitously, seemingly on a whim. But even though the lone actor may be socially inhibited and impetuous, he or she is presented as nevertheless intelligent, cautious, deeply secretive, and adept at planning and carrying out an attack, thus rendering the person a special threat to society. In reality, we now know this depiction misses the mark.

Fortunately, a more accurate portrait of the lone actor is emerging at this time. A particularly illuminating study was conducted by researchers Paul Gill, John Horgan, and Paige Deckert, who published their results in the *Journal of Forensic Sciences*.[4] Based on the cases of 119 individuals in Europe and the United States who sought to engage in lone-actor terrorism, the team analyzed the available information for both single perpetrators and isolated dyads. As mentioned earlier, the latter are comprised of two people who together conceive and execute a terrorist attack.

First and foremost, the research team found that there does not appear to be a reliably consistent, uniform profile of the lone-actor terrorist, although this may change as further studies are conducted. Other than the fact that over ninety-six percent of lone actors are male—a striking figure—those who carry out extremist attacks on their own tend to display a substantial degree of diversity. In terms of age, Gill and his collaborators found that it varied appreciably. In their sample, it ranged from fifteen to sixty-nine years, with thirty-three being the average age. The exception: those inspired by Islamist extremism. The mean age of terrorists holding al-Qaeda-related ideologies, in particular, was approximately ten years younger than those expressing non–Islamist beliefs.

An examination of the educational levels of this same pool of lone actors revealed that, as a whole, the group was well-educated. Three-fourths had attended college, and many of the terrorists, after graduating, proceeded to pursue masters' or doctoral degrees. In terms of those who held a militant Islamist ideology, they were the most likely to be highly educated, either being students or having already obtained college degrees.

Still, despite their relatively advanced levels of education, Gill and his colleagues discovered that their sample of lone actors did not perform as well as expected when it came to employment. Excluding those who were still attending college, approximately forty percent were unemployed. As for the remaining terrorists, the jobs that they held were less impressive than would be anticipated given their educational achievements.

Although it has not been confirmed, it is plausible that mental health issues may be a factor in the lone actors' low rate of employment; that emotional difficulties may interfere with their job performance and retention. In this regard, one study found that approximately thirty-one percent of lone actors had a history of mental disorder,[5] while another reported the figure to be slightly over forty precent.[6] For comparison, the World Health Organization estimates that twenty-five percent of the global population is affected by a mental disorder at some point.[7]

More precise investigations have discovered that lone-actor terrorists, compared to the general population, are more likely to be diagnosed with one of three mental conditions: schizophrenia, delusional disorder, or autism spectrum disorders (ASD).[8] In terms of the latter, autism *per se* is not believed to the issue. "Although individuals with ASD are not linked to violent behaviors, social interaction deficits impair an individual's ability to maintain functional relationships," write Emily Corner and her associates, who add that the individual with ASD may therefore turn to the internet for interaction.[9] These researchers noted that such was the case for the lone actors with autism in their study, who were prone to form intense online attachments. It is true, of course, that many people with symptoms of ASD do experience an enhanced sense of sanctuary and equality in the virtual world of cyberspace. "(P)eople with ASD have characterized the Internet as a liberating environment where they can interact with others on a more equal basis," write Christina Shane-Simpson and her colleagues, "partially due to perceptions of increased control over when, how, and with whom one interacts online."[10] Unfortunately, it is also online that the person may encounter and develop relationships with extremists, including recruiters acting on behalf of militant groups or terrorist organizations.

Concerning another aspect of the lone actor, criminal tendencies, studies have found that such extremists are more likely than members of the general population to have had run-ins with law enforcement. In one study, approximately forty-one percent of lone-actor terrorists had a history of criminal convictions, from driving while intoxicated to assault, and most of this number had served jail time.[11] Another research project, this one conducted by Bart Schuurman and his colleagues, reported that forty-six percent of the lone-actor terrorists in their analysis had a history of violent crime, including stabbings and other injurious acts.[12]

Not only are lone actors more likely than the general population to have had criminal convictions, however; they are also more likely than those terrorists who belong to actual terrorist organizations.[13] In part, this may be because terrorist groups prefer recruits with unblemished legal records, since such newcomers are less apt to be on the radar of law enforcement or intelligence agencies and thus unlikely to invite outside scrutiny of the organization. This may also be one of the reasons that an estimated ten percent of lone-actor terrorists have been rejected by, or expelled from, groups or networks that practice contentious politics.[14] If this is indeed the case, it may mean that some lone-actor terrorists end up alone by default, not by choice.

Along these same lines, the lone actor's increased chance of a mental disorder and its behavioral manifestations could likewise diminish the person's effectiveness within, or prevent his or her acceptance into, a terrorist group, as could the social difficulties from which some lone actors reportedly suffer. The fact is, the rate of mental disorder for terrorists who function in organizations, like ISIS, is quite low, even lower than that of the general population.[15] Presumably, this is because such organizations believe that recruits who display emotional instability, or who have a history of mental disturbance, are potential risks to the group's essential secrecy and well-ordered functioning.

That said, it must be kept in mind that the preponderance of lone-actor terrorists do not appear to be so socially inept or emotionally unstable as to be unable to interact productively with other people. In fact, Schuurman and his colleagues point out that lone actors, on closer inspection, appear to have many more attachments and interactions than was previously assumed. Even more important, they have more connections to other extremists and terrorist organizations.

"Although the term 'lone actor' implies a high or even complete degree of autonomy, these individuals are in actuality seldom completely isolated," writes the Schuurman team.[16] Like all of us, the lone-actor terrorist lives and functions within a social context, and it now appears that most such terrorists have direct or indirect, face-to-face or online, contact with other extremists or extremist organizations. The person's "loneness," it seems, is limited largely to the actual commission of the attack itself.[17] "For most lone actors, connections to others, be they virtual or physical, play an important and sometimes even critical role in the adoption and maintenance of their motivation to commit violence, as well as the practical skills that are necessary to carry out acts of terrorism," write Schuurman and his associates.[18] These researchers add that the services provided by those with whom the lone actor engages may range "from providing bomb-making advice and materials to offering post-attack safe houses."[19]

Illustrating the degree to which the lone actor seldom functions in a vacuum, the Schuurman group's study of fifty-five lone-actor terrorists found that eighty-six percent of them conveyed their extremist opinions and beliefs to family members, coworkers, friends, and people they encountered on the internet.[20] In many cases, they did so months or even years before devising a terrorist attack. Over a quarter, moreover, informed other people of their intentions to commit specific aggressive acts, such as violence against others.

Investigators further determined that lone-actor terrorists, as a whole, are not the brilliant, cunning figures of lore. Rather, they tend to be amateurish. For instance, nearly seventy-five percent of lone actors in one study failed to take adequate precautions to ensure the secrecy of their plans.[21] Instead, they revealed aspects of their plots to others, as well as displaying careless lapses, such as leaving guns, incendiary devices, or incriminating written materials, like manuals, in plain sight. In addition, the majority of lone actors made preparations for their attacks at locations close to home rather than at more distant, secluded spots, the result being that their questionable activities were more likely to be noticed and reported to the authorities. It may be partly for this reason that nearly half of the lone-actor terrorists in Schuurman's study came into contact with law enforcement at some point while readying for their attacks.[22]

Concerning the lone actor's decision to devise and carry out an assault, it appears that an event may trigger the person to do so; that he or she may have long harbored extremist beliefs and violent fantasies but that an identifiable occurrence sets the individual on the path to committing the assault. In forty-four percent of the Schuurman team's sample, triggering incidents could be identified, with the researchers pointing to, as examples, a personal trial of some sort or perhaps watching other people successfully carry out violent acts.[23] Paul Gill and his associates reported that a number of the lone actors in their research had lost their jobs or had been the victims of prejudice, physical assault, or other disturbance prior to deciding to devise their terrorist plots.[24]

In terms of targets and methods, lone actors, compared to those who belong to terrorist organizations, usually select ordinary citizens to kill or maim. They prefer everyday people—civilians—rather than more prominent targets that might be harder to reach or better protected. When political figures, government facilities, and the like are attacked, the perpetrators tend to be those who belong to terrorist organizations.

Turning to the choice of weapons, most lone-actor terrorists are inclined to use firearms in their attacks, and to a slightly lesser extent, incendiary devices.[25] Studies have revealed that many lone actors already possess firearms before they begin preparing for their offensives, such that this aspect of the mission is already in place. Beyond convenience, it may also be the case that they prefer firearms because guns do not kill the user, only the targets. And lone actors may be more feel more comfortable with firearms, twenty-six percent of lone-actor terrorists having had military experience, with most of this number having served in combat.[26] Incendiary devices, by comparison, must be specially devised for an attack, a skill set that the person may not possess. And there are, of course, significant risks involved in constructing a bomb, and premature detonations are not uncommon. Unless the plan is for a suicide attack, then, the terrorist may wish to use guns, knives, or even vehicles as weapons.

Selecting the type of weapon to be used, like learning to construct a bomb, is a task that can be accomplished online, the go-to source for budding lone-actor terrorists since the 1990s. Certainly the internet offers a surfeit of toxic information, material that is accessible to the everyday user, and this includes such controversial documents as the 1,500-page "terror and revolution" manual posted by Norway's notorious lone actor, Anders Breivik, who killed seventy-seven people.[27] But not only is it remarkably easy to access such information online. Today, a would-be terrorist, owing to developments like the Dark Web and to advances such as end-to-end encryption capabilities, is in a securer position to initiate contact and communicate directly with terrorist organizations themselves. As could be expected, ISIS and other groups are alert to these technological gifts and eager to capitalize on them. The result: the potential transformation of lone-actor terrorism. Such high-tech developments allow extremist networks to micromanage those attacks that are carried out by individuals who previously would have functioned more independently. As a result, what was once lone-actor terrorism is rapidly evolving into remote-control terrorism guided from afar, meaning that the former concept may soon become obsolete.

Virtual Planning, Remote Control Attacks, and Lone-Actor Terrorsim

The first identified case of this type occurred in France in April 2015, when a terrorist attempted to commit an attack in a village, an operation that looked as if it had been plotted by a perpetrator intent upon acting alone. Authorities later determined, however, that cyberplanners in Syria had been behind the failed assault, and had even arranged for the would-be terrorist to receive assistance within France itself. Indeed, ISIS's virtual planners sent messages to the extremist instructing him where to pick up weapons and a getaway car that sympathetic criminal elements in France had procured and positioned for him. Despite the fact that this particular mission flopped, the method itself quickly gained favor, meaning that more such operations would take place as the Islamist organization struggled to adapt to a number of existential challenges.

Challenges indeed. As the tide turned against the Islamic State in the face of the Syrian Democratic Front's onslaught, it became far more difficult for prospective terrorists to travel to Syria, meet up with the organization, and receive training. Western nations, by enhancing their security operations, had become more aware of the aspiring terrorists within their borders and thus more able to block their travel to the Middle East. Then too, Syrian and Iraqi border officials were now more diligent in spotting and refusing entry to suspicious arrivals. So it was that ISIS, weakened by these developments, started de-emphasizing the need for aspiring recruits to make the journey to the faltering caliphate and instead urged them to remain in their own countries. Here, on their home turf, they were less likely to be conspicuous and thus more able to opportunistically commit acts of violence. At the same time, ISIS commenced lending substantial, at times tangible, support to such extremists. Whereas groups like al-Qaeda and ISIS had long provided online inspiration and encouragement to those who would embrace their ideologies, the adoption of the "virtual planning model" to furnish practical help for terrorist attacks represented a critical extension in strategy.

Remote-Control Terrorism

The virtual planning approach, whose outcomes are referred to by such terms as "enabled attacks," "remote-control attacks," or, in French, "télécommande" (remote control) operations, does not involve a uniform, undeviating process. No standard, one-size-fits-all method exists for transforming lone actors into terror agents for an organization. Instead, the degree to which cyberplanners, or handlers, furnish guidance or instruction to the would-be terrorists with whom they interact in the cybersphere varies considerably, and for this reason such individuals do not fall into a clearly definable category. "(T)hey represent a hybrid, a midpoint between lone-actors and truly organizationally supported operations—a marriage of convenience if not necessity," writes Sam Mullins, professor of counterterrorism at George C. Marshall European Center for Security Studies.[28] Jen Easterly and Joshua Geltzer, formerly of the National Security Council, put it this way: "Direction from a terrorist group like the Islamic State … is a spectrum, not a dichotomy."[29]

In terms of the prominence of the virtual planning model within ISIS, the approach has fast become a principal component of the division that oversees terrorist operations outside of Syria and Iraq. Known as the Amniyat al-Kharji, this is the intelligence sector of ISIS that was discussed in Chapter 6. Within it, virtual planners are now integrated into the command structure, some of whom function as both traditional theater commanders and cyberplanners. And the benefits for ISIS are apparent: the opportunity to take its recruitment and radicalization platform to a global level, and to do so at little cost or risk to the organization.

Typically, a handler will befriend a potential recruit in a chat room or elsewhere on the internet, although it may be the aspiring recruit who initiates contact online with the handler. In the chat-room scenario, the cyberplanner forms and nurtures an ongoing relationship with the individual, offering encouragement and emotional support for the person's movement toward militant jihadism. Helping to assuage any doubts the would-be terrorist may develop, the handler may also apply some form of social pressure, such as peer pressure, to compel the individual to continue on the path to radical Islamism. It is common knowledge that peer pressure is most effective in influencing those in younger, rather than older, age groups, and ISIS recruits tend to fall into the former category.

Whereas a prospective recruit may be anywhere in the world as long as there is an internet connection, ISIS's virtual planners nearly always work from Syria or Iraq. Of course, they could perform their roles outside of these two countries, which may become the case as the organization continues being driven out of them. But whatever the location of ISIS's cyber-coaches, now or in the years ahead, they have online ties to support sources across the globe, the upshot being that they are often able to arrange for their assailants to receive local assistance.

In addition, the Islamic State's virtual planners are fluent in the languages spoken by the recruits, and many times hail from countries, such as Belgium and France, where prospective terrorists are apt to be situated. Also noteworthy, virtual planners do not use their real names when communicating with would-be attackers, nor do they reveal their nationalities, show their faces, or allow prospective terrorists to hear their voices. In this way, an attacker who is apprehended while preparing for a virtually-planned operation will be unable to identify the handler or disclose anything of value about the person.

To be sure, the virtual planning model is a smart, economical, low-risk approach by which groups like ISIS can formulate deadly attacks at distant locations, with the pay-offs for the organization—first and foremost, international attention—being considerable. And while those terrorists whom the Islamic State directs through the cybersphere have not, as a whole, been enormously effective to date, their attacks are potentially more lethal than those of the lone actors of the past who had no meaningful connections to a terrorist organization's command and control structure. "This model has helped transform lone attackers who rely heavily on the Internet from the bungling wannabes of a decade ago into something more dangerous," say Daveed Gartenstein-Ross and Madeleine Blackman.[30]

As mentioned earlier, the specific tasks that virtual planners perform vary according to the needs of the attacker. By and large, however, cyber-coaches are thoroughly involved in nearly all aspects a mission. "These terrorists are micromanaged in every decision, right down to the bullets they use to carry out their violence," reads a piece in the *Homeland Security News Wire*.[31]

Characteristically, the virtual planner, after recruiting and radicalizing the person, assumes the role of friend and confidant, justifying the use of violence and keeping the aspiring terrorist on course. The handler may also conceptualize the terror plot itself, select the targets, and establish the timing of the attack. Another critical role the cyberplanner may play centers on the type of weapons to be used, with the handler choosing the weaponry and providing the necessary guidance. For instance, if the would-be terrorist is constructing a bomb, the planner may point the person to either online or hands-on help, or may provide the bomb-making instructions directly. The cybercoach may also arrange for the attacker to obtain firearms. In one mission that was set to take place in Germany, an ISIS cybercoach sent a text message containing the GPS coordinates of a position where the terrorist would find firearms awaiting him. And finally, the cyberplanner may still be in contact with the attacker and actively furnishing instructions as the moment arrives to carry out the assault. In a separate mission in Germany, one in which the attacker used a machete in his assault, the virtual planner was in contact with the man minutes before the strike. "If you look at the communications between the attackers and the virtual plotters, you will see that there is a direct line of connection to the point where they are egging them on minutes, even seconds, before the individual carries out an attack," says terrorism analyst Nathaniel Barr.[32]

Besides working with individuals who, in the past, would have functioned as genuine lone-actor terrorists, virtual planners also introduce such individuals to one another, thereby creating dyads or small cells. The planners then manage these entities in the same fashion, groupings that may be even more dangerous than solitary individuals. Which brings us to the question of the threat posed by remote-control terrorists as a whole.

Many terrorism analysts are deeply concerned about the future of single-perpetrator, enabled attacks, and for several reasons. First, an attack, depending on the location, timing, and circumstances, does not have to be large or spectacular to be politically impactful and financially destructive. Second, a handful of small, crude strikes conducted simultaneously or in rapid succession may, collectively, be experienced by the public as a single, overpowering affront and be highly disruptive. Third, the virtual planning model, because it can be used to devise attacks anywhere in the world, may amplify the terrorist organization's image and publicize its reach. Indeed, the Islamic State has already used, or attempted to use, the virtual planning approach for offensives in Australia, Germany, Indonesia, France, Bangladesh, and even Ohio, New York, and Washington, D.C. The prospect of harm being visited upon disparate, unprotected locations is therefore quite real, even as it draws attention to the terrorist group's supposed power before an uneasy public.

That said, some analysts argue that the threat posed by the virtual planning model is not all that great, that it is being overstated, and that such exaggeration only serves to make ISIS and similar groups appear more formidable than is actually the case. One reason for this skepticism is that would-be terrorists, many of whose attempted attacks were amateurish in the past, will presumably continue being inexpert in the future.

9. Terrorism, Encrypted Extremism, and Remote Control Attacks 147

"Cybercoaches have little or no control over their charges who are very often naïve, voluble, incautious, gullible, incapable, and/or troubled—qualities that are often underappreciated, and sometimes even unacknowledged, in official, journalistic, and academic accounts," writes John Mueller of the Cato Institute.[33] Moreover, the cybercoach's lack of direct, face-to-face contact with the terrorist limits the degree to which the planner is able to assess the individual's dedication, just as the planner's lack of personal familiarity with the immediate site at which the individual expects to carry out an attack may hinder the former's ability to engineer the operation. The fact is, most remote-control terrorist attacks connected to ISIS have misfired, although they may become more successful in the years to come.

One thing seems certain, though: terrorist attacks will continue being conducted and the internet will continue playing a role in them. And while some of these strikes, perhaps most of them, will be limited in their destructiveness or may even fail, others will surely be successful and lethal.

At present, many counterterrorism experts are convinced that the virtual planning model represents a resilient strategy for the Islamic State and other terrorist outfits as well, and that the strategy will endure. And there is a related development that troubles them. "Of special concern to the FBI is the recent switch by ISIS supporters to encrypted communication via the Dark Web, which makes online monitoring almost impossible," write Mark Hamm and Ramón Spaaij.[34] Certainly the Islamic State's descent into the deeper, more hidden recesses of the internet, and the fact that cyber-planners are presently encouraging many of the organization's supporters on the Surface Web to migrate to it, is sobering.

The Dark Web

Cyberplanners and their online recruits, as mentioned earlier, are currently able to communicate securely through such applications as WhatsApp, Pidgin, and Telegram; instant-messaging software that is end-to-end encrypted and that can ensure that the untraceable messages sent from it self-destruct. Some such apps, most notably Telegram, also offer public channels and mechanisms for video sharing that can be used to spread propaganda. But there is another challenge that is vexing to counterterrorism experts as well: the Dark Web. Because it cannot be effectively penetrated, terrorist groups are increasingly drawn to it, both Islamist and non–Islamist. This provides an aspiring attacker—for instance, a lone actor seeking a connection to ISIS—not only with a means of communicating with the organization and its virtual planners, but also access to its online documents, restricted videos, and other materials.

As to the Dark Web itself, the internet is composed of tiers, and the tier with which most of us are familiar is known as the Surface Web. Accessible to everyone, the contents of this "open web," as it is also called, are indexed by standard search engines. Beneath the Surface Web, is another tier known as the Deep Web, which is up to 500 times larger. Comprising ninety-six percent of the internet and not directly accessible to the average user, its contents are not indexed by search engines such as Google. "You need to know the URL or have access permissions to view a deep-web site," says Mae Rice.[35] It is on the Deep Web that services such as online banking and web mail are located, along with paywall-protected businesses like video-on-demand and online newspapers. And lastly, within the Deep Web lies the Dark Web, which requires special software to access. The most prevalent software at this time is TOR, an acronym for "The Onion Router," an open-source browser that safeguards the anonymity of internet traffic by applying multi-layered encryption. Also referred to as the "darknet," the Dark Web was conceptualized by researchers at the U.S. Naval Research Lab as a means of shielding American intelligence communications on the internet. Once a user is on the Dark Web, which is not crawled or indexed, the person can browse sites without revealing his or her identity, although it is necessary to know where to find a given site and precisely how to access it. As could be expected, the impenetrability of the Dark Web is what makes it so attractive to extremist organizations like the Islamic State, which began relocating to it within the days of its terror attacks at the Bataclan Theatre, the Stade de France, and a café district in Paris.

"The rise of the Islamic State (also known as ISIS or ISIL), and especially the 13 November 2015 attacks in Paris," write Daniel Moore and Thomas Rid, "prompted more calls to deny cryptographically protected virtual safe spaces to terrorists."[36] This is because investigators determined that the terrorists in the Paris massacres had planned their attacks using encrypted Telegram messaging, at least in part. As a result, the authorities quickly shut down dozens of public channels on the Telegram application. And there was additional fallout for ISIS. The online social activist collective known as Anonymous set about pulling down hundreds of Islamic State-related websites as part of Operation Paris ("OpParis"), its hactivist campaign.[37] Not only that, it also expunged over 5,500 Twitter accounts that were affiliated with the terrorist outfit. "(E)xpect a total mobilization on our part," Anonymous declared.[38] For such reasons, ISIS set about transferring a significant share of its online operations to the Dark Web, including ISIS-related news, propaganda, fundraising efforts, and archives of video and textual materials for use by new recruits and others who might have a need for them. Soon it had constructed a home for itself on this layer of the internet, which was already a nest for an array of decentralized, encrypted, and illicit sites. "A recent study found that 57% of the Dark Web is occupied by illegal content like pornography, illicit finances, drug hubs, weapons trafficking, counterfeit currency, terrorist communication, and much more," writes Gabriel Weimann.[39] ISIS simply increased the amount of terrorist traffic that was traveling along this tier.

Here it should be noted that the Dark Web is also used by those who are not involved in criminal activities. While fifty-seven percent of its content may be illicit, the remaining forty-three percent is legal and sometimes even life-saving. For instance, the Dark Web is often employed by everyday people in nations having authoritarian governments; that is, autocratic regimes that surveil their citizens on the Surface Web. It also serves as a secure zone for journalists and for activists who may be under threat from totalitarian governments. Indeed, the Dark Web was a crucial tool for organizers and protestors during the Arab Spring uprisings of 2011; activists who otherwise would have had no means of planning political actions or otherwise expressing themselves without the risk of dire consequences. A neutral sector, the Dark Web, then, can be used for both corrupt and constructive purposes.

Returning now to our discussion of ISIS and the Dark Web, a new procedure emerged among the Islamic State's virtual planners: an inquisitive individual would track down information about militant jihadism and the Islamic State on the Surface Web, such as ISIS propaganda videos on Facebook or YouTube that display Syrian children who had been wounded, if inadvertently, by Western military forces. ISIS posts such videos on social media so as to reach as many people as possible and thus cast the widest net when seeking recruits. The curious individual would then join an online forum or discussion group centering on jihad-related issues or visit any of the large number of Twitter accounts, video websites, and extremists blogs that ISIS operates, directly or indirectly, on the internet. Within a portion of these posts the interested individual would likely encounter additional links to hidden channels. "It is inside those channels that the extremist group moves from semipublic propaganda to encrypted chats," write Stacy Meichtry and Sam Schechner.[40] From here, the recruit would be shifted into protected, one-on-one contact with an ISIS handler and, in many cases, relocated to the Dark Web. "Terrorists are increasingly using the hidden parts of the Internet to avoid surveillance, relying on the open web for recruiting but then moving to encryption and the Dark Web for more nefarious interactions," says Elizabeth Weise.[41] At this encoded level, the prospective recruit would be in a secure position to discuss travel to Syria and Iraq, for instance, or to undergo online grooming as a foreign-based terrorist to be is directed by the Islamic State.

In the ensuing chapters, four terrorists attacks are revisited, each of which transpired in France during the years 2015 or 2016. In most cases, the assailants were identified as lone actors within hours of the attacks, most notably by the news media, although investigators later uncovered connections, strong or weak, direct or indirect, to the Islamic State. Also uncovered in most of the cases were the internet-based alliances such as those previously described.

10

Normandy
The Slaying of a Parish Priest

Whereas any terrorist attack that kills or maims the innocent is distressing to people of conscience, some assaults inflict a special kind of anguish. When the casualties are children or the elderly, for instance, or when the victims have devoted their lives to the pursuit of peace, the loss can feel especially acute.

In summer of 2016, a brutal attack was launched in Normandy, a horrific confrontation that had as its target someone who bestrode two of these categories: an elderly Roman Catholic priest. As so often happens, the media, in a knee-jerk response, reported that an isolated dyad had carried out the strike, implying, in effect, that it had been a lone actor-type operation. But investigators soon learned that the pair of young men who set out to slay the priest were not a couple of bigoted buddies acting on a reckless whim. They had been introduced and, at the very least, persuaded by a French cybercoach based in Syria. At most, they were executing a remote control attack as described in Chapter 9. The reputed coach's name: Rachid Kassim.

Hailing from Roanne, France, the twenty-nine-year-old Kassim was the son of immigrants, his father being Yemeni and his mother, Algerian. A lonely child, he became a religious extremist in his teens, eventually being kicked out of his local mosque due to his menacing rhetoric. He also was removed from his job at a youth center for refusing to shake hands with women and for insisting that a prayer room be built on the premises. Then, for a while, Kassim was a struggling rap artist. "I'm a Terrorist," was the title of one of the many militant songs that he wrote and performed prior to taking the pivotal step of recording an album, one that flopped. Subsequent to this, Kassim abandoned his plans of becoming a professional singer, traveled to the Middle East with his wife and three children, and joined the Islamic State.[1]

Arriving in Syria in 2015, he joined the organization's intelligence division, the Amniyat, where he served as an online propagandist and virtual planner. A formidable voice on social media, most notably on Facebook and in his own influential chat group on Telegram, Kassim posted videos of himself decapitating hostages, threatening the life of French President François Hollande, and imploring youths in France to conduct terrorist missions in their communities. "He uses 15-year-old kids, whom he incites to commit attacks, kids who are his youngest brother's age" ("Il utilise des gamins de 15 ans, qu'il incite à commettre des attentats, des gamins qui ont l'âge de son plus jeune frère"), said one of Kassim's former friends.[2] With hundreds of devoted followers on his encrypted Telegram account, officials perceived Kassim, whose online moniker was "Lightsaber," to be a threat to France and pledged to bring him to justice. Not surprisingly, he quickly climbed to the top of the nation's most-wanted list of French citizens serving with ISIS in the Middle East. Certainly he had demonstrated his dangerousness, albeit in the cybersphere.

Earlier that year, for instance, French intelligence was monitoring the cellphone activity of a man named Larossi Abballa, a twenty-five-year-old Frenchman and ISIS sympathizer, when they discovered that he was a member of Kassim's encrypted Telegram chat group. Because officials did not yet have sufficient evidence to arrest Abballa on terrorism-related charges, however, he was able to roam free; that is, until June 13, 2016, when he stabbed to death a policeman and the policeman's girlfriend in their home in Magnanville, France. Afterward, he took hostage their three-year-old child. In the course of the ensuing standoff with the police, Abballa live-streamed himself from the deceased couple's home—the traumatized child was still in the house—during which he pledged his allegiance to the Islamic State and called upon other French citizens to carry out local attacks. Shot to death by elite French forces a few hours later, intelligence experts later concluded that Abballa's online contact with Rachid Kassim was likely a critical factor in the stabbings; that it may even have been a virtual, or remote control, attack.

During the same summer, Kassim, over the internet, introduced four women in France to one another, after which he explained to them how to acquire gas canisters and place them strategically in a car. He then directed this all-female cell to park the vehicle near Notre Dame Cathedral, detonate the car bomb, and thereby kill scores of bystanders. Fortunately, law enforcement was able to disrupt the plot shortly before it was due to be carried out.

Also during this period, French intelligence agents found that Kassim was communicating online from Syria with several other French citizens, mostly those in their teens. In fact, it was he who decided to bring together two of these young people for a lethal operation, the pair being strangers to one another who lived 430 miles apart. As for their terrorist strike, it would target a Catholic mass being celebrated at a church in Saint-Étienne-du-Rouvray, eighty miles northwest of Paris in Normandy. It would mark the first time that an ISIS-related attack had targeted a Christian church.

The Valor of Father Jacques Hamel

Thirty-thousand people live in Saint-Étienne-du-Rouvray, a town that was named in honor of Saint Stephen, the first Christian martyr. Situated on the edge of the Forêt de la Londe-Rouvray, an ancient forest, the working-class town is also a suburb of the city of Rouen, where, in the year 1431, Joan of Arc was condemned for heresy and burned at the stake.

Because the two ISIS-linked terrorists had scheduled their assault for late July 2016, it would occur during a time when many French people enjoy vacations away from home. This meant that Saint-Étienne-du-Rouvray, already a peaceful town, would be even more placid than usual. Furthermore, because a smaller number of residents would be present, fewer parishioners would be attending worship services at the two local churches. These consist of Église Saint-Étienne (Church of St. Stephen), a stone church dating back to the sixteenth century, and the more modern Église Sainte-Thérèse le Madrillet (Church of St. Teresa). As it happened, the summer escape may have been a blessing for many of the townspeople.

Among those who had left on holiday was the parish priest, Father Auguste Moanda Phuati. He had journeyed back to Congo, his homeland, and only recently returned to France. In his absence, he handed over certain church-related duties to Father Jacques Hamel, an eighty-five-year-old ecclesiastic who, although officially retired, wished to stay active in the church. "I'll work until my last breath," Father Hamel told a fellow priest.[3]

At 9:25 a.m. on an airless Tuesday morning, July 26, 2016, Father Hamel, once again, was at work. Outside the church, meanwhile, two young men were approaching, one of whom had just sent a text message to his mother. "Don't worry, everything is fine," it said. "I love you."[4]

Inside the Church of St. Stephen, Father Hamel finished celebrating the Mass, a ritual attended by a small number of holy sisters and parishioners. Standing at the foot of the altar, the elderly priest was still clad in his chasuble, the ornate vestment worn when performing the ritual. And it was at this serene moment that the two young men—both were nineteen years old—burst into the church and rushed toward him. Brandishing knives, a handgun, and what appeared to be an explosive device, the two terrorists forced Father Hamel to his knees even as he struggled against them and as the congregation yelled at the attackers. "Everyone was shouting 'stop, stop you don't know what you're doing,'" recalled Sister Danielle, a witness.[5] No match for the younger men's strength, Father Hamel ended up on his knees, and the aggressors proceeded with their mission. "(T)hey took over his place and started speaking Arabic," said Sister Danielle.[6]

Although the nuns and parishioners in the Church of St. Stephen had no way of knowing it, Father Hamel, during the preceding two months, had been haunted by a recurrent nightmare, according to a sibling in whom he confided. In it, he was walking home after a religious service when a group of strangers appeared out of the blue and pounced on him. As they were beating him, he looked around for help but there was no one to rescue him.

Father Hamel's sibling further noted that the priest, who seldom went to the movies, attended and was deeply moved by the film, *Of Gods and Men*. Set in 1996, it is based on the slaughter of Trappist monks by radical Islamic fundamentalists during the Algerian Civil War. "How is it … that these men could act with such vicious violence against these [holy] men who had lived in their community doing nothing but serving the poor, feeding the hungry and caring for the sick?" Father Hamel asked his loved one.[7] Answering his own question, he submitted that Satan had seized their minds and hearts.[8] And now, with terrorists subjugating Father Hamel himself in this venerated sixteenth-century place of worship, the priest's belief in a wellspring of evil once again asserted itself. "Be gone, Satan!" ("Va t'en Satan!"), he shouted.[9] Despite being on his knees, he managed to kick a foot outward at his assailants.

Continuing with their desecration, the two young Frenchmen now delivered from the altar a brief sermon in the Arabic language. "(T)he terrorists underlined the meaning of their actions by engaging in a ritual sacrifice of the priest before the altar and a mock homily," said Anthony Fisher, bioethicist and archbishop.[10] It was a calculated sacrilege against the Christian religion. Fisher added that Father Hamel was about to die "in odium fidei, that is in hatred of the faith," a term used to describe a martyr's death.[11]

As the terrorists presented their short sermon, they made sure to film it. Again, Father Hamel attempted to resist the pair, and it was at this juncture that one of the attackers slashed the priest's throat in what some believe may have been a bungled attempt to behead him.[12] "Allahu akbar!" shouted the killers as they carried out the execution, recounted the *Catholic World Report*.[13] Collapsing onto the floor, Father Hamel was facing upward and peering at a pair of holy sisters when he succumbed.

The terrorists next gathered up four people as hostages, three of them nuns and one, a parishioner. The latter was an eighty-six-year-old man, Guy Coponet, whom the assailants now forcibly recruited to help them with their perverse mission. His task was to take control of recording it.[14] To this end, a terrorist shoved a cellphone into Coponet's hand and demanded that he take videos or photos of the lifeless Father Hamel. Afterward, the attackers turned on Coponet himself, stabbing him four times in the throat and hip and leaving him for dead. Astutely, the wounded man played along, pretending to have perished. He ultimately survived.

Still holding the remaining hostages, the terrorists explained their reasons for striking the church and murdering Father Hamel. They accused Christians of purposely decimating the Muslim population, and insisted that ISIS aggression would continue until Western nations withdrew from Syria.

Sister Huguette Peron, a nun who was being held captive, recalled that one of the terrorists smiled at her during this time, a kind and gentle smile, and she said that he appeared to be happy. The same assailant also retrieved Sister Peron's cane when she asked for it, and the two briefly discussed their religious beliefs. It was a dialogue during which the young assailant displayed his lack of understanding of Christianity even as he maintained that Sister Huguette was confused in her beliefs. "Jesus cannot be God and a man," he informed her.[15] Unperturbed, the holy sister turned inward in prayer and primed her spiritual self for physical death, which she felt awaited her.[16]

Moments later, Sister Danielle dashed from the church and notified the police about the attack, who, in turn, activated a terrorism protocol. The BRI (Brigades de Recherche et d'Intervention) promptly appeared on the scene, surrounded the Church of St. Stephen, and attempted to negotiate with the attackers. When it became obvious that the latter had no interest in talking, the commandos tried to break into the church. They did not succeed, however, because the assailants were using the remaining three hostages to barricade the door. In any case, the incident was resolved moments later.

At 10:45 a.m., without warning, the terrorists darted out of the building, shouting praise to Allah and dragging the hostages as human shields. And the commandos let loose. "A number of shots were heard over a period of around 15 seconds as the incident came to an end," write Alix Culbertson and Katie Mansfield.[17] One witness reported hearing twenty gunshots.[18] Both terrorists lay dead. A search of their bodies revealed that their bomb was not real, but rather a kitchen timer affixed to a backpack.

Predictably, the shock to the normally peaceful community was instant and intense. The townspeople could not believe that the kindhearted man who had served them for so many years, who had become such a integral part of their lives, had been slayed in such a sadistic manner. In the ensuing hours, mourners gathered in the town square to share their grief. "When I heard the news of his death, it was like being hit on the head from above," said one resident.[19] Unlike Father Hamel's assailants, the priest was known for his warmth, generosity, devotion, and humility; a man who, even in his eighties, celebrated baptisms and marriages and attended the funerals of the residents of Saint-Étienne-du-Rouvray. Sebastiano Velardita, the eighty-four-year-old man in charge of the sacristy at St. Stephen's, added a bittersweet note, stating that his friend Father Hamel also appreciated a fine wine.[20]

Condemnation of the assassination was swift and stern, with denunciations coming from the Élysée Palace, the White House, and the Vatican. The Catholic daily, *La Croix*, issued a statement as well, one that centered on the distinctly anti–Christian nature of the operation and its figurative attack on the country as a whole. "The history of France is very associated with Catholics," wrote Guillaume Coubert, the newspaper's editor, "and to strike a church is to strike one of those elements that constitutes the identity of France."[21] Pope Francis also made a bold statement, one in which he upended the jihadists' claim of righteousness. "(T)o kill in the name of God is satanic," the pontiff declared.[22]

Within days, Father Hamel's own words, which had been published in a parish newsletter shortly before his murder, were recollected. "At these times," he wrote, "we should dig deep inside ourselves to hear God's invitation to take care of this world, to make it, where we live in it, a warmer, more human, more fraternal world."[23]

The Assailants

At the time of the terrorist attack, the BRI did not know the identities of the two assailants or if the pair was connected to a terrorist organization. Several hours later, however, police spokespersons cautiously began using terms like "Islamic State-inspired terrorists" and "ISIS sympathizers." This was because Amaq, the ISIS-linked propaganda and news outlet, released a statement after the vicious strike, one in which the Islamic State claimed ownership of the mission and referred to the killers as its combatants. Then, on Tuesday evening, French authorities publicly named Adel Kermiche as one of the terrorists. A French citizen, he was a resident of Saint-Étienne-du-Rouvray. His accomplice remained unknown.

The next day, ISIS posted a video that the terrorists had filmed before their attack at the church. In it, the two are sitting on a wooden staircase, one of them clad in camouflage gear and the other wearing a kufi covered by a red cloak. Smiling and speaking broken Arabic, they vow their allegiance to Abu Bakr al-Baghdadi and the Islamic State, while holding an electronic tablet displaying an ISIS flag on its screen. They also urge Muslims to obliterate France and other Western nations.

On Thursday, two days after the attack, officials made public the name of the second attacker: Abdel-Malik Petitjean. Because his face had been shot off during his confrontation with the BRI commandos, and because he had no criminal record and therefore no fingerprints were on file, his identity initially could not be determined. A search of Kermiche's home turned up Petitjean's identification card, however, with confirmation of the latter's identity being obtained through a DNA analysis performed on tissue extracted from the corpse.

As it turned out, Petitjean's mother could not accept that Abdel-Malik had participated in the killings. "I know my son," she told a reporter. "I know my child."[24] Even after the police informed her of the DNA results, she sent a text message to Abdel-Malik's cellphone asking him to call her. Incidentally, it had been Abdel-Malik who sent a message to this woman, his mother, in the minutes before the attack; the text in which he expressed his love for her.

As for Adel Kermiche's family, his relatives were not struggling with such denial. In fact, they had contacted French authorities about Adel a year earlier, on March 23, 2015, when the young man, who had become hostile toward others and obsessed with Islam, vanished.[25] He was en route to Syria.

Adel Kermiche

Born on March 25, 1997, into a working class family of Algerian descent, Adel Kermiche's early home life was a supportive one. He lived in Saint-Étienne-du-Rouvray with his mother and siblings, and he had an older sister who was a doctor.

Kermiche's neighbors remember him as a friendly, sociable boy who enjoyed playing with other children. Apparently, the neighbors' familiarity with him was only partial. According to Kermiche's legal file, when he was only six years old, he was hospitalized for unspecified psychological problems.[26] Subsequent to this, he received psychotropic medication and psychotherapy until the age of thirteen, when he was placed in a special school for behaviorally-disturbed youths.[27] "He was hyperactive, very nervous, he created trouble to get attention," said the father of one of Kermiche's classmates.[28] Such disparate opinions of him were typical.

Indeed, those who knew Kermiche during his adolescence either speak of his outward normality in certain respects—he was a fan of the singer Rihanna and *The Simpsons* television series—or of his purported intellectual and personality deficits. More specifically, they say he was neither a bright teen nor one who was interested in learning. Acquaintances further describe him as gullible and easily persuaded, and as rarely succeeding in anything he attempted. Considering that such descriptions were collected after he and his accomplice had murdered a beloved priest, the community's recollections may have focused on Kermiche's less attractive traits. One point upon which everyone agreed, however, is that his turn to militant Islamism was swift and comprehensive, and that it came in the wake of the al-Qaeda-inspired attack on the headquarters of *Charlie Hebdo* in Paris in January 2015. Kermiche suddenly severed ties to many of his friends and, seemingly identifying with the Kouachi brothers, turned to the internet, where he set about developing relationships with Islamist extremists.

Contributing to his radicalization, Kermiche encountered a twenty-six-year-old man at a local mosque one month later, an extremist who "turned his brain" ("tourné le cerveau"), in the words of Christophe Conevin.[29] The man disappeared soon afterward only to resurface a little later in a Syrian-Iraqi combat zone. Adel Bouauon was his name, although he would use Kermiche's name and French identification card at the Syrian border. Alerted to this turn of events, French authorities began keeping tabs on both Bouauon and Kermiche.

Also between January and March of 2015, Kermiche, who adopted the *nom de guerre* Abul Jaleel al-Hanafi at this juncture, wed numerous girls, pious young Muslims, then repudiated each marriage a few days later. In one case, he married a fifteen-year-old girl over the phone in a ten-minute ceremony that included an imam and two witnesses. One of his ex-wives proceeded to become a member of the all-female terrorist cell that was discussed earlier, the one that the aforementioned Rachid Kassim, the virtual planner in Syria, had organized and that had as its mission the car-bombing near Notre Dame Cathedral.

It would be on March 23, 2015, that Kermiche made his first attempt to travel to Syria. Intercepted in Munich using his brother's passport and suspected of being en route to Syria to join the Islamic State, German authorities deported the seventeen-year-old back to France, where he was indicted and placed under the control of the courts. French authorities, while he awaited trial, put him on probation, but Kermiche violated it on May 11, 2015, when he again tried to travel to Syria.

In the course of this second attempt, officials in Turkey intercepted and deported him back to France. Along the way, he was held in Switzerland, where his mother granted an interview to a Swiss newspaper, *Tribune de Genève*. In it, she revealed that she previously had told French authorities about her son's alarming transformation. "He was bewitched," she said, "like he was in a cult."[30] In fact, Kermiche's family had requested that he be required to wear an electronic device so that the authorities could monitor his whereabouts. Yet this was not to be. By all accounts, Kermiche's mother, siblings, and friends tried diligently to rescue him from militant Islamism. "They gave him everything in material terms, in terms of love," said Annie Geslin, a colleague of the mother.[31] But the worry remained, with some convinced that tragedy lay ahead. "Everyone knew that kid was a time bomb" ("Tout le monde savait que ce gosse, c'était une bomb à retardement"), said Foued, an acquaintance.[32]

Upon his return to France, Kermiche was held for ten months in pre-trial detention for criminal conspiracy to commit terrorist acts. He later wrote on his Telegram channel that a sheikh he met during his confinement had strongly influenced him. As well, Kermiche expressed his desire to organize a terrorist cell in the Rouen area.[33]

In March of 2016, and against the strident protests of the prosecutor, the court made a fateful decision: it permitted Adel Kermiche to be released from detention and placed under house arrest instead. Despite the fact that he had a documented history of mental disturbance, was still in the grip of militant jihadism, had tried twice to travel to Syria, and had previously violated a parole agreement, the judge purportedly believed the teen's claim that he had learned his lesson. Supporting the court's decision, it was pointed out that Kermiche had conducted himself suitably while being held in detention. Maybe such good conduct should have been expected. "Detainees for terrorism all behave well and have a systematic practice of lying" ("Les détenus pour terrorisme se comportment tous bien et ont une partique systématique du mensonge"), said a high-ranking officer at the prison.[34]

Concerning the terms of his release, Kermiche was to wear an electronic surveillance device on his ankle during his stint of home confinement. Unlike those worn by sex offenders and other potential threats to the community, however, the one assigned to Kermiche would not contain a GPS locator. This meant that the authorities would be unable to pinpoint his location. The court also stipulated that Kermiche's device be deactivated on weekdays between 8:30 a.m. and 12:30 p.m., so that he could leave his home and move about freely in the community.

Returning to his family's home in Saint-Étienne-du-Rouvray, the would-be terrorist did not find his former friends and neighbors to be very welcoming. They had not been impressed by his dramatic conversion to militant jihadism or by his attempts to travel to the ISIS caliphate. Complaining that he only spoke about radical Islamism, his friends said he was fixated on jihadism and they found him tiresome as a result. Then too, they questioned his knowledge of the Koran, asserting that he was unable to cite a verse when asked. Still others thought he was mentally disturbed. "He was crazy, he was talking to himself, he would say anything" ("Il était fou, il parlait tout seul, il disait n'importe quoi"), recalled a neighbor.[35] One annoyed acquaintance even admitted that he wanted to punch Kermiche, but was afraid that the budding Islamist might actually have connections to ISIS, so he refrained.[36] Most disturbing, though, was an ominous assertion Kermiche made to a one-time friend only two months before the murder of Father Hamel. "He talked about the Koran and Mecca and he told me 'I'm going to attack a church,'" said the teen, who did not take the threat seriously.[37]

After the BRI commandos liquidated Kermiche outside the Church of St. Stephen, the local mosque refused to be involved with preparing his body, his funeral service, or his burial, stating that it would not do so even if his family requested it. "What this youth did was filthy, he's no longer part of the community" ("Ce qu'a fait ce jeune, c'est immonde, il ne fait plus partie de la communauté"), said twenty-five-year-old Khalid El Armani, a local Muslim.[38]

As for the family, friends, and acquaintances of Kermiche's accomplice in the attack, Abdel-Malik Petitjean, they too were dumbstruck by the slaying of Father Hamel. They could not imagine that Petitjean, who they knew as a gentle and genial soul, would be capable of taking part in such a heinous deed. Unlike Kermiche's personal history, Petitjean had been free of mental instability and misconduct.

Abdel-Malik Petitjean

It was into a family of Algerian immigrants that Petitjean was born on November 14, 1996. He lived most of his short life in the French town of Saint-Dié-des-Vosges near the German border, spending his last years with his mother and siblings in the spa town of Aix-les-Bans in southeastern France. A seemingly ordinary child, pleasant and sociable, he remained so well into his teens, when he became drawn to science fiction films and video games like other youths his age. In 2015, he graduated from a vocational school and thereafter held a part-time sales job and worked as an airport baggage handler.[39]

In terms of his religious beliefs, Petitjean was a Muslim. Not known to hold extreme political or religious convictions, he seldom spoke about ISIS, although one of his former friends said that Petitjean was put off by the organization. "He was not radical at all," said this companion.[40] Along the same lines, a staff member at the local mosque portrayed Petitjean as a normal youth, one who got along well with others and never created problems. "All the believers are shocked because he was known for his kindness, his calm," said Djamel Tazghat, the mosque's manager.[41]

It remains unknown when or how Petitjean's conversion to militant

Islamism occurred. In the summer of 2016, he told his mother that he was going to visit a family member in northeastern France, but he instead traveled to Turkey, a gateway to the Islamic State stronghold. On June 10, Turkish authorities spotted him speaking to a man who was on their country's no-fly list. And it was at this point, unfortunately, that counterterrorism agents dropped the ball.

Turkish officials promptly notified their French counterparts that Petitjean was preparing to leave Turkey for Syria. They could not detain him because he had not committed a crime. The next day, however, the teen inexplicably flew back to France. Yet again, Turkish officials contacted their French colleagues and notified them of this latest action. Yet French officials, for their part, would later claim that Turkey had waited over a week to inform them of Petitjean's travels and therefore they were unaware that he had returned to France. An inexcusable cockup, it was not unique. Turkish officials had already been grumbling about other nations' failures when sending or receiving timely information about terrorists and their activities. "This is exactly why we have been highlighting the importance of intelligence sharing," complained a senior Turkish official.[42]

Due to the confusion, French authorities were not on the lookout for Petitjean, believing him to be in the Middle East. The teen, who was now using the name Ibn Omar as his *nom de guerre*, had given them the slip. It would be a month later that he and Kermiche would team up for the bloodstained attack at the Church of St. Stephen.

Impaired Intelligence

Although French officials maintain that they were unaware of it when the attack was committed, the terrorist operation in Saint-Étienne-du-Rouvray appears to have involved a cyberplanner in Syria. Certainly Adel Kermiche was active in the cybersphere prior to the assault, most notably on the Telegram app.

On a private forum on July 19, 2016, one week before the murder of Father Hamel, Kermiche posted an audio message in which he discussed the obstacles he encountered when trying to enter Syria and, by extension, the need for would-be terrorists to remain in their own countries and carry out attacks on the home front. He further noted the ease of doing so. "You take a knife, you go in a church, you cause carnage … you cut two or three heads and there you are, it's done," said Kermiche.[43]

The next day, he posted another audio message. Apologizing to ISIS, he explained that, until a week earlier, he had been opposed to the Islamic State. And it is true, he had argued against it on his Telegram channel, favoring al-Qaeda instead. At this point, however, Kermiche was declaring that his disdain for ISIS was behind him and that he was ready to act on its behalf.

Finally, one day before the attack, he returned to his Telegram channel and announced that "big stuff" ("des gros trucs") was about to occur, according to researcher Kyle Orton.[44] And at 8:30 a.m. on the morning of the assault, he posted his last message. "Download what is about to happen and share it en masse!!!!!" he wrote.[45]

Shortly after the murder of Father Hamel, officials announced that, just then, they had accessed and scrutinized Kermiche and Petitjean's internet activity, as well as that of the attackers' circles of friends. The upshot: police in the ensuing days and weeks would take into custody a handful of suspects, among them Farid K., a thirty-year-old cousin of Petitjean. "Farid knew very well … of his cousin's impending plans for violence," said a statement from the prosecutor's office, while conceding that he may not have known "the exact place or time."[46] Farid was placed in preventive detention on the grounds that he had been associating with terrorists with an eye toward participating in an act of political violence himself.

Another of those arrested was a twenty-one-year-old man who had traveled from Toulouse to Saint-Étienne-du-Rouvray so that he could be on hand while Kermiche and Petitjean were preparing to unleash their rage at the Church of St. Stephen. After making the 500-mile journey, the suspect stayed in the Normandy town on July 24 and July 25, leaving after the murder the next day. It had been on Telegram that this man communicated with Kermiche and Petitjean in the days leading up to the assault, thus confirming that fellow ISIS sympathizers in France did indeed have advance knowledge of the terrorists' scheme and perhaps played supportive roles in it. A crucial figure in the operation, however, was not in France but in Islamic State territory. It was Rachid Kassim, who was discussed at the outset of this chapter.

A week after the murder of Father Hamel, an unidentified man accessed Adel Kermiche's page on Telegram—presumably, Kermiche had provided this person with the password—and on it he posted an audio message in which he praised Petitjean and Kermiche for their lethal deeds. Shortly thereafter, this man's identity became known to the public when *L'Express* published an article about Rachid Kassim. In it, reporters revealed that it was his voice on Kermiche's Telegram channel.[47] And there was more. "(A)ccording to the [materials] collected by *L'Express*," wrote the authors, "Rachid Kassim is suspected, if not to be a sponsor, of having exercised at least a virtual influence in the acting out of the two young killers" ("[S]elon les éléments recueillis par *L'Express*, Rachid Kassim est suspecté, sinon d'être un commanditaire, d'avoir exercé au minimum une influence virtuelle dans le passage à l'acte des deux jeunes tueurs").[48] At the time of the *L'Express* article, the precise nature of the alliance among Kassim, Kermiche, and Petitjean was unclear, although investigators determined that the three of them had been conversing on Telegram.

Within a few weeks, analyses of communications obtained from the computer of Petitjean's sister suggested that Kassim had played a formative role.[49] "It is suspected that the two were put into contact with one another by Kassim, who is believed to have orchestrated the attack remotely," reported the Counter Extremism Project.[50] After Kassim introduced the pair, Petitjean contacted Kermiche on Chatogram, an encrypted app associated with Telegram, on the night of July 21–22, 2016. In their terse conversations, Kermiche asked Petitjean if he was hot. "Yes, boiling" ("Oui, bouillant"), replied Petitjean.[51] The pair thereafter discussed such matters as weaponry and transportation, with Petitjean agreeing to travel to Normandy to carry out the assault. It would be on July 23 in Saint-Étienne-du-Rouvray that the two assailants, for the first time, would meet face to face.

Regarding Rachid Kassim, while he was instrumental in teaming up the two terrorists, the details of the mission may have been left up to Kermiche and Petitjean themselves. In the virtual planning model, such leeway is sometimes extended, since the terrorists "on the ground" may be more knowledgeable than a distant cybercoach about their particular communities and therefore in a better position to make certain types of operational decisions. It further appears that ISIS did not provide any financial support, not even travel funds, nor did it furnish or make arrangements for weaponry. In all, then, it seems to have been a dyad operation set in motion by a handler in the Islamic State.

In the wake of the carnage at the Church of St. Stephen, the people of France were dismayed to learn about what appeared to be serious failures by the intelligence and law enforcement communities in preventing the incident. They discovered, for instance, that Abdel-Malik Petitjean, as noted earlier in the chapter, had tried to travel to Syria six weeks before the assault in Saint-Étienne-du-Rouvray, and that French intelligence officials did not know that he had returned to France; this, despite the fact that their counterparts in Turkey had notified them. Also, the public learned that both Kermiche and Petitjean had been on their nation's "fiche S," the national security watch list, and should have been under heightened scrutiny. Of course, with 20,000 individuals on the list, 4,000 of whom are considered dangerous, it was no doubt difficult to effectively monitor all of them, all of the time.

It was equally disconcerting for the French people to discover that a formal warning had been dispatched by the nation's anti-terrorism police, the UCLAT, four days before the onslaught at the place of worship.

On July 22, UCLAT, an acronym for "Unité de Coordination de la Lutte Anti-Terroriste" ("Coordination Unite of the Struggle Against Terrorism"), sent an alert to selected police precincts. Containing a photo of Abdel-Malik Petitjean, it identified him as an extremist who "could already be present in France and act alone or with other individuals" in perpetrating a terrorist attack.[52] Petitjean's name was not provided in the notice because the source of the tip-off, a foreign intelligence agency, was not privy to it, and French authorities did not recognize him. Since the image was not shared with the public, the aspiring terrorist's identity remained unknown to law enforcement officials until after the savage assault.

Perhaps the most glaring lapse, though, was the decision to release Kermiche from prison and place him on home confinement. In light of his long history of mental and behavioral instability as well as his recent legal history, one that included a parole violation, the court's decision was, to many, unfathomable. Among those who were flummoxed was François Heisbourg, a special advisor at the Fondation pour la Recherche Stratégique in Paris. "In my worst nightmares I didn't imagine that we would actually let loose an individual on furlough who would not be tracked by legitimate intelligence-gathering while he was condemned for terror-related activities with well-established radical credentials," said Heisbourg.[53]

Disturbing, too, was a subsequent exposé by Mediapart, the French online investigative journal, which revealed that an agent working for the Paris Police Prefecture Intelligence Unit had managed to tap into Kermiche's encrypted Telegram channel five days before the attack on the church. On Kermiche's page, which had 200 followers, the terrorist used the online moniker "@Jayyed," and claimed that he gave lessons at a mosque in the town of Saint-Étienne-du-Rouvray. Of course, this disclosure more or less revealed his general location. It was also on this page that Kermiche posted his ominous statement about attacking a church, a statement that was recounted earlier in this chapter ("You take a knife, you go in a church, you cause carnage ... you cut two or three heads and there you are, it's done.")

So it was that the vigilant agent in Paris alerted his superiors to what might well be a forthcoming attack on a church in or near Saint-Étienne-du-Rouvray. And he didn't stop there. The agent further advised them to contact the General Directorate for Interior Security, the French intelligence organization that specializes in counterterrorism, surveils threatening individuals and groups, and detects illegal cyber activity. Surprisingly, however, the agent's superiors did not follow through on his alarming report. In fact, it was only after Father Hamel was murdered that they finally took action, and it was self-serving. Revealing Kermiche's Telegram messages following the attack, officials claimed—falsely—that they had just acquired them. Moreover, they reportedly expected the Parisian agent to collaborate in a cover-up. "Officers cited by Mediapart said that after the murder, the agent was asked to post-date his notes and erase his computer's browser history to ensure that the blunder went unnoticed," writes Henry Samuel.[54] Rightly, Mediapart's exposé would lead to an investigation.

Additional inquiries and investigations were also conducted after the terrorist strike in Saint-Étienne-du-Rouvray, with the debate about the French government's ability, or inability, to protect the public picking up more steam. While numerous figures railed against what appeared to be the sloppiness of the various agencies in handling the threat posed by Kermiche and Petitjean, others highlighted the virtual impossibility of monitoring all of the thousands of potential terrorists in France. And whereas there were enhanced calls for restricting the rights of those who might conceivably commit terrorist acts, other voices insisted that France must respect and protect civil liberties, that it must refrain from suppressing the freedoms of the citizenry. "We can't give up on the rule of law in order to protect the rule of law," declared Interior Minister Bernard Cazeneuve.[55]

Even as François Hollande's government continued to be a magnet for scathing criticism owing to its seeming inability to safeguard the public, the French president would, within three days of the killing of Father Hamel, announce a plan that would bring into existence a new protective measure. In reality, it would be the re-institution of a very old one.

At the outset of the French Revolution in 1789, the nation formed a militia, the French National Guard. Disbanded in 1827, it was resurrected between 1831 and 1872. And it would be on October 12, 2016, that it would officially come alive for the third time, the catalyst being the threat that contemporary terrorism posed to the French people. Comprised of a combination of existing reserve forces, the measure was met with widespread approval, which is not surprising: both the military and the public, Parisians most of all, had been calling for such an entity since the massacre at *Charlie Hebdo* the previous year. "In the face of this threat that has never been greater in France and Europe, the government is absolutely determined [to defeat] terrorism," Hollande said.[56]

On the subject of Father Hamel, Pope Francis held a Mass for him on September 14, 2016. In the course of the ceremony, the pontiff pointed to a crucial moment during Father Hamel's slaying that he felt illustrated the battle between good and evil. "(I)n this man who accepted his martyrdom there, with the martyrdom of Christ, at the altar," said Pope Francis, "there is one thing that causes me to reflect a great deal: in the midst of the difficult moment that he experienced, in the midst also of this tragedy that he saw approaching, this gentle man, this good man, this man who strove for brotherhood, did not lose his clarity of thought and clearly said the name of the murderer, he said it very clearly: 'Be gone, Satan!'"[57]

The pontiff further announced that Father Hamel was to be considered for sainthood. Subsequent to this, it was decided that the case for canonization would be expedited, and, owing to the nature of Father Hamel's death, would likely proceed unimpeded. "Saints typically must be attributed with performing miracles in order to become canonized, but Hamel may manage to avoid that obstacle altogether because he died a martyr for the church," wrote Andrew Blake.[58]

As for the Church of Saint Stephen, it reopened on October 2, 2016, with a special penitential Mass, one that both Christians and local Muslims attended. The latter, who had long adored Father Hamel, were visibly grief-stricken. Besides honoring the late priest, the ceremony was also aimed at rectifying the terrorists' desecration of the church itself, Kermiche and Petitjean having committed their deplorable acts at the altar in the sanctuary, places of purity and safety in the Catholic faith. The Archbishop of Rouen, Dominique Lebrun, further made it known that the two terrorists had destroyed a cross, the symbol of Christ's crucifixion and resurrection. "The penitential rite," said Lebrun, who performed the cleaning ceremony, "symbolizes God's pardon through the gesture of sprinkling holy water on the walls, altar and the floor of the church at the place where Fr Hamel was killed and finally on the whole assembly."[59]

As of 2019, French authorities were still investigating the terrorist attack that was committed at the Church of St. Stephen. Most of all, they were continuing to explore whether Adel Kermiche and Abdel-Malik Petitjean had the help of accomplices in their deadly mission, as well as the extent to which Rachid Kassim, and thus ISIS, was directly involved in the operation. At this point, it appears that the truth may never be fully known.

11

Insanity by the Sea
The Bastille Day Ramming Attack

"I left the city, and I'm living in the Canary Islands now."[1] These were the words of Emilie Bromley, a woman who, no fault of her own, found herself at the scene of the second bloodiest terrorist attack on French soil. Carried out by one man, the monstrous assault targeted a spot along the Côte d'Azur packed with tens of thousands of men, women, and children on holiday. Besides the staggering death toll, it was an act of violence that resulted in an extension of President François Hollande's state of emergency, the one that the French leader had declared eight months earlier in the wake of the ISIS massacres at the Bataclan Theatre, the Stade de France, and a café district of Paris. As for the man who committed the atrocity, his name was Mohamed Lahouaiej-Bouhlel and he was thirty-one years old.

It was in the city of M'saken, in northeastern Tunisia, that Lahouaiej-Bouhlel was born on January 3, 1985. Because his father was a property owner and a livestock trader, the family of twelve was both financially secure and respected in the community. That said, its affluence and social standing did not always translate into a peaceful home life for young Lahouaiej-Bouhlel, according to his own accounts. "He told me at least three times that his father was mean to him," recalled a man who knew Lahouaiej-Bouhlel in adulthood.[2] Whatever the case, one point on which several people in M'saken concur is that Lahouaiej-Bouhlel was a volatile youth, one who was difficult for his parents to manage.

Hot-tempered and defiant as a boy, he was known to attack other children, an aggressiveness that persisted throughout his adolescence and reached its apex when he was between seventeen and nineteen years of age. "(H)e became angry, he shouted, he broke everything he found in front of him," recalled his father.[3]

Also during adolescence, Lahouaiej-Bouhlel appeared to be despondent much of the time and withdrew from others, unusual behavior for a youth and perhaps part of the reason that some saw him as aloof. "He didn't talk with all of the other young guys in the neighborhood," said one of his cousins, who claimed that Lahouaiej-Bouhlel was conceited.[4]

Due to his progressively more destructive outbursts, Lahouaiej-Bouhlel was booted out of the family home briefly when he was sixteen years old, and later, when he was nineteen, his father took him to a psychiatrist for an evaluation. The results suggested that young Lahouaiej-Bouhlel was in the early stages of a psychotic disorder. "He wasn't someone living in the real world," said the doctor who examined him.[5] At this juncture—the year was 2004—the psychiatrist prescribed antipsychotic and antidepressant medications, together with an anxiolytic for anxiety.

In terms of Lahouaiej-Bouhlel's education, he was a capable student during his high school years even in the face of the psychological problems he was experiencing. And he had hopes for the future. After graduating, he wished to pursue a college education abroad, but this was not to be. It seems that his father refused to finance Lahouaiej-Bouhlel's foreign studies, the family's prosperity notwithstanding, with the decision widening the gulf between the pair.[6] But although Lahouaiej-Bouhlel was frustrated by not being in a position to study abroad, he was not deterred, and soon he hatched an alternate plan.

Several months later, in 2005, he departed for Nice on the Côte d'Azur, the sunny French city being home to over 40,000 Tunisian immigrants. This included a tight-knit community from M'saken. Lahouaiej-Bouhlel's first cousin, a Tunisia-born woman by the name of Hajer Khalfallah, had also settled in Nice, and it may have been her presence in the city both as a relative and a French citizen that attracted him to it.[7] Whatever the case, the two tied the knot a few months after his arrival, and he was granted a residency permit due to his wife's citizenship status. Subsequent to this, the couple moved into a public-housing apartment in a northern district of the city, and over the course of the next decade formed a family of five.

From the start, religious differences were evident in the pair, but the disparities do not appear to have comprised a significant problem. Hajer was a practicing Muslim who dressed in a traditional hijab, while Lahouaiej-Bouhlel, even though he had been born into a Muslim family, had never been a religious man. Attesting to this fact, those in his hometown of M'saken could not remember having seen him in a mosque, a lack of interest in Islam that carried over to his years in Nice.

Here, in the seaside city, Lahouaiej-Bouhlel quickly came to be regarded as a notorious flirt, a handsome man who was narcissistic and self-absorbed. Considered by many locals to be a "gym rat," he spent much of his free time working out in health clubs. It was a passion for bodybuilding that he had long nurtured. Indeed, while undergoing the aforementioned psychiatric evaluation in Tunisia, Lahouaiej-Bouhlel told his doctor that he felt unattractive, even ugly, and for this reason planned to build up his body.[8] And sure enough, Lahouaiej-Bouhlel spent the ensuing years honing his physique, all the while making sure to flaunt his progress to those around him. And bodybuilding was not the only thing he relished.

Unlike observant Muslims, Lahouaiej-Bouhlel enjoyed pork, alcohol, recreational drugs, and a prolific extramarital sex life. There were also suggestions that he was aroused by rough sex, and that he may have been a "gentleman for hire," or male escort. "Some in Nice knew the man as one of the many playboy predators the city seems to beget—black hair slicked back off a shining brow, dress shoes tapering to varnished points, a dark shirt unbuttoned low to reveal the pectorals into which he had obsessively, unblushingly, invested himself," writes journalist Scott Sayare.[9] It was an image that would remain attached to Lahouaiej-Bouhlel throughout his time on the Côte d'Azur.

Among those widely rumored to be one of his patrons was Roger, an openly gay man in his seventies whom Lahouaiej-Bouhlel met at a health club. This man has asserted, however, that the two of them were not sexually intimate, that although he had made overtures toward Lahouaiej-Bouhlel, the younger man only sought companionship from from.[10] Roger further explained that he was a father figure to Lahouaiej-Bouhlel and his wife; an older, platonic friend who intervened when their relationship encountered rough waters. In this regard, Roger's presence may have been beneficial, since the married couple evidently spent quite a bit of time in such waters. In addition, Lahouaiej-Bouhlel found himself in turmoil outside the home as well.

In 2010, for instance, he took a position as a delivery truck driver for a beverage company, but soon began having difficulties on the job. For one thing, he fell asleep while driving. For another, his behavior brought complaints from the company's clients, who were put off by his swagger and braggadocio. But it would be during a company Christmas party in 2011 that Lahouaiej-Bouhlel's offensive behavior reached a flashpoint, a party following which both the waiters and waitresses complained that he had been sexually inappropriate toward them. Of course, this turn of events embarrassed the company, as well as bringing into view Lahouaiej-Bouhlel's sexual compulsiveness. When confronted, he denied the servers' allegations, while insisting that he was not sexually attracted to other men. All the same, the company terminated his employment, which provoked a fiery reaction and prompted the police to escort him off the premises.

During the same period, Lahouaiej-Bouhlel's marriage became marred by violence. While he had never shown much affection for his spouse or their children, he had now taken to hitting them. He even assaulted his mother-in-law at one point. The consequence of his violence: law enforcement was contacted repeatedly, according to François Molins, the magistrate and anti-terror prosecutor.[11] Moreover, as Lahouaiej-Bouhlel's home life deteriorated and his job prospects dwindled, he added other types of crime to his repertoire. "(T)hreats, violence, theft and acts of criminal damage," says Molins, were among the offenses listed on the rap sheet that Lahouaiej-Bouhlel acquired starting in 2010.[12] On the other hand, one set of illicit behaviors that he did not exhibit, at least publicly, was an affinity for militant Islamism.

While his marriage was falling apart—and while he was still living in the family apartment and battering his wife and children—Lahouaiej-Bouhlel complained to friends that his spouse, Hajer, had become disinterested in being intimate with him. Presumably, it was on this pretext that he began taking dance lessons. Attending classes several nights a week, he practiced the salsa and seduced the female students, many of whom found him genuinely appealing, if sexually preoccupied.

At home, meanwhile, Lahouaiej-Bouhlel's hostile actions toward his family grew steadily worse and more peculiar. Once, when Hajer left the apartment without his consent, he stabbed one of their children's teddy bears and ripped out the filling. On another occasion, he poured wine onto Hajer's face and urinated on her as she slept. He even defecated in their bed and smeared his feces on the walls. And while Hajer suspected that Lahouaiej-Bouhlel was subjecting her to these abuses in the hope that she would leave him, his bizarre actions also suggest a progressive mental illness.[13] In due course, Lahouaiej-Bouhlel did in fact move out of the apartment, and the couple thereafter pursued a divorce.

Nearly destitute by this point, Lahouaiej-Bouhlel relocated to a small flat in eastern Nice, where people found him daunting. "Neighbors … described him as a moody and aggressive oddball who never went to mosque," reported the *New York Times*.[14] Unfortunately, his physical outbursts persisted.

In January 2016, police arrested Lahouaiej-Bouhlel when his behavior careened out of control in public. It happened when a man complained aloud to Lahouaiej-Bouhlel that the latter's delivery truck was blocking traffic. Enraged, Lahouaiej-Bouhlel beat the man with a plank of wood wrenched from a shipping pallet. Three months later, a court convicted Lahouaiej-Bouhlel of assault and handed down a six-month sentence, but the sentence was suspended. Curiously, the court did not order him to undergo a mental health evaluation despite the numerous reports of domestic violence and now an assault on the streets of Paris. Had it done so, it may have helped prevent him from committing far greater violence in the very near future.

By summer, the future terrorist was no longer working full-time, having taken an extended vacation. It was a stint during which he spent his days riding his blue bicycle through the city. Also during this period, those who knew him noticed that Lahouaiej-Bouhlel appeared to be consumed by radical Islamism, abruptly growing a beard for religious reasons and listening to daily recitations of the Koran—at full volume on YouTube— in his sparsely furnished flat. Then too, he phoned and texted friends and acquaintances with aggravating frequency, confounding them at times with messages that made little sense. In short, his mental organization appeared to be fragmenting.

Ominously, it was at this juncture that Lahouaiej-Bouhlel sent a substantial sum of money—$150,000—to his family in Tunisia, the source of which was unclear as was the reason for the financial gift itself. Furthermore, it was a largesse that he dispensed illegally. "He gave cash to people he knew who were returning to our village and asked them to give it to the family," said his brother.[15] Lahouaiej-Bouhlel, it seems, knew he would never see these loved ones again.

Murder on the Esplanade

A few days later, Bastille Day arrived. Known in France as La Fête Nationale (The National Festival) or Le 14 Juillet (The Fourteenth of July), it marks the first major insurgency of the French Revolution and is celebrated throughout the country. In 2016, unfortunately, Lahouaiej-Bouhlel had his own plans for the French celebration, and they did not involve a demonstration of national pride. More the opposite: he plotted to target those who would gather to revel in the spectacular celebration that the city of Nice staged annually, a series of events that have long drawn both local residents and European tourists to this lush spot on the French Riviera. This year, the activities would include a concert, a parade, and, as the highlight of the festivities, a dazzling fireworks display over the sea.

As it happened, the holiday fell on a Thursday, a bright and warm one, and Lahouaiej-Bouhlel made the most of it. At midday, he dropped in on an aunt and uncle who lived in the city, and together they enjoyed a light meal. In addition, he visited the renowned esplanade by the sea, the Promenade des Anglais, where he snapped photos of himself in front of military vehicles.[16] Earlier, he had told his aunt that he planned to watch the fireworks exhibition from this vantage point.

Over four miles long, a generous segment of the Promenade des Anglais is lined with palm trees and arcs along the city's beaches. Sightseers, bicyclists, and skateboarders enjoy the breezy walkway, one that dates back nearly 200 years. Local families flock to it too, as would be the case on La Fête Nationale, when 30,000 people would gather to share in the excitement of the pyrotechnic display scheduled for 10:00 p.m. And while brief surges of rain had passed through on this spirited holiday, bouts that the crowds welcomed during the otherwise balmy month of July, the skies would clear in time for the fireworks.

After sundown, Mohamed Lahouaiej-Bouhlel peddled his bicycle to Auriol, a neighborhood in eastern Nice, where previously he had parked a white vehicle. A large, twenty-one-ton cargo truck, the Renault Premium was fitted to transport perishable items, such as frozen foods. He had rented it three days earlier in the nearby town of Saint-Laurent-du-Var. Stowing his bicycle inside the vehicle, surveillance footage would show that Lahouaiej-Bouhlel next drove to a neighborhood in Nice known as Magnan, located just north of the Promenade des Anglais, and waited. Meanwhile, a public party dubbed "The Prom" was in full swing on the esplanade, with bands blasting music and revelers dancing on the thirty-foot wide walkway. Then, right on schedule, fireworks lit up the night sky and the crowd exploded into cheers.

At 10:32 p.m., after the exhibition had reached its zenith, the throng of spectators left the coastline and began meandering back across the esplanade toward the city. And it was at this moment that Lahouaiej-Bouhlel made his move. Beginning at a thoroughfare a few blocks west of the crowd, he drove the cargo truck slowly along the Promenade des Anglais.

The first police officer to recognize what was happening was Christophe, a brawny veteran of the French military.[17] Calling in the incident at 10:33 p.m., Christophe and two other municipal officers set out to pursue the truck in a patrol car. Because they were in danger of running over pedestrians, however, the police had no choice but to suspend the chase.

When Lahouaiej-Bouhlel reached a checkpoint near the entrance to the pedestrian walkway, he veered onto it and turned off the truck's headlights. Although barriers separated the esplanade from vehicular traffic, they were of the steel variety. They were not made of concrete, the sort used at military installations and embassies, which vehicles can neither crush nor knock down.

Once he had circumvented the structures, Lahouaiej-Bouhlel drove over two people and was heading toward thousands more. Ambling along in the moonlight, these people, countless families among them, were unaware that a large truck was racing toward them. Suddenly, a loud popping sound erupted, which for many pedestrians was the first indication that anything was amiss. And whereas some mistook the cracking noise to be that of belated fireworks, those in Lahouaiej-Bouhlel's vicinity realized that the sound was coming from the wooden benches on the Promenade that were splintering and bursting as the vehicle plowed over them.

11. Insanity by the Sea

At this point, Lahouaiej-Bouhlel sped up to an estimated forty miles per hour, but as his lethal rampage progressed, he would accelerate even more. "I saw him—*bam, bam, bam*—hitting people," said a Canadian photographer.[18] Like other onlookers, the photographer assumed that the truck's brakes had failed, and that he was witnessing was a dreadful accident.

Another pedestrian, a British woman, glimpsed the truck's hood and bumper as the vehicle sped in her direction. "It had people on the front about to go under it," she recalled, "and then it went straight past with all these bodies on the [ground]."[19]

As Lahouaiej-Bouhlel cut a deadly swath through the throng, zigzagging left and right so as to slam into those straining to evade his path, a handful of bystanders at different points along the street and walkway tried to stop him. Among such courageous individuals was Franck, a forty-eight-year-old man on a motor scooter who has asked that his full name not be made public. In an account published by the *New York Times*, Franck reportedly drove alongside the refrigerator truck and succeeded in ramming it, but then he bounced off of it.[20] Scrambling to his feet, he sprinted back to the vehicle, climbed onto its running board, and attempted to open the driver's door. Unable to do so, he began hitting Lahouaiej-Bouhlel through the open window, prompting the latter to try to shoot him. Fortunately for Franck, Lahouaiej-Bouhlel's pistol failed to fire, but the terrorist did manage to strike Franck in the head with it, a blow that knocked the courageous civilian to the ground. A valiant effort, the City of Nice subsequently decorated Franck for his heroism, an act of bravery that cost him a broken rib and a back injury. Although he had been unable to stop Lahouaiej-Bouhlel's rampage, Franck took solace in the fact that his struggle with the assailant had momentarily prevented further deaths. "He was concentrating on me," said Franck. "In that moment he could not kill people."[21]

Two other men likewise tried to halt the terrorist's slaughter. One was Gwenaël Leriche, who, armed only with a pocket knife, attempted to enter the truck's cab and incapacitate Lahouaiej-Bouhlel. The other was Alexander Migues, who pursued the truck on his bicycle. Like Franck, both men were honored by city officials.[22]

As Lahouaiej-Bouhlel continued hurtling along the Promenade des Anglais, onlookers heard the shrieks of victims and the thuds of bodies glancing off the truck. "I saw bodies flying like bowling pins in its path," said journalist Damien Allemand.[23] Other casualties were dragged underneath the vehicle and mangled. As the macabre spectacle was unfolding, Lahouaiej-Bouhlel was observed to be grinning.[24]

Contributing to the madness, thousands of pedestrians, many of whom were visitors from other European nations, were unable to understand the warnings and panicked explanations of those around them due to language barriers. Then too, the refrigerator truck was travelling faster than those trying to outrun it, meaning that the vehicle had a marked advantage. And owing to its erratic course, those hoping to dodge the truck's path did not know in which direction to flee. "People were jumping into the sea to get away from the killing," said one eyewitness.[25] So it was that the darkness, the jumble of languages, and the unreality of the attack itself caused the potential victims to run with abandon, slamming into baby strollers and trampling children and the elderly.

As Lahouaiej-Bouhlel passed in front of the posh Negresco Hotel, he grabbed his revolver and fired off three rounds at law enforcement officers. Returning fire, the officers took off on foot, pursuing the cargo truck roughly 300 yards to a spot near another hotel and casino, the Palais de la Méditerranée (Hyatt Regency). It was at this location that Lahouaiej-Bouhlel, with little choice, began braking. Horribly, bodies had become tangled in the truck's axles, one tire was nearly flat, and the front bumper and hood had been torn off by the force of the bodies slamming into them. Sputtering, the truck slowed, then crawled, and finally sat idling. Here, in front of the Hyatt, the area was deserted except for a smattering of survivors hovering over their loved ones who lay injured or dead.

Lahouaiej-Bouhlel was now sitting behind the wheel of the motionless truck when a man, a civilian, suddenly materialized and tried to pummel him through the window. Lahouaiej-Bouhlel grabbed his pistol and fired at him, causing the man to lose his balance and tumble to the ground. Again, Lahouaiej-Bouhlel shot at him, but missed.

A small number of police officers now rushed to the vehicle and leapt into action. Without pausing to negotiate, they sprayed the cab with bullets, which Lahouaiej-Bouhlel tried to avoid by throwing himself across the passenger's seat. It was a pointless maneuver. A female officer who had stationed herself just outside the passenger door raised her firearm above her head and, aiming it down into cab, squeezed off eight rounds.[26] It was the end of the terrorist attack. The police had shot Lahouaiej-Bouhlel a total of sixteen times, leaving twenty-five bullet holes in windshield.

As the terrorist lay dead in his truck, experts began checking the vehicle for explosives. It was a realistic concern in light of the circumstances. In the end, their search did not uncover an incendiary device, but they did find Lahouaiej-Bouhlel's pistol, along with an imitation hand grenade and two plastic M16s. They also retrieved his cellphone, credit cards, driver's license, and identification card.

Meanwhile, survivors returned to the Promenade to hunt for their friends and loved ones. Casualties were strewn for over a mile, and the

11. Insanity by the Sea 175

carnage was unfathomable. "People were disemboweled, stripped naked of their clothes, mothers sprawled on the [ground] next to their dead children," said a British attorney vacationing in Nice.[27] It was a panorama of hell, far too much for survivors to absorb. "I saw one woman lying on the ground talking to her dead child," said another witness.[28] Others tried to prevent their surviving sons and daughters from being further traumatized by the grisly aftermath. "(A) dad had a toddler in his arms and had buried his face in his T-shirt for him not to see anything," said a fellow survivor at the scene.[29] In the coming hours, the trauma would persist as scores of the injured and maimed, teetering on the edge of life, were transported to local hospitals. Hotel Negresco, which Lahouaiej-Bouhlel has passed during his rampage, served as one the emergency triage sites, while the nearby Lenval Children's Hospital (Fondation Lenval Hôpital pour Enfants), treated scores of young casualties on this surreal evening.

In all, 434 people of all ages were wounded in the vehicle ramming attack.[30] A total of eighty-six people, many of them children and teens, died from their injuries.[31] Over 30 percent of those whom Lahouaiej-Bouhlel killed were Muslims, according to the Union of Muslims of the Alpes-Maritimes.[32] And nineteen different nations counted their own citizens among the fatalities.[33] "Terror basically aims at the whole society and at its freedom," said the president of a local French-Moroccan organization.[34] To be sure, Lahouaiej-Bouhlel had targeted a wide swath of the European community in this latest terrorist action.

At 4:00 a.m. on July 15, 2016—it was five and half hours after the attack—President François Hollande stood at the podium in the Élysée Palace and made a televised statement about the heinous incident. The French leader had just returned to Paris from Avignon to mourn the dead and reassure the public in the face of yet another terrorist atrocity on French soil. It was becoming a recurrent event.

In the Nice case, however, the attack presented law enforcement and counterterrorism experts with a new worry: the weaponization of vehicles. "You have to have a driver's license and that's it," says William McCants of the Brookings Institution about the requirement to obtain a vehicle.[35] As could be expected, the ease and effectiveness of Lahouaiej-Bouhlel's method would not go unnoticed by those seeking to inflict maximum damage on an unsuspecting public. In the ensuing months, vehicle ramming attacks were carried out in such diverse cities as London, Stockholm, Jerusalem, Berlin, Barcelona, and even Columbus, Ohio. In some of these episodes, ISIS claimed responsibility, as it did two days after Lahouaiej-Bouhlel's attack on the French Riviera. Declaring him to be a soldier, a statement on ISIS's propaganda and news source, Amaq, stated that he had answered the organization's call to target civilians in those nations fighting against the

Islamic State. The ISIS proclamation notwithstanding, the authorities did not believe that Lahouaiej-Bouhlel was associated with the organization or, for that matter, that he had been in contact with extremist individuals in France or elsewhere. Instead, he was thought to be emblematic of the mentally disturbed lone actor.

The Investigation

Within 24 hours, officials confirmed Lahouaiej-Bouhlel's identity, his fingerprints supporting the information on the identification documents he had left behind in the cargo truck. As stated earlier, the authorities were initially working under the assumption that he was a lone actor unaffiliated with a domestic or international terrorist outfit. Even though Lahouaiej-Bouhlel had a criminal record, his past offenses had been limited to assault, threats of assault, property damage, and theft. Violent acts stemming from political or religious ideologies were not on his rap sheet, and for this reason he was not a *fiche S* individual; that is, someone listed on France's national security watchlist.

While the nation was grieving during the seven days that followed the Nice attack, European and U.S. law enforcement and intelligence were vigorously examining Lahouaiej-Bouhlel's financial dealings, social media presence, cellphone texts, voicemails, images, and email messages. The result was a bounty of information. When François Molins, the Paris-based anti-terror prosecutor, updated the public on the inquiry on July 21, 2016, his revelations were at once surprising and unsettling. "The investigation since the night of July 14 has ... allowed us not only to confirm again the premeditated nature of Mohamed Labouaiej-Bouhlel's deadly act," Molins said, "but also to establish that he benefited from support and had accomplices in the preparation and carrying out of his criminal act."[36]

As so often happens in such cases, investigators retrieved unrelated, but nevertheless edifying, material on Labouaiej-Bouhlel's cellphone and computer, such as his communications with the men and women he picked up on dating websites. Besides their messages, he had saved photos and video clips of these past sex partners. More relevant to the investigation, however, was a trove of electronic communications, hundreds of them, to and from a handful of people who appeared to be collaborators in his terror plot. Furthermore, the messages suggested that the authorities and the media had been wrong: Labouaiej-Bouhlel's radicalization had been neither recent nor sudden. Rather, he had been flirting with jihadism and terrorism a year prior to his actions on the Promenade des Anglais.

While this discovery was instrumental in furthering the inquiry,

11. Insanity by the Sea

it also caused consternation in certain quarters. First and foremost, it re-focused public attention on France's counterterrorism apparatus, which was already the target of intense criticism owing to its perceived failure to detect and thwart previous terrorist operations. The *Wall Street Journal* summed up the situation thusly: "The disclosures raise the possibility that Lahouaiej-Bouhlel and his suspected accomplices were part of a broader jihadist group that went undetected, in what would be another security failing by French authorities after two major terror attacks over the past 18 months."[37] Within days, government agencies and political factions within France were sparring once again, hurling blame and demanding change.

Regarding the materials unearthed during the inquiry, the earliest message with significance to the case had been sent nearly nineteen months before the Nice attack. The date was January 10, 2015, three days after the al-Qaeda-affiliated massacre at *Charlie Hebdo* headquarters in Paris, when a grieving public was expressing its solidarity with the satirical magazine's victims by declaring, "Je Suis Charlie," or "I am Charlie." It turned out that not everyone was sympathetic to the murdered staffers. A forty-year-old French-Tunisian man named Mohamed Oualid (Walid) Ghraieb sent a text message to Lahouaiej-Bouhlel, presumably his friend, expressing the inverse sentiment. "I am not Charlie" ("Je ne suis pas Charlie") wrote Ghraieb.[38] "Let them go get fucked and may God do even more to them" ("Qu'ils aillent se faire enculer et que Dieu leur ajoute plus que ça").[39]

When the authorities interrogated Ghraieb about his relationship with Lahouaiej-Bouhlel, he insisted they were not close friends and seldom spoke to one another. For that matter, he claimed that periods of up to six months elapsed without the two of them having any contact. What Ghraieb did not know is that the police were already in possession of both men's phone records, and these records indicated that he and Lahouaiej-Bouhlel had made contact by phone on 1,278 occasions between July 2015, and July 2016.[40]

Incriminating, too, were the photos Lahouaiej-Bouhlel saved on his cellphone. Dated July 11 and July 13, 2016—one to three days before the carnage on the Promenade des Anglais—Ghraieb and Lahouaiej-Bouhlel are shown standing beside the white cargo truck to be used in the killings. Under questioning, Ghraieb conceded that he had been a passenger in the vehicle mere days before the attack, and that Lahouaiej-Bouhlel had previously sent him information about the car rental agency from which he planned to rent the truck.

Equally damning, police retrieved a video that Ghraieb had recorded in the wake of the truck assault, one focusing on the casualties, rescue workers, and reporters at the scene. In the midst of the horrific scene, he also snapped a photograph of himself. To be sure, Ghraieb appeared to be entangled in the terror plot, an ultra-violent scheme that seems to have been under consideration for quite some time.

Lending support to this notion, fifteen months before the Nice operation, Lahouaiej-Bouhlel saved an article on his cellphone pertaining to a drug called Captagon. In light of his subsequent actions, the article was of interest to investigators because they knew that militant jihadists frequently used Captagon, an illegal stimulant, when preparing for, and carrying out, terrorist missions in Iraq and Syria. Presumably, Lahouaiej-Bouhlel had stored this information for future reference.

And there was more. Seven weeks later, in July 2015—exactly one year before the attack—Lahouaiej-Bouhlel attended La Fête Nationale festivities on the Promenade des Anglais, where he took in the annual fireworks display in the course of the holiday. He also photographed the events, with investigators highlighting the fact that Lahouaiej-Bouhlel pointed his lens mainly at the crowds. A month later, he would again photograph a large public gathering on the Promenade des Anglais.[41]

Furthermore, it was during this period that Lahouaiej-Bouhlel was busily communicating with a second man, Chokri Chafroud. A thirty-seven-year-old Tunisian citizen living in France, Chafroud was adamant that he was simply an acquaintance of Lahouaiej-Bouhlel; that they were not chummy and that their personal contact had been negligible. When investigators confronted Chafroud with the evidence they had recovered from Lahouaiej-Bouhlel's devices, however, he admitted trying to mislead them.

Certainly, the material they presented to him was formidable. Not only was Lahouaiej-Bouhlel using Chafroud's photograph as the background image on his cellphone, but the pair had also contacted each other more than 150 times during the one-year period culminating in the Nice attack. Then too, there was the telltale message that Chafroud had sent to Lahouaiej-Bouhlel on April 4, 2016. "Load the truck with 2000 tons of iron and fuck, cut the brakes my friend, and I'll watch" ("Charge le camion de 2000 tonnes de fer et nique, coupe lui les freins mon ami, et moi je regarde"), Chafroud wrote.[42] Chafroud would later claim that he hadn't been serious when sending the message, that he was watching a Spider-Man movie when he wrote it and was a bit hyped.

Perhaps most damaging to Chafroud's claims of innocence, though, was the forensic evidence collected from the cargo truck, coupled with footage from closed-circuit cameras, both of which pointed directly to him. "His fingerprints were … found on the truck's passenger door, and he was recorded by a surveillance camera in the truck beside Mr. Lahouaiej-Bouhlel, on the promenade in Nice, less than three hours before the attack," reported the *New York Times*.[43] There was also a voicemail

Lahouaiej-Bouhlel had left for a third suspect only 18 minutes before the truck attack. "Bring more weapons, bring five of them to [Chafroud]."[44] Investigators believed this to mean that another terrorist mission was in the works, particularly since concurrent messages referred to the following month in suspicious terms.

As for this third suspect, the one with whom Lahouaiej-Bouhlel was communicating immediately before the ramming episode, it was his friend and cocaine dealer, Ramzi Arefa. A twenty-one-year-old native of Nice, Arefa had a history of violence, theft, and drug abuse, and had been convicted and sentenced six times between 2013 and 2015.[45] It was Arefa, investigators determined, who procured the handgun that Lahouaiej-Bouhlel used during the truck attack; a weapon Arefa acquired with the help of a sketchy Albanian couple, Artan Henaj and Enkeledja Zace. Police would also find an AK-47 and a supply of ammunition in the cellar of one of Arefa's associates.

In regard to another dubious figure, Rachid Kassim, the cyberplanner discussed in the previous chapter who operated out of ISIS-held territory in Syria, he posted a video on the internet in which he praised Lahouaiej-Bouhlel for carrying out the Nice attack. Kassim then beheaded a captive. There is no evidence to suggest, however, that Kassim had contact with, or even knew, Lahouaiej-Bouhlel, nor is he thought to have had any involvement in organizing the cargo truck assault. (Kassim would be killed in Iraq in 2017, the target of a U.S. airstrike.)

On July 21, 2016, after prosecutor François Molins presented portions of the evidence against the accused—Ghraieb, Chafroud, Arefa, Henaj, and Zace—he announced that the five had been indicted on charges that included possession and transportation of weapons, terrorist conspiracy, murder, and attempted murder. A sixth suspect would be indicted a few days later, Hamdi Zagar, another friend of Lahouaiej-Bouhlel. Like Mohamed Oualid Ghraieb, Zagar had been photographed standing by the cargo truck two days before the attack. Even more illuminating, investigators found that Zagar had sent two messages to Ramzi Arefa on July 6, 2016. They were simply dates, but they were vital ones: 7/14/16, which was the date of the impending attack in Nice, and 8/15/16. The latter reference alarmed counterterrorism officials, who believed it referred to a second terrorist operation to be conducted in mid–August. "Anti-Terrorist Subdirectorate investigators ... have, according to our sources, become almost certain that action was planned for that date" ("Les enquêteurs de sous-direction antiterroriste ... ont, selon nos informations, acquis la quasi-certitude qu'aucune action n'était prévue à cette date"), reported the French news site *La Chaîne Info*.[46] Still, investigators lacked concrete, irrefutable evidence that any of the suspects, including Zagar, knew specifically what Lahouaiej-Bouhlel was planning to do on the night of La Fête Nationale.

Following the announcement of the suspects' indictments, some were transferred from Nice to a special anti-terror complex in Paris. And while phone records revealed that Lahouaiej-Bouhlel had been in contact with other questionable figures in the coastal region, these people were not charged because it was not known if his interactions with them entailed potential terrorist activities. As one person close to the case explained, given the neighborhood in which Lahouaiej-Bouhlel lived, one that was home to many militant residents, his contacts with these individuals may have been innocuous or wholly coincidental.[47] In terms of Lahouaiej-Bouhlel's estranged wife, Hajer, she was detained, questioned, and released without being charged. In 2017 and 2018 respectively, and to considerable public opposition, Enkeledja Zace and Hamdi Zagar would be released and placed on probation. Artan Henaj would hang himself in prison.

A Tangle of Intentions

As the investigation of Lahouaiej-Bouhlel progressed, authorities found themselves baffled by some of the assailant's actions leading up to the Bastille Day attack. Not only did his behavior deviate from that displayed by other political or religious terrorists, but his motives appeared to be contradictory.

First and foremost, officials became convinced that Lahouaiej-Bouhlel was not a member of a formal terrorist organization, particularly ISIS. While he had, on one occasion, expressed support for its aim of having its own territory in the Middle East, he otherwise did not appear to have held strong opinions of, or a commitment to, the Islamic State. Similarly, while Lahouaiej-Bouhlel's cellphone and home computer held numerous videos of beheadings and other abhorrent punishments delivered by Islamists, videos that he showed to his friends presumably for enjoyment, it seems that he was drawn solely to the acts of violence themselves. The ideological pretexts for them did not appear to interest him. Indeed, Lahouaiej-Bouhlel's devices were found to also contain photos and videos of disastrous car wrecks and other gory incidents that were unrelated to radical jihadism.

Also weakening the pro–Islamist argument, Lahouaiej-Bouhlel did not leave behind the standard declaration, such as a written manifesto, a loyalty statement to ISIS, or a martyrdom video. He also carried out his Bastille Day attack in a crowd of 30,000 in a city having a large Muslim population. As noted earlier, over thirty-percent of those killed in his rampage were adherents of the Islamic faith. In that Lahouaiej-Bouhlel had surveilled and photographed the Promenade des Anglais on this same holiday a year in the advance, he would have known that a considerable share of the spectators had Middle Eastern and North African roots; that they or their forebears had come from nations having majority Muslim populations. The upshot: the massive gathering was most likely not the type that a true soldier of ISIS would target.

Perhaps the most perplexing feature of the case is the fact that Lahouaiej-Bouhlel appeared to have laid a trap for those whom the prosecutors would accuse of collaborating with him. As noted earlier, four of these individuals—Ghraieb, Chafroud, Arefa, and Zagar—initially insisted that they hardly knew Lahouaiej-Bouhlel, but eventually conceded that they had not been telling the truth about their relationships with him. Because they were facing serious charges in a terrorist investigation, they were attempting to downplay any substantial involvement with the perpetrator. That said, it does appear that Lahouaiej-Bouhlel may have set them up to some extent, in a sense handing them over to the authorities on the heels of his own death and for reasons known only to Lahouaiej-Bouhlel himself. Certainly, the defendants seemed to think that he had betrayed them. It should be noted that none of the suspects had a criminal record prior to the Nice attack with the exception of twenty-one-year-old Ramzi Arefa, the minor-league cocaine dealer, and none were known to have a history of suspicious Islamist activities or to belong to militant jihadist groups. Their records were clean.

Retrieving the contents of the cellphone that Lahouaiej-Bouhlel left in the cab of the cargo truck, investigators found that he had taken a photograph five hours before he set out on his killing spree, a photo that seemed as if he was deliberately pointing out his associates. The image was that of a handwritten document—a flowchart—connecting their names to telephone numbers and other incriminating information. One of the names was that of Ramzi Arefa, and it had three phone numbers associated with it. Another was Chokri Chafroud, which had five number issuing from it. In Lahouaiej-Bouhlel's apartment, moreover, investigators came across more handwritten pages containing additional names, street addresses, and telephone numbers in what looked like an outline of a criminal conspiracy.[48] Then too, in phone messages to three of his presumed collaborators, he made sure to mention the name of the car rental agency from which he had initially planned to rent the truck to be used in the killings. And this is not all. Lahouaiej-Bouhlel texted them, albeit incorrectly, the date of the upcoming attack on the Promenade des Anglais, as well as a subsequent date in mid–August, one that authorities believed to be that of the aforementioned follow-up terrorist operation. The point is, Lahouaiej-Bouhlel not only failed to take any measures to protect his friends' identities and their apparent involvement in the impending assault on the Promenade des Anglais; he seems to have ensured that the police would have easy access to an array of materials calculated to ensure their arrests and convictions.

Hamid Zagar was among those defendants who felt sure that Lahouaiej-Bouhlel had framed him. Making the case that the latter was mentally disturbed, Zagar told investigators it was Lahouaiej-Bouhlel's idea to photograph him in front of the white cargo truck two days before the attack. He added that he did not understand why Lahouaiej-Bouhlel wanted to do this, but that he complied. It will be recalled that Lahouaiej-Bouhlel also photographed Ghraieb beside the truck shortly before the assault. Like the conspiracy flowchart, this imagery, which casts serious doubt on both Zagar and Ghraieb's innocence, would be used in court.

According to Paris-based journalist Scott Sayare, in one phone message alone, Lahouaiej-Bouhlel effectively provided the authorities with the names of his associates, important elements of the terrorist scheme, and the street address of the weapons traffickers from whom Mohamed Oualid Ghraieb obtained the pistol that Lahouaiej-Bouhlel fired at police on the Promenade des Anglais.[49] If exposing his reputed collaborators was his intention, he surely succeeded.

As of early 2020, six of the original nine defendants were still behind bars and awaiting trial. And while the authorities had originally suspected that one of them, Chokri Chafroud, may have been radicalized in the past and subsequently mentored Lahouaiej-Bouhlel in Islamist militancy, they ultimately ruled it out. Psychologists, psychiatrists, and prison personnel who observed Chafroud for a four-month period concluded that he was not a religious extremist, that he was somewhat easily influenced himself, and that he never held such sway over Lahouaiej-Bouhlel.

In terms of the impending trials, they are expected to commence in late 2020. "It remains to be seen whether key characters such as Chafroud [will] be tried for complicity in assassination or criminal conspiracy in relation to a terrorist company" ("Reste à savoir si des personnages-clés tels que Chafroud seraient jugés pour complicités d'assassinats ou association de malfaiteurs en relation avec une entreprise terroriste)," writes journalist Christophe Cirone.[50]

After three years of investigations, what does appear certain is that Mohamed Lahouaiej-Bouhlel had no explicit links to ISIS or, for that matter, to anyone in the Iraqi-Syrian zone. Rather, he seems to have been an unstable, volatile man struggling with employment problems and a divorce, a figure who became bent on killing in a most brutal fashion scores of children and adults enjoying a national holiday. It also appears that he sought to ensure that the authorities would be able to identify and incarcerate his alleged collaborators, while he himself would be liquidated at the scene of the crime. It was a carefully crafted package of destruction, and it guaranteed that everyone involved would suffer—victims, perpetrator, and alleged collaborators.

In 2017, the city of Nice witnessed two developments of note. Both looked toward a better future.

The first event was an unofficial cleansing ceremony, and it took place at the "anti-shrine," as it was known. "The 'anti-shrine' [is] a pile of rubbish," writes Heather Welford, "erected on the spot where police shot terrorist Mohamed Lahouaiej-Bouhlel."[51] It seems the people of Nice decided to mark the location of the terrorist's death through the use of trash, and on this date it was hauled away. Also removed at this time was a makeshift sign, penned in English, that likewise observed where Lahouaiej-Bouhlel's had died, with instructions to spit on the site. So it was that the last physical reminders of the man and his heinous crime were eradicated on this warm summer day.

The second development was preventive. The city of Nice completed a project costing over $20 million, a project designed to protect public gatherings on the Promenade des Anglais. A mile of bollards, or posts, were implanted at a depth of over six feet, and have the capability to stop a twenty-ton truck in motion. Moreover, traveling by vehicle into this protected zone now requires approval. "Only authorised vehicles can get access to the area behind the bollards," explains Christian Estrosi, the mayor of Nice, "and they are only allowed in after visual verification by cameras which check [license] number plates."[52] It is a strategy that other European cities are likewise considering due to the disturbing increase in ramming attacks that have followed Lahouaiej-Bouhlel's fevered Bastille Day assault on the Côte d'Azur.

12

The Ramadan Murders

Ritualized Assault at an American-Owned Chemical Plant in France

"Oh, Allah make this month a month of victories for the Muslims everywhere and make it a month of disasters, defeats, and disgrace for the *kuffar* [nonbelievers] everywhere."[1] It was on June 23, 2015, one week into the Muslim holy month of Ramadan, that this audio message was released to the world, one in which the spokesman for the Islamic State called for a different kind of annual observance. Rather than the traditional acts of fasting and prayer, Abu Muhammad al-Adnani, the spokesman, was beseeching militant Islamists to commit acts of violence in part to commemorate the one-year anniversary of the self-proclaimed caliphate itself. "Be keen to conquer in this holy month and to become exposed to martyrdom," al-Adnani declared.[2] Specifically, the Islamic State, a Sunni insurgent organization, was entreating its adherents to target their fellow Sunnis who were fighting on the side of the U.S.-led coalition in the Middle East. In the crosshairs, too, were Shi'ites and Christians, with hostile actions to be carried out against them in Iraq, Syria, and Libya, among other nations.

Unfortunately, al-Adnani's call was heeded. During the 2015 Ramadan in the Nigerian city of Jos, a terrorist cell from Boko Haram, an affiliate of ISIS, targeted the city's Yantaya Mosque while a public reading of the Koran was underway. Worshippers died when an explosion by a suicide bomber ripped through the building, while those who managed to survive the blast subsequently found themselves face to face with heavily-armed terrorists. "(P)eople emerged from nowhere, five of them, holding sophisticated arms, shooting sporadically into the crowd," said one witness.[3]

In Raqqa, Syria, meanwhile, the ISIS caliphate murdered—crucified— scores of Muslim men for having committed such purported offenses as traveling during daylight hours, eating food, and drinking water. As could

184

be expected, the primitive executions shocked the world, but ISIS and its supporters defended their barbarity. In fact, the organization seemed pleased by the reaction and deemed the executions to be moral. In this regard, Anjem Choudary, a British Islamist and apologist for the Islamic State, has argued that punishments like crucifixion are not only ethical, but even merciful in the long term. In an interview with Graeme Wood of *The Atlantic*, Choudary emphasized the ends rather than the means. "(T)he [Islamic] state has an obligation to terrorize its enemies—a holy order to scare the shit out of them with beheadings and crucifixions and enslavement of women and children, because doing so hastens victory and avoids prolonged conflict," Wood writes, recapitulating Choudary's viewpoint.[4] Sadly, the world would witness further horrors as ad-Adnani's appeal for Ramadan carnage continued being answered.

On a single day—June 26, 2015—four separate terrorist attacks were committed in the East Africa, North Africa, the Middle East, and Europe. In Mogadishu, Somalia, the militant Islamist group al-Shabab rained havoc on the Jazeera Palace Hotel when a suicide bomber drove within thirty yards of the establishment. Detonating the bomb, the explosion demolished the hotel, which, in addition to offering lodging to travelers, housed the embassies of China, Egypt, and Qatar. Among the dead were a journalist, hotel staff members, and pedestrians and motorists unlucky enough to be in the vicinity of the seven-story building. And while it was never proven that the extremist group was responding directly to ISIS's appeal for violence during Ramadan, al-Shabab did announce its intention to escalate its attacks during the holy month in the wake the Islamic State's request.

On this same day, a Saudi Arabian member of ISIS with an incendiary devices strapped to his body stepped out of a car in front of the Imam al-Sadiq Mosque in Kuwait City, Kuwait. Inside, Shi'ite congregants were in the midst of afternoon prayers when the suicide bomber entered and discharged his explosive belt. Rejecting the worshippers as heretics, the Islamic State claimed responsibility for the blast, which killed twenty-seven people and injured over 200 more in what was the first ISIS strike in the Sunni-majority nation of Kuwait.

Even more civilians would be killed on this day when thirty-eight people, mainly women and men from England, Belgium, and Germany, perished in the worst terrorist offensive in the history of Tunisia. It happened at the Hotel Riu Imperial Marhaba, a resort situated on the Mediterranean Sea in the city of Sousse. Surveillance footage and an online statement by ISIS, which claimed responsibility for the attack, indicate that Abu Yehya Al Qirwani, a college student with no criminal record, carried out the assault.

Barefoot and clad in black shorts and a black tee-shirt, Al Qirwani, it is surmised, arrived by boat and walked along the seashore until he reached his destination, a private stretch of the beach reserved for guests of the luxury hotel. His plan, evidently, was to commence his rampage at this spot because it had fewer security guards than the front of the Riu Imperial Marhaba.

Clutching the Kalashnikov that he had concealed inside an umbrella, Al Qirwani began gunning down his prey—sunbathers. "Coming in the middle of the day during Ramadan, the [gunman] would have known the beaches would have been primarily used by non-fasting foreign tourists," writes researcher and author Charles Lister.[5] While the potential victims shrieked in horror and rushed back to the hotel in search of shelter, Al Qirwani continued his lethal stride. "He was shouting something, I don't know what he was shouting," said Glenn Whitehead from England.[6]

Inside the hotel, the scene was pandemonium. Although the gunman was still firing at sunbathers on the beach, many of those who had dashed into the hotel now mistook a handful of armed, plainclothes police officers for terrorists, intensifying the panic and galvanizing the crowd straining to escape upstairs to their rooms. "I was trying to be rational but it was hard with people pushing everybody trying to get on the elevator," recalled twenty-one-year-old Will Donaghy from Ireland.[7]

Minutes later, Al Qirwani became a casualty himself. Shot to death by the police, he lay sprawled in a lake of his own blood, the Kalashnikov by his side. Although questions remained as to how he had acquired the military-grade weapon, the authorities concluded that the attack was probably a lone-actor mass murder rather than a network operation.

As could be expected, condolences and pledges of support rolled in from around the world, including a message from the Élysée Palace in Paris. "France's President François Hollande," writes journalist Jamie Walker, "spoke to Tunisian President Beji Caid Essebsi after the attacks and they both vowed to step up co-ordination."[8] This was noteworthy in that France itself was subjected to an ISIS-inspired Ramadan strike on this same day.

A Beheading at L'Isle-d'Abeau

The assailant who committed the Ramadan attack in France was a thirty-five-year-old French citizen, Yassin Salhi, and his assault was truly macabre. It certainly stunned those who had come to know him as a friendly, easygoing father of three. But then Salhi had always been characterized by a peaceful, unruffled nature, a pervasive feature that could be traced back to his earliest days.

Formative Years

It was near the Swiss border in Pontarlier, France, that Yassin Salhi spent his formative years. A quiet boy, he obeyed his Moroccan mother and Algerian father, and was considered a "good kid" by most everyone who knew him. As for events during his childhood and adolescence, these years appear to be without incident until he reached the age of sixteen, at which time his father died. Perhaps it was partly because of this loss that Salhi developed an interest in the Arabic language, the teenager explaining that he was drawn to his father and mothers' North African roots. And indeed, Salhi, who had always been studious, learned to read and write Arabic after three years of private lessons. But while he possessed an attraction to the language of his forebears, he did not evince a similar curiosity about Islam, their religion. Instead, he was drawn to soccer. By all accounts, he was an ordinary youth in his interests, activities, and conduct.

When Salhi reached his mid-twenties, a man of a similar age moved to Pontarlier. Tall, blond-haired, and intimidating, Frédéric Jean Salvi was his name, and he had recently been released from prison in the nearby town of Besançon. Drug trafficking was the crime for which he had been incarcerated.

In Pontarlier, the two men became acquainted, attended the local mosque together, and before long began creating problems in the community. It seems that Salvi had converted to a radical brand of Islam during his stretch in prison, where the other inmates bestowed upon him the nickname, "Grand Ali." After his release, Salvi remained opinionated and outspoken about his religious and political beliefs, and, in the main, was regarded as aggressive, disrespectful, and offensive to others. The latter included those Muslims who did not share his extremist convictions. As for Yassin Salhi, he appears to have been influenced by, even radicalized by, this new friend.

In 2006, Salhi, his wife, and their children moved to the neighboring town of Besançon. Also at this juncture, French intelligence, which had been keeping tabs on Frédéric Jean Salvi after his discharge from prison, took notice of Yassin Salhi as well and placed his name on France's national security watch list. Although the precise reason for his presence on the *fiche S* has not been made public, it likely stemmed from his increasingly militant deeds in unison with those of Frédéric Salvi and the pair's expanding circle of radical Islamist comrades.

In one notable episode, Salvi, with Yassin Salhi and seven other militants in tow, accosted the imam at the Philippe-Grenier mosque in Pontarlier, the same house of worship where Salvi and Salhi attended services together when they first met.[9] But now Salvi jumped to his feet while the imam was delivering a sermon and set about condemning the man's words, disrupting the religious service. "He ordered the imam to stop, said his sermons were wrong," recalled Amar Remimi, the mosque's treasurer.[10] In response, the leadership barred Salvi from the premises for instigation. Salvi would later state that he was not alone in his ideological struggle with the mosque, that Yassin Salhi was at odds with it too. "He [Salhi] tried to install a radical movement in the mosque but it did not work," Salvi told the *Express*.[11] Whatever the truth of Salvi's claim, Yassin Salhi, formerly a subdued and amiable man, was clearly becoming more immoderate in his views, if not his actions.

Here it should be noted that another young Islamist also joined the Philippe-Grenier mosque at this time and befriended Yassin Salhi and Frédéric Salvi. A convert to Islam, his name was Sébastien-Younes Voyez-Zairi, he held a technical degree from a college in Besançon, and in due course he ostensibly would play a role in Salhi's extremist acts.[12]

Two years later, in 2008, a pair of important events took place. First, Frédéric Salvi left France, studied in Egypt, and thereafter allegedly helped set up terrorist operations in Jakarta, Indonesia. Subsequent to this, he moved to England. Second, French intelligence stopped monitoring Yassin Salhi, a lapse that would carry dreadful consequences. Government officials have explained that French intelligence services, being overburdened at this point, were known to cease surveilling potential risks after a two-year period if the individuals had not engaged in criminal activities. This was the case for Saïd and Cherif Kouachi, who massacred the *Charlie Hebdo* staff and whom French intelligence had ceased to monitor after a stretch of two outwardly uneventful years. Yet other officials have asserted that 2008 was also a singularly chaotic period for French intelligence due to a restructuring of services. It seems that President Nicolas Sarkozy merged two intelligence agencies at this juncture—each agency had been responsible in part for detecting domestic terrorist threats—and Yassin Salhi, among others, was dropped from the *fiche S* during the transition.[13] Salhi, then, may have simply slipped between the cracks, and for this reason was free to continue mutating into a dangerous extremist without interruption. It is plausible, too, that his transformation was accelerated during a journey that he and his family made to Syria in 2009, one that the authorities discovered only later and the details of which remain somewhat murky. What is known is that his transformation into a terrorist was nearing completion in 2014.

The Air Products Factory Attack

In December of that year, Yassin Salhi moved his family to Saint-Priest, a suburb of Lyon, where neighbors remember him as a mild-mannered man and the family as peaceful and unobtrusive. One acquaintance, a Muslim, added that he had never seen Salhi at the local mosque, although it is possible, of course, that Salhi attended services elsewhere.[14]

In terms of employment, Salhi drove a van for a private transport firm, ATC-Colicom in Chassieu, where he increasingly distanced himself from his coworkers who were opposed to ISIS. One employee, Abdel Karim, recounted Salhi's reaction when he, Karim, voiced his opinion of the Islamic State. "When I told him what I thought, from that day on, it was 'hello/goodbye.'"[15] Karim further suggested that Salhi's superficial geniality masked a more sinister nature.

The transport company was directed by a fifty-four-year-old man, Hervé Cornara, who occasionally accompanied Salhi on deliveries. As it happened, Cornara would escort him on this Friday morning during Ramadan, which the family was observing in the traditional fashion.[16] Also conventional, it appears, was Salhi's outward behavior at home with his loved ones in the early hours of this fateful day.

The tragic drama that was to come unfolded in this way: Salhi, concealing a long knife and a fake gun, drove his delivery van to the ATC-Colicom transport center in Chassieu. He arrived at 7:30 a.m. As he waited for Hervé Cornara to show up, he placed several canisters of flammable gas in back of the vehicle, having already hidden two flags—one was Islamic, the other Islamist—in the van as well.

Sometime after 8:00 a.m., the two men began the thirteen-mile drive to L'Isle-d'Abeau, the site of an Air Products factory, which was to be the target of Salhi's intended attack. An international venture based in Allentown, Pennsylvania, Air Products specializes in gases and chemicals for industrial use. "As the name indicates," reports the *Iran Times*, "the company's main business is breaking down the gases in the atmosphere and packaging them in pressurized canisters of oxygen, nitrogen, et cetera."[17] Due to the nature of its operation, the plant, situated in an industrial park, could comprise an appealing target for terrorists, and this fact had not escaped officials' notice. "According to French regulations applicable to zones where gases and chemicals are handled," write Catherine Lagrange and Michel Rose, "the site [was] required to implement security arrangements at the low end of the European Union's so-called 'Seveso' scale."[18]

The company's chairman, president, and chief executive officer was Seifi Ghasemi, a highly-regarded Iranian-American businessman who holds an engineering degree from Stanford University. The significance of Ghasemi's heritage in this case is uncertain, however. While Iran itself is predominantly Shi'ite and the country was fighting against ISIS at this juncture, it has not been established that Ghasemi, as the head of Air Products, was a factor in Salhi's decision to target the factory in the forthcoming attack. Along the same lines, it has not been determined that the company was selected because of its American proprietorship, the United States being another enemy of the Islamic State. Rather, these Iranian and American connections appear to have been coincidental. It almost certainly was the location, the accessibility, and the potential volatility of the chemical factory that made it such an attractive mark for Salhi.

Returning to the impending attack: the trip that Salhi and Cornara made from the transport center in Chassieu to the chemical plant in L'Isle-d'Abeau, ordinarily a brief one, took longer than usual on this day. The reason was because Salhi made an abrupt stopover that delayed their arrival. Pulling the van into a parking lot, he grabbed Hervé Cornara, struck him in the head with a car jack rendering him unconscious, then choked him to death. Salhi would later tell the police that he strangled the insentient man with one hand.[19]

Continuing on his way to the Air Products factory, Salhi, when he was one-third of a mile from the facility, pulled off road again. Coming to a halt in a secluded area, he used the long knife to cut off Cornara's head. (Forensics experts would later be unable to conclude whether Cornara was unconscious or deceased during the amputation.) Salhi next snapped a cellphone photo of himself with the severed head resting atop the victim's torso and, using the encrypted WhatsApp, sent the image to a thirty-year-old Frenchman in Syria. Propping the headless corpse in the passenger seat, Salhi then drove on toward the chemical factory.

Approaching the site, the assailant stopped a third and final time. Just outside the plant, he attached Cornara's head to a chain-link fence and positioned the two large flags on each side of it. One banner expressed the Islamic creed, or Shahada. "There is no god but Allah, and Muhammad is his messenger," it states.[20] As he had done with the selfie, Salhi photographed the grotesque display and sent the image to his contact in Syria.

The assailant now proceeded to the front gate of the Air Products plant, where security guards waved the van inside. Because Salhi made deliveries on a regular basis, he already possessed the necessary authorization to enter the installation. Unfortunately, the guards failed to notice that the man sitting next to him was headless, and the facility's closed-circuit surveillance cameras were unable to capture a distinct image of the mutilated passenger.

As Salhi drove into the industrial plant, surveillance footage showed his van speed up until it was racing toward an open hangar, one that was loaded with combustible gases and liquids. A tremendous explosion could be anticipated, of course, the canisters of flammable gas that Salhi had stashed in the back of van colliding with the drums of chemicals stored in the hangar. And yet, while the blast was impressive and destroyed most of the structure, it was not the lethal eruption that Salhi had evidently expected. Only two workers were wounded, and their injuries were not life-threatening.

Four minutes later—it was shortly before 10:00 a.m.—an on-site fire squad arrived at the conflagration, followed by local security forces from L'Isere. While the firefighters were containing the blaze, security forces tried to locate Salhi, who was nowhere in sight. Convinced that he had not perished in the inferno, the officers concluded he was still on the premises and perhaps attempting to trigger more destruction. And they were right. Because his attack had failed to obliterate the installation, an explosion that would have "martyred" Salhi himself, he was now trying to complete his lethal mission in another hangar that housed gases and acetone, a volatile organic solvent. "Video surveillance footage showed that Mr. Salhi had tried to open canisters containing flammables gases while shouting 'Allahu akbar,'" reported the *New York Times*.[21] As it turned out, his efforts were in vain. "(T)he suspected culprit was neutralized by someone from the security forces of L'Isere who had arrived at the scene and who had a lot of courage and kept his cool and proceeded to put the individual out of action," said Bernard Cazeneuve, France's Minister of the Interior at the time.[22]

Arrested and confined, Salhi performed poorly under interrogation. Perhaps because he thought he would perish in the blast, he had not prepared a cogent defense, and the answers that his attorney subsequently offered also did little to convince the authorities that Salhi was not a terrorist. When asked about the beheading of Hervé Cornara, for instance, Salhi claimed that he did not remember doing it, just as he claimed not to recall taking the photos he snapped at the crime scene. In another line of questioning, one designed to uncover the killer's motives, authorities asked Salhi's lawyer why his client had murdered Cornara, and the attorney replied that the homicide was personal. Salhi, he said, had become upset because Cornara, earlier that morning, reproached him for dropping a piece of equipment from a pallet. Of course, the fact that Salhi, before picking up Cornara at the ATC-Colicom transport center, had hidden a pair of flags in the van, banners that he appeared to have created himself and that involved painting on cloth, indicated that his actions were premeditated, as did the knife that he had brought along with him. When presented with this evidence, Salhi admitted having prepared for the killing on the previous day, but maintained that it stemmed from a personal antipathy toward his boss, not a terrorist impulse. It should be noted that there was no known antagonism between Salhi and Cornara, and that Cornara's son, who was in his early twenties at the time of the killing, said he had always found Salhi to be a friendly, likeable man.[23]

Challenging Salhi and his attorney's assertion that the murder was the product of a workplace spat, François Molins, the prosecutor in the case, pointed out that a homicidal act can be both personal and political; the two are not mutually exclusive. Most persuasive, though, the prosecutor drew attention to the method of the killing, the beheading and posting of the head, treated as a trophy, in public view and adorned by Islamist and Islamic flags. "That corresponds quite exactly with the instructions of Islamic State, which regularly calls for terrorist acts to be committed on French soil, especially the cutting of infidel's throats," Molins stated.[24] Accordingly, because Salhi appeared to have been responding to ISIS's public call to carry out acts of violence during the holy month of Ramadan, he would, in due course, be charged with murder and attempted murder associated with terrorism. All the same, Salhi would remain steadfast in his contention that he was merely settling a score and seeking a bit of attention, that his deeds had nothing to do with religion or politics.

The Investigation

The prosecutor, convinced that Salhi was lying, launched a formal terrorism investigation into the case and soon unearthed intriguing materials suggesting that the defendant had not acted alone in his actions. Among them were the messages Salhi sent to his French contact in Syria immediately after cutting off Cornara's head. Officials identified the recipient as Sébastien-Younes Voyez-Zairi, whom press reports referred to simply as Sébastien-Younes or Sébastien-Younes V-Z. This is the same man with whom Salhi had attended the Philippe-Grenier mosque in Pontarlier a few years earlier. The pair had been part of the militant Islamist clique headed by Frédéric Jean Salvi.

Probing further into Sébastien-Younes' background, investigators discovered that after he received the two photos of the beheaded victim, he purportedly contacted high-level figures in ISIS seeking authorization to release them. Furthermore, Sébastien-Younes sent a text message to his mother shortly after Salhi's attack, one in which he claimed a degree of responsibility for Salhi's murderous actions.[25] "He's a good brother to me," Sébastien-Younes wrote to his mother, adding "I'm one of the causes in what he did" ("C'est un bon frère à moi…. Je suis une des causes dans ce qu'il a fait").[26]

It appears that Sébastien-Younes' claims may be accurate. Eight months earlier, Sébastien-Younes told his loved ones in France that he was relocating to Belgium, where he planned "to repopulate the Islamic State."[27] In reality, he moved to Raqqa, Syria, with his wife and children, where he joined ISIS to fight on behalf of the terrorist organization. A month later, in December 2014, his father, concerned about Sébastien-Younes' sudden departure, notified French authorities, who set about searching Sébastien-Younes' former residence. Among other items, they found an edition of *Les Soldats de Lumièré*, the inflammatory 2004 jihadist autobiography.[28]

In terms of the relationship between Sébastien-Younes and Yassin Salhi, and, more importantly, whether the two collaborated on the Air Products terrorist plot perhaps in concert with others, this question has never been satisfactorily resolved. Also unanswered is the reason Salhi sent the gruesome images, especially the one of himself with his decapitated victim, to Sébastien-Younes in Syria. "The question is whether Yassin Salhi sent this photo to the person closest to jihadist circles he knew to promote his criminal act, or if it was a process of advocacy thought or even encouraged … on foreign soil" ("La question est de savoir si Yassin Salhi a envoyé cette photo à la personne la plus proche des cercles djihadistes qu'il connaissait pour valoriser son acte criminel, ou s'il s'agissait d'une démarche de revendication réfléchie, voire encouragée depuis l'étranger"), said a source close the investigation.[29]

In the end, the principal reason that a more satisfying closure was not achieved in this case has to do with Yassin Salhi himself and the fact that he had difficulty coping with solitary confinement at the daunting Fleury-Mérogis prison. At a legal proceeding on December 22, 2015, two weeks before he was slated to be released from pre-trial detention, the court informed Salhi that it was extending his confinement, that he would be serving another six months behind bars. Presumably, he would continue doing so in the isolation unit. And this turn of events appears to have been too much for him to bear. At some point later that day, Salhi evidently took his own life. At 9:15 p.m., prison guards found him hanged with his bedsheet, which had been affixed to the bars of his cell.

Not surprisingly, many people across France were comforted by the news of his death, although one woman was not: the wife of Hervé Cornara. She had been waiting to confront her husband's self-appointed executioner in court, and was disgusted by Salhi's apparent suicide. "He's a coward," she said, "and he's been a coward until the end."[30]

Salhi's death closed the door on further inquiries in the case, at least those that relied on his disclosures. If there had been more information locked inside him, such as how he knew to carry out his terrorist attack precisely on the same day as the trio of Ramadan attacks in other nations, he would not be divulging it.

13

Terror on the Tracks
Face-Off on a High-Speed Train to Paris

A few weeks after the beheading and car bombing at the Air Products plant in eastern France, another terrorist, seemingly acting alone, attempted an attack in a northern region of the country. In this episode, however, the outcome was different in that a cluster of onlookers intervened in what would come to be heralded worldwide as a sterling display of courage. And unique to the incident was its location, namely, aboard a high-speed train packed with passengers.

It happened on August 21, 2015, a Friday. In mid-afternoon, a train operated by Thalys International, a French-Belgian company, left the Amsterdam Centraal station in the Netherlands. Set to travel to Brussels, it would continue on its way to Paris, its terminus. Typically, the sleek train could complete the 320-mile trip in three and a half hours.

Boarding at Amsterdam Centraal on this summer afternoon were three American men. Growing up together in Sacramento, California, they had been classmates at a Christian school and had remained friends in the ensuing years. Two of them were serving in the military and the other was attending college. En route, three other men boarded the train: a French banker, a British computer consultant and grandfather, and a middle-aged Franco-American academic. These six travelers, all of them headed to Paris, would become the champions in this tale.

Arriving on schedule in Brussels shortly after 5:00 p.m., the train, designated Thalys #9364, took on another noteworthy Paris-bound passenger. A twenty-five-year-old man of Moroccan descent, he was dragging an oversized suitcase. Ayoub El Khazzani (also spelled el-Qahzzani) was his name, and he was on a terrorist watch list. Unfortunately, no intelligence services were watching on this ill-fated day; a startling lapse in light of his criminal background and recent journey to the Middle East.

Ayoub El Khazzani

Born and reared in Tétouan, Morocco, Ayoub El Khazzani moved with his mother and father to Spain in 2007. He was seventeen years old at the time. In due course, he was granted Spanish residency and lived with his parents for the next several years in Madrid and, later, the southern city of Algeciras.

Those who knew Khazzani, a part-time house painter, considered him to be an ordinary man. "He played and went to the beach with other guys; he was also looking for a job," is how Kamal Cheddad, a local Muslim leader, remembered him.[1] But Khazzani was a far cry from ordinary in at least one respect: Spanish police, in 2009, arrested him for narcotics trafficking on two occasions while he was living in Algeciras, a port city and major transit point between Spain and Morocco. Three years later, they collared him again for drug dealing, this time in Ceuta, an autonomous Spanish city on the coast of northwest Africa. It was through these illicit activities that Khazzani first drew the attention of Spanish authorities, who began tracking his movements.

More suspicion would arise when he set about establishing extremist ties in Algeciras, most notably with a handful of militant Islamists at the Taqwa mosque.[2] A controversial house of worship, law enforcement officials placed it under surveillance the day it was established, just as they placed Khazzani himself under surveillance when he became passionate about the Taqwa site. "Mr. El-Khazzani 'assiduously attended' a mosque in southern Spain known for radical proselytizing," says Paris prosecutor François Molins, "and in which Mr. El-Khazzani's brother was the treasurer."[3] Khazzani's radicalization, in conjunction with his criminal background, troubled Spanish politicians such as Antonio Sanz, who speculated that Khazzani's case may have been a "merger between radicalism and drug trafficking."[4] And it was because of Khazzani's disconcerting actions that Spanish counterterrorism agents shared their concerns with French officials in February 2014, a time when Khazzani was relocating to Paris to work for a mobile phone company.

Acting on their Spanish counterparts' warnings, French authorities placed Khazzani's name on the *fiche S* as a potential threat to national security. Even so, he was still free to roam about unimpeded, and he took advantage of his liberty. In the ensuing months, the prospective terrorist traveled to Belgium, specifically to the Molenbeek district in Brussels, the epicenter of Islamic State recruitment in Western Europe at the time. In addition, he traveled to Austria and Germany, and from there to Turkey on May 10, 2015. Because Khazzani was on a terrorist watch list, his arrival was duly noted by counterterrorism agents, but no action was taken because he had not committed a crime.

At this point in what was to become a protracted excursion, a two-week period remains unaccounted for, although it was later discovered that he spent a third week with ISIS in Syria. In a 2016 confession, Khazzani recounted that during his stint in the self-proclaimed caliphate, a masked fighter for the Islamic State recommended that he give thought to returning to Europe and conducting a terrorist operation.[5] Taking the proposal under consideration, Khazzani submitted to a crash course at an ISIS training camp, a course intended to teach him how to handle a Kalashnikov.

When the time arrived for him to reenter Europe, the prospective terrorist tried to leave from the Turkish city of Antakya, but a series of obstacles delayed his journey. Partly for this reason, ISIS in Syria dispatched a scout to create a new route for Khazzani, as well as to provide him with a seasoned traveling companion. This comrade was Abdelhamid Abaaoud, the organizer for the Islamic State who would soon become notorious for orchestrating the bloody attacks at the Bataclan Theatre, the Stade de France, and numerous cafés in Paris. As for the new route, Khazzani and Abaaoud would join the hordes of Syrians making their way through the Balkans, refugees struggling to escape the turmoil of the Middle East. In the end, it would prove to be an effective means of slipping back into Europe for future terrorists as well.

So it was that Khazzani and Abaaoud, by the first day of August, were installed in a Budapest hotel. And while TEK (Terrorelhárítási Központ), the Hungarian counterterrorism center, detected the pair's arrival, it did not share this crucial information with Western intelligence agencies. For this reason, the men's movements would thereafter remain a mystery to intelligence officers in France, among other vulnerable nations. And indeed, a few days later, Abaaoud drove to Vienna, while Khazzani boarded a train for the same destination, traveling separately so they would not be seen or filmed together. And here, in the Austrian capital where an apartment had been readied for them, Abaaoud disclosed to Khazzani that the ISIS leadership in Syria was now formally instructing Khazzani to carry out a terrorist strike and to begin bracing himself for it psychologically. The men concluded their journey in the Molenbeek district of Brussels as the moment approached for them to execute a sweeping act of political violence.

If Khazzani's 2016 confession is to be believed, the specifics of the terrorist mission were Abaaoud's handiwork. Abaaoud purportedly informed him that a Thalys train would be the target, and that he, Abaaoud, would gather the materials needed for the attack. He further instructed Khazzani to target American passengers on the train, supposedly adding that three to five members of the U.S. military would be seated in a first-class coach.[6] Here it should be noted that Western intelligence agencies have largely dismissed the latter assertion on the grounds that Abaaoud would not have had access to such information at this juncture. As to why Khazzani would make the claim, it is not unusual for members of the Islamic State to seed their confessions with misleading information. "Other ISIS operatives arrested in the West have shaped their accounts to suit their interests," writes Paul Cruickshank, "complicating the task of investigators."[7]

The Attack

In the days preceding the Thalys assault, Khazzani found lodging in two houses in the Molenbeek district, one of which belonged to his sister. Then, on the day of the attack, he left the latter's home and went to the Bruxelles-Midi train station, where he paid cash for a first-class ticket to Paris. The cost was €149 euros ($173). Although the ticket agent offered him a seat on an earlier train, Khazzani insisted on this later one. It was always jam-packed on a Friday afternoon, meaning, for the assailant, a higher body count. And while it is not known precisely when or how he did it, Khazzani also acquired a burner phone, a disposable and virtually untraceable cellphone.

Climbing aboard the train, the terrorist pulled behind him an oversized, wheeled suitcase, one in which a peculiar assortment of weapons was stashed. These were the items that Abaaoud had purportedly obtained for him. Among them was a box cutter, a bottle of gasoline, a hammer, an AKM (modified Kalashnikov automatic rifle) with a slant muzzle, and a nine-millimeter Luger semi-automatic pistol. Completing the mobile arsenal were 270 rounds, including a full cartridge for the Luger and eight fully-loaded magazines for the AKM. Selecting a seat toward the rear of the train, Khazzani stowed the suitcase in the overhead compartment as the train pulled out of the Brussels depot at 3:17 p.m. It was slated to arrive ninety minutes later in the French capital.

Thirty miles inside of France, as the high-speed train whisked toward the small industrial town of Oignies, Khazzani made his move. Rising from his seat and retrieving the suitcase, he entered a restroom situated between two coaches. Electric sliding-glass doors separated it from the passenger sections of the coaches.

Inside, he assembled the AKM. Also, to galvanize himself for the horror he was planning to let loose upon the 554 weekend travelers, Khazzani watched a YouTube video on his burner phone, a clip of an Islamist calling for violence against the so-called enemies of Islam. Presumably, it was because he was engaged in these final measures that Khazzani remained in the lavatory for such a long stretch of time, so long that one passenger, in particular, became inquisitive.

Mark Moogalian, a professor of English at the Sorbonne and a citizen of both France and the United States, was seated near the restroom. Sitting across from him was his wife, Isabella Risacher-Moogalian, who described Mark's curiosity on this day. "My husband told me he saw a man who he thought appeared strange because he went into the toilet with his bag and stayed there for a very long time," she said.[8] The fifty-one-year-old professor and musician continued keeping an eye on the restroom door.

Even closer to the lavatory was a twenty-eight-year-old banker, a Frenchman, who has chosen to remain anonymous and whom the authorities have designated "Damien A." in their reports of the incident.[9] He was just a few feet away, waiting for the restroom to become vacant.

At 5:35 p.m., Khazzani flung open the door and stood face to face with Damien. No longer wearing a shirt, the terrorist was gripping the Kalashnikov and, strapped to his chest, was the backpack holding his ammunition. Behind him sat the suitcase and canister of gasoline.

"I saw that he was shirtless," Damien told reporters shortly after the incident, adding that the gunman was "quite thin" ("J'ai vu qu'il était torse nu, assez fin").[10] Still in a mild state of shock while he was speaking to the press, Damien described his instinctive reaction as he stood opposite the armed man: the banker lunged at him and grabbed the AKM. A spur-of-the-moment intervention, it was audacious but unfortunately ineffective, because Khazzani, still clutching the assault weapon, knocked him to the ground and walked over him.

Those seated in the vicinity assumed the commotion was merely a heated exchange between a couple of passengers vying for the restroom. The train's controller, Michel Bruet, who was in an adjoining coach, likewise overheard the encounter and thought it was just a squabble—that is, until he saw the Kalashnikov. Realizing that something far more serious was afoot, the fifty-four-year-old train employee rushed at the gunman, who in turn threw Bruet into a door and decked him. "(H)e knocked me to the ground and pointed the handgun at me, then left the car," said Bruet.[11] Seconds later, the controller felt a bullet graze his arm as he, Bruet, sprinted to a special on-board chamber that was reserved for the crew. Accompanying him were a few passengers and a couple of the catering staff, whose company was under contract to Thalys. Once inside, they bolted the door and Bruet activated the emergency mechanism that would stop the train.

On their heels were fifteen other panicked passengers who also sought safety in the crew's chamber, but without success. For whatever reason, the people inside would not unlock the door. Among those desperate for entry was actor Jean-Hugues Anglade, star of films *Betty Blue* and *Killing Zoe* and the televised French crime drama *Braquo*. With him in the coach were his two children and his companion. Although Anglade and his fellow passengers banged on the door and shouted, it remained locked, causing them to feel abandoned.[12] And then the situation became even grimmer: Anglade looked back to find the terrorist tramping toward him and the others. "I thought it was the end, that we were going to die, that he was going to kill us all" ("J'ai pensé que c'était la fin, que nous allions mourir, qu'il allait tous nous tuer"), he said.[13] Desperate, Anglade broke a window with his hand, slicing his middle finger to the bone.

In the meantime, the vigilant Mark Moogalian had seen the altercation between the terrorist and the banker and now decided to take action himself. "Get out, this is serious," he warned his wife, who took cover behind two seats.[14] And with that, the Sorbonne professor ran to the lavatory.

Throwing himself at Khazzani, Moogalian wrenched the Kalashnikov out of the terrorist's hands, yelling to those around them that the assailant had been disarmed. But suddenly, a shot rang out. Khazzani had pulled out the Luger and shot Moogalian in the back with it, the bullet exiting through his neck. A potentially fatal wound, the hemorrhaging was instant and massive. "I'm hit, I'm hit," Moogalian called out to Isabella, who could see him from her vantage point couched between the seats.[15] Moogalian collapsed, dropping the AKM. He would later explain that he thought he was about to die, especially when the gunman walked over and picked up the assault rifle.[16] Smartly, the injured teacher pretended to be dead as Isabella hurried to him, tied her scarf around one of his wounds tourniquet-style, and shouted for a doctor.[17]

The sounds of the gunshot and shattering glass alerted more passengers to the threat, among them the American men mentioned earlier, prompting them to enter the fray. Isabella Risacher-Moogalian recalled the moment when she first became aware that the Americans were up and running toward the terrorist. "I hear one of them scream, 'Fuck this shit!'" ("J'entends l'un d'eux hurler, 'Fuck this shit!'"), she said.[18]

Throughout most of the trip, the Americans, having been unable to locate their first-class coach, had been sitting in the wrong one. It was well into the journey that they decided to switch cars in quest of a stronger Wi-Fi signal and, in this way, ended up in Coach 12, the correct one. It would also be the one in which they confronted Ayoud el Khazzani.

When the attack commenced, California-born Spencer Stone was catnapping in an aisle seat. A twenty-three-year-old Airman First Class in the United States Air Force, the six foot, four inch Stone was a member of the 65th Air Base Group as well as being a martial arts aficionado with training in jiu-jitsu. Sitting next to him in the window seat was his friend Aleksander "Alek" Skarlatos. Twenty two years old, Skarlatos was a member of the U.S. Army National Guard and had just wrapped up a deployment to Afghanistan. And across the aisle was their companion and former classmate, Anthony Sadler, who was also sitting by a window and wearing earbuds. Unlike them, the twenty-three-year-old Sadler was not in the military; he was studying kinesiology at Sacramento State University. By this point in their European sojourn, Sadler and Stone had toured Italy and Germany before meeting up with Skarlatos in the Netherlands and together boarding the high-speed train to France.

Suddenly there came a loud *thud*, followed by the sound of shattering glass. Wearing noise-cancelling headphones and drifting in and out of sleep, a weary Stone awakened to glimpse a figure in a uniform running toward the front of the coach. It was a man, and he appeared to be a member of the train's crew. Turning around to see what had happened, Airman Stone saw the shirtless terrorist walking up the aisle, clutching the AKM. At once, he knew the backpack strapped to the man's torso was loaded with ammunition.

Flashing a glance across the aisle at Sadler, Stone could see that his friend was puzzled by the commotion. Skarlatos, at this same moment, looked to the rear of the coach where he too spotted the armed extremist. But since it was Stone who was sitting in the aisle seat, it was he who was in the best position to move on the gunman.

"Spencer, go!" said Skarlatos.[19] His words notwithstanding, Skarlatos was thinking, "*Go—let's go*," a more collective impulse, according to a written account of the Thalys attack based on the men's recollections.[20] And sure enough, all three of them would go after the gunman in due course.

The first to act was Stone. Launching himself out of his seat, he raced down the aisle toward Khazzani, who aimed the Kalashnikov at him and squeezed the trigger. But nothing happened. Stone, hurtling into him, spun him around, put a headlock on him from behind, pulled him backwards over a pair of seats, and held him in place. In spite of being partially immobilized, Khazzani's hands remained free, so he pulled the Luger from the waistband of his pants. Skarlatos now appeared on the scene. Wresting the gun from Khazzani's hand, he pistol-whipped the terrorist, then tried to shoot him in the head but the weapon would not fire. Khazzani's Luger had only been able to fire a single shot, and this was the one that felled Mark Moogalian, who was hemorrhaging badly nearby. Bleeding, too, was Spencer Stone, having struck his head on the window while dragging Khazzani across the row of seats.

Stone would bleed even more profusely as the terrorist pulled out the box cutter and, reaching behind him, slashed Stone twice in the neck and once at the base of the thumb. And now Anthony Sadler was in the brawl, pummeling Khazzani until, moments later, Stone put a chokehold on the terrorist, who gradually lost unconsciousness. Subsequent to this, all three men, along with Chris Norman, a British IT consultant who had joined them, were on top of Khazzani, retraining him in the aisle of Coach 12.

Sadler, Norman, and Eric Tanty, an off-duty Thalys driver, tied up the assailant—Norman clutched Khazzani's left arm, and Tanty, the right one—using a shirt and a train employee's necktie.[21] As they were doing this, a small number of passengers climbed out of windows. The alarm having been activated, the train had stopped briefly, although it would soon resume its journey and divert to the town of Arras, twenty-three miles away. Those who disembarked here in the countryside would be left behind.

As these events were unfolding, Alek Skarlatos conducted a walk-through of the other coaches to ensure there were no additional gunmen or injured passengers, while Spencer Stone, although injured himself, tended to the wounds of Mark Moogalian. It was obvious that the Sorbonne professor would die without treatment, his carotid artery having been nicked, so the airman did his utmost to ensure that the man would survive until they reached Arras. Local paramedics could then take the reins. Isabella Risacher-Moogalian recalled Stone's precise actions. "He put his finger on the wound in the middle of [Mark's] neck and he stayed in that position for the whole journey until we got to Arras," she said, "so I think he really saved my husband's life."[22] The airman also talked to Moogalian in an effort to help the suffering passenger remain conscious and calm. "Hey man," Stone said to him, "after this we're going to go have a beer."[23] Stone has since reflected on his humane actions. "I didn't really care about my injuries at that point because of the adrenaline, I didn't feel them," he said, "I just thought that guy was gonna die, so I wanted to give him a fighting chance."[24]

To be sure, the train still had to make it to Arras, and fast, if Moogalian was to survive. And the sight that greeted the passengers as they arrived at the provincial station was intimidating to say the least. "Men and equipment prepared for urban warfare," recounts Anthony Sadler and his friends, "SWAT-style trucks, national police, dozens of people waiting, some in full combat gear."[25]

Without delay, the police escorted Sadler, Skarlatos, Norman, and other witnesses to the police station in Arras to be debriefed, while paramedics took over Stone's life-saving actions on Moogalian. The wounded professor would be airlifted to University Hospital in Lille, thirty miles away, and admitted to its intensive care unit. Airman Stone would likewise be treated in Lille, before being transferred to Ramstein Air Base in Germany and treated at the nearby Landstuhl Regional Medical Center. Both men would make satisfactory, if lengthy, recoveries.

As for the man behind the madness, Ayoub El Khazzani, five

heavily-armed policeman headed toward him in Coach 12, where he was lying in the aisle, in and out of consciousness. Sadler and his friends have described how the law enforcement officers seized him. "The police do not untie the terrorist or cuff him, they simply pick him up like he is and carry him, one policeman on each limb, right off the train."[26]

A few hours later, someone deactivated Khazzani's Facebook account. The police did not do it, nor did the terrorist, who was behind bars. The logical conclusion: a person who knew Khazzani well enough to also be privy to his Facebook password was trying to protect him. And this, of course, raised the possibility of a co-conspirator.

Investigation and Indictments

On this subject, Ayoub El Khazzani insisted otherwise, maintaining that he had acted alone. He further claimed that he was homeless, had been living on the streets of Brussels, and found the weapons-laden suitcase in a park where he slept; a green space near the Brussels depot. According to the assailant, his plan was to rob some of the train's passengers and escape through a window. Of course, such claims were dubious, but he remained steadfast in his version of events. Not surprisingly, then, when the authorities confronted him, insisting that he was a militant Islamist who had conducted a terrorist strike, albeit a botched one, he vehemently denied it. "(T)he suggestion makes him almost laugh," said his attorney, Sophie David.[27]

While investigators did not accept Khazzani's account of the attack, including the fact that was a lone actor, they would finally get their hands on substantiating materials in December 2016. Sixteen months after the assault, French intelligence services learned that Khazzani had traveled to Syria shortly before the Thalys attack and, along with Abdelhamid Abaaoud, returned by way of Hungary and the Balkans. As previously noted, the Hungarian intelligence service knew that the pair had entered its borders, but it did not report this critical development to its French counterpart or to other countries' counterterrorism organizations. And this is inexplicable, since both Khazzani and Abaaoud were on the terrorist watch lists of multiple nations in addition to France; countries that included Spain, Germany, and Belgium. Moreover, when French intelligence officers contacted their Hungarian colleagues after Khazzani's arrest and formally requested any information the Eastern European nation possessed about his recent activities, the Hungarians, once again, did not fulfill the request. It was only when the findings of an independent investigation were reported publicly in the *CTC Sentinel*, an American journal published by the Combatting Terrorism Center at the U.S.

Military Academy at West Point, that French intelligence services found out that the two militant Islamists were known to have been traveling together in Europe in the weeks leading up to the Thalys operation.[28] It was also with the publication of this article that Ayoub El Khazzani finally capitulated and began speaking the truth to investigators, more or less.

In terms of the more questionable aspects of his confession, Khazzani claimed that when he was aboard the train and preparing to carry out his acts of violence—he was now admitting that terrorism had been his true intention—he saw Spencer Stone coming down the aisle toward him and, in that instant, changed his mind about killing anyone. "When I saw his head," Khazzani said, "it blocked me, I could not shoot a human being."[29] It was an assertion that would become the assailant's new line of defense. Even so, the facts were clear: Khazzani did try to kill Stone using the Kalashnikov, with the bullet that forensics experts retrieved from the scene confirming it. "The bullet," write Anthony Sadler and his colleagues, "has a perfect, deep dent in the back."

> Just like it's supposed to, just like you'd see on a spent shell casing after a bullet had fired. Only this time the bullet didn't fire. It had a bad primer. The firing pin struck the bullet, but the chemical reaction that was supposed to initiate simply did not happen. The bullet simply did not ignite.[30]

Ultimately, Khazzani would be charged with membership in a terrorist organization, coupled with attempted murder and attempted mass murder. And although he would continue to insist that he had experienced a change of heart about killing the train's passengers, he would update this statement while awaiting trial. "El-Khazzani," reported the BBC, "told the judge that having seen what has happened in Syria since he has been in custody, he now regrets his failure to kill anyone."[31] It was not the sort of statement a court could be expected to take lightly.

Returning to the subject of accomplices, it will be noted that Khazzani's co-conspirator in the Thalys attack, Abdelhamid Abaaoud, was deceased by this point in 2016, having perished in a police raid on the Saint Denis apartment in which he was hiding in the days following the November 2015 Paris attacks. But while Abaaoud's direct involvement in the Thalys train attack escaped detection while he was living, four other accomplices, all of whom were still very much alive, would in due course be identified and arrested. And this development would put to rest Khazzani's claim that he had been a lone actor. It was only in executing the assault itself that had he been completely on his own. Prior to this, he had been in contact with a small circle of Islamist extremists. There were even suspicions that Khazzani may have had previous interactions with the Belgian ISIS cell in

Verviers, the one that the police raided in January 2015 in the wake of the *Charlie Hebdo* atrocity.³²

So it was that French authorities, in October 2016, charged a Moroccan man, Redouane Sebbar, with complicity in the Thalys assault. It turns out that Sebbar, a few days prior to Khazzani's terror operation, had taken the same Brussels-to-Paris trip on the same train that would be the target of the assault.³³ He was casing it, most likely. And this is significant in that Sebbar was already known to have been a close comrade of Abdelhamid Abaaoud.

A year later, in October 2017, Belgian police seized another person, Youssef Siraj, and charged him with providing lodging in Molenbeek to Khazzani immediately before the Thalys attack. Siraq was subsequently handed over to law enforcement officers in France. As well, Belgian authorities accused still another individual of helping organize the Thalys assault, Mohamed Bakkali, and likewise extradited him to France with the stipulation that he be returned to Belgium to serve any prison sentence that might be forthcoming.³⁴

And lastly, in 2018, Germany extradited Bilal Chatra to France, the suspected ISIS scout who established the route through the Balkans for Khazzani and Abbaoud.³⁵ Among other deeds, investigators believed Bilal relayed information about unguarded border crossings to the pair so they could return safely to Western Europe. At the time of extradition, Chatra was twenty one years old and a citizen of Algeria.

As of September 2019, Ayoub El Khazzani and his four alleged accomplices were incarcerated and awaiting trial in France. And it was at this juncture that a French court granted an unusual request by the defendant. For the benefit of Khazzani, it agreed to stage a reenactment of the train attack at an undisclosed location.³⁶ And while the three American men who took down the assailant did not participate, fifteen other witnesses did take part in the exercise. Also on hand were the judges involved in the case. As to whether or not the reenactment will have an impact on the court's verdict, it remains to be seen, although it may be stated with certainty that the physical evidence and witness testimonies remain very damning.

Concluding with a look at the heroes of this tale, in recognition of Damien A. and Mark Moogalian's noble, self-sacrificing, and intrepid actions, French President Francois Hollande awarded them the Légion d'honneur—the Legion of Honor. France's highest order of merit, Napoleon Bonaparte established the decoration in 1802.³⁷ President Hollande also bestowed the Légion d'honneur upon Spencer Stone, Alek Skarlatos, Anthony Sadler, and Chris Norman. By any measure, all six men had demonstrated extraordinary courage during the assault on the Thalys train.

Then too, the terrorist incident, dreadful though it was, culminated in new friendships abroad for the trio of young Americans, producing in them a bond with France and the French people. In time, the three requested citizenship in the European nation, even as they planned to retain their U.S. citizenship as well. "(T)his attack has had such an impact on our lives," Alek Skarlatos told Agence France-Presse, "that for us it means a lot to be able to travel freely between these two countries and even to buy a house and live there one day if [we] want."[38] Exceptionally gracious in his response to their request was the new president of France, Emmanuel Macron, who granted the men French citizenship. "France is proud and happy to welcome you," Macron wrote in their official letters of naturalization.[39] Declaring that they now had the same rights as all other citizens of France, Macron invited their active participation in the French republic.[40]

Epilogue—France Today
Emotional Scars, Enhanced Security, and the Question of Future Attacks

On an October afternoon in 2018, I paid a visit to the Bataclan Theatre on the Boulevard Voltaire. Apart from the bold anti-terrorism announcement posted on its front door, a government-issued notice indicating that increased security measures were in effect because the site was still considered a potential target of terrorism, the renowned venue showed no remnants of the horror that was unleashed on November 13, 2015. Certainly, my partner Michael and I were hard-pressed, on this bright autumn day, to envision the bloodbath that had occurred on that tragic night. And yet, in conversations with lifelong Parisians who were in the capital city when the attacks occurred, I discovered that the mere mention of the onslaught, even four years afterward, was often met with mournful looks and, occasionally, hints of discomfort with the topic itself.

The fact is, the city of Paris, and France more generally, have never truly recovered from the two-year spate of mass killings that blindsided the nation. In important respects, the city and country have changed. This does not mean, however, that the terrorists "won." Those behind the assaults—al-Qaeda, the Islamic State, and, in some cases, their devotees acting unofficially on the organizations' behalf—did not, in fact, achieve their purported aims. France, for instance, did not withdraw its troops from Syria as ISIS demanded, nor did the French people relinquish their so-called liberal lifestyles to submit to the strict mandates of radical Islamists, as both al-Qaeda and ISIS wished. Rather, the 2015–2016 rash of savagery was a war in which there were no victors, only victims.

Ironically, one casualty appears to have been France's sizable and authentic Muslim community, authentic in the sense that it follows the globally-recognized tenets of the Islamic faith, rejecting the distorted interpretations and indiscriminate violence of Muslim extremists. Owing to the al-Qaeda and ISIS attacks, many conventional, law-abiding Muslims watched as their communities became bruised by the mounting tendency of France's non–Muslim citizens to view their Islamic compatriots, collectively, as suspect.

Then too, the legislation that the government enacted during and after the Islamist assaults vexed many civil liberties advocates, who expressed concerns about the impact such exceptional legal measures appeared to be having on adherents of the Islamic faith. "With the ... attacks in France being driven by extremist religious motives, there are legitimate fears that the country's Muslim population will be increasingly bearing the brunt of the exceptional becoming the 'new normal,'" wrote Roxane De Rebetz De Massol and Maartje Van Der Woude in the journal *Critical Studies in Terrorism*.[1] This is not to understate the fact that other minority groups also appear to be at risk of being adversely affected by the country's new anti-terrorism measures.

It is an ongoing controversy that began with the national state of emergency that President Hollande enacted on November 13, 2015, the night of the ISIS massacres at the Bataclan Theatre and five other Paris venues. The declaration handed sweeping new powers to prosecutors and law enforcement officers with the understanding that it was to be a short-term, comprehensive effort to detect and prevent further acts of religious or political violence. Generally speaking, the emergency declaration streamlined the requirements and procedures involved in surveilling, seizing, and detaining suspects by sidestepping the standard administrative practices and judicial authorizations that could slow down or stall such activities. Unfortunately, misuses and abuses of the state of emergency were soon reported. "In one house raid," reported *Human Rights Watch*, "police broke four of a disabled man's teeth before they realized he wasn't the person they were looking for."[2] In another, police in Nice stormed a family's apartment in the pre-dawn hours, in the process firing into an open window. The barrage of gunfire caused wooden objects to shatter, with wood fragments striking a six-year-old girl in the neck and ear. The police were at the wrong address, it turned out.[3]

So it was that several months after the November 13th attacks—the date was June 3, 2016—the Hollande administration, in a move to upgrade the existing regulations to better address the terrorism crisis, adopted the "Law Reinforcing the Fight Against Organized Crime, Terrorism and its Financing." In effect, the law was to be superimposed over the original state of emergency, which was to remain in place for the time being. And while the public generally viewed the new 2016 law favorably, some within the judicial system were troubled by various aspects of it, as were civil liberties advocates. Their overarching objection was that Hollande's reforms appeared to be an attempt to make permanent many of the controversial elements of the temporary state of emergency. "They say the government is trying to institutionalize exceptional measures that were made possible when a state of emergency was declared after last year's attacks," reported the *New York Times*.[4]

To be sure, the provisions in the 2016 anti-terrorism law were tough. For starters, the legislation relaxed the existing surveillance regulations, permitting prosecutors and police officers to wiretap telephones and acquire internet data without a court's permission, employ hidden cameras, and surreptitiously install microphones and cameras in prison cells. It also granted law enforcement officers access to cutting-edge technology that was previously available only to those in the nation's intelligence agencies. And it criminalized citizens who consulted jihadist websites on a regular basis, with exemptions for journalists and academic researchers. The punishment: €30,000 ($33,500 USD) and up to two years in prison. (In 2017, a court would rule the latter component—punishment for viewing militant jihadi websites—unconstitutional.[5])

In addition, law enforcement officers were given greater latitude when using lethal force if there was reason to believe that a suspect might be engaging in a grievous assault. As well, the police could detain individuals for up to four hours without access to an attorney, and could place those returning from Iraq or Syria under house arrest for a month.

While most of the citizenry supported these reforms despite the challenges they posed to civil liberties, people in France did, by this point, want the original state of emergency lifted. And they were not alone. Among the political figures who also desired it was Emmanuel Macron, who pledged to end the state of emergency if he were elected. And indeed, when he won the presidency, Macron's administration proposed a second set of reforms, which were approved on October 31, 2017. In this way, the two-year emergency declaration was finally discontinued.

Like the first set of reforms, however, these new principles and regulations were provocative. Titled, the "Law Reinforcing Internal Security and the Fight Against Terrorism," Macron's new law merely codified numerous components of the state of emergency rather than replacing them with less intrusive, less restrictive measures, the upshot being that it granted ordinary police officers extraordinary license on a permanent basis.[6] "These powers include the ability to shut down mosques, raid private property, conduct warrantless stop-and-frisk operations, and restrict movement of individuals deemed potential national security threats with electronic surveillance tags," journalist Sarah Harvard wrote at the time.[7] Indeed, several thousands of searches were subsequently conducted, along with hundreds of raids and house arrests, the establishment of scores of "protection zones," most often in minority neighborhoods, and closures of mosques and other gathering spots.[8] In some cases, the authorities permitted mosques that were under suspicion to re-open if they agreed to install surveillance cameras and other equipment. And yet these police actions, excessive though they were, did prove valuable in some cases. For instance, they led, within a short time frame, to five hundred illegal weapons being seized, forty of them being weapons of war.[9] Yet only a handful of indictments were forthcoming from the thousands of raids and searches. The issue, then, was one of priorities; that of individual liberties vs. public safety.

On this matter, some experts have argued that it is possible to achieve both aims, that they are not mutually exclusive. Rym Khadhraoui of Amnesty International, the human rights organization, was one expert who weighed in on the subject. "Whilst protecting people from violent attacks is vital," Khadhraoui stated, "side-stepping the criminal justice system in order to target people on the assumption that they might commit crimes in the future is absurd and unjust."[10]

In response to the concerns being voiced about the measures, the French government, in 2018, extended an invitation to Fionnuala D. Ni Aolain, the United Nations' Special Rapporteur on the protection of human rights. Ni Aolain's task during her nine-day visit was to assess the anti-terrorism law's impact on human rights. And her findings were disconcerting. While acknowledging that extreme events, like threats of mass violence, may call for extreme responses, Ni Aolain was forthright in her criticism of the way in which the anti-terrorism measures were being applied in France. "It is clear," she stated, "that the French Muslim community have been the community primarily subject to exceptional measures both during the state of emergency and the new law in tandem with other counter-terrorism measures."[11] She continued,

> It is deeply concerning that the Muslim minority community is being constructed as a *per se* 'suspect community' through the sustained and broad application of a counter-terrorism law…. There is no doubt that the state may lawfully engage in restrictions to protect public order, but a clear tipping point to exceptionality arises when counter-terrorism measures engage profound, sustained and potentially disproportionate effects on the enjoyment of fundamental human rights and civil liberties.[12]

Ni Aolain's observations bring us back to that which was stated earlier in the Epilogue, namely that the jihadi terrorists who conducted the 2015–2016 strikes, nearly all of whom are now dead, left behind for non-radicalized French Muslims a social and political situation that is undoubtedly worse than it was before the attacks. It is one that threatens to alienate France's Muslim population, widening the gulf between the country's non–Muslims and Muslims while breeding bitterness and resentment in the latter. In turn, French Muslims may now become less inclined to trust, and thus confide in, law enforcement and counterterrorism officials, leaving the authorities with fewer sources in the Islamic community to report suspicious activities. And the latter group, ordinary members of the community, are often the ones who are in the best position to detect possible threats and alert the authorities to them. Obviously, distancing this segment of the population runs counter to France's strenuous efforts to prevent terrorism, since human intelligence—HUMINT—is most often the key to averting it.

In this regard, Christophe Castaner, Minister of the Interior, revealed in late 2019 that between the years 2003 and 2019, a total of 59 terrorist plots were thwarted in France—an impressive number—and that fifty-eight of them, or ninety-nine percent—had been detected, first and foremost, through HUMINT.[13] Other methods, such as electronic surveillance, tended to be most effective when used in a supportive capacity for HUMINT.

Presumably, the French government will continue fine-tuning its anti-terrorism measures. This should include a concentrated effort to regain the trust of, and liaise with, the Muslim community in recognizing terrorist threats, viewing members of the Islamic faith as partners in fighting terrorism rather than as potential perpetrators of it. As well, it should better ensure that all French citizens, regardless of religious affiliation, skin color, or other personal quality, enjoy those rights enshrined in the nation's Constitution, while also being protected from extremist violence.

Chapter Notes

Prologue

1. Adam Nossiter, "In Paris Knife Attack, Police Ask How They Missed a Killer in Their Midst," *New York Times*, October 5, 2019.
2. Adam Nossiter, Aurelien Breeden, and Elian Peltier, "Knife Attack at Paris Police Headquarters Leaves 4 Dead," *New York Times*, October 3, 2019.
3. Rachel Donadio, "The Unending Disquiet after Attacks in Paris," *The Atlantic*, October 9, 2019.
4. Conrad Hackett, "5 Facts About the Muslim Population in Europe," PerResearch.org. (Pew Research Center), November 29, 2017, https://www.pewresearch.org/fact-tank/2017/11/29/5-facts-about-the-muslim-population-in-europe/.
5. Michel Gurfinkiel, "Islam in France: The French Way of Life Is in Danger," *Middle East Quarterly* 4, no. 1 (March 1997): 19–29.
6. Ibid.
7. Yasmine Ryan, "Uncovering Algeria's Civil War," Aljazeera.com, November 18, 2010, https://www.aljazeera.com/indepth/2010/11/2010118122224407570.html.
8. Seymour Hersch, "Torture at Abu Ghraib," *The New Yorker*, May 10, 2004.
9. Victoria Craw and Wire Reports, "National Front Leader Marine Le Pen Tipped for French Presidential Run Following Terror Attacks," News.com.au, January 23, 2015, https://www.news.com.au/finance/work/leaders/national-front-leader-marine-le-pen-tipped-for-french-presidential-run-following-terror-attacks/news-story/e772a1f86fa2e8e322bfa25ebe9c0fdc.
10. Cindy Pom, "France Faces the Daunting Task of Curbing Prison Radicalization to Prevent 'ISIS 2.0.,'" *Pittsburgh Post-Gazette*, January 10, 2019.
11. Dina Temple-Raston, "French Prisons Prove to Be Effective Incubators for Islamic Extremism," NPR.com, January 22, 2015, https://www.npr.org/sections/parallels/2015/01/22/379081047/french-prisons-prove-to-be-effective-incubators-for-islamic-extremism.
12. "Jihadism in French Prisons: Caged Fervour," *The Economist*, September 17, 2016.

Chapter 1

1. Emma Hurt, "The Freedom to Be Funny: Reflecting on France's Tradition of Satire," *La Jeune Politique*, January 23, 2015.
2. Laurence Grove, "French Cartooning: A History," *Jewish Quarterly*, Spring 2015, https://www.jewishquarterly.org/2015/02/french-cartooning-a-history/.
3. Project Gutenberg, *Les Cent Nouvelles Nouvelles*. n.d. Gutenberg.org, accessed 12/7/18, http://www.gutenberg.org/files/18575/18575-h/18575-h.htm.
4. Alice Robb, "There Is No 'Charlie Hebdo' in America," *New Republic*, January 8, 2015.
5. British Broadcasting Corp., "Charlie Hebdo: Gun Attack on French Magazine Kills 12," BBC.com, January 7, 2015. https://www.bbc.com/news/world-europe-30710883.
6. Jonathan Jones, "Daumier's Satirical Art Hits with the Force of a Drone Attack," *The Guardian*, October 29, 2013.
7. Amy Wiese Forbes, *The Satiric Decade: Satire and the Rise of Republicanism in France, 1830–1840* (Lanham, Maryland: Lexington Books, 2010).

8. *Ibid.*, 44.
9. Michael L. J. Wilson, "Portrait of the Artist as a Louis XIII Chair," in *Montmartre and the Making of Mass Culture*, ed. Gabriel P. Weisberg (New Brunswick, New Jersey: Rutgers University Press, 2001), 182.
10. Robert Zaretsky, "'Charlie Hebdo,' Houellebecq, and France's Pungent Satirical Tradition," *Chronicle of Higher Education*, January 9, 2015.
11. Janet Whitmore, "Absurdist Humor in Bohemia," in *Montmartre and the Making of Mass Culture*, ed. Gabriel P. Weisberg. (New Brunswick, New Jersey: Rutgers University Press, 2001), 221.
12. *Ibid.*, 207.
13. *Ibid.*, 221.
14. Tony Husband, ed., *Cartoons of World War II* (London: Arcturus, 2015), 9.
15. *Ibid.*, 19.
16. Victor S. Navasky, *The Art of Controversy* (New York: Alfred A. Knopf, 2013).
17. *Ibid.*, 18.
18. *Ibid.*, xxi.
19. *Ibid.*, 45.
20. *Ibid.*, 22.
21. British Broadcasting Corp., "Charlie Hebdo: Gun Attack on French Magazine Kills 12," BBC.com, January 7, 2015. https://www.bbc.com/news/world-europe-30710883.

Chapter 2

1. Peter Hervik, *The Annoying Difference: The Emergence of Danish Neonationalism, Neoracism, and Populism in the Post-1989 World* (New York: Berghahn Books, 2011), 1.
2. Samantha Ruth Brown, "Denmark Already Had a Muslim Ban. It Was Just Called Something Else," *Washington Post*, March 23, 2017.
3. "Kurt Westergaard, Free Speech, and Leftist Refuseniks," *The National Post*, October 5, 2009.
4. *Ibid.*
5. *Ibid.*
6. Peter Hervik and Malmö University, *The Danish Muhammad Cartoon Conflict— Current Themes in IMER Research, no. 13* (Malmö, Sweden: Malmö Institute for Studies of Migration, Diversity and Welfare— Malmö University, 2012).
7. Mona Konwal Sheikh and Manni Crone, "Muslims as a Danish Security Issue," in *Islam in Denmark: The Challenge of Diversity*, ed. Jørgen S. Neilson. (Lanham, Maryland: Lexington Books, 2011) 178.
8. Hervik, *The Annoying Difference*, 179.
9. Daniel Burke, "Why Images of Mohammed Offend Muslims," CNN.com, Updated May 4, 2015, https://www.cnn.com/2015/05/04/living/islam-prophet-images/index.html.
10. Hervik, *The Annoying Difference*, 181.
11. *Ibid.*
12. *Ibid.*, 183.
13. Flemming Rose, "Why I Published Those Cartoons," *Washington Post*, February 19, 2006.
14. Peter Hervik and Malmö University, *The Danish Muhammad Cartoon Conflict*, 35.
15. Bob Simon (Correspondent), "Rewind: Danish Newspaper Satirizes Islam," CBS News—60 Minutes Overtime, CBSNews.com, January 1, 2015 (transcript of earlier television program, titled "State of Denmark; aired February 19, 2006), https://www.cbsnews.com/news/danish-newspaper-satirizes-islam/.
16. Simon, "Rewind: Danish Newspaper Satirizes Islam."
17. Michael Coren, "The 'Draw Mohammad' Contest Was Not an Attempt to Start a Conversation But a Single Act of Bravado," *The National Post*, May 7, 2015.
18. *Ibid.*
19. Hervik and Malmö University, *The Danish Muhammad Cartoon Conflict*, 38.
20. Hervik, *The Annoying Difference*, 185.
21. John Ward Anderson, "Cartoons of Prophet Met with Outrage," *Washington Post*, January 31, 2006.
22. "Shahada," Berkley Center for Religion, Peace, and World Affairs. n.d., BerkleyCenter.Georgetown.edu (Georgetown University website), accessed January 14, 2018, https://berkleycenter.georgetown.edu/essays/shahada.
23. Kaare Sørensen, *The Mind of a Terrorist: David Headly, the Mumbai Massacre, and His European Revenge* (New York: Arcade Publishing), 2016, 67.
24. Peter McGraw and Joel Warner, "The Danish Cartoon Crisis of 2005 and 2006: 10 Things You Didn't Know about the Original

Muhammad Controversy," *Huffington Post*, September 5, 2012.

25. Adam Taylor, "Why Would Terrorists Kill Cartoonists?" *Washington Post*, January 7, 2015.

26. John Ward Anderson, "Cartoons of Prophet Met with Outrage."

27. Nicholas Watt, "Danish Paper Sorry for Muhammad Cartoons," *The Guardian*, January 31, 2006.

28. Sørensen, *The Mind of a Terrorist*, 68–69.

29. Marie Louise Sjølie, "The Danish Cartoonist Who Survived an Axe Attack," *The Guardian*, January 4, 2010.

30. Jérôme Lambert and Philippe Picard, "Charlie Hebdo, before the Massacre," *New York Times*, January 9, 2015.

31. Catherine Taibi, "These Are the Charlie Hebdo Cartoons That Terrorists Thought Were Worth Killing Over," *Huffington Post*, December 6, 2017.

32. "Prophet Mohammed Cartoons Controversy: Timeline," *The Telegraph*, May 4, 2015.

33. Craig W. Smith, "French Court Rules for Newspaper That Printed Muhammad Cartoons," *New York Times*, March 23, 2007.

34. Gwladys Fouché, "Cartoon Court Case Begins," *The Guardian*, February 7, 2007.

35. Gregory Viscusi, "French Muslims File Suit Over Alleged Racism," *Bloomberg News* (Reprinted in *The New York Sun*, February 7, 2007).

36. Associated Press, "Paper Cleared in Muhammad Drawings Case," *Washington Post*, March 22, 2007.

37. Thierry Leveque, "French Court Clears Weekly in Mohammad Cartoon Row," Reuters.com, March 22, 2007, https://www.reuters.com/article/industry-france-cartoons-trial-dc/french-court-clears-weekly-in-mohammad-cartoon-row-idUSL2212067120070322.

38. "Charlie Hebdo: Procès," Charlie-Hebdo.fr (*Charlie Hebdo* website), accessed 1/5/20, https://charliehebdo.fr/pages/proces/, *Charlie Hebdo* (website), 2018, https://charliehebdo.fr/en/trials/.

39. "French Satirical Newspaper 'Charlie Hebdo' Wins Second Trial Over Controversial Cartoon Ban Request," NewswireToday.com, February 9, 2007, https://www.newswiretoday.com/news/13842/.

Chapter 3

1. "Attentat à Charlie Hebdo: Pontoise Pleure Charb," *Le Parisien*, January 7, 2015.
2. *Ibid.*
3. *Ibid.*
4. Olivier Delcroix, "Charb, Insolent Volontaire," *Le Figaro*, January 7, 2015.
5. *Ibid.*
6. *Ibid.*
7. Jean-Marie Colombani, "Nous Sommes Tous Américains," *Le Monde*, May 23, 2007.
8. Stéphane Charbonnier, *Charlie Hebdo Magazine* (cover cartoon), September 19, 2001.
9. *Ibid.*
10. Charb (Charbonnier, Stéphane), *Open Letter: On Blasphemy, Islamophobia, and the True Enemies of Free Expression* (New York: Little, Brown, 2015), 15.
11. "Muhammad Depictions: French Satirical Paper Reportedly Attacked," *Der Spiegel*, November 2, 2011.
12. Soeren Kern, "100 Lashes If You Don't Die Laughing," *Gatestone Institute National Policy Council*, November 3, 2011, https://www.gatestoneinstitute.org/2560/islam-free-speech-lashes.
13. David Jolly, "Satirical Magazine Is Firebombed in Paris," *New York Times*, November 2, 2011.
14. British Broadcasting Corp., "French Satirical Paper Charlie Hebdo Attacked in Paris," BBCNews.com, November 2, 2011, https://www.bbc.com/news/world-europe-15550350.
15. Associated Press, "French Satirical Magazine Office Fire Bombed Ahead of 'Muhammad Edition,'" FoxNews.com, updated December 4, 2015, https://www.foxnews.com/world/french-satirical-magazine-office-fire-bombed-ahead-of-muhammad-edition.
16. "French Satirical Paper Charlie Hebdo Attacked in Paris," *BBC News*, November 2, 2011.
17. Lizzie Deardon, "Charlie Hebdo Attack: Former Editor Philippe Val Urges People to Use Laughter as the 'Ultimate Weapon' against Extremists," *The Independent*, January 7, 2015.
18. Elaine Teng, "The Last Time 'Charlie Hebdo' Was Attacked by Terrorists, Its Response Was Perfect," *New Republic*, January 7, 2015.

19. Richard Esposito, Brian Ross, and Cindy Galli, "Anti-Islam Film Producer Wrote Script in Prison: Authorities," ABC-News.go.com, September 13, 2012, https://abcnews.go.com/Blotter/anti-islam-film-producer-wrote-script-prison-authorities/story?id=17230609.

20. Jon Wiener, "Defend Charlie Hebdo's Publishing Disgusting Cartoons about Muslims? Yes. Give Them an Award for It? No," *The Nation*, May 1, 2015.

21. Steven K Baum, "Antisemitic Incidents from Around the World, January—June 2015: A Selected List," *Journal for the Study of Antisemitism* 7, no. 1 (2015), 17.

22. "Muhammad Depictions: French Satirical Paper Reportedly Attacked," *Der Spiegel*, November 2, 2011.

23. Anne Penketh and Julian Borger, "Fight Intimidation with Controversy: Charlie Hebdo's Response to Critics," *The Guardian*, January 7, 2015.

24. Nicolas Vinocur, "Cartoons in French Weekly Fuel Mohammad Furor," Reuters.com, September 19, 2012, https://www.reuters.com/article/us-protests-france/cartoons-in-french-weekly-fuel-mohammad-furor-idUSBRE88I0BU20120919.

25. Kern, "100 Lashes If You Don't Die Laughing."

Chapter 4

1. John Litchfield, "Paris Attacks: Why the Charlie Hebdo Gunmen Saïd and Chérif Kouachi Made an Unlikely Terror Cell," *The Independent*, January 18, 2015.

2. Ibid,

3. Marion Van Renterghem, "Les Freres Kouachi: Une Jeunesse Française," *Le Monde*, February 13, 2015.

4. Rukmini Callimachi and Jim Yardley, "From Amateur to Ruthless Jihadist in France: Chérif and Saïd Kouachi's Path to Paris Attack at Charlie Hebdo," *New York Times*, January 17, 2015.

5. Litchfield, "Paris Attacks."

6. Van Renterghem, "Les Freres Kouachi: Une Jeunesse Française."

7. Callimachi and Yardley, "From Amateur to Ruthless Jihadist in France."

8. Van Renterghem, "Les Freres Kouachi."

9. Ibid.

10. Associated Press, "French Muslims Flock to, from Iraq's Battlefields," NBCNews.com, updated March 30, 2008, http://www.nbcnews.com/id/23872546/ns/world_news-islam_in_europe/t/french-muslims-flock-iraqs-battlefields/.

11. "Searching for Answers in the 'Charlie Hebdo' Attacks: Charlie Hebdo Attackers Radicalized in Search for Identity," *Der Spiegel*, January 19, 2015.

12. Angelique Chrisafis, "Charlie Hebdo Attackers: Born, Raised, and Radicalised in France," *The Guardian*, January 12, 2015.

13. Spiegel Staff, "Searching for Answers in the 'Charlie Hebdo' Attacks: Charlie Hebdo Attackers Radicalized in Search of Identity."

14. Usama Hasan, "Viewpoint: What Do Radical Islamists Actually Believe In?" BBCNews.com, May 24, 2013, https://www.bbc.com/news/magazine-22640614.

15. Chris Pleasance, "'They Were Too Weak to Resist Jihad,' Says Former Boarding School Teacher: How Kouachi Brothers Went from Football-Loving Teenager with No Interest in Religion to Extremist Killers," *Daily Mail*, January 12, 2015.

16. Max Kutner, "Meet Farid Benyettou, the Man Who Trained Paris Attack Suspect Cherif Kouachi," *Newsweek*, January 8, 2015.

17. Mark Houser, "French Muslims Battle Internal, External Strife," *Pittsburgh Tribune*, May 29, 2005.

18. Spiegel Staff, "Searching for Answers in the 'Charlie Hebdo' Attacks: Charlie Hebdo Attackers Radicalized in Search of Identity."

19. Kutner, "Meet Farid Benyettou."

20. Spiegel Staff, "Searching for Answers in the 'Charlie Hebdo' Attacks."

21. Jim Yardley, "Jihadism Born in a Paris Park and Fueled in the Prison Yard," *New York Times*, January 11, 2015.

22. Flore Olive with Karim Baouz, "Chérif et Saïd Kouachi: Le Voyage sans Issue de Deux Paumés," *Paris Match*, January 11, 2015.

23. Scott Sayare, "The Ultimate Terrorist Factory," *Harper's Magazine*, January 2016.

24. Ibid.

25. Josh Halliday, Duncan Gardham, and Julian Borger, "Mentor of Charlie Hebdo Gunmen Has Been UK-based," *The Guardian*, January 11, 2015.

26. Alexandria Sage and Chine Labbé,

"French Attacks Inquiry Centers on Prison 'Sorcerer' Beghal," Reuters.com, January 15, 2015, https://www.reuters.com/article/us-france-shooting-beghal-insight/french-attacks-inquiry-centers-on-prison-sorcerer-beghal-idUSKBN0KO28G20150115.
27. Jon Henley, "Paris Plot Reveals Link to Terror Chief," *The Guardian*, October 2, 2001.
28. Henley, "Paris Plot Reveals Link to Terror Chief."
29. "Leader of U.S. Embassy Bomb Plot Gets 10 Years," *New York Times*, March 15, 2005.
30. Sayare, "The Ultimate Terrorist Factory."
31. Callimachi and Yardley, "From Amateur to Ruthless Jihadist in France."
32. Sayare, "The Ultimate Terrorist Factory."
33. James Bruce, "For ISIS, Prisons Have Become Terror Incubators," *The Arab Weekly* (UK), January 15, 2017.
34. Dina Temple-Raston, "French Prisons Prove to Be Effective Incubators for Islamic Extremism," NPR.com, January 22, 2015, https://www.npr.org/sections/parallels/2015/01/22/379081047/french-prisons-prove-to-be-effective-incubators-for-islamic-extremism.
35. Callimachi and Yardley, "From Amateur to Ruthless Jihadist in France."
36. Sayare, "The Ultimate Terrorist Factory."
37. British Broadcasting Corp., "Paris Attacks: Suspects' Profiles," BBC.com, January 12, 2015, https://www.bbc.com/news/world-europe-30722038.
38. Andrew Higgins, "French Police Say Suspect in Attack Evolved from Petty Criminal to Terrorist," *New York Times*, January 10, 2015.
39. Scott Shane, "In New Era of Terrorism, Voices from Yemen Echoes," *New York Times*, January 10, 2015.
40. Shane, "In New Era of Terrorism, Voices from Yemen Echoes."
41. Mark Hosenball, "Suspect Sought in Paris Attack Had Training in Yemen—Sources," Reuters.com, January 8, 2015, https://www.reuters.com/article/france-shooting-yemen/suspect-sought-in-paris-attack-had-trained-in-yemen-sources-idUSL1N0UN1PJ20150108.
42. Mark MacKinnon, "Neighbour Says Suspects in Paris Shooting Had 'Cache of Arms,'" *The Globe and Mail*, March 25, 2017.
43. Vivienne Walt, "Mentor of Charlie Hebdo Gunman Says He Was Obsessed with Violence," *TIME Magazine*, January 13, 2015.

Chapter 5

1. Griff Witte and Anthony Folala, "Charlie Hebdo Suspect Said to Surrender: Two Others at Large After Paris Terror Attack," *Washington Post*, January 7, 2015.
2. "Un Ancien de Charlie Hebdo Accuse Charb," *L'Express*, January 15, 2015.
3. Amelia Smith, "Stephane Charbonnier Was on Al-Qaeda 'Hit List' Circulated on Social Media," *Newsweek*, January 8, 2015.
4. *Je Suis Charlie*, written and directed by Daniel Leconte and Emmanuel Leconte (Paris: Films en Stock, 2015) https://www.amazon.com/Je-Suis-Charlie-Elisabeth-Badinter/dp/B01AYSRVUO.
5. Liz Alderman, "Recounting a Bustling Office at Charlie Hebdo, Then a 'Vision of Horror,'" *New York Times*, January 9, 2015.
6. Kiran Moodley, "Charlie Hebdo Survivor: 'I Turned Around and My World Tumbled,'" *The Independent*, January 14, 2015.
7. Australian Broadcasting Corp., Agence France-Presse, and Reuters, "Charlie Hebdo Shooting: Track How Events Unfolded," ABC.net.au, January 8, 2015, https://www.abc.net.au/news/2015-01-08/paris-newspaper-attack-mapped/6006110.
8. *Je Suis Charlie*, Leconte and Leconte.
9. Ibid.
10. Michael Koziol, "Charlie Hebdo Survivor Simon Fieschi Marries Australian Girlfriend Maisie Dubosarsky in Paris," *The Sydney Morning Herald*, October 3, 2015.
11. *Je Suis Charlie*, Leconte and Leconte.
12. Ibid.
13. Ibid.
14. "Assaulting Democracy: The Deep Repercussions of the Charlie Hebdo Attack," *Der Spiegel*, January 9, 2015.
15. *Three Days of Terror: The Charlie Hebdo Attacks*, Dan Reed, director (Paris/

London: Premières Lignes Télévision and AMOS Pictures, with the participation of Home Box Office (ë), British Broadcasting Corp. (BBC), and France Télévisions, 2016).
16. Alderman, "Recounting a Bustling Office at Charlie Hebdo."
17. *Je Suis Charlie*, Leconte and Leconte.
18. *Charlie Hebdo: 3 Days That Shook Paris*, Ursula Macfarlane, director (London: Films of Record, 2015).
19. *Ibid.*
20. "Charlie Hebdo: Gun Attack on French Magazine Kills 12," *BBC News*, January 7, 2015.
21. Jake Tapper, "The Lead with Jake Tapper: Mapping the Paris Terror Attack," Youtube.com (CNN Channel), January 7, 2015, https://www.youtube.com/watch?v=9BHQSSUyeOE.
22. Randi Kaye, "Anderson Cooper 360 Degrees: Two of the Suspects in the Shootings in 'Charlie Hebdo' Office in Paris Identified," CNN.com, aired January 8, 2015, http://transcripts.cnn.com/TRANSCRIPTS/1501/08/acd.02.html.
23. *Charlie Hebdo: 3 Days That Shook Paris*, Ursula Macfarlane, director.
24. "Victims of the Terror Attacks in Paris," *New York Times*, January 11, 2015, https://www.nytimes.com/2015/01/12/world/europe/terror-attacks-in-paris-the-victims.html.
25. British Broadcasting Corp., "Paris Shootings: Ahmed Merabet's Killers 'Pretend Muslims' Says brother," BBC.com, January 10, 2015, https://www.bbc.com/news/av/world-europe-30762153/paris-shootings-ahmed-merabet-s-killers-pretend-muslims-says-brother.
26. Kim Willsher, "Charlie Hebdo Attack: Fallen Policeman Ahmed Merabet Buried in Bobigny," *The Guardian*, January 13, 2015.
27. Luke Harding, "Charlie Hebdo Timeline: How Events Have Unfolded," *The Guardian*, January 9, 2015.
28. "Terror from the Fringes: Searching for Answers in the "Charlie Hebdo" Attacks—Part 5: The Bewilderment of the Terrorists' Friends," *Der Spiegel*, January 19, 2015.
29. François Hollande, "Attack against Charlie Hebdo Statement by Mr. François Hollande, President of the Republic," *Élysée Palace*, January 7, 2015, https://www.diplomatie.gouv.fr/en/the-ministry-and-its-network/events/article/attack-against-charlie-hebdo.
30. *Ibid.*
31. Kim Willsher, "John Kerry Declares 'Profound Emotion' for France in Paris Address," *The Guardian*, January 16, 2015.
32. Peter Allen, "Student Who Was Cleared of Being Getaway Driver in Charlie Hebdo Attacks Is Arrested as He 'Tries to Join Islamic State in Syria,'" *Daily Mail*, August 7, 2016.
33. Agence France-Presse, "Teen 'In Shock' after Wrongly Linked to Charlie Hebdo Attack," NDTV.com, January 13, 2015, https://www.ndtv.com/world-news/teen-in-shock-after-wrongly-linked-to-charlie-hebdo-attack-726332.
34. Edward Mickolus, *Terrorism Worldwide, 2016* (Jefferson, NC: McFarland, 2018).
35. Melodie Bouchard, "In Photos: 'I Am Charlie' Vigil Held in Paris for Murdered 'Charlie Hebdo' Journalists," Vice.com, January 7, 2015, https://www.vice.com/en_us/article/gyn7d9/in-photos-i-am-charlie-vigil-held-in-paris-for-murdered-charlie-hebdo-journalists.
36. Sarah Ann Harris, "Shooting of Paris Police Officer Linked to Charlie Hebdo Massacre," *Daily Express*, January 9, 2015.
37. Tariq Ramadan, "Search Narrows for Charlie Hebdo Suspects," Aljazeera.com, January 8, 2015, https://www.aljazeera.com/news/europe/2015/01/police-locate-suspects-behind-paris-attack-2015181093491033O.html.
38. Kim Willsher and Alexandra Topping, "Police Converge on Area North-East of Paris in Hunt for Charlie Hebdo Gunmen," *The Guardian*, January 8, 2015.
39. *Charlie Hebdo: 3 Days That Shook Paris*, Ursula Macfarlane, director.
40. *Ibid.*
41. *Three Days of Terror*, Dan Reed, director.
42. National Broadcasting Network, "Paris Killer Cherif Kouachi Gave Interview to TV Channel before He Died," NBCNews.com, updated January 9, 2015, https://www.nbcnews.com/storyline/paris-magazine-attack/paris-killer-cherif-kouachi-gave-interview-tv-channel-he-died-n283206.
43. *Ibid.*
44. *Three Days of Terror*, Dan Reed, director.

45. Robert Mendick, Nicola Harley, and Harriet Alexander, "Amid the Terror, a Hero Who Lost His Life by Fighting Back," *The Telegraph*, January 10, 2015.
46. Shiryn Solny, "Footage Shows Hyper Cacher Terrorist Kill Shopper after Victim Revealed He Was Jewish," *The Algemeiner*, February 26, 2015.
47. *Three Days of Terror*, Dan Reed, director.
48. Jason Hanna and Margot Haddad, "Cherif Kouachi Texted Coulibaly an Hour before Paris Attacks Began," CNN.com, updated February 17, 2015, https://www.cnn.com/2015/02/17/world/france-charlie-hebdo-attacks/index.html.
49. "Paris Shooting: Armed Man Takes Hostages in Paris Kosher Store," *Sydney Morning Herald*, January 10, 2015.
50. Daniel L. Byman and Jennifer R. Williams, "ISIS vs. Al Qaeda: Jihadism's Global Civil War," Brookings.edu (The Brookings Institution), February 24, 2015, https://www.brookings.edu/articles/isis-vs-al-qaeda-jihadisms-global-civil-war/.
51. Byman and Williams, "ISIS vs. Al Qaeda."
52. Julian Borger, "Paris Gunman Amedy Coulibaly Declared Allegiance to ISIS," *The Guardian*, January 11, 2015.
53. Lizzie Dearden, "Paris Shootings: How the Sieges with Charlie Hebdo Killers at Dammartin-en-Goele Print Works and Jewish Grocer Ended," *The Independent*, January 9, 2015.
54. "Paris Shooting," *Sydney Morning Herald*.
55. "Hyper Cacher Victim's Father Knew His Son 'Would Fight,'" *Times of Israel*, January 16, 2015.
56. Griff Witte, "In a Kosher Grocery Store in Paris, Terror Takes a Deadly Toll," *Washington Post*, January 9, 2015.
57. Harriet Alexander, "Paris Attacks: Special Forces Hit Amedy Coulibaly with 40 Bullets," *The Telegraph*, January 11, 2015.
58. Mariano Castillo, "Following the Tangled and Treacherous Trail after France Terror Attack," CNN.com, updated January 15, 2015, https://www.cnn.com/2015/01/13/europe/france-charlie-hebdo-attack-trail/index.html.
59. Ibid.
60. Catherine E. Shoichet and Josh Levs, "Al Qaeda Branch Claims Charlie Hebdo Attack Was Years in the Making," CNN.com, January 21, 2015, https://www.cnn.com/2015/01/14/europe/charlie-hebdo-france-attacks/index.html.
61. Adam Withnall, "Were Paris Attacks the First Case of al-Qaeda and Isis Working Together? Six Questions Raised in Aftermath of France Shootings," *The Independent*, January 13, 2015.
62. Vivienne Walt, "Paris March in Solidarity against Terror Attacks Was Largest in French History," *TIME Magazine*, January 11, 2015.
63. "Salman Rushdie Condemns Attack on Charlie Hebdo," EnglishPen.org., January 7, 2015, https://www.englishpen.org/campaigns/salman-rushdie-condemns-attack-on-charlie-hebdo/.
64. "Voltaire Quotes," Brainy Quote (website). n.d., accessed November 17, 2018. https://www.brainyquote.com/quotes/voltaire_125630.

Chapter 6

1. Lizzie Dearden, "Abdelhamid Abaaoud: What We Know About Belgian Man Identified as Suspected Paris Attacks 'Mastermind,'" *The Independent*, November 16, 2015.
2. Robert Chalmers, "Is Molenbeek Really a No-Go Zone?" *Gentleman's Quarterly* (GQ), June 21, 2007.
3. David Connett, "Paris Attacks: 'Mastermind' of Attacks Abelhamid Abaaoud Turned Back on 'Fantastic' Life, Says Father," *The Independent*, November 16, 2015.
4. "Abdelhamid Abaaoud, L'Homme le Plus Recherché de Belgique a Fréquenté Une École Huppée," SudInfo.be, January 21, 2015, https://www.sudinfo.be/art/1194729/article/2015-01-20/abdelhamid-abaaoud-l-homme-le-plus-recherche-de-belgique-a-frequente-une-ecole-h.
5. Andrew Higgins and Kimiko de Freytas-Tamura, "An ISIS Militant from Belgium Whose Own Family Wanted Him Dead," *New York Times*, November 17, 2015.
6. Agence France-Presse, "Abaaoud: From School Bully to Terrorist Plotter," TheLocal.fr, November 19, 2015. https://www.thelocal.fr/20151119/the-terrorist-whose-family-prayed-he-was-dead.

7. Guy Van Vlierden, "Profile: Paris Attack Ringleader Abdelhamid Abaaoud," *CTC Sentinel* 8, issue 11 (November/December 2015), 30.
8. *Ibid.*
9. Associated Press, "Tracing the Roots of European Terror: What Led a Young Belgian to Become an ISIS Terrorist," *Haaretz*, February 4, 2018.
10. *Ibid.*
11. Weinman, Edward, "Inside ISIS," *Connecticut College Magazine*, Fall 2016.
12. Paul Cruickshank, "A View from the CT Foxhole: An Interview with Alain Grignard, Brussels Federal Police," *CTC Sentinel* 8, issue 8 (August 2015), 8.
13. *Ibid.*
14. *Ibid.*
15. Van Vlierden, "Profile: Paris Attack Ringleader Abdelhamid Abaaoud," 30.
16. Elise Vincent, "Ce Que les Services Belges Savaient d'Abdelhamid Abaaoud," *Le Monde*, November 20, 2015.
17. Jérémie Pham-Lê, Claire Hache, and Boris Thiolay, "Le Petit Frère d'Abaaoud, Younès, Donné Pour Mort en Zone Irako-Syrienne," *L'Express*, January 24, 2018.
18. News Wires, "Brother of Paris Attacker Abaaoud Jailed in Morocco," France24.com, May 7, 2016, https://www.france24.com/en/20160507-brother-paris-attacker-abaaoud-jailed-morocco.
19. Mariano Castillo and Paul Cruickshank, "Who Was Abdelhamid Abaaoud, Suspected Ringleader of Paris Attack?" CNN.com, updated November 19, 2015, https://www.cnn.com/2015/11/16/europe/paris-terror-attack-mastermind-abdelhamid-abaaoud/index.html.
20. Dearden, "Abdelhamid Abaaoud."
21. Daveed Gartenstein-Ross and Nathaniel Barr, "Recent Attacks Illuminate the Islamic State's Europe Attack Network," Jamestown.org, April 27, 2016, https://jamestown.org/program/hot-issue-recent-attacks-illuminate-the-islamic-states-europe-attack-network/.
22. Isabel Summerson (producer), Phillip Adams (interviewer), Christoph Reuter (guest), and Martin Chulov (guest), "How Religious Is the Islamic State?" (transcript), ABC.net.au, May 7, 2015, https://www.abc.net.au/radionational/programs/latenightlive/haji-bakr-and-the-islamic-state/6453494.

23. Christoph Reuter, "Secret Files Reveal the Structure of Islamic State," *Der Spiegel*, April 18, 2015.
24. *Ibid.*
25. Anne Speckhard and Ahmet S. Yayla, "The ISIS Emni: Origins and Inner Workings of ISIS's Intelligence Apparatus," *Perspectives on Terrorism* 11, issue 1 (February 2017), 4.
26. Margo Haddad, Erin McLaughlin, and Tim Hume, "France Identifies Suspected Coordinator of Paris, Brussels Attacks," CNN.com, November 8, 2016, https://www.cnn.com/2016/11/08/europe/paris-brussels-attacks-suspected-coordinator/index.html.
27. Amnesty International Health and Human Rights Team, "Health Professional Action: Prisoner in Need of Urgent Medical Care—Iraq," *Amnesty International*, September 9, 2010, https://www.amnesty.org/download/Documents/40000/mde140112010en.pdf.
28. Castillo and Cruickshank, "Who Was Abdelhamid Abaaoud, Suspected Ringleader of Paris Attack?"
29. *Ibid*
30. Suzanne Lynch, "Belgium Police Kill Two That Authorities Claim Were on Verge of Terrorist Attack," *Irish Times*, January 16, 2015.
31. Josh Halliday and Jonathan Bucks. "Abdelhamid Abaaoud: What We Know about the Paris Attacks 'Mastermind,'" *The Guardian*, November 18, 2015.
32. Henry Samuel, "Paris Attacks Ringleader Visited Britain 'To Plan UK Attacks,' Believes Top French Judge," *The Telegraph*, January 11, 2016.
33. Soren Seelow, "Abdelhamid Abaaoud, L'Instigateur Présumé des Attentats Tué à Saint-Denis," *Le Monde*, November 16, 2015.
34. Peter Taylor, John O'Kane, and Ceri Isfryn, "IS in Europe: The Race to the Death," BBC.com, March 23, 2016, https://www.bbc.com/news/magazine-35872562.
35. Seelow, "Abdelhamid Abaaoud."
36. Matthew Campbell et al., "Gay Sex, Drugs, Then Suicidal Slaughter," *Sunday Times* (London), November 22, 2015.
37. *Ibid.*
38. Camilla Turner and Matthew Holehouse, "Paris Attacks Suicide Bomber 'Drank, Smoked and Ran Drugs Den,'" *The Telegraph*, November 16, 2015.

39. *Ibid.*
40. British Broadcasting Corp., "Paris Attacks: Who Were the Attackers?" BBC.com, April 27, 2016, https://www.bbc.com/news/world-europe-34832512.
41. Hannah Roberts, "The Pot-Smoking Paris Suicide Bomber: Ex-Wife Reveals 'Blood Brother' Terrorist Was a Jobless Layabout Who Spent His Time Taking Drugs and Sleeping … and Never Went to the Mosque," *Daily Mail*, November 17, 2015.
42. Roberts, "The Pot-Smoking Paris Suicide Bomber."
43. Claire Schaffner, "Foued Mohamed-Aggad, un Enfant de Wissembourg 'Sans Historie,'" France3.com, December 10, 2015, https://france3-regions.francetvinfo.fr/grand-est/bas-rhin/foued-mohamed-aggad-un-enfant-de-wissembourg-sans-histoire-879235.html.
44. *Ibid.*
45. Cécile Bouanchaud, "Qui Est Foued Mohamed-Aggad, le Troisième Kamikaze du Bataclan?" Europe1.fr, December 10, 2015, https://www.europe1.fr/faits-divers/qui-est-foued-mohamed-aggad-le-troisieme-kamikaze-du-bataclan-2633591.
46. Sud Ouest Staff with AFP, "Attentats de Paris: Inhumé Pour Noël, Amimour, l'Introverti Devenu Assassin au Bataclan," *Sud Ouest*, December 27, 2015.
47. Chine Labbé, Marie-Louise Gumuchian, and Matthias Blamont, "Insight—Bus Driver Who Turned Paris Attacker Skipped Police Watch," Reuters.com, November 20, 2105, https://www.reuters.com/article/uk-france-shooting-amimour-insight/insight-bus-driver-who-turned-paris-attacker-skipped-police-watch-idUKKCN0T91KC20151120.
48. *Ibid.*
49. Stéphanie Marteau, "Le Père D'Un des Kamikazes Avait Tenté, en Vain, de le Ramener de Syrie," *Le Monde*, November 16, 2015.
50. Lexi Finnigan and Gregory Walton, "Paris Attacks: Stade de France Bomber Bilal Hadfi Was 'Unambitious Loner Who Failed His Exams,'" *The Independent*, November 17, 2015.
51. Sewell Chan and Milan Schreuer, "School's Warnings About Paris Attacker Were Not Passed On," *New York Times*, December 26, 2015.
52. Andrew Blake, "Bilal Hadi, Paris Terrorist, Left Social Media Clues before Attacks," *Washington Times*, November 20, 2015.
53. Jay Newton-Small, "Paris Attacker Is an Example of France's Homegrown Terrorists," *TIME Magazine*, November 16, 2015.

Chapter 7

1. Alex Berezow, "How Chemists Plan to Sniff Out Bombs," BBC.com, December 25, 2015, https://www.bbc.com/news/science-environment-35022731.
2. Bea Perks and Lionel Milgrom, "UK Government Clamp Down on Online Bomb-Making Instructions," *Chemistry World*, July 20, 2005.
3. Laurence Peter, "Paris Attacks: Key Questions after Abaaoud Killed," BBC.com, November 24, 2015, https://www.bbc.com/news/world-europe-34866144.
4. Eric Schmitt, "Paris Attacks and Other Assaults Seen as Evidence of a Shift by ISIS," *New York Times*, November 22, 2015.
5. Miranda Tomic, "Case Study: Perimeter Security at Stade-de-France," MSASecurity.net, August 31, 2017, http://www.msasecurity.net/security-and-counterterrorism-blog/case-study-perimeter-security-at-stade-de-france.
6. Paul Cruickshank, "The Inside Story of the Paris Attack," CNN.com, updated March 22, 2016, https://www.cnn.com/2016/03/21/europe/inside-paris-terror-attack/index.html.
7. Joshua Robinson and Inti Landauro, "Attacker Tried to Enter Paris Stadium but Was Turned Away," *Wall Street Journal*, November 15, 2015.
8. Aimie Rigas, "Eyewitness Franck Benarroch Reveals Frenzied Aftermath of Paris Explosions, Shootings," *Huffington Post Australia*, November 14, 2015.
9. Alissa J. Rubin, "Paris: One Year On," *New York Times*, November 12, 2015.
10. Jules Naudet and Gédéon Naudet, directors, *November 13: Attack on Paris* (*13 Novembre: Fluctuat Nec Mergitur*), Episode 1, Netflix/Propagate/No School Productions (Los Gatos, California, 2018), https://www.netflix.com/title/80190297.
11. Rohan Banerjee and Adam Shergold, "Suicide Attacks Near Stade de France Leave Three People Dead as Explosions Are Heard during Friendly Victory over

Germany and Paris Is Rocked by Coordinated Terrorist Strikes on Six Targets," *Daily Mail*, November 14, 2015.
12. Ibid.
13. Ibid.
14. Ibid.
15. Cruickshank, "The Inside Story of the Paris Attack."
16. Sam Borden, "As Paris Attacks Unfolded, Players and Fans at Soccer Stadium Remained Unaware," *New York Times*, November 14, 2105.
17. Rubin, "Paris: One Year On."
18. Robin Panfili, "'At the First Explosion, We Didn't Suspect Anything': An Eyewitness Account from the Stade de France," *Slate*, November 14, 2015.
19. Andrew Higgins and Milan Schreuer, "Attackers in Paris 'Did Not Give Anybody a Chance,'" *New York Times*, November 14, 2015.
20. David Hills, "France Players Praised for Staying with Germany Team in Stade de France," *The Guardian*, November 14, 2015.
21. Rubin, "Paris: One Year On."
22. Kevin Ponniah, "Le Carillon: Paris Bar Regulars Left Reeling after Attack," BBC.com, November 14, 2015, https://www.bbc.com/news/world-europe-34822605.
23. Jake Wallis Simons et al., "'I Saw a Hole in Her Face, and Realised She'd Been Shot': Gunman Dressed in Black Picked Off Terrified Diners Firing 'Professional Bursts' of Shots in Cafe Shooting Rampage," *Daily Mail*, November 14, 2015.
24. Robert A. Burke, *Counter-Terrorism for Emergency Responders* (Boca Raton, Florida: CRC Press, 2017), 426.
25. John Masanauskas, "Paris Attacks: Diners Killed in Le Carillon and Le Petit Cambodge Restaurants," *Herald Sun*, November 14, 2015.
26. Simons et al., "'I Saw a Hole in Her Face.'"
27. Masanauskas, "Paris Attacks: Diners Killed in Le Carillon."
28. Simons et al., "'I Saw a Hole in Her Face.'"
29. Burke, *Counter-Terrorism for Emergency Responders*, 426.
30. Julia Pascual, "Au Carillon, 'On N'avait Rien pour Aider, Rien Que Nos Mains,'" *Le Monde*, November 18, 2015.
31. Ibid.
32. Fidelma Cook and Flory Drury, "'For a Mum to Bury Her Child Is the Hardest Thing. Burying Two Is Unthinkable': Mother Pays Tribute to Her 'Beautiful' Identical Twins Killed in Carillon Bar Massacre," *Daily Mail*, November 19, 2015.
33. British Broadcasting Corp., "Paris Attacks: What Happened on the Night," BBC.com, December 9, 2015, https://www.bbc.com/news/world-europe-34818994.
34. Lori Hinnant, "Timeline of Paris Attacks: How a Half-hour of Horror Washes Paris in Blood," *Associated Press*, November 14, 2015. https://www.deseret.com/2015/11/15/20487314/timeline-of-paris-attacks-how-a-half-hour-of-horror-washes-paris-in-blood.
35. Naudet and Naudet, *November 13*, Episode 1.
36. Simons et al., "'I Saw a Hole in Her Face.'"
37. Rubin, "Paris: One Year On."
38. British Broadcasting Corp., "Paris Attacks: Who Were the Victims?" BBC.com, November 27, 2015, https://www.bbc.com/news/world-europe-34821813.
39. Times of Israel Staff, Associated Press, and Jewish Telegraphic Agency, "Jewish Paris Cafe Owner Loses Wife, Friends in Terror Attack," *The Times of Israel*, November 17, 2015.
40. Dan Bilefsky, "After Paris Attacks, Ties That Bind Patrons at a Cafe Also Burn," *New York Times*, November 25, 2015.
41. Alexandra Ma and Rowaida Abdelaziz, "Mourning the Arab Victims of the Paris Attacks," *Huffington Post*, November 18, 2015.
42. Anne Penketh, "Paris Attacks: The Muslim Victims of Terrorist Bullets," *The Guardian*, November 18, 2015.
43. Naudet and Naudet, *November 13*, Episode 1.
44. Ibid.
45. Marie-Louise Gumuchian and Pauline Mevel, "Exclusive: In Paris Attack, Nurse Discovers the Man He Tried to Save Was Bomber," Reuters.com, November 21, 2015, https://www.reuters.com/article/us-france-shooting-nurse-bomber/exclusive-in-paris-attack-nurse-discovers-the-man-he-tried-to-save-was-bomber-idUSKCN0TA00N20151121.
46. Jess Staufenberg, "Video Shows Nurse Giving Suicide Bomber CPR at Paris Café After Failed Attack," *The Independent*, November 21, 2015.
47. Patrick Sawer and Lexi Finnigan,

"Paris Attacks: Gunmen May Still Be on the Loose as Kalashnikovs and Empty Magazines Found in Abandoned Car in City Suburb," *The Telegraph*, November 15, 2015.

48. Angelique Chrisafis, "'It Looked Like a Battlefield': The Full Story of What Happened in the Bataclan," *The Guardian*, November 20, 2015.

49. "Eagles of Death Metal," Genius Media Group. n.d., Genius.com, accessed February 3, 2019, https://genius.com/artists/Eagles-of-death-metal.

50. "'On Est Parti, On Commence,' le Dernier SMS d'un des Kamikazes du Bataclan," *Le Point*, November 19, 2015, https://www.lepoint.fr/societe/on-est-parti-on-commence-le-dernier-sms-d-un-des-kamikazes-du-bataclan-18-11-2015-1982655_23.php.

51. "Three Hours of Terror in Paris, Moment by Moment," *New York Times*, November 9, 2016,

52. Fahmi B., "Sur la Livre: Fusillade à Paris," *Libération*, November 14, 2015.

53. "Paris Attacks: Eagles of Death Metal Reveal How They Escaped from Bataclan Theatre," ABC.net.au, November 25, 2015, https://www.abc.net.au/news/2015-11-26/eagles-of-death-metal-vice-interview/6975940

54. Daniel Kreps, "Eagles of Death Metal Merch Manager Nick Alexander Killed in Paris Attack," *Rolling Stone*, November 14, 2015.

55. Kory Grow, "Nearly 100 Dead After Paris Concert Terrorist Attack," *Rolling Stone*, November 13, 2015.

56. Emmanuelle Saliba, Nancy Ing, and Elisha Fieldstadt, "Multiple Paris Terror Attacks Leave at Least 120 Dead," NBCNews.com, November 14, 2015, https://www.nbcnews.com/storyline/paris-terror-attacks/french-police-report-paris-shootout-explosion-n463186.

57. British Broadcasting Corp., "Paris Attacks: Eyewitness Accounts," BBC.com, November 16, 2015, https://www.bbc.com/news/world-europe-34813570.

58. Naomi Shavin, "Photographer Cristian Movilă's Eyewitness Photos of the Attack on Paris and Its Aftermath," *Smithsonian Magazine*, November 19, 2015.

59. "The World" Staff, "A Bataclan Survivor Asks a Rocker to Understand the Complexities of Terrorism," PRI.org, May 25, 2016, https://www.pri.org/stories/2016-05-25/bataclan-survivor-asks-rocker-understand-complexities-terrorism.

60. "As It Happened: Over 120 Dead in Paris Attacks," TheLocal.fr, November 13, 2015.

61. Wolf Blitzer, Wolf (host/interviewer), "Concert Witness Julien Pearce Full," Facebook.com (CNN/Anderson Cooper 360 page), aired on November 1, 2015, https://www.facebook.com/watch/?v=10156332669095533.

62. James Purtill, "Paris Attacks: Australian Man Recounts Desperate Bataclan Theatre Escape with 12yo Son," ABC.net.au, updated November 15, 2015, https://www.abc.net.au/news/2015-11-16/australian-man-recounts-surviving-bataclan-attack-with-12yo-son/6942976.

63. Paul Cruickshank, "The Inside Story of the Paris and Brussels Attacks," CNN.com, updated October 30, 2017, https://www.cnn.com/2016/03/30/europe/inside-paris-brussels-terror-attacks/index.html.

64. Claire Lomas, "Paris Survivor of Suicide Bomb Was 'Saved by Phone,'" *The Telegraph*, November 14, 2015.

65. Zlata Rodionova, "Paris Attacks Anniversary: 'Open the Door, I Am Here to Rescue You,' Isis Gunman Told Bataclan Survivor," *The Independent*, November 12, 2016.

66. Rukmini Callimachi, Alissa J. Rubin, and Laure Fourquet, "A View of ISIS's Evolution in New Details of Paris Attacks," *New York Times*, March 19, 2016.

67. France 24, "Bataclan Victims to File Legal Complaint Over 'Inadequate' Police Response," France 24.com, June 9, 2018, https://www.france24.com/en/20180608-bataclan-victims-file-legal-complaint-over-inadequate-police-response.

68. Ibid.

69. Sébastien Pietrasanta, *Commission d'Enquête Relative aux Moyens Mis en Œuvre par l'État pour Lutter Contre le Terrorisme Depuis le 7 Janvier 2015* (Paris, France: Assemblée Nationale, July 5, 2016), http://www2.assemblee-nationale.fr/14/autres-commissions/commissions-d-enquete/moyens-pour-lutter-contre-le-terrorisme/(block)/28447.

70. Emmanuel Jarry/Reuters, "Des Victimes du 13/11 Portent Plainte pour Non-Assistance," *Challenges* (French language), June 8, 2018, https://www.challenges.fr/top-news/des-victimes-

du-13-11-portent-plainte-pour-non-assistance_592740.

71. Henry Samuel, "Paris Attack: Office Recounts Killing Bataclan Terrorist Then Calling Wife to Say 'Goodbye,'" *The Telegraph*, December 15, 2015.

72. Naudet and Naudet, *November 13: Attack on Paris* (*13 Novembre: Fluctuat Nec Mergitur*), Episode 2. Netflix/Propagate/No School Productions. Los Gatos, California, 2018. https://www.netflix.com/title/80190097.

73. Samuel, "Paris Attack."

74. Angelique Chrisafis et al., "Witness Accounts from across Paris: 'I Saw My Final Hour Unfurl Before Me,'" *The Guardian*, November 13, 2015.

75. Naudet and Naudet, *November 13*, Episode 2.

76. Chrisafis et al., "Witness Accounts."

77. Naudet and Naudet, *November 13*, Episode 2.

78. Ibid.

79. Derek Blasberg, "Paris Attacks Survivor Isobel Bowdery Shares Her Story," *Vanity Fair*, December 4, 2015.

80. Emiland Guillerme, Ben Laffin, and Spencer Wolff, "Surviving Paris: Pulled from the Gunfire," NYTimes.com (New York Times videos), November 15, 2015, https://www.nytimes.com/video/world/europe/100000004038181/surviving-paris-pulled-from-the-gunfire.html.

81. Emmy Mack, "Aussie Victim of Paris Attacks Recounts Harrowing Scenes Inside the Bataclan Theatre," MusicFeeds.com.au, November 23, 2015, https://musicfeeds.com.au/news/aussie-victim-paris-attacks-recounts-harrowing-scenes-inside-bataclan-theatre/

82. Simon Piel, "Au Bataclan, Deux Heures d'Intervention Policière sans Négociation," *Le Monde*, November 16, 2015.

83. Lester Holt (host/interviewer), "'Hell on Earth': Leader of Bataclan Raid Describes What He Saw Inside," NBCNews.com, November 19, 2015. https://www.nbcnews.com/nightly-news/video/hell-on-earth-leader-of-bataclan-raid-describes-what-he-saw-inside-570073667878.

84. Rubin, "Paris: One Year On."

85. Associated Press, "Eyewitnesses Construct Minute-By-Minute Account of Paris Attacks," *Macleans*, November 15, 2015.

86. Angelique Chrisafis, "Doctor Who Treated Paris Wounded and Charlie Hebdo Victims Calls for Unity," *The Guardian*, November 15, 2015.

87. Lucie Aubourg, "This Is What Happened at the Bataclan Concert Hall During the Paris Attacks," Vice.com, November 25, 2015, https://www.vice.com/en_us/article/ev9bnm/this-is-what-happened-at-the-bataclan-concert-hall-during-the-paris-attacks.

88. Sophie Shevardnadze (host/interviewer), "Terrorist Leader Said, 'Don't Be Afraid, You'll Die in a Few Minutes'—Paris Attack Survivor," RT.com, November 20, 2015, https://www.rt.com/shows/sophieco/322796-france-terrorist-attacks-isis/.

89. Burke, *Counter-Terrorism for Emergency Responders*.

90. Cassandra Vinograd and Nancy Ing, "Paris Attacks: Commando Captain Shares Details of Bataclan, Saint-Denis Raids," NBCNews.com, updated November 20, 2015, https://www.nbcnews.com/storyline/paris-terror-attacks/paris-attacks-commando-captain-shares-details-france-raids-n466461.

91. Burke, *Counter-Terrorism for Emergency Responders*.

92. Julia Razil, "'J'Étais Otage, J'ai Crié aux Flics de ne pas Rentrer,'" *La Provence* (Marseille), November 16, 2105.

93. British Broadcasting Corp., "Who Was Third Bataclan Attacker Foued Mohamed-Aggad?" BBC.com, December 9, 2015, https://www.bbc.com/news/world-europe-35055304.

94. British Broadcasting Corp., "Paris Attacks: Who Were the Victims?" BBC.com, November 27, 2015, November 27, 2015, https://www.bbc.com/news/world-europe-34821813.

95. Mary Brophy Marcus, "Injuries from Paris Attacks Will Take Long to Heal," CBSNews.com, November 19, 2015, https://www.cbsnews.com/news/injuries-from-paris-attacks-will-take-long-to-heal/.

96. Rukmini Callimachi, "ISIS Claims Responsibility, Calling Paris Attacks 'First of the Storm,'" *New York Times*, November 14, 2015.

Chapter 8

1. Emily Greenhouse, "Life and Death on the Boulevard Voltaire," *New Republic*, November 15, 2015.

2. Smitha Mundasad, "Paris Attacks: Doctor Describes Moment First Casualties Arrived," BBCNews.com, November 19, 2015, https://www.bbc.com/news/health-34845730.
3. Martin Hirsch et al., "The Medical Response to Multisite Terrorist Attacks," *The Lancet* 386 (December 19/26, 2015), 2536, http://dx.doi.org/10.1016/S0140-6736(15)01063-6.
4. Ibid., 2538.
5. "Emergency Responders in Paris Train for Terrorist Attacks Just Days before Actual Event," MedTrust.com, December 15, 2015, http://ridemedtrust.com/emergency-responders-in-paris-train-for-terrorist-attack-just-days-before-actual-event/.
6. Hirsch et al., "The Medical Response to Multisite Terrorist Attacks," 2536.
7. Ibid., 2538.
8. Indra Warnes, "Twenty Bataclan Victims Still in Hospital as Survivors Vow 'Isis Will Not Kill Us Again,'" *Daily Express*, November 12, 2016.
9. "Bataclan Survivor Commits Suicide Two Years after Terror Attack," TheLocal.fr, November 27, 2017, https://www.thelocal.fr/20171127/paris-bataclan-survivor-commits-suicide-two-years-after-terror-attack.
10. Y. P. Motreff et al., "Mental Health Impact among First Responders following the November 2015 Paris Terror Attacks: Philippe Pirard," *European Journal of Public Health* 27, issue suppl. 3 (November 2017): 490, https://doi.org/10.1093/eurpub/ckx186.254.
11. Carla De Stefano, et al., "Early Psychological Impact of Paris Terrorist Attacks on Healthcare Emergency Staff: A Cross-Sectional Study," *Depression and Anxiety* 35, issue 3 (March 2018), 185.
12. Swati Sharma, "'It Is Horror': French President Hollande's Remarks After Paris Attacks," *Washington Post*, November 13, 2015.
13. "As It Happened: Over 120 Dead In Paris Attacks," TheLocal.fr, November 13, 2015, https://www.thelocal.fr/20151113/several-dead-in-paris-shootings.
14. Nicolas Boring, "France: Special Security Measures Declared Unconstitutional," *Library of Congress—Global Legal Monitor*, December 20, 2017, https://www.loc.gov/law/foreign-news/article/france-special-security-measures-declared-unconstitutional/.
15. Ibid.
16. Rose Troup Buchanan, "Paris Terror: Muslim Leaders Around the World Condemn 'Heinous' Attacks," *The Independent*, November 14, 2015.
17. Alissa J. Rubin, and Anne Barnard, "France Strikes ISIS Targets in Syria in Retaliation for Attacks," *New York Times*, November 16, 2015.
18. Ibid.
19. Ben Brumfield, Tim Lister, and Nick Paton Walsh, "French Jets Bomb ISIS Stronghold of Raqqa, Syria; Few May Have Been Killed," CNN.com, updated November 16, 2015, https://www.cnn.com/2015/11/16/middleeast/france-raqqa-airstrikes-on-isis/index.html.
20. Benoît Floc'h, "Au Centre de Recrutement des Armées: 'Ce Coup-là, Je M'Engage,'" *Le Monde*, November 19, 2015.
21. Ibid.
22. Ibid.
23. Caroline Taix and Adam Plowright, "Paris Defendant: 'No One Told Me' Terrorists Rented My Flat," *Times of Israel*, January 26, 2018.
24. Kim Willsher, "Hasna Aitboulahcen: Police Examine Remains of 'Cowgirl' Turned Suicide Bomber," *The Guardian*, November 20, 2015.
25. Willa Frej, "Another Cafe Targeted in Paris Attacks Reopens, Ushering in Springtime," *Huffington Post*, March 21, 2016.
26. Lauren Messman, "Banksy Mural Is Stolen from Bataclan, Site of Paris Attacks," *New York Times*, January 27, 2019.

Chapter 9

1. Rukmini Callimachi, "ISIS Caliphate Crumbles as Last Village in Syria Falls," *New York Times*, March 23, 2019.
2. Adam Withnall, "ISIS Official Calls for 'Lone Wolf' Attacks in U.S. And Europe during Ramadan," *The Independent*, May 22, 2017.
3. Ben Hubbard, "ISIS Uses Ramadan as Calling for New Terrorist Attacks," *New York Times*, July 3, 2016.
4. Paul Gill, John Horgan, and Paige Deckert, "Bombing Alone: Tracing the Motivations and Antecedent Behaviors of Lone-Actor Terrorists," *Journal of Forensic Sciences* 59, issue 2 (December 6, 2013).

5. Ibid.
6. Jeff Gruenewald, Steve Chermak, and Joshua Freilich, "Distinguishing 'Loner' Attacks from Other Domestic Extremist Violence," *Criminology & Public Policy* 12, issue 1 (February 2013).
7. "Mental Disorders Affect One in Four People," WHO.int (World Health Organization), 2001, https://www.who.int/whr/2001/media_centre/press_release/en/.
8. Emily Corner, Paul Gill, and Oliver Mason, "Mental Health Disorders and the Terrorist: A Research Note Probing Selection Effects and Disorder Prevalence," *Studies in Conflict & Terrorism* 39, no. 6 (2016).
9. Ibid., 564.
10. Christina Shane-Simpson, Patricia Brooks, Rita Obeid, Ellen-ge Denton, and Kristen Gillespie-Lynch, "Associations Between Compulsive Internet Use and the Autism Spectrum," *Research in Autism Spectrum Disorders* 23 (2016).
11. Gill, Horgan, and Deckert, "Bombing Alone."
12. Bart Schuurman, Edwin Bakker, Paul Gill, and Noémi Bouhana, "Lone Actor Terrorist Attack Planning and Preparation: A Data-Driven Analysis," *Journal of Forensic Sciences* 63, no. 4 (2017), 154.
13. Gill, Horgan, and Deckert, "Bombing Alone."
14. Ibid.
15. Corner et al., "Mental Health Disorders."
16. Schuurman et al., "Lone Actor Terrorist Attack Planning," 1193.
17. Ibid.,
18. Bart Schuurman et al., "End of the Lone Wolf: The Typology That Should Not Have Been," *Studies in Conflict & Terrorism* 42, no. 8 (2019), 773.
19. Ibid., 773.
20. Schuurman et al., "Lone Actor Terrorist Attack Planning."
21. Ibid.
22. Ibid.
23. Ibid.
24. Paul Gill, "Seven Findings on Lone-Actor Terrorism," PSU.edu (International Center for the Study of Terrorism at Pennsylvania State University), February 6, 2013, https://sites.psu.edu/icst/2013/02/06/seven-findings-on-lone-actor-terrorists/.
25. Schuurman et al., "Lone Actor Terrorist Attack Planning."
26. Gill, "Seven Findings on Lone-Actor Terrorism."
27. Andrew Berwick (AKA Anders Behring Breivik), "2083—A European Declaration of Independence," PublicIntelligence.net, accessed January 6, 2020, https://publicintelligence.net/anders-behring-breiviks-complete-manifesto-2083-a-european-declaration-of-independence/
28. Sam Mullins, "Lone-Actor vs. Remote-Controlled Jihadi Terrorism: Rethinking the Threat to the West," WarOnTheRocks.com, April 20, 2017, https://warontherocks.com/2017/04/lone-actor-vs-remote-controlled-jihadi-terrorism-rethinking-the-threat-to-the-west/.
29. Jen Easterly and Joshua A. Geltzer, "The Islamic State and the End of Lone-Wolf Terrorism," *Foreign Policy*, May 23, 2017.
30. Daveed Gartenstein-Ross and Madeleine Blackman, "ISIL's Virtual Planners: A Critical Terrorist Innovation," WarOnTheRocks.com, January 4, 2017, https://warontherocks.com/2017/01/isils-virtual-planners-a-critical-terrorist-innovation/.
31. Homeland Security News Wire, "Remote-Controlled Terrorism," HomelandSecurityNewsWire.com, February 7, 2017, http://www.homelandsecuritynewswire.com/dr20170207-remotecontrolled-terrorism.
32. Rumini Callimachi, "Not 'Lone Wolves' After All: How ISIS Guides World's Terror Plots from Afar," *New York Times*, February 4, 2017.
33. John Mueller, "The Cybercoaching of Terrorists: Cause for Alarm?" *CTC Sentinel* (October 2017), 29.
34. Mark Hamm and Rámon Spaaij, *The Age of Lone Wolf Terrorism* (*Studies in Transgression*) (New York: Columbia University Press, 2017), 262
35. Mae Rice, "The Deep Web Is the 99% of the Internet You Can't Google," Curiosity.com, May 22, 2018, https://curiosity.com/topics/the-deep-web-is-the-99-of-the-internet-you-cant-google-curiosity/.
36. Daniel Moore and Thomas Rid, "Cryptopolitik and the Darknet," *Survival: Global Politics and Strategy* 58, issue 1 (2016).
37. Gabriel Weimann, "Terrorist Migration to the Dark Web." *Perspectives on Terrorism* 10, no. 3 (June 2016).
38. Jonathan Hepburn, "Anonymous

'Hactivist' Group Claims 5,500 Islamic State-Affiliated Twitter Accounts Down in #OpParis," ABC.net.au, updated January 24, 2016, https://www.abc.net.au/news/2015-11-18/anonymous-being-opparis-against-islamic-state/6952826.
39. Weimann, "Terrorist Migration to the Dark Web."
40. Stacy Meichtry and Sam Schechner, "How Islamic State Weaponized the Chat App to Direct Attacks on the West," *Wall Street Journal*, October 20, 2016.
41. Elizabeth Weise, "Terrorists Use the Dark Web to Hide," *USA Today*, March 27, 2017.

Chapter 10

1. Bethan McKernan, "France's Most Wanted ISIS Fighter Killed in Iraq Leaves Final Message Accusing His Leaders of Hypocrisy," *The Independent*, February 16, 2017.
2. Michel Peyrard, "Rachid Kassim: Enquête sur le Donneur D'Ordre de Daech," *Paris Match*, September 23, 2016.
3. Adam Nossiter and Hannah Olivennes, "Jacques Hamel, 85, a Beloved French Priest, Killed in His Church," *New York Times*, July 26, 2016.
4. Jamie Schram and Yaron Steinbuch, "France Was Warned About Terrorist Who Killed Priest in Church Attack," *New York Post*, July 28, 2016.
5. Kim Willsher and Julian Borger, "ISIS Attackers Forced French Priest to Kneel before He Was Murdered, Hostage Says," *The Guardian*, July 26, 2016.
6. France 24. "France Church Attack: Nun Who Witnessed ISIS Terrorists' Assault Recounts Priest Murder," YouTube.com (France 24 Channel), July 26, 2016, https://www.youtube.com/watch?v=GnOuYvbQPAo.
7. Nicholas Zinos, "Father Jacques Hamel, Europe's First 21-Century Martyr," *America: The Jesuit Review*, July 26, 2018.
8. Ibid.
9. Jean-Marie Guénois, "'Va-t'en Satan!'" … Les Derniers Mots du Père Hamel Remettent L'Église Face à la Question du Mal," *Le Figaro*, July 25, 2017.
10. Terry Mattingly, "The Symbolic Death of Father Jacques Hamel." UExpress.com, August 3, 2016, https://www.uexpress.com/on-religion/2016/8/3/the-symbolic-death-of-father-jacques.
11. "Fr Hamel Was Martyred 'In Odium Fidei,' Says Archbishop Fisher," *Catholic Herald*, July 27, 2016.
12. Mattingly, "The Symbolic Death of Father Jacques Hamel."
13. Samuel Gregg, "The Passion of Father Jacques Hamel," *Catholic World Report*, August 17, 2018.
14. "Abdel Malik Petitjean," Counter Extremism Project, Counterextremism.com, accessed July 11, 2019, https://www.counterextremism.com/extremists/abdel-malik-petitjean.
15. "France Church Attackers 'Smiled' and Talked of Peace, Nun Says," *The Guardian*, July 30, 2016.
16. Ibid.
17. Alix Culbertson and Katie Mansfield, "Normandy Attack: Murdered Priest Was 'Treasured' by the Community for Nearly 60 Years," *Daily Express*, July 26, 2016.
18. France 24, "Priest Killed in France 'Was Always There for Others,'" France24.com, modified July 27, 2016, https://www.france24.com/en/20160726-profile-france-priest-killed-group-attack-jacques-hamel.
19. "British Broadcasting Corp., "France Church Attack: Priest Killed by Two 'IS Militants,'" BBC.com, July 26, 2016, https://www.bbc.com/news/world-europe-36892785.
20. Inti Landauro and William Horobin, "For Parishioners in French Town, Slain Priest Was Model of Dedication," *Wall Street Journal*, July 26, 2016.
21. Adam Nossiter, Alissa J. Rubin, and Benoit Morenne, "ISIS Says Its 'Soldiers' Attacked Church in France, Killing Priest," *New York Times*, July 26, 2016.
22. Christopher White, "The Martyrdom of Jacques Hamel," *Wall Street Journal*, July 20, 2017.
23. Landauro and Horobin, "For Parishioners in French Town, Slain Priest Was Model of Dedication."
24. The Local/Agence France-Presse, "Mother of French Priest Killer Left Stunned and in Denial." TheLocal.fr, July 28, 2016, https://www.thelocal.fr/20160728/french-priest-murderer-he-was-a-gentle-child.
25. Inti Landauro, "French Priest Killer Adel Kermiche Was Under Police

Monitoring," *Wall Street Journal*, July 26, 2016.

26. Nicolas Jacquard and Anthony Lieures, "C'Était une Bombe à Retardement," *Le Parisien*, July 27, 2016.

27. Michel Rose, "French Church Attacker: From Troubled Childhood to Altar Killer," Reuters.com, July 29, 2016, https://www.reuters.com/article/us-europe-attacks-france-killer/french-church-attacker-from-troubled-childhood-to-altar-killer-idUSKCN1091U5.

28. *Ibid.*

29. Christophe Cornevin, "Adel Kermiche, un Ado Perturbé Devenu Terroriste," *Le Figaro*, July 28, 2016.

30. France 24, "One French Church Attacker Identified as Teen Under House Arrest," France24.com, July 26, 2016, https://www.france24.com/en/20160726-france-church-attack-teen-under-house-arrest-identified-syria.

31. CBS News and the Associated Press, "New Details Emerge About Teen Killer of French Priest," CBSNews.com, July 27, 2016, https://www.cbsnews.com/news/new-details-emerge-about-french-priests-teen-killer/.

32. Jacquard and Lieures, "C'Était une Bombe a à Retardement."

33. Kim Willsher, "Police in French Priest Murder Case Investigate Messaging App Link," *The Guardian*, July 31, 2016.

34. Paule Gonzalès, "Saint-Étienne-Du-Rouvray: Mis en Examen en 2015, Adel Kermiche a Été Libéré en 2016," *Le Figaro*, July 26, 2016.

35. Delphine de Mallevoüe, "'Fou,' 'Ordinaire,' les Mots des Voisins d'Adel Kermiche," *Le Figaro*, July 27, 2016.

36. "French Church Killer Adel Kermiche: 'A Ticking Time Bomb,'" *The Guardian*, July 27, 2016.

37. *Ibid.*

38. "La Mosquée de Saint-Etienne-du-Rouvray Refuse d'Inhumer Adel Kermiche," *Le Parisien*, July 29, 2016.

39. "Abdel Malik Petitjean," Counter Extremism Project.

40. British Broadcasting Corp., "France Church Attack: 'Gentle' Boy Who Became a Killer," BBC.com, July 28, 2016, https://www.bbc.com/news/world-europe-36914706.

41. Jack Moore, "Abel Malik Petitjean: What We Know About Second ISIS-Inspired Priest Attacker," *Newsweek*, July 28, 2016.

42. Noemie Bisserbe and Emre Peker, "Intelligence Lapse Hindered Search for Second French Church Assailant," *Wall Street Journal*, July 28, 2016.

43. Kim Willsher, "Police in French Priest Murder Case Investigate Messaging App Link."

44. Kyle Orton, "The Islamic State Guided the Normandy Church Attack," KyleOrton.com ("Kyle Orton's Blog"), August 22, 2016, https://kyleorton1991.wordpress.com/2016/08/22/the-islamic-state-guided-the-normandy-church-attack/#_ftn37.

45. Jason Murdock, "French Police Investigating ISIS Murder of Catholic Priest Probe Telegram App," *International Business Times*, July 31, 2016.

46. France 24, "Cousin of French Church Attacker Charged and Detained," France24.com, August 1, 2016, https://www.france24.com/en/20160801-cousin-church-attacker-charged-detained.

47. Jérémie Pham-Lê, Victor Garcia, and Claire Hache, "Rachid Kassim, le Djihadiste Qui a Inspiré les Assassins du Père Hamel," *L'Express* (France), August 18, 2016.

48. *Ibid.*

49. Raphaël Tual, "Attentat de Saint-Étienne-du-Rouvray. Les Messages Glaçants Échangés par les Tueurs," Actu.fr (Normandy edition). November 9, 2016. https://actu.fr/normandie/saint-etienne-du-rouvray_76575/attentat-de-saint-etienne-du-rouvray-les-messages-glacants-echanges-par-les-tueurs_809003.html.

50. "Adel Kermiche," Counter Extremism Project, Counterextremism.com, accessed July 11, 2019, https://www.counterextremism.com/extremists/adel-kermiche.

51. Elise Vincent, "Saint-Etienne-Du-Rouvray, Histoire d'une Haine Fulgurante," *Le Monde*, November 8, 2016.

52. Lori Hinnant, and Elaine Ganley, "-French ID 2nd Church Attacker; Police Had Warning About Him," APNews.com, July 28, 2016, https://apnews.com/f3dbc2f65ffb43b086f3490164dc5d8b.

53. James McAuley and Brian Murphy, "Islamic State Says Militant 'Soldiers' Carried Out Normandy Church Attack," *Washington Post*, July 26, 2016.

54. Henry Samuel, "French Intelligence 'Doctored Files' to Cover Up Failings Over Islamist Murder of Priest," *The Telegraph*, January 5, 2018.

55. Alissa J. Rubin and Adam Nossiter, "French Ask Whether Priest's Killer, Listed as a Threat, Could Have Been Stopped," *New York Times*, July 27, 2016.
56. "Hollande Says France Will Form National Guard," *Press TV*, July 28, 2016, https://www.presstv.com/Detail/2016/07/28/477325/France-Hollande-Daesh-terror-attack.
57. Pope Francis, "Holy Mass in Suffrage of Father Jacques Hamel," *Libreria Editrice Vaticana* (Vatican Publishing House), September 14, 2016, https://w2.vatican.va/content/francesco/en/cotidie/2016/documents/papa-francesco-cotidie_20160914_p-jacques-hamel.html.
58. Andrew Blake, "Pope Francis Sets the Stage for Canonizing the French Priest Killed in Terror Attack," *Washington Times*, September 14, 2016.
59. Global Pulse Staff, "Five Year Wait for Fr Hamel's Canonization Cause Dispensed," *Le Croix International*, October 3, 2016.

Chapter 11

1. Alissa J. Rubin, and Breeden Aurelie, "France Remembers the Nice Attack: 'We Will Never Find the Words,'" *New York Times*, July 14, 2017.
2. Jack Moore, "Nice Attacker Mohamed Lahouaiej-Bouhlel Spoke Often of His Troubled Childhood, Friend Reveals," *Newsweek*, August 7, 2016.
3. Vivien Walt, "Was the Nice Attacker Really a Jihadist?" *TIME Magazine*, July 16, 2016.
4. Tarek Amara, "Shock in Tunisian Hometown of Nice Attacker," Reuters.com, July 15, 2016, https://www.reuters.com/article/us-europe-attacks-nice-hometown/shock-in-tunisian-hometown-of-nice-attacker-idUSKCN0ZV2X5.
5. Adam Nossiter, Alissa J. Rubin, and Lilia Blaise, "Years Before Truck Rampage in Nice, Attacker Wasn't 'Living in the Real World,'" *New York Times*, July 24, 2016.
6. Scott Sayare, "The Untold Story of the Bastille Day Attacker," *Gentleman's Quarterly* (*GQ*), January 24, 2017.
7. Sayare, "The Untold Story of the Bastille Day Attacker."
8. Nossiter, Rubin, and Blaise, "Years before Truck Rampage in Nice, Attacker Wasn't 'Living in the Real World.'"
9. Sayare, "The Untold Story of the Bastille Day Attacker."
10. Ibid.
11. Agence France-Presse, "What Do We Know About the Nice Attacker?" TheLocal.fr, July 17, 2016, https://www.thelocal.fr/20160717/nice-attacker-body-building-drug-taking-womanising.
12. Ibid.
13. Sayare, "The Untold Story of the Bastille Day Attacker."
14. "Truck Attack in Nice, France: What We Know, and What We Don't," *New York Times*, July 15, 2016.
15. Neil Frankland, "Disturbing Picture Emerges of Nice Killer," *The New Daily* (Australia), July 18, 2016.
16. Sayare, "The Untold Story of the Bastille Day Attacker."
17. Ibid.
18. Stacy Meichtry, Joshua Robinson, and Mike Bird, "How a Tunisian Immigrant Staged the Simple, Deadly Attack in Nice," *Wall Street Journal*, July 15, 2016.
19. Anthony Bond, "Traumatised Nice Terror Attack Eyewitness Says She'll 'Never Forget Wild Screams of Children' Killed in Bastille Day Massacre," *The Mirror*, July 15, 2016.
20. Alissa J. Rubin, "'It Had To Be Stopped': Heroes Rise amid France Terror Attacks," *Wall Street Journal*, August 22, 2016.
21. Ibid.
22. Ibid.
23. Hassan Morajea, and Sam Schechner, "From Celebration to Horror in Nice," *Wall Street Journal*, July 14, 2016.
24. Sayare, "The Untold Story of the Bastille Day Attacker."
25. Peter Mikelbank, "France Attack: Eyewitness Says 'There Was a Trail of Bodies,'" *People Magazine*, July 15, 2016.
26. Sayare, "The Untold Story of the Bastille Day Attacker."
27. British Broadcasting Corp., "Nice Attack: Witnesses Describe Bastille Day Horror," BBC.com, July 15, 2016, https://www.bbc.com/news/world-europe-36801431.
28. Ibid.
29. Nick Hopkins, Angelique Chrisafis, and Sofia Fischer, "Bastille Day Attack: 'Hysterical Crowds Were Running from Death,'" *The Guardian*, July 15, 2016.
30. "Remembering the Nice Attack: July 14, 2016," Counter Extremism Project,

Counterextremism.com, accessed May 4, 2019, https://www.counterextremism.com/remembering-nice-attack.
31. Sayare, "The Untold Story of the Bastille Day Attacker."
32. Alissa J. Rubin and Lilia Blaise, "A Third of Nice Truck Attack's Dead Were Muslim, Group Says," *New York Times*, July 19, 2016.
33. Sayare, "The Untold Story of the Bastille Day Attacker."
34. Rubin and Blaise, "A Third of Nice Truck Attack's Dead Were Muslim."
35. Damian Paletta, "Truck Attack in Nice Shows Limits of Global Hunt for Terrorism," *Wall Street Journal*, July 14, 2016.
36. Kim Willsher, "French Prosecutor Says Killer of 84 in Nice Had Accomplices and Planned Attack for Months," *Los Angeles Times*, July 21, 2016.
37. William Horobin and Matthew Dalton, "Attacker in Nice Conspired for Months," *Wall Street Journal*, July 21, 2016.
38. "'Je Ne Suis Pas Charlie, Je Suis Content …'": Le Message d'un Complice de Lahouaiej Bouhlel," LCI.fr, July 21, 2016, https://www.lci.fr/france/je-ne-suis-pas-charlie-je-suis-content-le-message-dun-complice-de-lahouaiej-bouhlel-1266910.html.
39. Sylvain Mouillard et al., "Les Profils Troubles des Proches du Tueur de Nice," *Libération*, October 2, 2016.
40. Sayare, "The Untold Story of the Bastille Day Attacker."
41. Horobin and Dalton, "Attacker in Nice Conspired for Months."
42. "Attentat de Nice: Les Curieuses Contradictions de L'Entourage du Tueur au Camion," *L'Express*, October 2, 2016.
43. Aurelien Breeden, "Attacker in Nice Plotted for Months and Had Accomplices, French Prosecutor Says," *New York Times*, July 21, 2016.
44. David Chazan et al., "Nice Terror Attack: 'Soldier of Islam' Bouhlel 'Took Drugs and Used Dating Sites to Pick Up Men and Women,'" *The Telegraph*, July 17, 2016.
45. Breeden, "Attacker in Nice Plotted for Months."
46. William Molinié, "Attentat de Nice: Un Proche du Terroriste Remis en Liberté," LCI.fr, October 25, 2018, https://www.lci.fr/justice/info-lci-attentat-de-nice-un-proche-du-terroriste-mohamed-lahouaiej-bouhlel-remis-en-liberte-2102562.html.
47. Chazan et al., "Nice Terror Attack: 'Soldier of Islam' Bouhlel."
48. Sayare, "The Untold Story of the Bastille Day Attacker."
49. *Ibid.*
50. Christophe Cirone, "Attentat De Nice: Le 'Mentor Influent' Ne Serait Pas Radicalisé," *Monaco-Matin*, March 4, 2019.
51. Heather Welford, "Nice Attack One Year On: 'How Can Anyone Bear to Visit the Beach?'" *New Statesman America*, July 14, 2017.
52. Jonathan Reilly, "New Ring of Steel: France Unveils New £16.5 Million Anti-Terror Barriers in Nice at the Scene of Truck Attack—Could London Be Next?" *The Sun*, June 11, 2017.

Chapter 12

1. "The Failure of ISIS's Ramadan Offensive," MEI.edu (Middle East Institute), August 6, 2015, https://www.mei.edu/publications/failure-isiss-ramadan-offensive.
2. Ali Abdelaty and Suleiman al-Khalidi, "Islamic State Urges Followers to Escalate Attacks in Ramadan," Reuters.com, June 23, 2015, https://www.reuters.com/article/mideast-crisis-ramadan/islamic-state-urges-followers-to-escalate-attacks-in-ramadan-idINKBN0P325620150623
3. Adam Nossiter, "Boko Haram's Civilian Attacks in Nigeria Intensify," *New York Times*, July 6, 2015.
4. Graeme Wood, "What ISIS Really Wants," *The Atlantic*, March 2015.
5. Charles Lister, "Jihad in Ramadan: Terror Attacks in Kuwait, Tunisia, and France as ISIS Launches a New Syrian Offensive," Brookings.edu, June 26, 2015, https://www.brookings.edu/blog/markaz/2015/06/26/jihad-in-ramadan-terror-attacks-in-kuwait-tunisia-and-france-as-isis-launches-a-new-syrian-offensive/.
6. Chris Stephen, Esther Addley, and Julian Borger, "Dozens Killed After Terror Attacks in Tunisia, Kuwait and France," *The Guardian*, June 26, 2015.
7. Radhouane Addala and Tamer El-Ghobashy, "Attack on Tunisian Hotel Leaves Dozens Dead," *Wall Street Journal*, June 27, 2015.

8. Jamie Walker, "ISIS Claims Spreading Attacks," *The Australian*, June 28, 2015.
9. Alissa J. Rubin, "Suspect in Attack in France Had Ties to Radical Islamist," *New York Times*, June 27, 2015.
10. Rubin, "Suspect in Attack in France Had Ties to Radical Islamist."
11. Alix Culbertson, "French Man Accused of Brainwashing ISIS Lorry Driver Who Beheaded Boss Lives in Leicester," *Daily Express*, July 3, 2015.
12. Fred Jiminez, "Radicalisation: Les Précédents Cas en Franche-Comté," *L'Est Republicain*, December 13, 2018.
13. Rubin, "Suspect in Attack in France Had Ties to Radical Islamist."
14. James Reevell et al., "France Attack 26 June 2015: As It Happened," BBC.com, June 26, 2015, https://www.bbc.com/news/live/world-europe-33287095.
15. "Suspect Arrested in Connection with Attack on French Factory Described As 'Wolf in Sheep's Clothing,'" Newstalk.com, June 27, 2015, https://www.newstalk.com/news/suspect-arrested-in-connection-with-attack-on-french-factory-described-as-wolf-in-sheeps-clothing-651340.
16. Reevell et al., "France Attack 26 June 2015."
17. "Iranian-American Heads Firm Where Beheading Carried Out in France," *Iran Times*, July 3, 2015.
18. Catherine Lagrange and Michel Rose, "Delivery Man Beheads Boss in Suspected Islamist Attack on French Gas Site," Reuters.com, June 26, 2015, https://www.reuters.com/article/us-france-blast/delivery-man-beheads-boss-in-suspected-islamist-attack-on-french-gas-site-idUSKBN0P60XR20150626.
19. Matthias Verbergt and Stacy Meichtry, "Suspect in France Attack Apparently Acted on Call from Islamic State, Prosecutors Say," *Wall Street Journal*, June 30, 2015.
20. Adam Taylor, "Why Would Terrorists Kill Cartoonists?" *Washington Post*, January 7, 2015.
21. Sewell Chan, "Frenchman Held in Jihadist Killing Commits Suicide," *New York Times*, December 23, 2015.
22. Reevell et al., "France Attack 26 June 2015."
23. Rubin, "Suspect in Attack in France Had Ties to Radical Islamist."
24. Verbergt and Meichtry, "Suspect in France Attack Apparently Acted on Call."
25. Ibid.
26. Le Figaro, "Attentat en Isère: 'C'est Comme Si J'Avais Enfanté un Monstre,' Témoigne la Mère de Yunes," *Le Figaro*, July 1, 2015.
27. D. B. with Agence France-Presse, "Attentat en Isère: Qui Est Sébastien-Younès, le Destinataire du Selfie Macabre?" *20 Minutes* (France), updated June 30, 2015, https://www.20minutes.fr/societe/1641627-20150629-attentat-isere-sebastien-younes-destinataire-selfie-macabre.
28. Guy Van Vlierden, "The Enduring Influence of Malika El Aroud, Belgium's 'Black Widow of Jihad,'" EERadicalization.com (European Eye on Radicalization), October 18, 2018, https://eeradicalization.com/the-enduring-influence-of-malika-el-aroud-belgiums-black-widow-of-jihad/.
29. Soren Seelow, "Attaque dans l'Isère: Les Motivations Troubles de Yassin Salhi," *Le Monde*, June 28, 2019.
30. Damien Sharkov, "French Beheading Suspect Hangs Himself in Prison," *Newsweek*, December 23, 2015.

Chapter 13

1. Jim Bittermann and Bryony Jones, "France Train Attack: What We Know About Ayoub El Khazzani," CNN.com, modified January 8, 2018, https://www.cnn.com/2015/08/24/europe/france-train-attack-what-we-know-about-suspect/index.html.
2. Adam Nossiter, "French Train Attack Suspect Viewed Jihadist Video, Official Says," *New York Times*, August 25, 2015.
3. Matthew Dalton, Inti Landauro, and Sam Schechner, "Train Gunman Watched Jihadist Video before Attack, French Prosecutor Says," *Wall Street Journal*, August 25, 2015.
4. Raphael Minder, "Scrutiny Falls on a Spanish Mosque after Foiled Train Attack," *New York Times*, August 27, 2015.
5. Paul Cruickshank, "Train Attack Suspect Confesses After Revelations in Academic Journal," CNN.com, updated December 19, 2016. https://www.cnn.com/2016/12/19/europe/isis-train-attack-suspect-confession/index.html.

6. Ibid.
7. Ibid.
8. David Barrett, "Revealed: The Mystery Man Who Tackled AK-47 Assault Rifle from Train Gunman," *The Telegraph*, August 25, 2015.
9. Stephanie Dube Dwilson, "Mark Moogalian & Damien A., Mystery Belgium Train Heroes: 5 Fast Facts You Need to Know," Heavy.com, May 29, 2018, https://heavy.com/news/2015/08/mark-moogalian-damien-a-thalys-france-paris-belgium-train-attack-heroes-legion-medal-terrorist-gunman-sorbonne-spencer-stone-skarlatos/.
10. Matthieu Suc, "Attaque dans Le Thalys: 'J'ai Levé la Tête et J'ai Vu un Gars Avec un AK-47,'" *Le Monde*, August 24, 2015.
11. Agence France-Presse, "What Happened on the Paris-Bound Terror Train?" TheLocal.fr, August 26, 2015, https://www.thelocal.fr/20150826/what-exactly-happened-on-the-paris-bound-terror-train.
12. Emilie Blachere, "Anglade: 'Rendre Hommage à Leur Courage Héroïque,'" *Paris Match*, August 22, 2015.
13. Ibid.
14. Associated Press and Network Writers, "French-American Mark Moogalian Is New High-Speed Train Attack Hero," News.com.au, August 26, 2015, https://www.news.com.au/world/frenchamerican-mark-moogalian-is-new-highspeed-train-attack-hero/news-story/146d22a604bb3ba0ae37f600d3ada203.
15. CBS News and the Associated Press, "Train Shooting Victim Played Dead before Gunman Was Overpowered," CBSNews.com, August 26, 2015, https://www.cbsnews.com/news/france-train-shooting-victim-mark-moogalian-recounts-suspects-strange-behavior/.
16. Ibid.
17. Barrett, "Revealed: The Mystery Man Who Tackled AK-47 Assault Rifle from Train Gunman."
18. Emilie Cabot, "Thalys: 'Je N'Avais Qu'une Idée en Tête: Lui Arracher Son Arme,' Raconte Mark Moogalian," *Le Journal du Dimanche*, June 20, 2017.
19. Anthony Sadler et al., *The 15:17 to Paris: The True Story of a Terrorist, a Train, and Three American Heroes* (New York: Public Affairs Perseus Books, 2016).

20. Ibid.
21. Agence France-Presse, "What Happened on the Paris-Bound Terror Train?"
22. Amanda Holpuch, "France Train Attack: American-French Citizen Was Shot Trying to Tackle Gunman," *The Guardian*, August 25, 2015.
23. Greg Keller, "Moogalian Recounts Train Attack in French Magazine Interview," APNews.com, August 26, 2015, https://apnews.com/e79bb15573d7462b928229513b209ca6.
24. Jennifer Hlad, "Stopping Terror on the Tracks," *Air Force Magazine* (November 2015), 26.
25. Sadler et al., *The 15:17 to Paris*, 224.
26. Ibid.
27. Don Melvin, "Train Gunman Had Terrorist Intent, French Prosecutor Says," CNN.com, updated January 8, 2018, https://www.cnn.com/2015/08/25/europe/france-train-attack/index.html.
28. Jean-Charles Brisard and Kévin Jackson, "The Islamic State's External Operations and the French-Belgian Nexus," *CTC Sentinel* 9, issue 11 (November/December 2016).
29. L'Obs with Agence France-Presse, "L'Attaque du Thalys Reconstituée Alors Que L'enquête Touche à Sa Fin," *L'Obs* (magazine), September 18, 2019, https://www.nouvelobs.com/topnews/20190918.AFP4917/l-attaque-du-thalys-reconstituee-alors-que-l-enquete-touche-a-sa-fin.html.
30. Sadler et al., *The 15:17 to Paris*, 159.
31. British Broadcasting Corp., "France Thalys Train Attack Gunman Was 'Unable to Kill,'" BBCNews.com, May 9, 2018, https://www.bbc.com/news/world-europe-44053410.
32. Isabelle Fraser et al, "France Train Attack: As It Happened Saturday August 22," *The Telegraph*, August 23, 2015.
33. Agence France-Presse, "Moroccan Extradited to France Over 2015 Train Attack," France24.com, November 3, 2017, https://www.france24.com/en/20171103-moroccan-extradited-france-over-2015-train-attack.
34. Francois Lenoir, "Belgium Transfers to France Man Linked to Foiled Train Attack," RFI.com, February 2, 2018, http://www.rfi.fr/en/france/20180202-belgium-transfers-france-man-linked-foiled-train-attack.
35. Agence France-Presse, "Moroccan Extradited to France."

36. L'Obs with Agence France-Presse, "L'Attaque du Thalys Reconstituée."
37. Dwilson, "Mark Moogalian & Damien A."
38. Le Parisien with Agence France-Presse, "Attentat Déjoué du Thalys: Les 3 Héros Américains Ont Reçu la Nationalité Française," *Le Parisien*, February 1, 2019.
39. News Wires, "Americans Who Thwarted Train Terror Attack Become French Citizens," France24.com, January 2, 2019, https://www.france24.com/en/20190201-americans-who-thwarted-thalys-train-terror-attack-become-french-citizens.
40. *Ibid.*

Epilogue

1. Roxane De Rebetz De Massol and Maartje Van Der Woude, "Marianne's Liberty in Jeopardy? A French Analysis on Recent Counterterrorism Legal Developments," *Critical Studies on Terrorism* (2019), 2, https://doi.org/10.1080/17539153.2019.1633838.
2. "France: Abuses Under State of Emergency," *Human Rights Watch*, February 3, 2016, https://www.hrw.org/news/2016/02/03/france-abuses-under-state-emergency.
3. *Ibid.*
4. Aurelien Breeden, "French Authorities Given Broader Powers to Fight Terrorism," *New York Times,* May 25, 2016.
5. Chloe Farand, "France Scraps Law Making 'Regular' Visits to Jihadi Websites an Offence," *The Independent*, February 10, 2017.
6. De Rebetz De Massol and Van Der Woude, "Marianne's Liberty in Jeopardy?"
7. Sarah A. Harvard, "Emmanuel Macron's Anti-Terror Law Is a Throwback to the Bad Days of Colonialism," *The New Republic*, November 1, 2017.
8. De Rebetz De Massol and Van Der Woude, "Marianne's Liberty in Jeopardy?"
9. "Etat d'Urgence: 3.021 Perquisitions, 500 Armes Découvertes," BFMTV.com (BFM Television, France), January 12, 2016, https://www.bfmtv.com/societe/etat-d-urgence-3-021-perquisitions-500-armes-decouvertes-942797.html.
10. "France: 'Dehumanising' Counter-Terror Measures Being Used to Unjustly Punish People—New Report," *Amnesty International*, November 22, 2018, https://www.amnesty.org.uk/press-releases/france-dehumanising-counter-terror-measures-being-used-unjustly-punish-people-new.
11. "France: UN Expert Says New Terrorism Laws May Undermine Fundamental Rights and Freedoms." *Office of the United Nations High Commissioner for Human Rights* (OHCHR), May 23, 2018, https://www.ohchr.org/en/NewsEvents/Pages/DisplayNews.aspx?NewsID=23130&LangID=E.
12. *Ibid.*
13. Jacques Follorou, "58 des 59 Attentats Déjoués depuis Six Ans l'Ont Été Grâce au Renseignement Humain," *Le Monde*, October 15, 2019.

Bibliography

Abdelaty, Ali, and Suleiman al-Khalidi. "Islamic State Urges Followers to Escalate Attacks in Ramadan." Reuters.com. June 23, 2015. https://www.reuters.com/article/mideast-crisis-ramadan/islamic-state-urges-followers-to-escalate-attacks-in-ramadan-idINKBN0P325620150623.

"Abdelhamid Abaaoud, L'Homme le Plus Recherché de Belgique a Fréquenté Une École Huppée." Sudinfo.be (Groupe Sudpresse Belgium). January 21, 2015. https://www.sudinfo.be/art/1194729/article/2015-01-20/abdelhamid-abaaoud-l-homme-le-plus-recherche-de-belgique-a-frequente-une-ecole-h.

Addala, Radhouane and Tamer El-Ghobashy. "Attack on Tunisian Hotel Leaves Dozens Dead." *Wall Street Journal,* June 27, 2015.

Agence France-Presse. "Abaaoud: From School Bully to Terrorist Plotter." TheLocal.fr. November 19, 2015. https://www.thelocal.fr/20151119/the-terrorist-whose-family-prayed-he-was-dead.

Agence France-Presse. "Moroccan Extradited to France Over 2015 Train Attack." France24.com. November 3, 2017. https://www.france24.com/en/20171103-moroccan-extradited-france-over-2015-train-attack.

Agence France-Presse. "Relative of Hebdo Killer Indicted on Terror Charges in France." *Times of Israel,* August 28, 2016.

Agence France-Presse. "Teen 'In Shock' after Wrongly Linked to Charlie Hebdo Attack." NDTV.com (New Delhi Television). January 13, 2015. https://www.ndtv.com/world-news/teen-in-shock-after-wrongly-linked-to-charlie-hebdo-attack-726332.

Agence France-Presse. "What Do We Know About the Nice Attacker?" TheLocal.fr. July 17, 2016. https://www.thelocal.fr/20160717/nice-attacker-body-building-drug-taking-womanising.

Agence France-Presse. "What Happened on the Paris-Bound Terror Train?" TheLocal.fr. August 26, 2015. https://www.thelocal.fr/20150826/what-exactly-happened-on-the-paris-bound-terror-train.

Alderman, Liz. "Recounting a Bustling Office at Charlie Hebdo, Then a 'Vision of Horror.'" *New York Times,* January 9, 2015.

Alexander, Harriet. "Paris Attacks: Special Forces Hit Amedy Coulibaly with 40 Bullets." *The Telegraph,* January 11, 2015.

Allen, Peter. "Student Who Was Cleared of Being Getaway Driver in Charlie Hebdo Attacks Is Arrested as He 'Tries to Join Islamic State in Syria.'" *Daily Mail,* August 7, 2016.

Amara, Tarek. "Shock in Tunisian Hometown of Nice Attacker." Reuters.com. July 15, 2016. https://www.reuters.com/article/us-europe-attacks-nice-hometown/shock-in-tunisian-hometown-of-nice-attacker-idUSKCN0ZV2X5.

Amnesty International Health and Human Rights Team. "Health Professional Action: Prisoner in Need of Urgent Medical Care—Iraq." *Amnesty International,* September 9, 2010. https://www.amnesty.org/download/Documents/40000/mde140112010en.pdf.

"Un Ancien de Charlie Hebdo Accuse Charb." *L'Express,* January 15, 2015.

Anderson, John Ward. "Cartoons of Prophet Met with Outrage." *Washington Post,* January 31, 2006.

"As It Happened: Over 120 Dead in Paris

Attacks." TheLocal.fr. November 13, 2015. https://www.thelocal.fr/20151113/several-dead-in-paris-shootings

"Assaulting Democracy: The Deep Repercussions of the Charlie Hebdo Attack." *Der Spiegel,* January 9, 2015.

Associated Press. "Eyewitnesses Construct Minute-By-Minute Account of Paris Attacks." *Macleans,* November 15, 2015.

Associated Press. "French Muslims Flock to, from Iraq's Battlefields." NBCNews.com. Updated March 30, 2008. http://www.nbcnews.com/id/23872546/ns/world_news-islam_in_europe/t/french-muslims-flock-iraqs-battlefields/.

Associated Press. "French Satirical Magazine Office Fire Bombed Ahead of 'Muhammad Edition.'" FoxNews.com. Updated December 4, 2015. https://www.foxnews.com/world/french-satirical-magazine-office-fire-bombed-ahead-of-muhammad-edition.

Associated Press. "Paper Cleared in Muhammad Drawings Case." *Washington Post,* March 22, 2007.

Associated Press. "Tracing the Roots of European Terror: What Led a Young Belgian to Become an ISIS Terrorist." *Haaretz,* February 4, 2018.

Associated Press and Network Writers. "French-American Mark Moogalian Is New High-Speed Train Attack Hero." News.com.au. August 26, 2015. https://www.news.com.au/world/french-american-mark-moogalian-is-new-highspeed-train-attack-hero/news-story/146d22a604bb3ba0ae37f600d3ada203.

"Attentat à Charlie Hebdo: Pontoise Pleure Charb." *Le Parisien,* January 7, 2015.

"Attentat de Nice: Les Curieuses Contradictions de L'Entourage du Tueur au Camion." *L'Express,* October 2, 2016.

Aubourg, Lucie. "This Is What Happened at the Bataclan Concert Hall during the Paris Attacks." Vice.com (Vice News). November 25, 2015. https://www.vice.com/en_us/article/ev9bnm/this-is-what-happened-at-the-bataclan-concert-hall-during-the-paris-attacks.

Australian Broadcasting Corp., Agence France-Presse, and Reuters. "Charlie Hebdo Shooting: Track How Events Unfolded." ABC.net.au. January 8, 2015. https://www.abc.net.au/news/2015-01-08/paris-newspaper-attack-mapped/6006110.

B., Fahmi. "Sur la Live: Fusillade à Paris." *Libération,* November 14, 2015.

Banerjee, Rohan, and Adam Shergold. "Suicide Attacks Near Stade de France Leave Three People Dead as Explosions Are Heard During Friendly Victory Over Germany and Paris Is Rocked by Coordinated Terrorist Strikes on Six Targets." *Daily Mail,* November 14, 2015.

Barrett, David. "Revealed: The Mystery Man Who Tackled AK-47 Assault Rifle from Train Gunman." *The Telegraph,* August 25, 2015.

"Bataclan Survivor Commits Suicide Two Years After Terror Attack." TheLocal.fr. November 27, 2017. https://www.thelocal.fr/20171127/paris-bataclan-survivor-commits-suicide-two-years-after-terror-attack.

Baum, Steven K. "Antisemitic Incidents from Around the World, January—June 2015: A Selected List." *Journal for the Study of Antisemitism* 7, no. 1 (2015): 16–29.

Berezow, Alex. "How Chemists Plan to Sniff Out Bombs." BBC.com. December 25, 2015. https://www.bbc.com/news/science-environment-35022731.

Berkley Center for Religion, Peace, and World Affairs. n.d. "Shahada." BerkleyCenter.Georgetown.edu (Georgetown University website). Accessed January 14, 2018. https://berkleycenter.georgetown.edu/essays/shahada.

Berwick, Andrew (AKA Anders Behring Breivik). "2083—A European Declaration of Independence." PublicIntelligence.net. Accessed January 6, 2020. https://publicintelligence.net/anders-behring-breiviks-complete-manifesto-2083-a-european-declaration-of-independence/

Bilefsky, Dan. "After Paris Attacks, Ties That Bind Patrons at a Cafe Also Burn." *New York Times,* November 25, 2015.

Bisserbe, Noemie, and Emre Peker. "Intelligence Lapse Hindered Search for Second French Church Assailant." *Wall Street Journal,* July 28, 2016.

Bittermann, Jim, and Bryony Jones. "France Train Attack: What We Know About Ayoub El Khazzani." CNN.com. Modified January 8, 2018. https://www.cnn.com/2015/08/24/europe/france-train-attack-what-we-know-about-suspect/index.html.

Blachere, Emilie. "Anglade: 'Rendre Hommage à Leur Courage Héroïque.'" *Paris Match,* August 22, 2015.

Blake, Andrew. "Bilal Hadi, Paris Terrorist, Left Social Media Clues before Attacks." *Washington Times,* November 20, 2015.

Blake, Andrew. "Pope Francis Sets the Stage for Canonizing the French Priest Killed in Terror Attack." *Washington Times,* September 14, 2016.

Blasberg, Derek. "Paris Attacks Survivor Isobel Bowdery Shares Her Story." *Vanity Fair,* December 4, 2015.

Blitzer, Wolf (host/interviewer). "Concert Witness Julien Pearce Full." Facebook.com (CNN/Anderson Cooper 360 page). Aired on November 13, 2015. https://www.facebook.com/watch/?v=10156332669095533.

Bond, Anthony. "Traumatised Nice Terror Attack Eyewitness Says She'll 'Never Forget Wild Screams of Children' Killed in Bastille Day Massacre." *The Mirror,* July 15, 2016.

Borden, Sam. "As Paris Attacks Unfolded, Players and Fans at Soccer Stadium Remained Unaware." *New York Times,* November 14, 2105.

Borger, Julian. "Paris Gunman Amedy Coulibaly Declared Allegiance to Isis." *The Guardian,* January 11, 2015.

Boring, Nicolas. "France: Special Security Measures Declared Unconstitutional." *Library of Congress—Global Legal Monitor,* December 20, 2017. https://www.loc.gov/law/foreign-news/article/france-special-security-measures-declared-unconstitutional/

Bouanchaud, Cécile. "Qui Est Foued Mohamed-Aggad, le Troisième Kamikaze du Bataclan?" Europe1.fr (Europe 1, radio station). December 10, 2015. https://www.europe1.fr/faits-divers/qui-est-foued-mohamed-aggad-le-troisieme-kamikaze-du-bataclan-2633591.

Bouchard, Melodie. "In Photos: 'I Am Charlie' Vigil Held in Paris for Murdered 'Charlie Hebdo' Journalists." Vice.com (Vice News), January 7, 2015. https://www.vice.com/en_us/article/gyn7d9/in-photos-i-am-charlie-vigil-held-in-paris-for-murdered-charlie-hebdo-journalists.

Brainy Quote (website). n.d. "Voltaire Quotes." Accessed November 17, 2018. https://www.brainyquote.com/quotes/voltaire_125630.

Breeden, Aurelien. "Attacker in Nice Plotted for Months and Had Accomplices, French Prosecutor Says." *New York Times,* July 21, 2016.

Breeden, Aurelien. "French Authorities Given Broader Powers to Fight Terrorism." *New York Times,* May 25, 2016.

Brisard, Jean-Charles, and Kévin Jackson. "The Islamic State's External Operations and the French-Belgian Nexus." *CTC Sentinel* 9, issue 11 (November/December 2016): 8–15.

British Broadcasting Corp. "Charlie Hebdo: Gun Attack on French Magazine Kills 12." BBC.com. January 7, 2015. https://www.bbc.com/news/world-europe-30710883.

British Broadcasting Corp. "France Church Attack: 'Gentle' Boy Who Became a Killer." BBC.com. July 28, 2016. https://www.bbc.com/news/world-europe-36914706.

British Broadcasting Corp. "France Church Attack: Priest Killed by Two 'IS Militants.'" BBC.com. July 26, 2016. https://www.bbc.com/news/world-europe-36892785.

British Broadcasting Corp. "France Thalys Train Attack Gunman Was 'Unable to Kill.'" BBC.com. May 9, 2018. https://bbc.com/news/world-europe-44053410.

British Broadcasting Corp. "French Satirical Paper Charlie Hebdo Attacked in Paris." BBC.com. November 2, 2011. https://www.bbc.com/news/world-europe-15550350.

British Broadcasting Corp. "Nice Attack: Lorry Driver Confirmed as Mohamed Lahouaiej-Bouhlel." BBC.com. July 15, 2016. https://www.bbc.com/news/world-europe 36808020.

British Broadcasting Corp. "Nice Attack: Witnesses Describe Bastille Day Horror." BBC.com. July 15, 2016. https://www.bbc.com/news/world-europe-36801431.

British Broadcasting Corp. "Paris Attacks: Eyewitness Accounts." BBC.com. November 16, 2015. https://www.bbc.com/news/world-europe-34813570.

British Broadcasting Corp. "Paris Attacks: Suspects' Profiles." BBC.com. January 12, 2015. https://www.bbc.com/news/world-europe-30722038.

British Broadcasting Corp. "Paris Attacks: What Happened on the Night." BBC.com. December 9, 2015. https://www.bbc.com/news/world-europe-34818994.

British Broadcasting Corp. "Paris Attacks: Who Were the Attackers?" BBC.com.

April 27, 2016. https://www.bbc.com/news/world-europe-34832512.
British Broadcasting Corp. "Paris Attacks: Who Were the Victims?" BBC.com. November 27, 2015. https://www.bbc.com/news/world-europe-34821813.
British Broadcasting Corp. "Paris Shootings: Ahmed Merabet's Killers 'Pretend Muslims' Says brother." BBC.com. January 10, 2015. https://www.bbc.com/news/av/world-europe-30762153/paris-shootings-ahmed-merabet-s-killers-pretend-muslims-says-brother.
British Broadcasting Corp. "Who Was Third Bataclan Attacker Foued Mohamed-Aggad?" BBC.com. December 9, 2015. https://www.bbc.com/news/world-europe-35055304.
Brown, Samantha Ruth. "Denmark Already Had a Muslim Ban. It Was Just Called Something Else." *Washington Post*, March 23, 2017.
Bruce, James. "For ISIS, Prisons Have Become Terror Incubators." *The Arab Weekly* (UK), January 15, 2017.
Brumfield, Ben, Tim Lister, and Nick Paton Walsh. "French Jets Bomb ISIS Stronghold of Raqqa, Syria; Few May Have Been Killed." CNN.com. Updated November 16, 2015. https://www.cnn.com/2015/11/16/middleeast/france-raqqa-airstrikes-on-isis/index.html
Buchanan, Rose Troup. "Paris Terror: Muslim Leaders Around the World Condemn 'Heinous' Attacks." *The Independent*, November 14, 2015.
Burke, Daniel. "Why Images of Mohammed Offend Muslims." CNN.com. Updated May 4, 2015. https://www.cnn.com/2015/05/04/living/islam-prophet-images/index.html.
Burke, Robert A. *Counter-Terrorism for Emergency Responders*. Boca Raton, Florida: CRC Press, 2017.
Byman, Daniel L., and Jennifer R. Williams. "ISIS vs. Al Qaeda: Jihadism's Global Civil War." Brookings.edu (The Brookings Institution), February 24, 2015. https://www.brookings.edu/articles/isis-vs-al-qaeda-jihadisms-global-civil-war/.
Cabot, Emilie. "Thalys: 'Je N'Avais Qu'une Idée en Tête: Lui Arracher Son Arme,' Raconte Mark Moogalian." *Le Journal du Dimanche*, June 20, 2017.
Callimachi, Rukmini. "ISIS Caliphate Crumbles as Last Village in Syria Falls." *New York Times*, March 23, 2019.
Callimachi, Rukmini. "ISIS Claims Responsibility, Calling Paris Attacks 'First of the Storm.'" *New York Times*, November 14, 2015.
Callimachi, Rukmini, Alissa J. Rubin, and Laure Fourquet. "A View of ISIS's Evolution in New Details of Paris Attacks." *New York Times*, March 19, 2016.
Callimachi, Rukmini, and Jim Yardley. "From Amateur to Ruthless Jihadist in France: Chérif and Saïd Kouachi's Path to Paris Attack at Charlie Hebdo." *New York Times*, January 17, 2015.
Callimachi, Rumini. "Not 'Lone Wolves' After All: How ISIS Guides World's Terror Plots from Afar." *New York Times*, February 4, 2017.
Campbell, Matthew, Bojan Pancevski, Tony Allen-Mills, and Nicola Smith. "Gay Sex, Drugs, Then Suicidal Slaughter." *The Sunday Times* (London), November 22, 2015.
Carbajal, Doreen, and Suzanne Daley. "Proud to Offend, Charlie Hebdo Carries the Torch of Political Provocation." *New York Times*, January 7, 2015.
Castillo, Mariano. "Following the Tangled and Treacherous Trail After France Terror Attack." CNN.com. Updated January 15, 2015. https://www.cnn.com/2015/01/13/europe/france-charlie-hebdo-attack-trail/index.html.
Castillo, Mariano, and Paul Cruickshank. "Who Was Abdelhamid Abaaoud, Suspected Ringleader of Paris Attack?" CNN.com. Updated November 19, 2015. https://www.cnn.com/2015/11/16/europe/paris-terror-attack-mastermind-abdelhamid-abaaoud/index.html.
CBS News and the Associated Press. "New Details Emerge About Teen Killer of French Priest." CBSNews.com. July 27, 2016. https://www.cbsnews.com/news/new-details-emerge-about-french-priests-teen-killer/.
CBS News and the Associated Press. "Train Shooting Victim Played Dead before Gunman Was Overpowered." CBSNews.com. August 26, 2015. https://www.cbsnews.com/news/france-train-shooting-victim-mark-moogalian-recounts-suspects-strange-behavior/.
Chalmers, Robert. "Is Molenbeek Really a No-Go Zone?" *Gentleman's Quarterly* (*GQ*), June 21, 2007.

Chan, Sewell. "Frenchman Held in Jihadist Killing Commits Suicide." *New York Times,* December 23, 2015.

Chan, Sewell, and Milan Schreuer. "School's Warnings About Paris Attacker Were Not Passed On." *New York Times,* December 26, 2015.

Charb (Charbonnier, Stéphane). *Open Letter: On Blasphemy, Islamophobia, and the True Enemies of Free Expression.* New York: Little, Brown, 2015.

Charbonnier, Stéphane. *Charlie Hebdo Magazine* (cover cartoon), September 19, 2001.

"Charlie Hebdo: Procès." CharlieHebdo.fr (*Charlie Hebdo* website). Accessed 1/5/20. https://charliehebdo.fr/pages/proces/.

Chazan, David, Lydia Willgress, Jannat Jalil, Tom Morgan, Camilla Turner, Peter Allen, James Rothwell, Martin Evans, and Saphora Smith. "Nice Terror Attack: 'Soldier of Islam' Bouhlel 'Took Drugs and Used Dating Sites to Pick Up Men and Women.'" *The Telegraph,* July 17, 2016.

Chrisafis, Angelique. "Charlie Hebdo Attackers: Born, Raised, and Radicalised in France." *The Guardian,* January 12, 2015.

Chrisafis, Angelique. "Doctor Who Treated Paris Wounded and Charlie Hebdo Victims Calls for Unity." *The Guardian,* November 15, 2015.

Chrisafis, Angelique. "'It Looked Like a Battlefield': The Full Story of What Happened in the Bataclan." *The Guardian,* November 20, 2015.

Chrisafis, Angelique, Jessica Reed, Raya Jalabi, and Nicky Woolf. "Witness Accounts from Across Paris: 'I Saw My Final Hour Unfurl Before Me.'" *The Guardian,* November 13, 2015.

Cirone, Christophe. "Attentat De Nice: Le 'Mentor Influent' Ne Serait Pas Radicalisé." *Monaco-Matin,* March 4, 2019.

Colombani, Jean-Marie. "Nous Sommes Tous Américains." *Le Monde,* May 23, 2007.

Connett, David. "Paris Attacks: 'Mastermind' of Attacks Abelhamid Abaaoud Turned Back on 'Fantastic' Life, Says Father." *The Independent,* November 16, 2015.

Cook, Fidelma, and Flory Drury. "'For a Mum to Bury Her Child Is the Hardest Thing. Burying Two Is Unthinkable': Mother Pays Tribute to Her 'Beautiful' Identical Twins Killed in Carillon Bar Massacre." *Daily Mail,* November 19, 2015.

Coren, Michael. "The 'Draw Mohammad' Contest Was Not an Attempt to Start a Conversation But a Single Act of Bravado." *National Post,* May 7, 2015.

Corner, Emily, Paul Gill, and Oliver Mason. "Mental Health Disorders and the Terrorist: A Research Note Probing Selection Effects and Disorder Prevalence." *Studies in Conflict & Terrorism* 39, no. 6 (2016): 560–568.

Cornevin, Christophe. "Adel Kermiche, un Ado Perturbé Devenu Terroriste." *Le Figaro,* July 28, 2016.

Counter Extremism Project. "Abdel Malik Petitjean." Counterextremism.com. Accessed July 11, 2019. https://www.counterextremism.com/extremists/abdel-malik-petitjean.

Counter Extremism Project. "Adel Kermiche." Counterextremism.com. Accessed July 11, 2019. https://www.counterextremism.com/extremists/adel-kermiche.

Counter Extremism Project. "Remembering the Nice Attack: July 14, 2016." Counterextremism.com. Accessed May 4, 2019. https://www.counterextremism.com/remembering-nice-attack.

Craw, Victoria, and Wire Reports. "National Front Leader Marine Le Pen Tipped for French Presidential Run Following Terror Attacks." News.com.au. January 23, 2015. https://www.news.com.au/finance/work/leaders/national-front-leader-marine-le-pen-tipped-for-french-presidential-run-following-terror-attacks/news-story/e772a1f86fa2e8e322bfa25ebe9c0fdc

Cruickshank, Paul. "The Inside Story of the Paris and Brussels Attacks." CNN.com. Updated October 30, 2017. https://www.cnn.com/2016/03/30/europe/inside-paris-brussels-terror-attacks/index.html.

Cruickshank, Paul. "The Inside Story of the Paris Attack." CNN.com. Updated March 22, 2016. https://www.cnn.com/2016/03/21/europe/inside-paris-terror-attack/index.html.

Cruickshank, Paul. "Train Attack Suspect Confesses After Revelations in Academic Journal." CNN.com. Updated

December 19, 2016. https://www.cnn.com/2016/12/19/europe/isis-train-attack-suspect-confession/index.html.
Cruickshank, Paul. "A View from the CT Foxhole: An Interview with Alain Grignard, Brussels Federal Police." *CTC Sentinel* 8, issue 8 (August 2015): 7–10.
Culbertson, Alix. "French Man Accused of Brainwashing ISIS Lorry Driver Who Beheaded Boss Lives in Leicester." *Daily Express*, July 3, 2015.
Culbertson, Alix, and Katie Mansfield. "Normandy Attack: Murdered Priest Was 'Treasured' by the Community for Nearly 60 Years." *Daily Express*, July 26, 2016.
D. B. with Agence France-Presse. "Attentat en Isère: Qui Est Sébastien-Younès, le Destinataire du Selfie Macabre?" *20 Minutes* (France), updated June 30, 2015. https://www.20minutes.fr/societe/1641627-20150629-attentat-isere-sebastien-younes-destinataire-selfie-macabre.
Dalton, Matthew, Inti Landauro, and Sam Schechner. "Train Gunman Watched Jihadist Video Before Attack, French Prosecutor Says." *Wall Street Journal*, August 25, 2015.
Dearden, Lizzie. "Abdelhamid Abaaoud: What We Know About Belgian Man Identified as Suspected Paris Attacks 'Mastermind.'" *The Independent*, November 16, 2015.
Dearden, Lizzie. "Charlie Hebdo Attack: Former Editor Philippe Val Urges People to Use Laughter as the 'Ultimate Weapon' against Extremists." *The Independent*, January 7, 2015.
Dearden, Lizzie. "Paris Shootings: How the Sieges with Charlie Hebdo Killers at Dammartin-en-Goele Print Works and Jewish Grocer Ended." *The Independent*, January 9, 2015.
Delcroix, Olivier. "Charb, Insolent Volontaire." *Le Figaro*, January 7, 2015.
De Mallevoüe, Delphine. "'Fou,' 'Ordinaire,' les Mots des Voisins d'Adel Kermiche." *Le Figaro*, July 27, 2016.
De Rebetz De Massol, Roxane, and Maartje Van Der Woude. "Marianne's Liberty in Jeopardy? A French Analysis on Recent Counterterrorism Legal Developments." *Critical Studies on Terrorism* (2019): 1–23. https://doi.org/10.1080/17539153.2019.1633838.

De Stefano, Carla, Massimiliano Orri, Jean Marc Agostinucci, Haroun Zouaghi, Frederic Lapostolle, Thierry Baubet, and Frederic Adnet. "Early Psychological Impact of Paris Terrorist Attacks on Healthcare Emergency Staff: A Cross-Sectional Study." *Depression and Anxiety* 35, issue 3 (March 2018): 185–282.
Donadio, Rachel. "The Unending Disquiet after Attacks in Paris." *The Atlantic*, October 9, 2019.
Dwilson, Stephanie Dube. "Mark Moogalian & Damien A., Mystery Belgium Train Heroes: 5 Fast Facts You Need to Know." Heavy.com. May 29, 2018. https://heavy.com/news/2015/08/mark-moogalian-damien-a-thalys-france-paris-belgium-train-attack-heroes-legion-medal-terrorist-gunman-sorbonne-spencer-stone-skarlatos/.
Easterly, Jen, and Joshua A. Geltzer. "The Islamic State and the End of Lone-Wolf Terrorism." *Foreign Policy*, May 23, 2017.
English PEN Staff. "Salman Rushdie Condemns Attack on Charlie Hebdo." EnglishPen.org. January 7, 2015. https://www.englishpen.org/campaigns/salman-rushdie-condemns-attack-on-charlie-hebdo/.
Esposito, Richard, Brian Ross, and Cindy Galli. "Anti-Islam Film Producer Wrote Script in Prison: Authorities." ABCNews.go.com (ABC News). September 13, 2012. https://abcnews.go.com/Blotter/anti-islam-film-producer-wrote-script-prison-authorities/story?id=17230609.
"Etat d'Urgence: 3.021 Perquisitions, 500 Armes Découvertes." BFMTV.com (BFM Television, France), January 12, 2016. https://www.bfmtv.com/societe/etat-d-urgence-3-021-perquisitions-500-armes-decouvertes-942797.html.
"The Failure of ISIS's Ramadan Offensive." MEI.edu (Middle East Institute). August 6, 2015. https://www.mei.edu/publications/failure-isiss-ramadan-offensive.
Farand, Chloe. "France Scraps Law Making 'Regular' Visits to Jihadi Websites an Offence." *The Independent*, February 10, 2017.
Le Figaro. "Attentat en Isère: 'C'est Comme Si J'Avais Enfanté un Monstre,' Témoigne la Mère de Yunes." *Le Figaro*, July 1, 2015.
Finnigan, Lexi, and Gregory Walton. "Paris

Attacks: Stade de France Bomber Bilal Hadfi Was 'Unambitious Loner Who Failed His Exams.'" *The Independent,* November 17, 2015.

Floc'h, Benoît. "Au Centre de Recrutement des Armées: 'Ce Coup-Là, Je M'Engage.'" *Le Monde,* November 19, 2015.

Follorou, Jacques. "58 des 59 Attentats Déjoués depuis Six Ans l'Ont Été Grâce au Renseignement Humain." *Le Monde,* October 15, 2019.

Forbes, Amy Wiese. *The Satiric Decade: Satire and the Rise of Republicanism in France, 1830–1840.* Lanham, Maryland: Lexington Books, 2010.

Fouché, Gwladys. "Cartoon Court Case Begins." *The Guardian,* February 7, 2007.

"Fr Hamel Was Martyred 'In Odium Fidei,' Says Archbishop Fisher." *Catholic Herald,* July 27, 2016.

"France: Abuses Under State of Emergency." *Human Rights Watch,* February 3, 2016. https://www.hrw.org/news/2016/02/03/france-abuses-under-state-emergency.

"France Church Attackers 'Smiled' and Talked of Peace, Nun Says." *The Guardian,* July 30, 2016.

"France: 'Dehumanising' Counter-Terror Measures Being Used to Unjustly Punish People—New Report." *Amnesty International,* November 22, 2018. https://www.amnesty.org.uk/press-releases/france-dehumanising-counter-terror-measures-being-used-unjustly-punish-people-new.

France 24. "Bataclan Victims to File Legal Complaint Over 'Inadequate' Police Response." France24.com. June 9, 2018. https://www.france24.com/en/20180608-bataclan-victims-file-legal-complaint-over-inadequate-police-response.

France 24. "Cousin of French Church Attacker Charged and Detained." France24.com. August 1, 2016. https://www.france24.com/en/20160801-cousin-church-attacker-charged-detained.

France 24. "France Church Attack: Nun Who Witnessed ISIS Terrorists' Assault Recounts Priest Murder." YouTube.com (France 24 Channel). July 26, 2016. https://www.youtube.com/watch?v=GnOuYvbQPAo.

France 24. "One French Church Attacker Identified as Teen Under House Arrest." France24.com. July 26, 2016. https://www.france24.com/en/20160726-france-church-attack-teen-under-house-arrest-identified-syria.

France 24. "Priest Killed in France 'Was Always There for Others.'" France24.com. Modified July 27, 2016. https://www.france24.com/en/20160726-profile-france-priest-killed-group-attack-jacques-hamel.

"France: UN Expert Says New Terrorism Laws May Undermine Fundamental Rights and Freedoms." *Office of the United Nations High Commissioner for Human Rights (OHCHR),* May 23, 2018. https://www.ohchr.org/en/NewsEvents/Pages/DisplayNews.aspx?NewsID=23130&LangID=E.

Frankland, Neil. "Disturbing Picture Emerges of Nice Killer." *The New Daily* (Australia), July 18, 2016.

Fraser, Isabelle, David Lawler, Barney Henderson, Andrew Marszal, James Rothwell, and David Millward. "France Train Attack: As It Happened Saturday August 22." *The Telegraph,* August 23, 2015.

Frej, Willa. "Another Cafe Targeted in Paris Attacks Reopens, Ushering in Springtime." *Huffington Post,* March 21, 2016.

"French Church Killer Adel Kermiche: 'A Ticking Time Bomb.'" *The Guardian,* July 27, 2016.

"French Satirical Newspaper 'Charlie Hebdo' Wins Second Trial over Controversial Cartoon Ban Request." NewswireToday.com. February 9, 2007. https://www.newswiretoday.com/news/13842/.

Gartenstein-Ross, Daveed, and Madeleine Blackman. "ISIL's Virtual Planners: A Critical Terrorist Innovation." WarOnTheRocks.com. January 4, 2017. https://warontherocks.com/2017/01/isils-virtual-planners-a-critical-terrorist-innovation/.

Gartenstein-Ross, Daveed, and Nathaniel Barr. "Recent Attacks Illuminate the Islamic State's Europe Attack Network." Jamestown.org. April 27, 2016. https://jamestown.org/program/hot-issue-recent-attacks-illuminate-the-islamic-states-europe-attack-network/.

Gauthier-Villars, David, Asa Fitch, and Raja Abdulrahim. "Islamic State Releases Video Calling Grocery Store Gunman Its 'Soldier.'" *Wall Street Journal,* January 11, 2015.

Genius Media Group. n.d. "Eagles of Death Metal." Genius.com. Accessed

February 3, 2019. https://genius.com/artists/eagles-of-death-metal.

Gill, Paul. "Seven Findings on Lone-Actor Terrorism." PSU.edu (International Center for the Study of Terrorism at Pennsylvania State University). February 6, 2013. https://sites.psu.edu/icst/2013/02/06/seven-findings-on-lone-actor-terrorists/

Gill, Paul, John Horgan, and Paige Deckert. "Bombing Alone: Tracing the Motivations and Antecedent Behaviors of Lone-Actor Terrorists." *Journal of Forensic Sciences* 59, issue 2 (December 6, 2013): 425–435.

Global Pulse Staff. "Five Year Wait for Fr Hamel's Canonization Cause Dispensed." *Le Croix International,* October 3, 2016.

Gonzalès, Paule. "Saint-Étienne-Du-Rouvray: Mis en Examen en 2015, Adel Kermiche a Été Libéré en 2016." *Le Figaro,* July 26, 2016.

Greenhouse, Emily. "Life and Death on the Boulevard Voltaire." *New Republic,* November 15, 2015.

Gregg, Samuel. "The Passion of Father Jacques Hamel." *Catholic World Report,* August 17, 2018.

Grove, Laurence. "French Cartooning: A History." *Jewish Quarterly,* Spring 2015. https://www.jewishquarterly.org/2015/02/french-cartooning-a-history/.

Grow, Kory. "Nearly 100 Dead After Paris Concert Terrorist Attack." *Rolling Stone,* November 13, 2015.

Gruenewald, Jeff, Steve Chermak, and Joshua Freilich. "Distinguishing 'Loner' Attacks from Other Domestic Extremist Violence." *Criminology & Public Policy* 12, issue 1 (February 2013): 65–91.

Guénois, Jean-Marie. "'Va-t'en Satan!'… Les Derniers Mots du Père Hamel Remettent L'Église Face à la Question du Mal." *Le Figaro,* July 25, 2017.

Guillerme, Emiland, Ben Laffin, and Spencer Wolff. "Surviving Paris: Pulled from the Gunfire." NYTimes.com (*New York Times* videos). November 15, 2015. https://www.nytimes.com/video/world/europe/100000004038181/surviving-paris-pulled-from-the-gunfire.html.

Gumuchian, Marie-Louise, and Pauline Mevel. "Exclusive: In Paris Attack, Nurse Discovers the Man He Tried to Save Was Bomber." Reuters.com. November 21, 2015. https://www.reuters.com/article/us-france-shooting-nurse-bomber/exclusive-in-paris-attack-nurse-discovers-the-man-he-tried-to-save-was-bomber-idUSKCN0TA00N20151121.

Gurfinkiel, Michel. "Islam in France: The French Way of Life Is in Danger." *Middle East Quarterly* 4, no. 1 (March 1997): 19–29.

Hackett, Conrad. "5 Facts About the Muslim Population in Europe." PewResearch.org (Pew Research Center). November 29, 2017. https://www.pewresearch.org/fact-tank/2017/11/29/5-facts-about-the-muslim-population-in-europe/.

Haddad, Margot, Erin McLaughlin, and Tim Hume. "France Identifies Suspected Coordinator of Paris, Brussels Attacks." CNN.com. Updated November 8, 2016. https://www.cnn.com/2016/11/08/europe/paris-brussels-attacks-suspected-coordinator/index.html.

Halliday, Josh, and Jonathan Bucks. "Abdelhamid Abaaoud: What We Know about the Paris Attacks 'Mastermind.'" *The Guardian,* November 18, 2015.

Halliday, Josh, Duncan Gardham, and Julian Borger. "Mentor of Charlie Hebdo Gunmen Has Been UK-based." *The Guardian,* January 11, 2015.

Hamm, Mark, and Rámon Spaaij. *The Age of Lone Wolf Terrorism* (*Studies in Transgression*). New York: Columbia University Press, 2017.

Hanna, Jason, and Margot Haddad. "Cherif Kouachi Texted Coulibaly an Hour Before Paris Attacks Began." CNN.com. Updated February 17, 2015. https://www.cnn.com/2015/02/17/world/france-charlie-hebdo-attacks/index.html.

Harding, Luke. "Charlie Hebdo Timeline: How Events Have Unfolded." *The Guardian,* January 9, 2015.

Harris, Sarah Ann. "Shooting of Paris Police Officer Linked to Charlie Hebdo Massacre." *Daily Express,* January 9, 2015.

Harvard, Sarah A. "Emmanuel Macron's Anti-Terror Law Is a Throwback to the Bad Days of Colonialism." *The New Republic,* November 1, 2017.

Hasan, Usama. "Viewpoint: What Do Radical Islamists Actually Believe In?" BBC.com. May 24, 2013. https://www.bbc.com/news/magazine-22640614.

Henley, Jon. "Paris Plot Reveals Link to Terror Chief." *The Guardian,* October 2, 2001.

Hepburn, Jonathan. "Anonymous 'Hactivist' Group Claims 5,500 Islamic State-Affiliated Twitter Accounts Down in #OpParis." ABC.net.au (Australian Broadcasting Corp.) Updated January 24, 2016. https://www.abc.net.au/news/2015-11-18/anonymous-being-opparis-against-islamic-state/6952826.

Hersch, Seymour. "Torture at Abu Ghraib." *The New Yorker*, May 10, 2004.

Hervik, Peter. *The Annoying Difference: The Emergence of Danish Neonationalism, Neoracism, and Populism in the Post-1989 World*. New York: Berghahn Books, 2011.

Hervik, Peter, and Malmö University. *The Danish Muhammad Cartoon Conflict—Current Themes in IMER Research*, no. 13. Malmö, Sweden: Malmö Institute for Studies of Migration, Diversity and Welfare; Malmö University, 2012.

Higgins, Andrew. "French Police Say Suspect in Attack Evolved from Petty Criminal to Terrorist." *New York Times*, January 10, 2015.

Higgins, Andrew, and Kimiko de Freytas-Tamura. "An ISIS Militant from Belgium Whose Own Family Wanted Him Dead." *New York Times*, November 17, 2015.

Higgins, Andrew, and Milan Schreuer. "Attackers in Paris 'Did Not Give Anybody a Chance.'" *New York Times*, November 14, 2015.

Hills, David. "France Players Praised for Staying with Germany Team in Stade de France." *The Guardian*, November 14, 2015.

Hinnant, Lori. "Timeline of Paris Attacks: How a Half-hour of Horror Washes Paris in Blood." *Associated Press*, November 14, 2015. https://www.deseret.com/2015/11/15/20487314/timeline-of-paris-attacks-how-a-half-hour-of-horror-washes-paris-in-blood.

Hinnant, Lori, and Elaine Ganley. "French ID 2nd Church Attacker; Police Had Warning About Him." APNews.com (Associated Press News). July 28, 2016. https://apnews.com/f3dbc2f65ffb43b086f3490164dc5d8b.

Hirsch, Martin, Pierre Carli, Rémy Nizard, Bruno Riou, Barouyr Baroudjian, Thierry Baubet, Vibol Chhor, Charlotte Chollet-Xemard, Nicolas Dantchev, Nadia Fleury, Jean-Paul Fontaine, Youri Yordanov, Maurice Raphael, Catherine Paugam Burtz, and Antoine Lafont. "The Medical Response to Multisite Terrorist Attacks in Paris." *The Lancet* 386 (December 19/26, 2015): 2535–2538. http://dx.doi.org/10.1016/S0140-6736(15)01063-6.

Hlad, Jennifer. "Stopping Terror on the Tracks." *Air Force Magazine* (November 2015), 24–28.

Hollande, François. "Attack Against Charlie Hebdo Statement by Mr. François Hollande, President of the Republic." *Élysée Palace*, January 7, 2015. https://www.diplomatie.gouv.fr/en/the-ministry-and-its-network/events/article/attack-against-charlie-hebdo.

"Hollande Says France Will Form National Guard." PressTV.com. July 28, 2016. https://www.presstv.com/Detail/2016/07/28/477325/France-Hollande-Daesh-terror-attack.

Holpuch, Amanda. "France Train Attack: American-French Citizen Was Shot Trying to Tackle Gunman." *The Guardian*, August 25, 2015.

Holt, Lester (host/interviewer). "'Hell on Earth': Leader of Bataclan Raid Describes What He Saw Inside." NBCNews.com. November 19, 2015. https://www.nbcnews.com/nightly-news/video/hell-on-earth-leader-of-bataclan-raid-describes-what-he-saw-inside-570073667878.

Homeland Security News Wire. "Remote-Controlled Terrorism." HomelandSecurityNewsWire.com. February 7, 2017. http://www.homelandsecuritynewswire.com/dr20170207-remotecontrolledterrorism.

Hopkins, Nick, Angelique Chrisafis, and Sofia Fischer. "Bastille Day Attack: 'Hysterical Crowds Were Running from Death.'" *The Guardian*, July 15, 2016.

Horobin, William, and Matthew Dalton. "Attacker in Nice Conspired for Months." *Wall Street Journal*, July 21, 2016.

Hosenball, Mark. "Suspect Sought in Paris Attack Had Training in Yemen—Sources." Reuters.com. January 8, 2015. https://www.reuters.com/article/france-shooting-yemen/suspect-sought-in-paris-attack-had-trained-in-yemen-sources-idUSL1N0UN1PJ20150108.

Houser, Mark. "French Muslims Battle Internal, External Strife." *Pittsburgh Tribune*, May 29, 2005.

Hubbard, Ben. "ISIS Uses Ramadan as

Calling for New Terrorist Attacks." *New York Times,* July 3, 2016.

Hurt, Emma. "The Freedom to Be Funny: Reflecting on France's Tradition of Satire." *La Jeune Politique,* January 23, 2015.

Husband, Tony, ed. *Cartoons of World War II.* London: Arcturus, 2015.

"Hyper Cacher Victim's Father Knew His Son 'Would Fight.'" *Times of Israel,* January 16, 2015.

"Iranian-American Heads Firm Where Beheading Carried Out in France." *Iran Times,* July 3, 2015.

Jacquard, Nicolas, and Anthony Lieures. "C'Était une Bombe à Retardement." *Le Parisien,* July 27, 2016.

Jarry, Emmanuel/Reuters. "Des Victimes du 13/11 Portent Plainte pour Non-Assistance." *Challenges* (French language). June 8, 2018. https://www.challenges.fr/top-news/des-victimes-du-13-11-portent-plainte-pour-non-assistance_592740.

"'Je Ne Suis Pas Charlie, Je Suis Content …'": Le Message d'un Complice de Lahouaiej Bouhlel." LCI.fr. July 21, 2016. https://www.lci.fr/france/je-ne-suis-pas-charlie-je-suis-content-le-message-dun-complice-de-lahouaiej-bouhlel-1266910.html.

"Jihadism in French Prisons: Caged Fervour." *The Economist,* September 17, 2016.

Jiminez, Fred. "Radicalisation: Les Précédents Cas en Franche-Comté." *L'Est Republican,* December 13, 2018.

Jolly, David. "Satirical Magazine Is Firebombed in Paris." *New York Times,* November 2, 2011.

Jones, Jonathan. "Daumier's Satirical Art Hits with the Force of a Drone Attack." *The Guardian,* October 29, 2013.

Kaye, Randi. "Anderson Cooper 360 Degrees: Two of the Suspects in the Shootings in 'Charlie Hebdo' Office in Paris Identified." CNN.com. Aired January 8, 2015. http://transcripts.cnn.com/TRANSCRIPTS/1501/08/acd.02.html.

Keller, Greg. "Moogalian Recounts Train Attack in French Magazine Interview." APNews.com (Associated Press News). August 26, 2015. https://apnews.com/e79bb15573d7462b928229513b209ca6

Kern, Soeren. "100 Lashes If You Don't Die Laughing." *Gatestone Institute National Policy Council,* November 3, 2011. https://www.gatestoneinstitute.org/2560/islam-free-speech-lashes.

Koziol, Michael. "Charlie Hebdo Survivor Simon Fieschi Marries Australian Girlfriend Maisie Dubosarsky in Paris." *The Sydney Morning Herald,* October 3, 2015.

Kreps, Daniel. "Eagles of Death Metal Merch Manager Nick Alexander Killed in Paris Attack." *Rolling Stone,* November 14, 2015.

"Kurt Westergaard, Free Speech, and Leftist Refuseniks." *The National Post,* October 5, 2009.

Kutner, Max. "Meet Farid Benyettou, the Man Who Trained Paris Attack Suspect Cherif Kouachi." *Newsweek,* January 8, 2015.

Labbé, Chine, Marie-Louise Gumuchian, and Matthias Blamont. "Insight—Bus Driver Who Turned Paris Attacker Skipped Police Watch." Reuters.com. November 20, 2015. https://www.reuters.com/article/uk-france-shooting-amimour-insight/insight-bus-driver-who-turned-paris-attacker-skipped-police-watch-idUKKCN0T91KC20151120

Lagrange, Catherine, and Michel Rose. "Delivery Man Beheads Boss in Suspected Islamist Attack on French Gas Site." Reuters.com. June 26, 2015. https://www.reuters.com/article/us-france-blast/delivery-man-beheads-boss-in-suspected-islamist-attack-on-french-gas-site-idUSKBN0P60XR20150626.

Lambert, Jérôme, and Philippe Picard. "Charlie Hebdo, before the Massacre." *New York Times,* January 9, 2015.

Landauro, Inti. "French Priest Killer Adel Kermiche Was Under Police Monitoring." *Wall Street Journal,* July 26, 2016.

Landauro, Inti, and William Horobin. "For Parishioners in French Town, Slain Priest Was Model of Dedication." *Wall Street Journal,* July 26, 2016.

"Leader of U.S. Embassy Bomb Plot Gets 10 Years." *New York Times,* March 15, 2005.

Leconte, Daniel, and Emmanuel Leconte, dirs. *Je Suis Charlie.* Paris: Films en Stock, 2015.

Lenoir, Francois. "Belgium Transfers to France Man Linked to Foiled Train Attack." RFI.fr (Radio France Internationale). Modified February 2, 2018. http://www.rfi.fr/en/france/20180202-belgium-transfers-france-man-linked-foiled-train-attack.

Leveque, Thierry. "French Court Clears Weekly in Mohammad Cartoon Row."

Reuters.com. March 22, 2007. https://www.reuters.com/article/industry-france-cartoons-trial-dc/french-court-clears-weekly-in-mohammad-cartoon-row-idUSL2212067120070322.

Lister, Charles. "Jihad in Ramadan: Terror Attacks in Kuwait, Tunisia, and France as ISIS Launches a New Syrian Offensive." Brookings.edu (The Brookings Institution). June 26, 2015. https://www.brookings.edu/blog/markaz/2015/06/26/jihad-in-ramadan-terror-attacks-in-kuwait-tunisia-and-france-as-isis-launches-a-new-syrian-offensive/.

Litchfield, John. "Paris Attacks: Why the Charlie Hebdo Gunmen Saïd and Chérif Kouachi Made an Unlikely Terror Cell." *The Independent*, January 18, 2015.

The Local/Agence France-Presse. "Mother of French Priest Killer Left Stunned and in Denial." TheLocal.fr. July 28, 2016. https://www.thelocal.fr/20160728/french-priest-murderer-he-was-a-gentle-child.

Lomas, Claire. "Paris Survivor of Suicide Bomb Was 'Saved by Phone.'" *The Telegraph*, November 14, 2015.

Lynch, Suzanne. "Belgium Police Kill Two That Authorities Claim Were on Verge of Terrorist Attack." *Irish Times*, January 16, 2015.

Ma, Alexandra, and Rowaida Abdelaziz. "Mourning the Arab Victims of the Paris Attacks." *Huffington Post*, November 18, 2015.

Macfarlane, Ursula, dir. *Charlie Hebdo: 3 Days That Shook Paris*. London: Films of Record, 2015.

Mack, Emmy. "Aussie Victim of Paris Attacks Recounts Harrowing Scenes Inside the Bataclan Theatre." MusicFeeds.com.au. November 23, 2015. https://musicfeeds.com.au/news/aussie-victim-paris-attacks-recounts-harrowing-scenes-inside-bataclan-theatre/

MacKinnon, Mark. "Neighbour Says Suspects in Paris Shooting Had 'Cache of Arms.'" *The Globe and Mail*, March 25, 2017.

Marcus, Mary Brophy. "Injuries from Paris Attacks Will Take Long to Heal." CBSNews.com. November 19, 2015. https://www.cbsnews.com/news/injuries-from-paris-attacks-will-take-long-to-heal/.

Marteau, Stéphanie. "Le Père d'Un des Kamikazes Avait Tenté, en Vain, de le Ramener de Syrie." *Le Monde*, November 16, 2015.

Masanauskas, John. "Paris Attacks: Diners Killed in Le Carillon and Le Petit Cambodge Restaurants." *Herald Sun*, November 14, 2015.

Mattingly, Terry. "The Symbolic Death of Father Jacques Hamel." UExpress.com. August 3, 2016. https://www.uexpress.com/on-religion/2016/8/3/the-symbolic-death-of-father-jacques.

McAuley, James, and Brian Murphy. "Islamic State Says Militant 'Soldiers' Carried Out Normandy Church Attack." *Washington Post*, July 26, 2016.

McGraw, Peter, and Joel Warner. "The Danish Cartoon Crisis of 2005 and 2006: 10 Things You Didn't Know about the Original Muhammad Controversy." *Huffington Post*, September 5, 2012.

McKernan, Bethan. "France's Most Wanted ISIS Fighter Killed in Iraq Leaves Final Message Accusing His Leaders of Hypocrisy." *The Independent*, February 16, 2017.

MedTrust Emergency Response. "Emergency Responders in Paris Train for Terrorist Attacks Just Days before Actual Event." MedTrust.com. December 15, 2015. http://ridemedtrust.com/emergency-responders-in-paris-train-for-terrorist-attack-just-days-before-actual-event/.

Meichtry, Stacy, and Sam Schechner. "How Islamic State Weaponized the Chat App to Direct Attacks on the West." *Wall Street Journal*, October 20, 2016.

Meichtry, Stacy, Joshua Robinson, and Mike Bird. "How a Tunisian Immigrant Staged the Simple, Deadly Attack in Nice." *Wall Street Journal*, July 15, 2016.

Melvin, Don. "Train Gunman Had Terrorist Intent, French Prosecutor Says." CNN.com. Updated January 8, 2018. https://www.cnn.com/2015/08/25/europe/france-train-attack/index.html.

Mendick, Robert, Nicola Harley, and Harriet Alexander. "Amid the Terror, a Hero Who Lost His Life by Fighting Back." *The Telegraph*, January 10, 2015.

"Mental Disorders Affect One in Four People." WHO.int (World Health Organization). 2001. https://www.who.int/whr/2001/media_centre/press_release/en/.

Messman, Lauren. "Banksy Mural Is Stolen

from Bataclan, Site of Paris Attacks." *New York Times,* January 27, 2019.

Mickolus, Edward. *Terrorism Worldwide, 2016.* Jefferson, NC: McFarland, 2018.

Mikelbank, Peter. "France Attack: Eyewitness Says 'There Was a Trail of Bodies.'" *People Magazine,* July 15, 2016.

Minder, Raphael. "Scrutiny Falls on a Spanish Mosque After Foiled Train Attack." *New York Times,* August 27, 2015.

Molinié, William. "Attentat de Nice: Un Proche du Terroriste Remis en Liberté." LCI.fr. October 25, 2018. https://www.lci.fr/justice/info-lci-attentat-de-nice-un-proche-du-terroriste-mohamed-lahouaiej-bouhlel-remis-en-liberte-2102562.html.

Moodley, Kiran. "Charlie Hebdo Survivor: 'I Turned Around and My World Tumbled.'" *The Independent,* January 14, 2015.

Moore, Daniel, and Thomas Rid. "Cryptopolitik and the Darknet." *Survival: Global Politics and Strategy* 58, issue 1 (2016): 7–38.

Moore, Jack. "Abel Malik Petitjean: What We Know About Second ISIS-Inspired Priest Attacker." *Newsweek,* July 28, 2016.

Moore, Jack. "Nice Attacker Mohamed Lahouaiej-Bouhlel Spoke Often of His Troubled Childhood, Friend Reveals." *Newsweek,* August 7, 2016.

Morajea, Hassan, and Sam Schechner. "From Celebration to Horror in Nice." *Wall Street Journal,* July 14, 2016.

"La Mosquée de Saint-Etienne-du-Rouvray Refuse d'Inhumer Adel Kermiche." *Le Parisien,* July 29, 2016.

Motreff, Y., P. Pirard, T. Baubet, A. Ravaud, P. Chauvin, and S. Vandentorren. "Mental Health Impact Among First Responders Following the November 2015 Paris Terror Attacks: Philippe Pirard." *European Journal of Public Health* 27, issue suppl. 3 (November 2017): 490. https://doi.org/10.1093/eurpub/ckx186.254.

Mouillard, Sylvain, Willy Le Devin, Ismaël Halissat, and Julie Brafman. "Les Profils Troubles des Proches du Tueur de Nice." *Libération,* October 2, 2016.

Mueller, John. "The Cybercoaching of Terrorists: Cause for Alarm?" *CTC Sentinel* (October 2017): 29–35.

"Muhammad Depictions: French Satirical Paper Reportedly Attacked." *Der Spiegel,* November 2, 2011.

Mullins, Sam. "Lone-Actor vs. Remote-Controlled Jihadi Terrorism: Rethinking the Threat to the West." WarOnTheRocks.com. April 20, 2017. https://warontherocks.com/2017/04/lone-actor-vs-remote-controlled-jihadi-terrorism-rethinking-the-threat-to-the-west/.

Mundasad, Smitha. "Paris Attacks: Doctor Describes Moment First Casualties Arrived." BBC.com. November 19, 2015. https://www.bbc.com/news/health-34845730.

Murdock, Jason. "French Police Investigating ISIS Murder of Catholic Priest Probe Telegram App." *International Business Times,* July 31, 2016.

National Broadcasting Network. "Paris Killer Cherif Kouachi Gave Interview to TV Channel Before He Died." NBCNews.com. Updated January 9, 2015. https://www.nbcnews.com/storyline/paris-magazine-attack/paris-killer-cherif-kouachi-gave-interview-tv-channel-he-died-n283206.

Naudet, Jules, and Gédéon Naudet, dirs. *November 13: Attack on Paris* (13 *Novembre: Fluctuat Nec Mergitur*), Episode 1. Netflix/Propagate/No School Productions. Los Gatos, California, 2018. https://www.netflix.com/title/80190097.

Naudet, Jules, and Gédéon Naudet, dirs. *November 13: Attack on Paris* (13 *Novembre: Fluctuat Nec Mergitur*), Episode 2. Netflix/Propagate/No School Productions. Los Gatos, California, 2018. https://www.netflix.com/title/80190097.

Navasky, Victor S. *The Art of Controversy.* New York: Alfred A. Knopf, 2013.

News Wires. "Americans Who Thwarted Train Terror Attack Become French Citizens." France24.com. January 2, 2019. https://www.france24.com/en/20190201-americans-who-thwarted-thalys-train-terror-attack-become-french-citizens.

News Wires. "Brother of Paris Attacker Abaaoud Jailed in Morocco." France24.com. May 7, 2016. https://www.france24.com/en/20160507-brother-paris-attacker-abaaoud-jailed-morocco.

Newton-Small, Jay. "Paris Attacker Is an Example of France's Homegrown Terrorists." *TIME Magazine,* November 16, 2015.

Nossiter, Adam. "Boko Haram's Civilian

Attacks in Nigeria Intensify." *New York Times,* July 6, 2015.

Nossiter, Adam. "French Train Attack Suspect Viewed Jihadist Video, Official Says." *New York Times,* August 25, 2015.

Nossiter, Adam. "In Paris Knife Attack, Police Ask How They Missed a Killer in Their Midst." *New York Times,* October 5, 2019.

Nossiter, Adam, Alissa J. Rubin, and Benoit Morenne. "ISIS Says Its 'Soldiers' Attacked Church in France, Killing Priest." *New York Times,* July 26, 2016.

Nossiter, Adam, Alissa J. Rubin, and Lilia Blaise. "Years Before Truck Rampage in Nice, Attacker Wasn't 'Living in the Real World.'" *New York Times,* July 24, 2016.

Nossiter, Adam, and Hannah Olivennes. "Jacques Hamel, 85, a Beloved French Priest, Killed in His Church." *New York Times,* July 26, 2016.

Nossiter, Adam, Aurelien Breeden, and Elian Peltier. "Knife Attack at Paris Police Headquarters Leaves 4 Dead." *New York Times,* October 3, 2019.

L'Obs with Agence France-Presse. "L'Attaque du Thalys Reconstituée Alors Que L'enquête Touche à Sa Fin." *L'Obs* (magazine), September 18, 2019. https://www.nouvelobs.com/topnews/20190918.AFP4917/l-attaque-du-thalys-reconstituee-alors-que-l-enquete-touche-a-sa-fin.html.

Olive, Flore, with Karim Baouz. "Chérif et Saïd Kouachi: Le Voyage sans Issue de Deux Paumés." *Paris Match,* January 11, 2015.

"'On Est Pari, On Commence,' le Denier SMS d'un des Kamikazes du Bataclan." *Le Point* (magazine), November 19, 2015.

Orton, Kyle. "The Islamic State Guided the Normandy Church Attack." KyleOrton.com ("Kyle Orton's Blog"). August 22, 2016. https://kyleorton1991.wordpress.com/2016/08/22/the-islamic-state-guided-the-normandy-church-attack/#_ftn37.

Paletta, Damian. "Truck Attack in Nice Shows Limits of Global Hunt for Terrorism." *Wall Street Journal,* July 14, 2016.

Panfili, Robin. "'At the First Explosion, We Didn't Suspect Anything': An Eyewitness Account from the Stade de France." *Slate,* November 14, 2015.

"Paris Attacks: Eagles of Death Metal Reveal How They Escaped from Bataclan Theatre." ABC.net.au (Australian Broadcasting Corp.). November 25, 2015. https://www.abc.net.au/news/2015-11-26/eagles-of-death-metal-vice-interview/6975940

"Paris Shooting: Armed Man Takes Hostages in Paris Kosher Store." *Sydney Morning Herald,* January 10, 2015.

Le Parisien with Agence France-Presse. "Attentat Déjoué du Thalys: Les 3 Héros Américains Ont Reçu la Nationalité Française." *Le Parisien,* February 1, 2019.

Pascual, Julia. "Au Carillon, 'On N'avait Rien pour Aider, Rien Que Nos Mains.'" *Le Monde,* November 18, 2015.

Penketh, Anne. "Paris Attacks: The Muslim Victims of Terrorist Bullets." *The Guardian,* November 18, 2015.

Penketh, Anne, and Julian Borger. "Fight Intimidation with Controversy: Charlie Hebdo's Response to Critics." *The Guardian,* January 7, 2015.

Perks, Bea, and Lionel Milgrom. "UK Government Clamp Down on Online Bomb-Making Instructions." *Chemistry World,* July 20, 2005.

Peter, Laurence. "Paris Attacks: Key Questions after Abaaoud Killed." BBC.com. November 24, 2015. https://www.bbc.com/news/world-europe-34866144.

Peyrard, Michel. "Rachid Kassim: Enquête sur le Donneur D'Ordre de Daech." *Paris Match,* September 23, 2016.

Pham-Lê, Jérémie, Claire Hache, and Boris Thiolay. "Le Petit Frère d'Abaaoud, Younès, Donné Pour Mort en Zone Irako-Syrienne." *L'Express,* January 24, 2018.

Pham-Lê, Jérémie, Victor Garcia, and Claire Hache. "Rachid Kassim, le Djihadiste Qui a Inspiré les Assassins du Père Hamel." *L'Express* (France), August 18, 2016.

Piel, Simon. "Au Bataclan, Deux Heures d'Intervention Policière sans Négociation." *Le Monde,* November 16, 2015.

Pietrasanta, Sébastien. *Commission d'Enquête Relative aux Moyens Mis en Œuvre par l'État pour Lutter Contre le Terrorisme Depuis le 7 Janvier 2015.* Paris, France: Assemblée Nationale, July 5, 2016. http://www2.assemblee-nationale.fr/14/autres-commissions/commissions-d-enquete/moyens-pour-lutter-contre-le-terrorisme/(block)/28447.

Pleasance, Chris. "'They Were Too Weak to Resist Jihad,' Says Former Boarding School Teacher: How Kouachi Brothers Went from Football-Loving Teenager with No Interest in Religion to Extremist Killers." *Daily Mail*, January 12, 2015.

Pom, Cindy. "France Faces the Daunting Task of Curbing Prison Radicalization to Prevent 'ISIS 2.0.'" *Pittsburgh Post-Gazette*, January 10, 2019.

Ponniah, Kevin. "Le Carillon: Paris Bar Regulars Left Reeling After Attack." BBC.com. November 14, 2015. https://www.bbc.com/news/world-europe-34822605.

Pope Francis. "Holy Mass in Suffrage of Father Jacques Hamel." *Libreria Editrice Vaticana* (Vatican Publishing House), September 14, 2016. https://w2.vatican.va/content/francesco/en/cotidie/2016/documents/papa-francesco-cotidie_20160914_p-jacques-hamel.html.

Project Gutenberg. *Les Cent Nouvelles Nouvelles*. n.d. Gutenberg.org. Accessed 12/7/18. http://www.gutenberg.org/files/18575/18575-h/18575-h.htm.

"Prophet Mohammed Cartoons Controversy: Timeline." *The Telegraph*, May 4, 2015.

Purtill, James. "Paris Attacks: Australian Man Recounts Desperate Bataclan Theatre Escape with 12yo Son." ABC.net.au (Australian Broadcasting Corp.). Updated November 15, 2015. https://www.abc.net.au/news/2015-11-16/australian-man-recounts-surviving-bataclan-attack-with-12yo-son/6942976.

Ramadan, Tariq. "Search Narrows for Charlie Hebdo Suspects." Aljazeera.com (Al Jazeera English). January 8, 2015. https://www.aljazeera.com/news/europe/2015/01/police-locate-suspects-behind-paris-attack-20151810934910330.html.

Rayner, Gordon. "Paris Shooting at Charlie Hebdo Office: How Terrorist Attack Unfolded." *The Telegraph*, January 7, 2015.

Razil, Julia. "'J'Étais Otage, J'ai Crié aux Flics de ne pas Rentrer.'" *La Provence* (Marseille), November 16, 2105.

Reed, Dan, dir. *Three Days of Terror: The Charlie Hebdo Attacks*. Paris/London: Premières Lignes Télévision and AMOS Pictures, with the participation of Home Box Office (ë), British Broadcasting Corp. (BBC), and France Télévisions, 2016.

Reevell, James, Bernadette McCague, Ayeshea Perera, Penny Spiller, Alex Kleiderman, and Roland Hughes. "France Attack 26 June 2015: As It Happened." BBC.com. June 26, 2015. https://www.bbc.com/news/live/world-europe-33287095.

Reilly, Jonathan. "New Ring of Steel: France Unveils New £16.5 Million Anti-Terror Barriers in Nice at the Scene of Truck Attack—Could London Be Next?" *The Sun*, June 11, 2017.

Renterghem, Marion Van. "Les Freres Kouachi: Une Jeunesse Française." *Le Monde*, February 13, 2015.

Reuter, Christoph. "Secret Files Reveal the Structure of Islamic State." *Der Spiegel*, April 18, 2015.

Rice, Mae. "The Deep Web Is the 99% of the Internet You Can't Google." Curiosity.com. May 22, 2018. https://curiosity.com/topics/the-deep-web-is-the-99-of-the-internet-you-cant-google-curiosity/.

Rigas, Aimie. "Eyewitness Franck Benarroch Reveals Frenzied Aftermath of Paris Explosions, Shootings." *Huffington Post Australia*, November 14, 2015.

Robb, Alice. "There Is No 'Charlie Hebdo' in America." *New Republic*, January 8, 2015.

Roberts, Hannah. "The Pot-Smoking Paris Suicide Bomber: Ex-Wife Reveals 'Blood Brother' Terrorist Was a Jobless Layabout Who Spent His Time Taking Drugs and Sleeping. .. and Never Went to the Mosque." *Daily Mail*, November 17, 2015.

Robinson, Joshua, and Inti Landauro. "Attacker Tried to Enter Paris Stadium but Was Turned Away." *Wall Street Journal*, November 15, 2015.

Rodionova, Zlata. "Paris Attacks Anniversary: 'Open The Door, I Am Here to Rescue You,' Isis Gunman Told Bataclan Survivor." *The Independent*, November 12, 2016.

Rose, Flemming. "Why I Published Those Cartoons." *Washington Post*, February 19, 2006.

Rose, Michel. "French Church Attacker: From Troubled Childhood to Altar Killer." Reuters.com. July 29, 2016. https://www.reuters.com/article/us-europe-attacks-france-killer/french-church-attacker-from-troubled-childhood-to-altar-killer-idUSKCN1091U5.

Rubin, Alissa J. "'It Had to Be Stopped': Heroes Rise amid France Terror Attacks." *Wall Street Journal*, August 22, 2016.

Rubin, Alissa J. "Paris: One Year On." *New York Times*, November 12, 2015.
Rubin, Alissa J. "Suspect in Attack in France Had Ties to Radical Islamist." *New York Times*, June 27, 2015.
Rubin, Alissa J., and Adam Nossiter. "French Ask Whether Priest's Killer, Listed as a Threat, Could Have Been Stopped." *New York Times*, July 27, 2016.
Rubin, Alissa J., and Anne Barnard. "France Strikes ISIS Targets in Syria in Retaliation for Attacks." *New York Times*, November 16, 2015.
Rubin, Alissa J., and Breeden Aurelie. "France Remembers the Nice Attack: 'We Will Never Find the Words.'" *New York Times*, July 14, 2017.
Rubin, Alissa J., and Lilia Blaise. "A Third of Nice Truck Attack's Dead Were Muslim, Group Says." *New York Times*, July 19, 2016.
Ryan, Yasmine. "Uncovering Algeria's Civil War." Aljazeera.com (Al Jazeera English). November 18, 2010. https://www.aljazeera.com/indepth/2010/11/2010118122224407570.html.
Sadler, Anthony, Alek Skarlatos, Spencer Stone, and Jeffrey E. Stern. *The 15:17 to Paris: The True Story of a Terrorist, a Train, and Three American Heroes*. New York: Public Affairs Perseus Books, 2016.
Sage, Alexandria, and Chine Labbé. "French Attacks Inquiry Centers on Prison 'Sorcerer' Beghal." Reuters.com. January 15, 2015. https://www.reuters.com/article/us-france-shooting-beghal-insight/french-attacks-inquiry-centers-on-prison-sorcerer-beghal-idUSKBN0KO28G20150115.
Saliba, Emmanuelle, Nancy Ing, and Elisha Fieldstadt. "Multiple Paris Terror Attacks Leave at Least 120 Dead." NBCNews.com. November 14, 2015. https://www.nbcnews.com/storyline/paris-terror-attacks/french-police-report-paris-shootout-explosion-n463186.
Samuel, Henry. "French Intelligence 'Doctored Files' to Cover Up Failings Over Islamist Murder of Priest." *The Telegraph*, January 5, 2018.
Samuel, Henry. "Paris Attack: Office Recounts Killing Bataclan Terrorist Then Calling Wife to Say 'Goodbye.'" *The Telegraph*, December 15, 2015.
Samuel, Henry. "Paris Attacks Ringleader Visited Britain 'To Plan UK Attacks,'

Believes Top French Judge." *The Telegraph*, January 11, 2016.
Sawer, Patrick, and Lexi Finnigan. "Paris Attacks: Gunmen May Still Be on the Loose as Kalashnikovs and Empty Magazines Found in Abandoned Car in City Suburb." *The Telegraph*, November 15, 2015.
Sayare, Scott. "The Ultimate Terrorist Factory." *Harper's Magazine*, January 2016.
Sayare, Scott. "The Untold Story of the Bastille Day Attacker." *Gentleman's Quarterly (GQ)*, January 24, 2017.
Schaffner, Claire. "Foued Mohamed-Aggad, un Enfant de Wissembourg 'Sans Historie.'" France3.com (public television channel, France). December 10, 2015. https://france3-regions.francetvinfo.fr/grand-est/bas-rhin/foued-mohamed-aggad-un-enfant-de-wissembourg-sans-histoire-879235.html.
Schmitt, Eric. "Paris Attacks and Other Assaults Seen as Evidence of a Shift by ISIS." *New York Times*, November 22, 2015.
Schram, Jamie, and Yaron Steinbuch. "France Was Warned about Terrorist Who Killed Priest in Church Attack." *New York Post*, July 28, 2016.
Schuurman, Bart, Edwin Bakker, Paul Gill, and Noémi Bouhana. "Lone Actor Terrorist Attack Planning and Preparation: A Data-Driven Analysis." *Journal of Forensic Sciences* 63, no. 4 (2017): 1191–1200.
Schuurman, Bart, Lasse Lindekilde, Stefan Malthaner, Francis O'Connor, Paul Gill and Noémie Bouhana. "End of the Lone Wolf: The Typology That Should Not Have Been." *Studies in Conflict & Terrorism* 42, no. 8 (2019): 771–778.
"Searching for Answers in the 'Charlie Hebdo' Attacks: Charlie Hebdo Attackers Radicalized in Search for Identity." *Der Spiegel*, January 19, 2015.
Seelow, Soren. "Abdelhamid Abaaoud, L'Instigateur Présumé des Attentats Tué à Saint-Denis." *Le Monde*, November 16, 2015.
Seelow, Soren. "Attaque dans l'Isère: Les Motivations Troubles de Yassin Salhi." *Le Monde*, June 28, 2019.
Shane, Scott. "In New Era of Terrorism, Voices from Yemen Echoes." *New York Times*, January 10, 2015.
Shane-Simpson, Christina, Patricia Brooks,

Rita Obeid, Rita, Ellen-ge Denton, and Kristen Gillespie-Lynch. "Associations Between Compulsive Internet Use and the Autism Spectrum." *Research in Autism Spectrum Disorders* 23 (2016): 152–165.

Sharkov, Damien. "French Beheading Suspect Hangs Himself in Prison." *Newsweek*, December 23, 2015.

Sharma, Swati. "'It Is Horror': French President Hollande's Remarks After Paris Attacks." *Washington Post*, November 13, 2015.

Shavin, Naomi. "Photographer Cristian Movilă's Eyewitness Photos of the Attack on Paris and Its Aftermath." *Smithsonian Magazine*, November 19, 2015.

Sheikh, Mona Konwal, and Manni Crone. "Muslims as a Danish Security Issue." In *Islam in Denmark: The Challenge of Diversity*, edited by Jørgen S. Neilson. Lanham, Maryland: Lexington Books, 2011.

Shevardnadze, Sophie (host/interviewer). "Terrorist Leader Said, 'Don't Be Afraid, You'll Die in a Few Minutes'—Paris Attack Survivor." RT.com (*Sophia & Co.* [television news series, English] on *RT* [television network, Russia]). Aired November 20, 2015. https://www.rt.com/shows/sophieco/322796-france-terrorist-attacks-isis/.

Shoichet, Catherine E., and Josh Levs. "Al Qaeda Branch Claims Charlie Hebdo Attack Was Years in the Making." CNN.com. January 21, 2015. https://www.cnn.com/2015/01/14/europe/charlie-hebdo-france-attacks/index.html.

Simon, Bob (Correspondent). "Rewind: Danish Newspaper Satirizes Islam." CBS News—60 Minutes Overtime. CBSNews.com. January 1, 2015. (Transcript of earlier television program, titled "State of Denmark; air date February 19, 2006). https://www.cbsnews.com/news/danish-newspaper-satirizes-islam/.

Simons, Jake Wallis, Jenny Stanton, Julian Robinson, and Stephanie Linning. "'I Saw a Hole in Her Face, and Realised She'd Been Shot': Gunman Dressed in Black Picked Off Terrified Diners Firing 'Professional Bursts' of Shots in Cafe Shooting Rampage." *Daily Mail*, November 14, 2015.

Sjølie, Marie Louise. "The Danish Cartoonist Who Survived an Axe Attack." *The Guardian*, January 4, 2010.

Smith, Amelia. "Stephane Charbonnier Was on Al-Qaeda 'Hit List' Circulated on Social Media." *Newsweek*, January 8, 2015.

Smith, Craig W. "French Court Rules for Newspaper That Printed Muhammad Cartoons." *New York Times*, March 23, 2007.

Solny, Shiryn. "Footage Shows Hyper Cacher Terrorist Kill Shopper After Victim Revealed He Was Jewish." *The Algemeiner*, February 26, 2015.

Sørensen, Kaare. *The Mind of a Terrorist: David Headly, the Mumbai Massacre, and His European Revenge*. New York: Arcade Publishing, 2016.

Speckhard, Anne, and Ahmet S. Yayla. "The ISIS Emni: Origins and Inner Workings of ISIS's Intelligence Apparatus." *Perspectives on Terrorism* 11, issue 1 (February 2017): 2–16.

Staufenberg, Jess. "Video Shows Nurse Giving Suicide Bomber CPR at Paris Café After Failed Attack." *The Independent*, November 21, 2015.

Stephen, Chris, Esther Addley, and Julian Borger. "Dozens Killed After Terror Attacks in Tunisia, Kuwait and France." *The Guardian*, June 26, 2015.

Suc, Matthieu. "Attaque dans Le Thalys: 'J'ai Levé la Tête et J'ai Vu un Gars Avec un AK-47.'" *Le Monde*, August 24, 2015.

Sud Ouest Staff with AFP. "Attentats de Paris: Inhumé Pour Noël, Amimour, l'Introverti Devenu Assassin au Bataclan." *Sud Ouest*, December 27, 2015.

Summerson, Isabel (producer), Phillip Adams (interviewer), Christoph Reuter (guest), and Martin Chulov (guest). "How Religious Is the Islamic State?" (transcript). ABC.net.au (Australian Broadcasting Corp.—Radio National). May 7, 2015. https://www.abc.net.au/radionational/programs/latenightlive/haji-bakr-and-the-islamic-state/6453494.

"Suspect Arrested in Connection with Attack on French Factory Described As 'Wolf in Sheep's Clothing.'" Newstalk.com (independent radio station, Ireland). June 27, 2015. https://www.newstalk.com/news/suspect-arrested-in-connection-with-attack-on-french-factory-described-as-wolf-in-sheeps-clothing-651340.

Taibi, Catherine. "These Are the Charlie

Hebdo Cartoons That Terrorists Thought Were Worth Killing Over." *Huffington Post*, December 6, 2017.

Taix, Caroline, and Adam Plowright. "Paris Defendant: 'No One Told Me' Terrorists Rented My Flat." *Times of Israel*, January 26, 2018.

Tapper, Jake. "The Lead with Jake Tapper: Mapping the Paris Terror Attack." YouTube.com (CNN Channel). January 7, 2015. https://www.youtube.com/watch?v=9BHQSSUyeOE.

Taylor, Adam. "Why Would Terrorists Kill Cartoonists?" *Washington Post*, January 7, 2015.

Taylor, Peter, John O'Kane, and Ceri Isfryn. "IS in Europe: The Race to the Death." BBC.com. March 23, 2016. https://www.bbc.com/news/magazine-35872562.

Temple-Raston, Dina. "French Prisons Prove to Be Effective Incubators for Islamic Extremism." NPR.org (National Public Radio). January 22, 2015. https://www.npr.org/sections/parallels/2015/01/22/379081047/french-prisons-prove-to-be-effective-incubators-for-islamic-extremism.

Teng, Elaine. "The Last Time 'Charlie Hebdo' Was Attacked by Terrorists, Its Response Was Perfect." *New Republic*, January 7, 2015.

"Terror from the Fringes: Searching for Answers in the "Charlie Hebdo" Attacks—Part 5: The Bewilderment of the Terrorists' Friends." *Der Spiegel*, January 19, 2015.

"Three Hours of Terror in Paris, Moment by Moment." *New York Times*, November 9, 2016.

Times of Israel Staff, Associated Press, and Jewish Telegraphic Agency. "Jewish Paris Cafe Owner Loses Wife, Friends in Terror Attack." *The Times of Israel*, November 17, 2015.

Tomic, Miranda. "Case Study: Perimeter Security at Stade-de-France." MSA Security.net. August 31, 2017. http://www.msasecurity.net/security-and-counterterrorism-blog/case-study-perimeter-security-at-stade-de-france.

"Truck Attack in Nice, France: What We Know, and What We Don't." *New York Times*, July 15, 2016.

Tual, Raphaël. "Attentat de Saint-Étienne-du-Rouvray. Les Messages Glaçants Échangés par les Tueurs." Actu.fr (Normandy edition). November 9, 2016. https://actu.fr/normandie/saint-etienne-du-rouvray_76575/attentat-de-saint-etienne-du-rouvray-les-messages-glacants-echanges-par-les-tueurs_809003.html.

Turner, Camilla, and Matthew Holehouse. "Paris Attacks Suicide Bomber 'Drank, Smoked and Ran Drugs Den.'" *The Telegraph*, November 16, 2015.

Van Vlierden, Guy. "The Enduring Influence of Malika El Aroud, Belgium's 'Black Widow of Jihad.'" EERadicalization.com (European Eye on Radicalization). October 18, 2018. https://eeradicalization.com/the-enduring-influence-of-malika-el-aroud-belgiums-black-widow-of-jihad/.

Van Vlierden, Guy. "Profile: Paris Attack Ringleader Abdelhamid Abaaoud." *CTC Sentinel* 8, issue 11 (November/December 2015): 30–33.

Verbergt, Matthias, and Stacy Meichtry. "Suspect in France Attack Apparently Acted on Call from Islamic State, Prosecutors Say." *Wall Street Journal*, June 30, 2015.

"Victims of the Terror Attacks in Paris." *New York Times*, January 11, 2015. https://www.nytimes.com/2015/01/12/world/europe/terror-attacks-in-paris-the-victims.html.

Vincent, Elise. "Ce Que les Services Belges Savaient d'Abdelhamid Abaaoud." *Le Monde*, November 20, 2015.

Vincent, Elise. "Saint-Etienne-Du-Rouvray, Histoire d'une Haine Fulgurante." *Le Monde*, November 8, 2015.

Vinocur, Nicholas. "Cartoons in French Weekly Fuel Mohammad Furor." Reuters.com. September 19, 2012. https://www.reuters.com/article/us-protests-france/cartoons-in-french-weekly-fuel-mohammad-furor-idUSBRE88I0BU20120919.

Vinograd, Cassandra, and Nancy Ing. "Paris Attacks: Commando Captain Shares Details of Bataclan, Saint-Denis Raids." NBCNews.com. Updated November 20, 2015. https://www.nbcnews.com/storyline/paris-terror-attacks/paris-attacks-commando-captain-shares-details-france-raids-n466461.

Viscusi, Gregory. "French Muslims File Suit Over Alleged Racism." *Bloomberg News* (Reprinted in *New York Sun*, February 7, 2007). https://www.nysun.com/

foreign/french-muslims-file-suit-over-alleged-racism/48136/.
Walker, Jamie. "ISIS Claims Spreading Attacks." *The Australian,* June 28, 2015.
Walt, Vivien. "Was the Nice Attacker Really a Jihadist?" *TIME Magazine,* July 16, 2016.
Walt, Vivienne. "Mentor of Charlie Hebdo Gunman Says He Was Obsessed with Violence." *TIME Magazine,* January 13, 2015.
Walt, Vivienne. "Paris March in Solidarity against Terror Attacks Was Largest in French History." *TIME Magazine,* January 11, 2015.
Warnes, Indra. "Twenty Bataclan Victims Still in Hospital as Survivors Vow 'Isis Will Not Kill Us Again.'" *Daily Express,* November 12, 2016.
Watt, Nicholas. "Danish Paper Sorry for Muhammad Cartoons," *The Guardian,* January 31, 2006.
Weimann, Gabriel. "Terrorist Migration to the Dark Web." *Perspectives on Terrorism* 10, no. 3 (June 2016): 40–44.
Weinman, Edward. "Inside ISIS." *Connecticut College Magazine,* Fall 2016.
Weise, Elizabeth. "Terrorists Use the Dark Web to Hide." *USA Today,* March 27, 2017.
Welford, Heather. "Nice Attack One Year On: 'How Can Anyone Bear to Visit the Beach?'" *New Statesman America,* July 14, 2017.
White, Christopher. "The Martyrdom of Jacques Hamel." *Wall Street Journal,* July 20, 2017.
Whitmore, Janet. "Absurdist Humor in Bohemia." In *Montmartre and the Making of Mass Culture,* edited by Gabriel P. Weisberg, 205–222. New Brunswick, New Jersey: Rutgers University Press, 2001.
Wiener, Jon. "Defend Charlie Hebdo's Publishing Disgusting Cartoons about Muslims? Yes. Give Them an Award for It? No." *The Nation,* May 1, 2015.
Willsher, Kim. "Charlie Hebdo Attack: Fallen Policeman Ahmed Merabet Buried in Bobigny." *The Guardian,* January 13, 2015.
Willsher, Kim. "French Prosecutor Says Killer of 84 in Nice Had Accomplices and Planned Attack for Months." *Los Angeles Times,* July 21, 2016.
Willsher, Kim. "Hasna Aitboulahcen: Police Examine Remains of 'Cowgirl' Turned Suicide Bomber." *The Guardian,* November 20, 2015.
Willsher, Kim. "John Kerry Declares 'Profound Emotion' for France in Paris Address." *The Guardian,* January 16, 2015.
Willsher, Kim. "Police in French Priest Murder Case Investigate Messaging App Link." *The Guardian,* July 31, 2016.
Willsher, Kim, and Alexandra Topping. "Police Converge on Area North-East of Paris in Hunt for Charlie Hebdo Gunmen." *The Guardian,* January 8, 2015.
Willsher, Kim, and Julian Borger. "ISIS Attackers Forced French Priest to Kneel Before He Was Murdered, Hostage Says." *The Guardian,* July 26, 2016.
Wilson, Michael L. J. "Portrait of the Artist as a Louis XIII Chair." In *Montmartre and the Making of Mass Culture,* edited by Gabriel P. Weisberg, 180–204. New Brunswick, New Jersey: Rutgers University Press, 2001.
Withnall, Adam. "ISIS Official Calls for 'Lone Wolf' Attacks in US and Europe during Ramadan." *The Independent,* May 22, 2016.
Withnall, Adam. "Were Paris Attacks the First Case of al-Qaeda and Isis Working Together? Six Questions Raised in Aftermath of France Shootings." *The Independent,* January 13, 2015.
Witte, Griff. "In a Kosher Grocery Store in Paris, Terror Takes a Deadly Toll." *Washington Post,* January 9, 2015.
Witte, Griff, and Anthony Folala. "Charlie Hebdo Suspect Said to Surrender: Two Others at Large After Paris Terror Attack." *Washington Post,* January 7, 2015.
Wood, Graeme. "What ISIS Really Wants." *The Atlantic,* March 2015.
"The World" Staff. "A Bataclan Survivor Asks a Rocker to Understand the Complexities of Terrorism." PRI.org (Public Radio International, "The World" program). May 25, 2016. https://www.pri.org/stories/2016-05-25/bataclan-survivor-asks-rocker-understand-complexities-terrorism.
Yardley, Jim. "Jihadism Born in a Paris Park and Fueled in the Prison Yard." *New York Times,* January 11, 2015.
Zaretsky, Robert. "'Charlie Hebdo,' Houellebecq, and France's Pungent Satirical Tradition." *Chronicle of Higher Education,* January 9, 2015.
Zinos, Nicholas. "Father Jacques Hamel, Europe's First 21-Century Martyr." *America: The Jesuit Review,* July 26, 2018.

Index

À la Bonne Bière 105
Abaaoud, Abdelhamid 72, 130; arrests during adolescence 77; childhood 74, 76–77; death 131–132; Paris attacks 96, 97, 98, 99, 103, 105, 107, 108; radicalization 76–80; roles in ISIS 81, 82, 83–87
Abaaoud, Badi 75, 76
Abaaoud, Omar 74, 75, 76, 79, 80
Abaaoud, Yassine 79, 80
Abaaoud, Younes 80
Abballa, Larossi 152
Abbas, Mahmoud 71
Abdeslam, Brahim 87–88, 89, 96, 98, 103, 107, 130
Abdeslam, Salah 87–89, 129–130, 132
Abdulmutallab, Umar Farouk 48
Abu Ghraib Prison 4, 43, 82
Abul Jaleel al-Hanafi see Kermiche, Adel
Adda'wa Mosque (Paris) 40
Adnani, Abu Mohammed al- 82, 83
Afghanistan 4, 21, 45, 63, 76, 86, 94, 137, 200
Air Products 188, 189, 190, 193, 194
Aix-les-Bans, France 160
Akrouh, Chakib 90, 103, 107, 108, 129, 130, 131, 132
Alexander, Nick 110
Alfortville, France 96
Algeciras, Spain 95
Algerian Civil War 4, 48, 154
Allah 2, 17, 20, 40, 42, 55, 63, 107, 155, 184, 190
Al-Qaeda in the Arabian Peninsula (AQAP) 48, 49, 69
Al-Rusafa Prison 82, 83
Al-Shabab 185
American Airlines 125
Amimour, Mohamed 92
Amimour, Samy 91–92, 108, 113, 114
Amn al-Askari 81
Amn al-Dawla 81
Amn al-Kharji see Emni
Amn Dakhili 81
Amniyat 81, 144, 152
Amsterdam Centraal 194
Anderlecht (municipality) 76

Anglade Jean-Hugues 198, 199
Ansi, Nasr Ibn Ali al- 69
Antakya, Turkey 196
anti-shrine 183
APHP see Assistance Publique-Hôpitaux de Paris
AQAP see al-Qaeda in the Arabian Peninsula
Arab Spring 149
Arc de Triomphe 61
Arefa, Ramzi 179, 181
Arras, France 201
ASD see autism spectrum disorder(s)
Assad, Bashar al- 127
assassination squads (November 13 attacks) 87–95
Assistance Publique-Hôpitaux de Paris (APHP) 122
Atar, Oussama (AKA Abu Ahmad) 82, 83, 95
ATC-Colicom 189, 191
Attia, Mona Omar 20
Attiyah, Khaled al- 127
autism spectrum disorder(s) (ASD) 140
Awlaki, Anwar al- 48, 49, 63, 69

B., Fahmi (witness) 110
Baghdadi, Abu Bakr al- 82, 85, 156
Bakkali, Mohamed 204
Bakr, Haji (Samir Abd Muhammad Al-Khlifawi and Haji Bakr al-Baghdadi; "Lord of the Shadows") 81, 82
Balkan Peninsula see Balkans
Balkans (Balkan Peninsula) 196, 203, 204
Banghalem, Salim 83
Banksy 132–134
Bargine, Franck 102
Baroudjian, Barouyr 104
Basile, Sam see Basseley, Nakoula
Basseley, Nakoula (Sam Basile) 32
Bastille Day see La Fête National
Bathily, Lassana 66–68
Bayern Munich Football Club (FC Bayern München) 100

251

Index

Beghal, Djamel 43–48
Les Béguines (bar) 88, 89
Belgian Intelligence *see* State Security Services—Belgium
Belkacem, Smaïn Aït Ali 48
BELKACEM Project 48
La Belle Époque 11
La Belle Équipe (bistro) 105–107, 114, 132
Benarroch, Franck 99
Bendaoud, Jawad 130
Benyettou, Farid 40–43, 49
Besançon, France 187
Betty Blue (film) 198
Biden, Joe 58
bin Laden, Osama 21, 22, 29, 45, 46
Blitzer, Wolf 112
Bluitgen, Kåre 17, 18, 19, 20
Bobigny, France 96, 129
Boko Haram 93, 184
Bouchnak, Thameur 43
Boulahcen, Hasna Aït 130
Boutinaud, Phillippe 100
Bowdery, Isobel 115
Braham, Philippe 65
Braquo (television drama) 199
Brehaut, Charlotte 104
BRI *see* Research and Intervention Brigade
Brigade de Recherche et d'Intervention *see* Research and Intervention Brigade
Brigade des sapeurs-pompiers de Paris *see* Paris Fire Brigade
Brinsolaro, Franck 52, 55
Bruet, Michel 198
Bruxelles-Midi (train station) 197
Buffalo Bill Cody 108
Bush, George W. 4
Buttes-Chaumont Gang 39, 41, 52
Buttes-Chaumont Jihadist Network 42, 57
Buttes-Chaumont Park (Paris) 39, 40

Cabu 13, 14, 23, 24, 51, 55
Cabu, Jean Maurice Jules *see* Cabu
Calciu, Ciprian 106
Cameron, David 71
Camp Bucca 82
Captagon 178
La Caricature (magazine) 10
Le Carillon (bar) 107, 132; terrorist attack 103–105
La Casa Nostra (café) 105
Castaner, Christophe 210
Catalano, Michel 62, 62, 68
Cayat, Elsa 51, 55
Cazeneuve, Bernard 84, 124, 165, 191
Les Cent Nouvelles Nouvelles 9
Chafroud, Chokri 178, 179, 181, 182
Champs-Elysées 61
Charb *see* Charbonnier, Stéphane
Charbonnier, Denise 26

Charbonnier, Michel 26
Charbonnier, Stéphane 29, 31, 32, 33 34; childhood 26–27; publishing career 14, 25–28; views on religion 30, 32
Charia Hebdo (parody) 30–31
Le Charivari (magazine) 10
Charles de Gaulle Airport 63
Charlie Brown (cartoon) 13
Charlie Hebdo (magazine) 1, 2, 9, 10; attack on 8, 50–64, 67–70; bombing 31, 33; history 11–14
Le Chat Noir (cabaret) 11
Chatra, Bilal 204
Cheney, Dick 4
Chevalier, Maurice 108
Choudary, Anjem 185
Christophe (policeman) 176
Church of St. Stephen (Église Saint-Étienne) 153, 154, 155, 160, 161, 162, 163, 166
Church of St. Teresa (Église Sainte-Thérèse le Madrillet) 153
Claude Pompidou Foundation 36
Coco *see* Rey, Corrine
Cohen, Yohan 65, 67
Collège Lakanal 37
Collège Saint-Pierre (Brussels) 76
Le Comptoir Voltaire (restaurant) 107
Coponet, Guy 154, 155
Cornara, Hervé 189, 190, 191, 192, 193
Coulibaly, Amedy 46, 47, 48; attack on Hyper Cacher market 64–67; attack on policewoman 60–62; death 67, 68, 69, 70
Coupris, Marc 115
Création Tendance Découverte 62, 69
Crépy-en-Valois (municipality) 61, 62
Croix-Rouge district (Reims) 57
cyber handler *see* cybercoach
cybercoach (cyber handler, virtual planner) 145–147, 151, 163

Dabiq (magazine) 86
Damien A. (witness) 198, 204
Dammartin-en-Goëlle (municipality) 62
Danielle (witness) 154
Danish Security and Intelligence Service 138
dark web 143, 147–149
Daumier, Honoré 10, 11, 33
deep web 148
de Gaulle, Charles 13
Deschamps, Didier 101
DGSI *see* General Directorate for Internal Security
Diakite, Asta 102
Diarra, Lassana 102
Didi (security officer) 111
Disneyland Paris (Euro Disney) 125
DNA analysis 62, 82, 132, 157
Donaghy, Will 186
Dorio, Julian 110
Draw Muhammad contest 19–20, 21

Dubosarsky, Maisie 54
Duchatel, Marie-Charles 11

Eagles of Death Metal (band) 109, 110, 112, 115
L'Echo des savanes (magazine) 27
Les Editions Rotative 23
Église Saint-Étienne *see* Church of St. Stephen
Eiffel Tower 125
El Iraki, Ismaël 111
El Khazzani, Ayoub (Ayoub el-Qahzzani) 194, 195–197, 199, 201, 202, 203, 204
Élysée Palace 58, 156, 175, 186
Emergency Declaration (13 November 2015 attacks) 124–126, 129, 207, 208
Emni (Amn al-Kharji) 80, 81, 82, 83, 84, 85, 95
enabled attacks *see* remote control terrorism
Ennahda 30
Essebsi, Beji Caid 186
Euro Disney *see* Disneyland Paris

Farid K. (cousin of terrorist) 162
FC Bayern München *see* Bayern Munich Football Club
Fenech, Georges 113
La Fête National (Bastille Day; Le 14 Juillet) 171
Le 14 Juillet *see* La Fête National
Le Petite Cambodge (restaurant) 103, 104
fiche S 163, 176, 187, 188, 195
Fieschi, Simon 54
Le Figaro (newspaper) 28
Finsbury Park Mosque 44
Firansi, Abu Suleyman al- 95
Fleury-Mérogis Prison 43, 46, 47, 193
Fluide Glacial (magazine) 27
FN *see* Front National
La Fonda (residential facility) 36, 37
Fondation Lenval Hôpital pour Enfants *see* Lenval Children's Hospital
Fondation pour la Recherche Stratégique 164
Forêt de la Londe-Rouvray 153
France Inter (radio channel) 25
Franck (witness) 173
French Football Federation 99
French Muslims (organization, formerly Union of Islamic Organizations of France) 23, 127
French National Police 66
French Revolution 10, 165, 171
Front National (FN) 5

Gaillard, Gérard 51, 55
Ganz, Jeremy 53
Gargantua (caricature) 11
Gauthier (witness) 115
Gazette d'Utopia (periodical) 27
Gebaly, Salah Emad el- 120

Geele, Muhudiin Mohamed 22
General Directorate for Internal Security (DGSI) 98
Ghasemi, Seifi 189
Ghlam, Sid Ahmed 84
Ghraieb, Mohamed Oualid (Walid) 177, 178, 179, 181, 182
GIA *see* Islamic Armed Group
GIGN *see* National Gendarmerie Intervention Group
Grand Ali *see* Salvi, Frédéric Jean
Grand Mosque of Paris 23
Griezmann, Antoine 102
Griezmann, Maud 102
Groupe d'intervention de la Gendarmerie nationale *see* National Gendarmerie Intervention Group
Guéant, Claude 31
Gueguen, Sylvie 44
Guyomard, Anne 120
Guyomard, Pierre-Yves 120

Hadfi, Bilal 93–94, 98, 99, 100
Hakim, Boubaker al- 42
Hakim, Redouane al- 42
Les Halles (Paris) 101
Hame, Reda 86
Hamel, Jacques 153, 154, 155, 156, 160, 181, 165, 166
Hamyd, Mourad 58, 59
Hamza, Abu 45
Hara-Kiri (magazine) 13, 14
Hara-Kiri Hebdo (magazine) 13
Harpon, Mickaël 1, 2
Hattab, Yoav 66, 67
Heisbourg, François 164
Henaj, Artan 179, 180
Hersch, Seymour 4
Hervik, Peter 18, 19
Hitler, Adolf 12
Hollande, François 54, 57, 58, 96, 99, 100, 120, 124, 126, 127, 152, 165, 167, 175, 186, 204, 207; statement on Charlie Hebdo massacre 58
Holocaust 5
Honoré *see* Honoré, Philippe
Honoré, Philippe ("Honoré") 51, 55
Hôpital Saint-Antoine 122
Horace 9
Hotel Riu Imperial Marhaba 185–186
Houd, Djamila 106
L'Humanité (newspaper) 27
Hyper Cacher (market) 64–67, 68, 69, 70

Ibn Omar *see* Petitjean, Abdel-Malik
Ibnolmobarak, Mohamed Amine 105
Imam al-Sadiq Mosque (Kuwait) 185
The Innocence of Muslims (video) 32, 33
Inspire (publication) 51
Iraq, Western military campaigns in 4, 41, 63, 76, 81, 110, 179

Index

Iraqi, Ali al- *see* Mahmod, M. al-
Iraqi, Ukasah al- *see* Mohammad, Ahmad al-
ISIS caliphate 4, 81, 82, 118, 135, 143, 159, 184, 196; recruitment in prisons 77–79
ISIS, U.S.–French military action against (2014–2019) 4–5
Islamic Armed Group (GIA) 48
L'Isle-d'Abeau, France 186, 189
isolated dyad 138, 139, 146, 151, 163

Janaszak, Pierre 118
Janvier, Eugene 11
Je Suis Charlie 55, 177
Jean-Philippe, Clarissa 60
Jewish Museum (Brussels) 85
Joan of Arc 153
Jos, Nigeria 184
Juste, Carsten 20, 21
Juvenal 9
Juvin, Philippe 117
Jyllands-Posten (JP) 16; cartoon controversy 17–22

Karim, Abdel 189
Kassim, Rachid ("Lightsaber") 151, 152, 158, 162, 163, 166, 179
Kermiche, Adel (Abul Jaleel al-Hanafi) 156, 157–160, 161, 162, 163, 164, 165, 166
Khalfallah, Hajer 168
Khlifawi, Samir Abd Muhammad al- *see* Bakr, Haji
Killing Zoe (film) 198
King Abdulla II of Jordan 71
King Louis-Philippe I 10, 11
Koran (Qu'ran) 5, 17, 40, 49, 75, 81, 159, 160, 171, 184
Kouachi, Aïcha 35, 36, 37
Kouachi, Chabanne 35
Kouachi, Chérif upbringing 35–37; radicalization 38–44, 46
Kouachi, Freiha 35, 36
Kouachi, Izzana 47, 49, 59
Kouachi, Mokhtar 35
Kouachi, Saïd upbringing 35–37; radicalization 38–44, 43, 49
Kouachi, Salima 35
Kouachi, Soumya 49
Kraftwerk (band) 108
Kuwait City, Kuwait 185

Lahouaiej-Bouhlel, Mohamed 176, 177, 178, 179, 180, 181, 182; aggressive tendencies 169–171; background 167–169; terrorist attack 171–176
Lambert, Jérôme 23
Lançon, Philippe 52
Landstuhl Regional Medical Center 201
Langlois, Matthieu 116, 117
Laurent (witness) 60
Lavrov, Sergei 71

Law Reinforcing Internal Security and the Fight Against Terrorism 208
Law Reinforcing the Fight Against Organized Crime, Terrorism and Its Financing 207
Leader, John 112
Lebrun, Dominique 166
Lefranc, Jacques 22
Léger, Laurent 51, 55
Légion d'honneur (Legion of Honor) 204
Legion of Honor *see* Légion d'honneur
Le Graët, Noël 99
Le Guen, Kelly 112
Lenval Children's Hospital (Fondation Lenval Hôpital pour Enfants) 175
Le Pen, Jean-Marie 5
Le Ray, Bruno 113, 114
Leriche, Gwenaël (eyewitness) 173
Lightsaber *see* Kassim, Rachid
Lilian (employee) 62, 63, 68
lone actor terrorist: definitions 138
lone wolf terrorist *see* lone actor terrorist
Lord of the Shadows *see* Haji Bakr
Louvre Museum 101
Löw, Joachim 101
Luz *see* Luzier, Rénald
Luzier, Rénald ("Luz") 31
Lycée Camille Pissarro 27

Macron, Emmanuel 205, 208
Magazinet (newspaper) 21
Magnanville, France 152
Mahi, Dniel 79
Mahmod, M. al- (Ali al-Iraqi) 91, 98, 99, 100
Maris, Bernard 55
Marks, James 128
Maurice et Patapon (cartoon) 28
McDonald's Restaurant 101
Meaud, Charlotte 105
Meaud, Emilie 105
Mecca, Saudi Arabia 105, 160
Merabet, Ahmed 56, 57, 68
Merabet, Malek 57
Merkel, Angela 71
Migues, Alexander 173
Mogadishu, Somalia 185
Mohamad (uncle of Kouachi brothers) 37, 38, 39
Mohamed-Aggad, Foued 89–90, 108, 110, 111, 112, 114, 115, 116, 117, 118, 119
Mohammad, Ahmad al- (Ukasah al-Iraqi) 91
Molenbeek 74, 77, 79, 81, 87, 88, 89, 90, 129, 132, 195, 196, 197, 204; history 75–76
Molins, François 170, 176, 179, 192, 195
Montmartre 11
Montrouge 60
Moogalian, Mark 198, 199, 200, 201, 204
Morocco 74, 80, 93, 105, 195
Mostefaï, Ismaël Omar 94–95, 108, 110, 111, 112, 114, 115, 116, 118, 119
Mosul, Iraq 92

Movilă, Cristian 11
Muhammad (prophet) 8, 15, 16, 17, 18, 19, 20, 22, 23, 30, 32, 56, 63, 66, 69, 190
Muslim immigrants (Belgium) 75, 79, 87, 88, 91
Muslim immigrants (Denmark) 15, 16, 17, 18
Muslim immigrants (France) 3, 5, 38, 39, 40, 57, 66, 130, 151, 160, 168
Muslims-by-culture (*kulturmuslimerne*) 17
Muslims-by-practice 17

Nakoula, Nakoula Basseley 32
National Front *see* Front National
National Gendarmerie Intervention Group (Groupe d'intervention de la Gendarmerie nationale; (GIGN) 61, 62, 63, 68
Navasky, Victor S. 12–13
Negresco Hotel 174, 175
Nemmouch, Mehdi 84, 85
Netanyahu, Benjamin 71
Ni Aolain, Fionnuala D. 209
Nice, France 168, 169, 170, 171, 172, 173, 175, 176, 177, 178, 179, 180, 181, 183, 207
Nicolino, Fabrice 52, 55
Noemi (hostage) 67
Norman, Chris 201, 204
Notre Dame Cathedral (Notre-Dame) 2, 29, 152, 158
Nouvelles du Val-d'Oise (newspaper) 27

Obama, Barack 33, 58, 127
O'Connor, Michael 111
Of Gods and Men (film) 154
Offenbach, Jacques 108
Oignies, France 198
The Onion Router (TOR) 147
Open Letter: On Blasphemy, Islamophobia, and the True Enemies of Free Expression (book) 30
open web *see* surface web
Operation Paris (OpParis) 148
Operation Sentinelle 113
OpParis *see* Operation Paris
Organization of the Islamic Conference 21
Ourrad, Mustapha 55, 57

Palais de la Méditerranée (Hyatt Regency) 174
Panfili, Robin 102
Paris Fire Brigade 100, 111
Paris Police Headquarters 1–2
Paris Police Prefecture 164
Paris railway bombings (1995) 48
Passage Saint-Pierre-Amelot 111
Pelloux, Patrick 117
The Pentagon 4, 29, 45
Peron, Huguette 155
Petitjean, Abdel-Malik (Ibn Omar) 157, 160–161, 162, 163, 164, 165, 166
Philippe-Grenier Mosque 187, 188, 192

Phuati, Auguste Moanda 153
Piaf, Edith 108
Picard, Philippe 23
Pidgin (app) 147
Place de la République 59, 61, 70, 121
Pompidou Center 101
Pontoise, France 26
Pop, Lacramioara 106
Pope Francis 156, 165
Premières Lignes Télévision 53
Premisler, Sylvie 27
Prevost-Desprez, Isabelle 80
Prince (performer) 108
The Prom (event) 172
Promenade des Anglais 171, 172, 173, 176, 177, 178, 181, 182, 183

Qatada, Abu 45
Qatar 127, 185
Qirwani, Abu Yehya al- 185, 186
Qu'ran *see* Koran

Radio France 25
RAID *see* Research, Assistance, Intervention, Dissuasion
Ramadan 137, 184, 185, 186, 189, 192, 193
Ramstein Air Base 201
Raqqa, Syria 86, 92, 128, 184, 192
Rasmussen, Anders Fogh 20, 21
Recherche, Assistance, Intervention, Dissuasion *see* Research, Assistance, Intervention, Dissuasion
Reibenberg, Gregory 106
remote control terrorism 143; defined 144, online recruitment process 144–146
Renaud, Michel 52, 55
Research and Intervention Brigade (Brigade de Recherche et d'Intervention) (BRI) 66, 67, 68, 114, 116, 117, 118, 119, 155, 156, 157, 160
Research, Assistance, Intervention, Dissuasion (Research, Assistance, Intervention, Dissuasion) (RAID) 116, 117, 129, 131
Rey, Corinne ("Coco") 50, 51, 53, 54, 69
Rihanna 157
Risacher-Moogalian, Isabelle 198, 199, 201
Roger (friend) 169
Rose, Flemming 18
Rouhani, Hassan 127
Rushdie, Salmon 51, 71

Saada, François-Michel 64
Saadi, Abdallah 107
Saadi, Halima 106
Saadi, Hodda 106
Saadi, Khaled 106–107
Sabah, Sabah al- 127
Sacramento, California 194, 200
Sadler, Anthony 200, 201, 202, 203, 204
Safran, Denis 116

Saint-Denis raid 130–132, 203
Saint-Étienne-du-Rouvray 153, 156, 157, 159, 162, 163, 164, 165
Saint-Laurent-du-Var, France 172
Saint Stephen 153
Salafism 40, 41, 75
Salhi, Yassin 186, 193; background 187–188; terrorist attack 188–192
Salvi, Frédéric Jean ("Grand Ali") 187, 188, 192
San'a Institute for the Arabic Language 48
Sarkozy, Nicolas 24, 188
SDF *see* Syrian Democratic Front
Sébastien-Younes VZ *see* Voyez-Zairi, Sébastien-Younes
Sebbar, Redouane 204
Sharia (Islamic law) 30, 31
The Simpsons (television series) 157
Siraj, Youssef 204
60 Minutes (television program) 19
Skarlatos, Aleksander ("Alek") 199, 200, 201, 204, 205
Les Soldats de Lumièrè (book) 193
solo terrorist 138
Sourisseau, Laurent ("Riss") 51, 54, 55, 69
Sousse, Tunisia 185
Stade de France 96, 98–102, 103, 117, 120, 129, 130, 148, 167, 196
Stasi 81
State Security Services-Belgium (Belgian Intelligence) 79
Stone, Spencer 199, 200, 201, 203, 204
surface web (open web) 147, 148, 149
Syria, Western military campaign in 4, 63, 76, 83, 90, 110, 118, 121, 127, 128, 155, 206
Syrian Civil War 76, 90, 93, 95
Syrian Democratic Front (SDF) 136, 143

Tanty, Eric 201
Taqwa Mosque (Algeciras, Spain) 195
TATP *see* triacetone triperoxide
TEK *see* Terrorelhárítási Központ
telecommande attacks *see* remote control terrorism
Telegram (app) 147, 148, 152, 159, 161, 162, 163, 164
Télérama (magazine) 27
Terrorelhárítási Központ (TEK) 196
Thalys International SCRL 194, 196, 197, 198, 200, 201, 202, 203, 204
13 Onze 15—Fraternité et verité (support organization) 123
TOR *see* The Onion Router
Toulouse, France 129–162
Tourtier, Jean-Pierre 100
Trabelsi, Nizar 45
triacetone triperoxide (TATP) 97
Twin Towers *see* World Trade Center

UCLAT *see* Unité de Coordination de la Lutte Anti-Terroriste

Union of Islamic Organizations of France *see* French Muslims
Union of Muslims of the Alpes-Maritimes 175
Unité de Coordination de la Lutte Anti-Terroriste (UCLAT) 163, 164
United Nations Climate Change Conference (Paris) 98
U.S. Naval Research Lab 148
University Hospital (Lille, France) 201

Val, Phillipe 14, 23, 24, 25, 31
Valls, Manuel 58, 124
Vatican 156
Velardita, Sebastiano 156
Verlhac, Bernard ("Tignous") 51, 55
Verviers ISIS cell 85, 203–204
Villejuif, France 84
Villers-Cotterêts (municipality) 60, 61
Vinson, Sigolène 51, 55
virtual planner *see* cybercoach
virtual planning approach *see* remote control terrorism
Voltaire 9, 10, 33, 71
Voyez-Zairi, Sébastien-Younes (Sébastien-Younes VZ) 192, 193

War of Independence (Algeria) 44
Washington, DC 146
Watson, Jenny 111
Westergaard, Kurt 16, 17, 18, 20, 22, 23, 24, 51
WhatsApp (app) 147, 190
White House 4, 33, 156
White Miles (band) 109
White Plan 122–123
Widodo, Joko 127
Wilson, Helen 110
The Wizard of Oz (film) 22
wolf pack 138
Wolinski, Georges 13, 14, 51, 55
World Health Organization (WHO) 139
World Trade Center (Twin Towers) 4, 29, 45, 50, 76
World War I 12, 74
World War II 3, 124, 142, 143

xenophobia 5

Yantaya Mosque 184
Yordanov, Youri 122
YouTube 149, 171, 197

Zace, Enkeledja 179, 180
Zagar, Hamdi 179, 180, 181, 182
Zemmouri, Youssef 40
Zerkani, Khalid 79
Zouheir (security guard) 99
Zubeida, Abu 45